PULSE

Teacher's Book

1

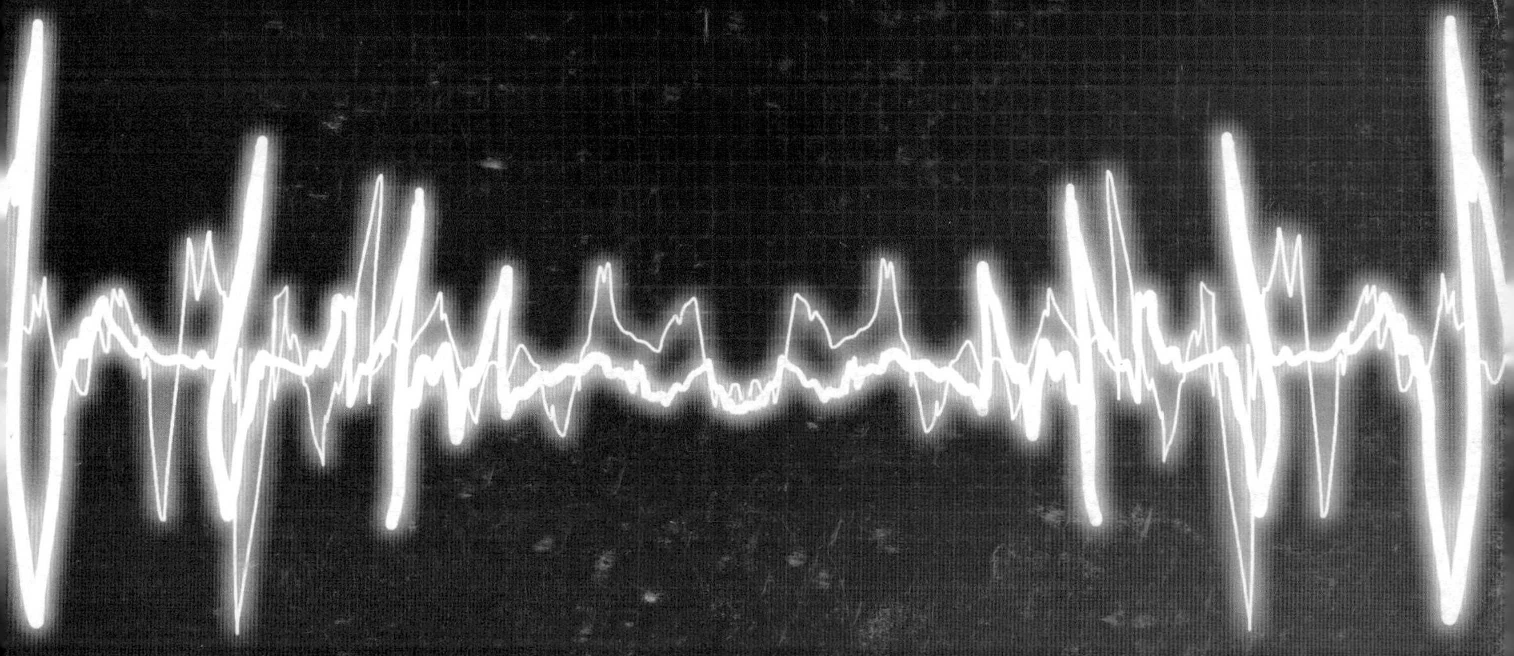

Tim Bowen

MACMILLAN

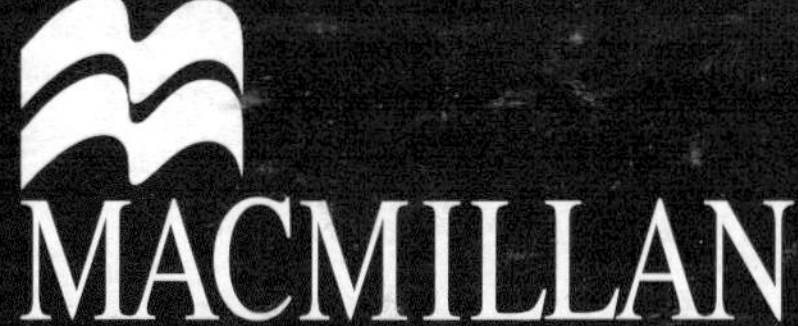

Macmillan Education
4 Crinan Street, London N1 9XW, UK
A division of Macmillan Publishers Limited
Companies and representatives throughout the world

ISBN 978-0-230-43914-6

Written by Tim Bowen
The author has asserted his rights to be identified as the author of this work in accordance with the Copyright, Designs and Patents Act 1988.

First published 2014

Designed by James Osborne
Cover design by Andrew Oliver

Student's Book acknowledgements:
Original design by Andrew Oliver
Designed by Designers Collective
Illustrated by Beach pp4, 97; Mark Draisey pp44, 54, 64; Mark Willey pp14, 24, 34, 56, 64, 66, 68, 78, 88, 98.
Picture research by Sally Cole

The authors and publishers would like to thank the following for permission to reproduce their photographic material:

Alamy/AA World Travel Library p65(hostel), Alamy/Apex News and Pictures Agency p55(cl), Alamy/P. Armstrong p79(bcl), Alamy/Big Cheese Photo LLC p52(pool), Alamy/Blend Images pp20(tr), 20(c), Alamy/M.Booth pp20(a), 35(r), Alamy/J.Collins pp14(tl), Alamy/Corbis Premium RF p23(d), Alamy/Corbis Super RF p53(mb), Alamy/Cultura Creative p52(gym), Alamy/Cultura RM p109(bl), Alamy/B.Daemmrich p26(tl), Alamy/I.Dagnall p99(br), Alamy/D. Davis p70(c), Alamy/D.Dempster Photography p46(b), Alamy/DK p56(bml), Alamy/Design Pics Inc p122(cl), Alamy/Fancy pp53(t), 53(b), Alamy/Corbis Flirt p23(g), Alamy/S.French pp48(flip-flops), 65(mobile home), Alamy/Fresh Start Images p30(cl), Alamy/fstop p41, Alamy/Golden Pixels LLC p47(tr), Alamy/D.Hancock p56(bmr), Alamy/T.Harris p111, Alamy/P.Hays p46(c), Alamy/W.Hutchinson p66(cr), Alamy/Image 100 p53(tm), Alamy/Imagebroker pp48(sweatshirt), 90(cl), Alamy/Imars p72(cl), Alamy/Image Source p118(br), Alamy/Incamerastock p80(tr), Alamy/Johner Images p25, Alamy/Kuttig People 2 p109(cr), Alamy/V.Mares p86(r), Alamy/I.Masterton p56(bl), Alamy/MBI pp28, 108, Alamy/R.McGouey p65(cabin), Alamy/K.Morris pp46(a), 98(br), Alamy/P.Muhly p98(bl), Alamy/Newsphoto p88(br), Alamy/D.Nottingham p100(r), Alamy/R.Parkes p98(bc), Alamy/Photolibrary Wales p70(tr), 54(r), Alamy/M.Richardson p100(l), Alamy/C.Ryan p103, Alamy/D.Sabljak p88(fiddle), Alamy/N.Setchfield p112, Alamy/A.Sherratt p38, Alamy/D. Shironosov p109(br), Alamy/S.Skjold pp20(e), 100(c), Alamy/Somos Images p23(b), Alamy/J.Spencer p65(lighthouse), Alamy/Stockfolio p65(hotel), Alamy/Stockimages p48(sunglasses), Alamy/T.Taulman p79(br), Alamy/The National Trust Photo Library p65(farm), Alamy/R.Torres p75(tr), Alamy/D.Valla FRPS p88(harp), Alamy/Z.Waters p110, Alamy/Zuma Wire Service p47(br), Alamy/Yokohama p76; Brand X Pictures p51; Corbis pp29, 45(a), 114(bl), Corbis/Ableimages p4(tr), Corbis/M.Ashton/AMA p40(b), Corbis/Blend Images p77(bc), Corbis/Elizabeth Whiting & Associates p62(br), Corbis/Glow Images p62(tr), Corbis/Juice Images pp6(tr), 20(b), Corbis/Ocean pp71, 106(bl), 123(bl), Corbis/T.Pannell p39, Corbis/P.Rees p60(bl), Corbis/P.Simon p52(park), Corbis/A.Summer p45(c), Corbis/J.Tepper p24(tr), Corbis/S.Tischler p84(br), Corbis/S.Wackerhagen p34(c); Dance Action Zone Leeds p31(tr); Digital Vision/Punchstock p32; Etnies pp63(tl, 63(tr); Falls Communications/ShurTechBrands LLC p43; FLPA/T. de Roy/Minden Pictures p77(tl); Getty Images pp26(cl), 86(cr), Getty Images/AFP pp21(cm), 33(5), 33(shotput), 33(hurdles), 33(high jump), 33(running), 34(l), 93, 40(bl), Getty Images/Age Fotostock pp30(l), 52(bowling), Getty Images/Allsport Concepts p30(c), Getty Images/ AWL Images p88(bagpipes), Getty Images/Blend Images pp87(cl),106(br), Getty Images/Bluestone Productions p122(bc), Getty Images/DK p48(hat), Getty Images/Getty Images Entertainment pp42(l), 50(1), 50(2), 88(cr), 92, 104(br), Getty Images/Film Magic pp19(bl), 42(r), Getty Images/Garden Picture Library p65(tent), Getty Images/Image Bank pp19(br), 20(f), Getty Images/Image Source pp107, 23(h), 116, Getty Images/Lonely Planet Images p88(drums), Getty Images/NBC/Universal p84(cr), Getty Images/Getty Images News p75(tm), Getty Images/Photodisc p115, GettyImages/Photographers Choice pp48(mug), 118(bl), Getty Images/PM Images p30(cr), Getty Images/Redferns pp72(cr), 104(bl), Getty/Riser p61, Getty Images/Getty Images Sport pp32, 33(javelin), 35(l),77(cr), 40(br), Getty Images/Sports Illustrated p33(long jump), Getty Images/Stockbyte p120, Getty Images/Stockfood Creative p60(tr), Getty Images/Stone pp94(r), 102(tr), Getty Images/Taxi pp26(tr), 45(b), 52(café), 66(cl), 67, 83, Getty Images/Time & Life Pictures p86(bl), Getty Images/Upper Cut Images p90(cr), Getty Images/Workbook Stock pp23(a), 102(tl), 121, 123(cl), Getty Images/Britain on View pp24(c), 48(socks); Image Source pp23(c),114(br); Liverpool Echo/Liverpool Signing Choir p85(l); Mary Evans Picture Library pp89(br), 89(c); Newsteam/Birmingham Post & Mailp22(cr); Rex Features/S. Bell p21(tl), Rex Features/G.Bevilacqua p7(br), Rex Features/D.Caudery/Future Publishing p14(br), Rex Features/CBS/Everett pp77(cl), 82, Rex Features/Col Pics/Everett p10(cmr), Rex Features/N.Cunard p22(bl), Rex Features/W.Disney/Everett p10(cr), Rex Features/Everett Collection pp14(tcr), 78(cr), RexFeatures/20thCentury Fox/Everett pp11(c), 11(cr), 13(tr), 15(bcm), 18(tr), 18(cr), Rex Features/F1Online p14(cr), Rex Features/N.Haynes p34(tr), Rex Features/J.Hordle p21(tr), Rex Features/ITV p77(br), Rex Features/N. Jorgensen p11(tl), Rex Features/MCPix Ltd p50(3), Rex Features/Moviestore Collection pp10(cml), 14(bcr), 79(cl), Rex Features/New Line/Everett pp10(cl), 11(tcm), 11(tr), Rex Features/G.Robinson p31(l), Rex Features/J.Selwyn/Evening Standard p113, Rex Features/Sony Pics/Everett Collection p15(br), Rex Features/ Startracks Photo p12(bl), Rex Features/USPS p78(cl); Ronald Grant Archive/Columbia Pictures p15(bcr), Ronald Grant Archive/Walt Disney Pictures p78(tr); Science Photo Library/M.Chillmaid p23(f), Science Photo Library/Maximillian Stock p57; Sony Music p104(cr); Superstock pp33(3), 33(1), 55(c), 72(c), Superstock/Age Fotostock pp23(e), 65(castle), 65(villa), Superstock/Blue jean Images p87(br), Superstock/P.Bona p33(4), Superstock/Flirt p87(tl), Superstock/M.Grebler p33(6), Superstock/Hemis.fr p6(tl), Superstock/Imagebroker p65(caravans), Superstock/Image Source p52(cinema), Superstock/Loop Images p65(barge), Superstock/A. Michael p36(l), Superstock/Moodboard p94(c), Superstock/Prisma p56(br), Superstock/Robert Harding Picture Library p65(apartment), Superstock/Stockbroker pp20(d), 94(l), Superstock/Stockbroker/Purestock p55(tr), Superstock/Universal Images Group p99(tr), Superstock/Waterframe p36(r), Superstock/K.Weatherly p33(2), Superstock/Westend61 p87(cr); The Guardian/The Purcell School p85(r); The Kobal Collection/MGM p13(br), The Kobal Collection/Paramount/Bad Robot p16(tl), The Kobal Collection/Universal p16(tm), The Kobal Collection/Walt Disney Pictures/Walden Media p13(cr); Xbox p74. Commissioned photos by Studio8 pp5, 8, 9, 16, 17, 26, 27, 36, 37, 48, 49, 58, 59, 68, 69, 81, 82, 90, 91, 95, 100, 101.
Thanks to Chris, Ellie, Kai, Molly, Annabelle Mitchell, Emmy Happisburgh, Josh Parris, Louis Cordice and Roxanne Rickets.
The authors and publishers are grateful for permission to reprint the following copyright material: Stuck at Prom® text and images reproduced by permission of ShurTech Brands, LLC; quote by Joe English reproduced by permission of Dazl Diamonds on behalf of Joe English; facts from website http://fabulousmag.co.uk/2012/04/08/im-not-proud-of-my-figure/ reproduced by permission of News International; quote by Leona Lewis from www.brit.croydon.sch.uk reproduced by permission of Modest! Management; extracts from www.skatestudyhouse.com reproduced by permission of Skate Study House; the designer Gil Le Bon Delapointe designed the whole building inside (the skate furniture and transitions) and outside (the "ribbon" concept) quotes and facts by Paige Wheeler from www.paigewheeler.co.uk reproduced by permission of Dionne Tomlinson and Andy Wheeler.

Material curricular para la Educación Secundaria Obligatoria del área de Lengua Extranjera, Inglés, que corresponde al proyecto presentado para su supervisión y/o aprobación / homologación / registro en las Entidades de Educación de las Comunidades Autónomas.

Pulse conforms to the objectives set by the Common European Framework of Reference and its recommendations for the evaluation of language competence.

Printed and bound in Spain by Grafoprint
2018 2017 2016 2015 2014

10 9 8 7 6 5 4 3 2 1

CONTENTS

INTRODUCING PULSE

Pulse is a four-level ESO course which contains a wide range of up-to-date, real-world material of genuine interest to teenagers. With its fast-paced approach and use of authentic texts, topics and language, *Pulse* maximizes students' interest and provides sufficient challenge for twenty-first century learners.

The main aims of *Pulse* are to ensure your students fully develop their language competence, to teach tools and strategies for lifelong learning inside and outside the classroom, and to train students in exam skills, which will be valuable for ESO and beyond.

To achieve this, *Pulse* offers:

Linguistic content

Vocabulary and grammar in context

Pulse takes an inductive approach to vocabulary, ensuring that new lexis is introduced gradually and practised thoroughly. To ensure a challenging and meaningful learning experience, *Pulse* uses a variety of methods to present and practise vocabulary, including contextual presentations. Vocabulary sets are recorded on the Class Audio CD so that students can practise pronunciation.

Grammar structures are presented in a range of authentic-style texts that provide the context essential for understanding meaning. Clear grammar tables provide students with easy-to-navigate reference.

Integrated skills

With its integrated approach to skills, *Pulse* encourages students to develop their receptive and productive skills in parallel. Each unit of the *Student's Book* features an innovative **Integrated skills** spread which presents fully-integrated practice of reading, listening, writing and speaking to improve students' communication skills in a real-world context. Receptive skills are developed through an authentic reading text, followed by an engaging listening activity. The topical link continues with the coverage of productive skills: a videoed speaking model provides the basis for carefully-structured written and spoken production.

Reading

Pulse contains a rich variety of reading texts of interest to teenage learners. A range of text types introduce students to different types of reading material in an appropriately graded, structured way.

Writing: Interaction and production

Pulse takes a highly structured approach to writing. Students first interact with model compositions, before following step-by-step tasks which emphasize that good writing requires planning, drafting and rewriting.

Listening

Listening can be one of the most difficult skills to develop, so *Pulse* provides learners with the support they need before and during listening to aid comprehension and improve confidence.

Speaking: Interaction and production

Pulse gets students talking through **Express yourself** activities, which provide frequent opportunities to interact and exchange opinions.

The **Integrated skills** spread provides a fully-interactive speaking model in the *Digital Course*, which allows students to watch video clips of British people interacting in everyday situations. Through a series of step-by-step tasks, students are supported through production and practice of their own dialogues.

Lifelong learning skills

Self-study and self-evaluation

Pulse promotes learner autonomy by encouraging students to take an active role in their own learning.

To this end, *Pulse* provides self-study reference and practice material in both the *Student's Book* and the *Workbook*. The **Self-study bank** in the *Workbook* contains a wealth of extension and consolidation activities to reinforce and expand upon what students learn in class, plus **Wordlists, Speaking reference** and **Pronunciation reference**.

Students are encouraged to evaluate their own learning through the **Self-evaluation** charts at the end of each *Workbook* unit. *Pulse* also promotes group evaluation of the **Collaborative projects** in the *Student's Book*.

Learning strategies

Pulse places high importance on developing learning strategies. The **Learning to Learn tips** provide useful learning ideas, while the **Analyse** boxes encourage students to reflect on the differences between their own language and English. In levels 3 and 4, *Pulse* also teaches critical thinking.

Socio-cultural awareness and life skills

Pulse aims to equip students with the socio-cultural awareness and skills they need to become more informed global citizens. Using a carefully-developed approach, the focus moves from cultural awareness (levels 1 and 2) to social awareness (level 3) to life skills (level 4). The *Digital Course* includes video clips of cultural and social footage designed to supplement the corresponding pages in the Student's Book. These videos provide a window into the culture and society of many English-speaking countries, and are accompanied by worksheets in the *Teacher's Resource File*.

Cross-curricular contents

In levels 1 and 2 the **Grammar in context** activities in the *Student's Book* have a CLIL focus, each related to a different school subject. In addition, the *Teacher's Book* highlights links to other subjects on the school curriculum. In levels 3 and 4, the focus changes to literature. Each activity is based on a different graded Macmillan Reader, with extra information in the *Teacher's Book* for those who wish to use the Reader in class or as homework. Teachers can also find useful extra resources and information on how to exploit these and other Readers in class at www.macmillanreaders.com.

Digital competence

Pulse promotes digital competence in numerous ways. These include searching the internet to complete **Web quests**, and using software packages and online tools for productive tasks in the **Collaborative projects**. Students will expand their knowledge of web tools through the **Digital competence worksheets** in the *Teacher's Resource File*. The *Student Website* gives access to additional online practice activities for language development. Students also have access to **interactive digital material**, which trains them to use digital learning tools independently.

Evaluation material for teachers

Pulse provides teachers with all the necessary resources for continuous evaluation of linguistic skills and for evaluation of all the key competences. Learning outcomes can be evaluated using the *Tests and Exams Multi-ROM*, the *CEFR Skills Exam Generator* and the **External exam trainer** section of the *Student's Book* and *Workbook*.

Pulse endeavours to provide students with the skills they need for exam success by training them how to approach a wide range of exam tasks covering all four skills. The External exam trainer provides model answers and breaks down exam tasks in a step-by-step way in order to build students' confidence in exam situations.

Council of Europe and key competences

Pulse has been developed following the legal guidelines set out by the Council of Europe, whose curricular objective is not just teaching a language itself, but teaching how to communicate through it. Following the Council of Europe's Common European Framework of Reference for Languages (CEFR), students must be able to carry out progressive communication tasks in order to gradually develop their communicative competence in a foreign language.

The course contents of *Pulse* have been designed not only to fulfil the linguistic and communicative competences identified below, but also to develop skills in all key competences.

CLC Competence in linguistic communication
CMST Competence in mathematics, science and technology
DC Digital competence
L2L Learning to learn
SCC Social and civic competences
SIE Sense of initiative and entrepreneurship
CAE Cultural awareness and expression

Support and solutions for teachers

Pulse has a full range of components to support teachers and offer solutions for classroom challenges. These include:

Teacher's Book

Teacher's Resource File with Audio CD

Teacher's Resource File Multi-ROM

Digital Course

Class Audio CDs

Tests and Exams Pack

OVERVIEW OF COMPONENTS

Pulse Student's Book 1

The *Student's Book* includes:

- A six-page starter unit
- Nine ten-page units
- Three Collaborative projects
- An External exam trainer focusing on listening and speaking tasks

The Teacher's *Digital Course* features a fully-interactive version of the *Student's Book*, which is compatible with al devices including interactive whiteboards.

Vocabulary and Speaking

The **Think about it** activity engages students and encourages vocabulary recall.

The first vocabulary set is presented using a variety of techniques including photos and authentic contexts. They are recorded on the *Class Audio CD* for pronunciation practice.

The **Express yourself** discussion feature gets students talking and using topic vocabulary.

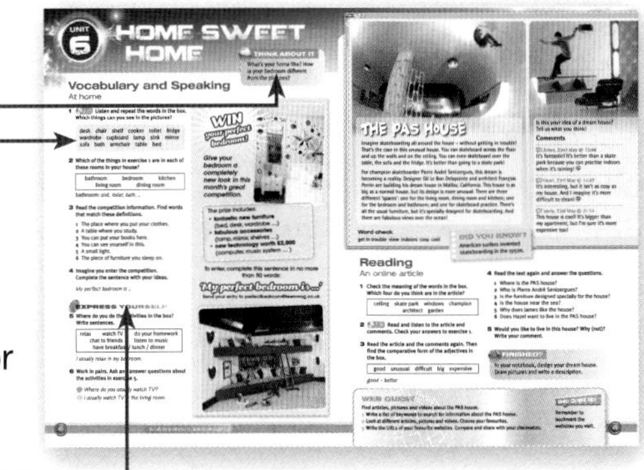

Reading

Reading texts present language in context and cover many real-world topics. *Pulse* uses a variety of text types, from web articles to magazine interviews. Reading texts are recorded on the *Class Audio CD*.

Grammar

Grammar is presented through clear grammar tables at the start of the page. Graded exercises help students practise what they learn.

The **Analyse** feature encourages students to reflect on the differences between grammar in English and their own language.

Each grammar section is linked to pronunciation tasks in the **Pronunciation lab** at the back of the book.

Vocabulary and Listenin

The second vocabulary set is presented and practised.

An extended listening text develops listening skills while recycling target language in context.

Cultural awareness

The Cultural awareness reading text highlights an aspect of life in different English-speaking countries.

Each Cultural awareness page is linked to a **culture video** with footage of real life in the English-speaking world. The videos are accompanied by worksheets.

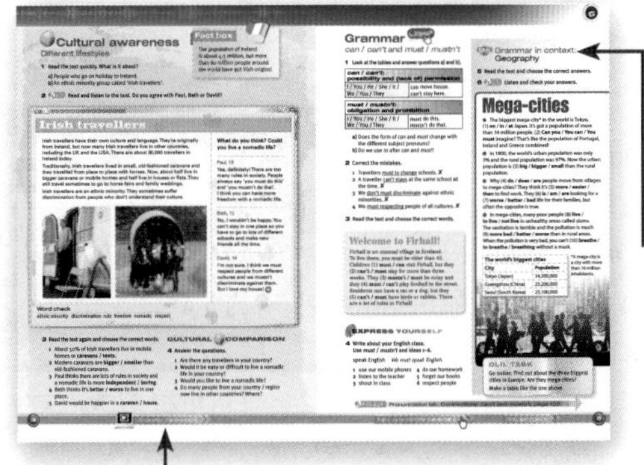

Grammar

The second grammar page presents and practises the new language.

All grammar presented in the unit is practised through the extended **Grammar in context** activity. Each exercise has a **CLIL** focus, covering different subjects from the school curriculum.

Integrated skills

A short real-world **reading** text engages students with the topic and practises comprehension.

Students **listen** to an authentic functional situation and test their understanding.

Students then watch a **videoed dialogue** of an everyday situation such as asking for directions.

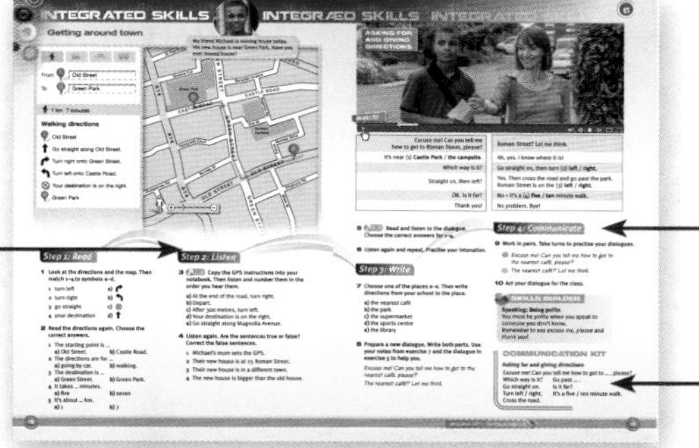

After listening to or watching the dialogue, students **write** their own conversation.

Working in pairs, students practise **speaking** by acting out their new dialogues.

The **Communication kit** provides functional language for easy reference.

Writing

The **Writing** page provides a model for different text types.

A specific language point is highlighted in the **Writing focus** box and practised.

The **Writing task** guides students through the preparation and production of their own text.

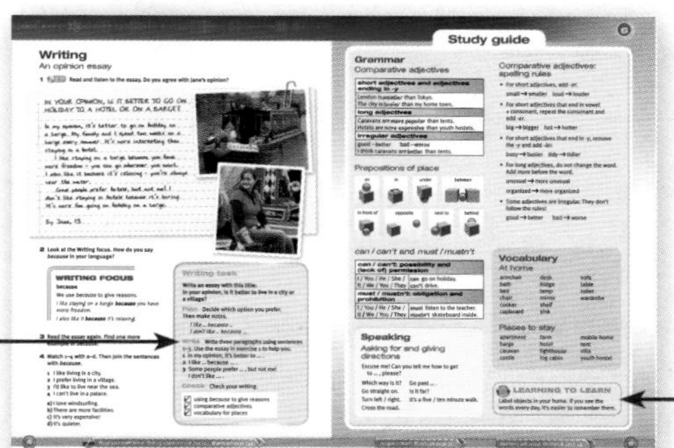

Study guide

The **Study guide** is a useful reference of all language presented in the unit.

It also encourages learner autonomy through the **Learning to Learn** tips.

Collaborative projects

These provide an opportunity for students to work collaboratively and develop their **digital competence** by creating a project using software packages or web tools.

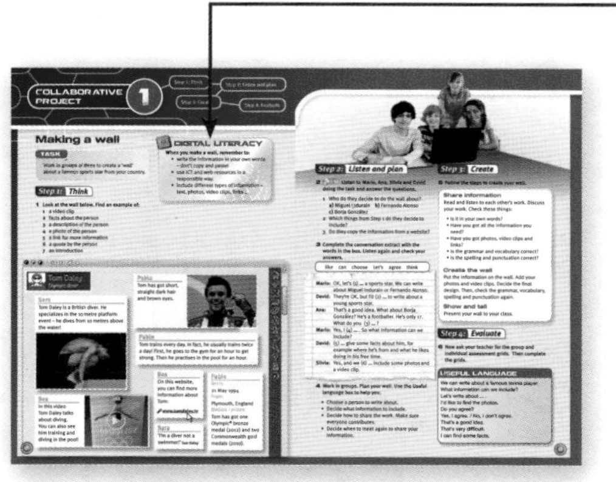

The **Digital literacy** feature gives students tips on improving their digital skills.

External exam trainer

On the **Your exam preparation** page, students are presented with a typical exam task and prepare to answer it.

The **Model exam** gives students a clear example of a model question and answer.

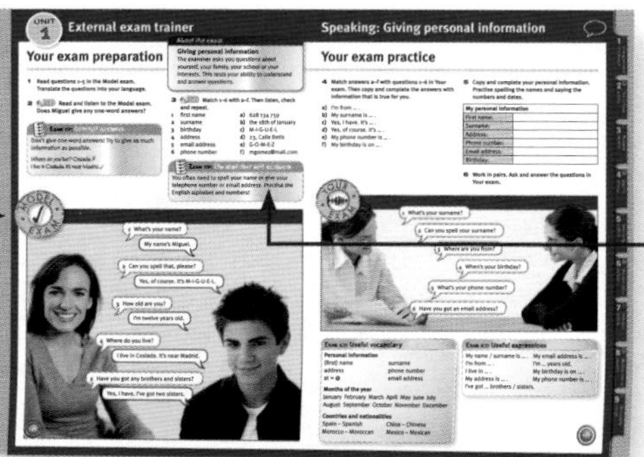

On the **Your exam practice** page students get the opportunity to put their exam strategies into action.

Exam tips give students advice and techniques to help them answer exam questions successfully.

Pulse Workbook 1

The *Workbook* includes:

- Practice activities testing all language presented in the Student's Book
- A full-colour Self-study bank including further practice, extension activities and reference material
- Online audio

The **Workbook** is available in three editions: English, Castilian and Catalan. The Teacher's *Digital Course* features a fully-interactive version of the *Workbook*, which is compatible with all devices including interactive whiteboards.

Vocabulary 1

A variety of activities and tasks ensure successful revision of the vocabulary sets from the *Student's Book.*

Express yourself activities provide students with personalization opportunities.

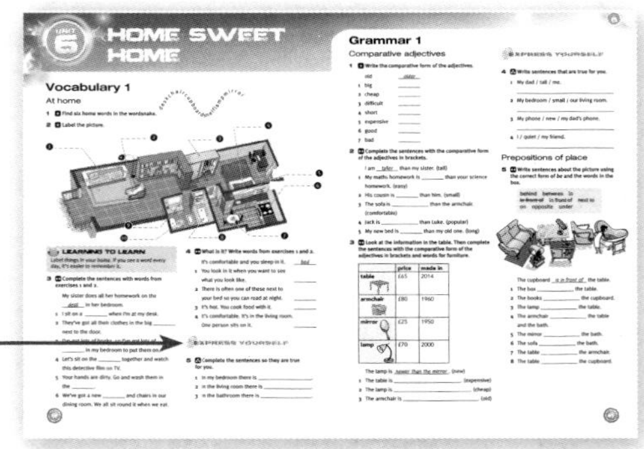
HOME SWEET HOME

Vocabulary 1

Grammar 1

Grammar 1

Clear, easy-to-follow exercises provide students with extensive practice of all the grammar taught in *Pulse*.

Vocabulary 2

The second vocabulary set is practised with a range of activities and tasks.

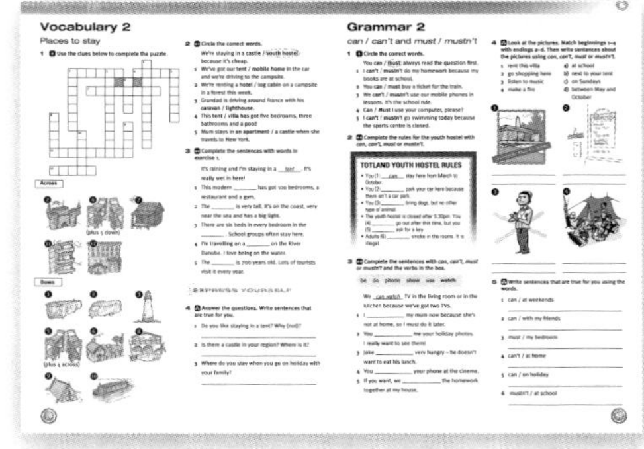
Vocabulary 2

Grammar 2

Grammar 2

The Grammar 2 page offers thorough practice of the second grammar point presented in the *Student's Book* unit.

Reading

A wide variety of texts on theme-related topics and thorough practice of all question types.

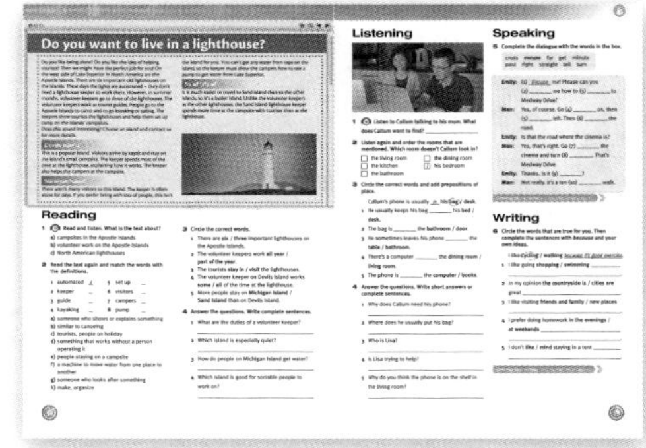
Do you want to live in a lighthouse?

Reading

Listening

Speaking

Writing

Communication skills

A broad range of **listening** texts and tasks link thematically to the units.

Speaking activities test students' recall of the functional language presented in the *Student's Book*.

Progress check

The Progress check provides an in-depth test of all vocabulary and grammar covered in the unit.

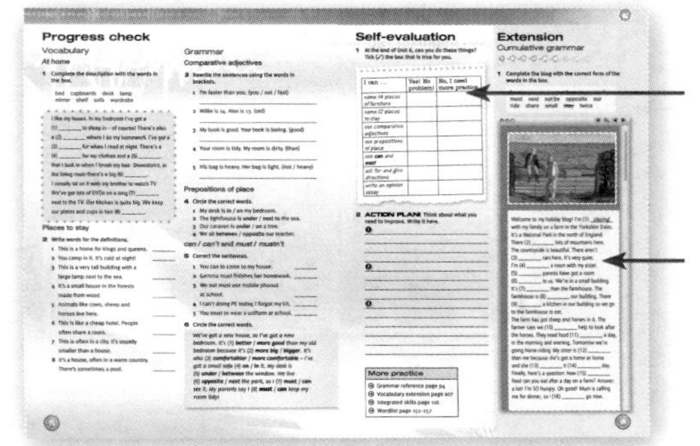
Progress check

Self-evaluation

Extension

Self-evaluation and Extension

Students use the **chart** to evaluate their progress before creating an **action plan** for improvement.

The **extension** text provides **cumulative** practice of grammar covered throughout the book.

'he *Self-study bank* includes:

- Grammar reference and practice
- Vocabulary extension
- Integrated skills
- Writing reference and practice
- External exam trainer
- Speaking reference
- Pronunciation reference
- Wordlist
- Irregular verb list

Grammar reference

'he **Grammar reference** section provides extended grammar tables and explanations of all grammar covered in level 1 of *Pulse*. It is available in three language versions: English, Castilian and Catalan.

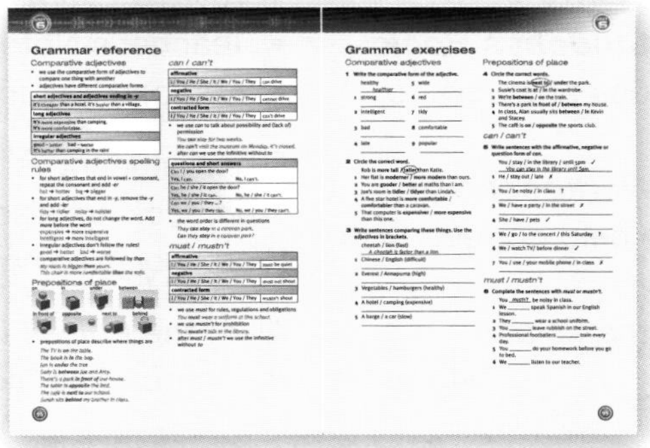

Grammar practice exercises are provided directly opposite the relevant Grammar reference pages.

Vocabulary extension

Vocabulary extension pages use visuals to present a new lexical set related to the topic of each unit. The vocabulary is recorded so that students can listen and then practise their pronunciation.

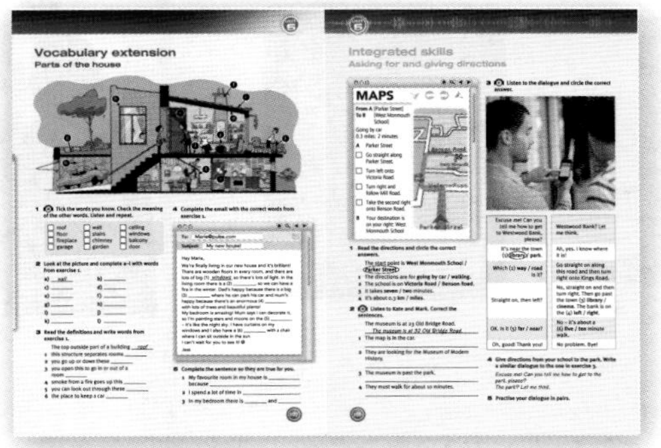

Integrated skills

The **Integrated skills** pages feature reading, listening, writing and speaking exercises that build on the Integrated skills section in the *Student's Book* through at-home practice.

Writing reference

An **annotated model text** linked to the unit topic shows students what they need to include in their own written work.

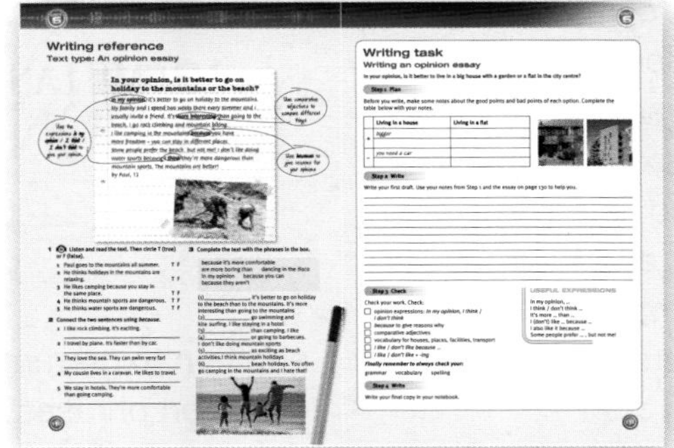

Writing tasks are broken down into steps to help students plan, prepare and produce their own writing texts at home.

External exam trainer

The **External exam trainer** section covers Reading and Writing exam tasks typical of external exams.

The **Model exam** gives students a clear example of a model question and answer.

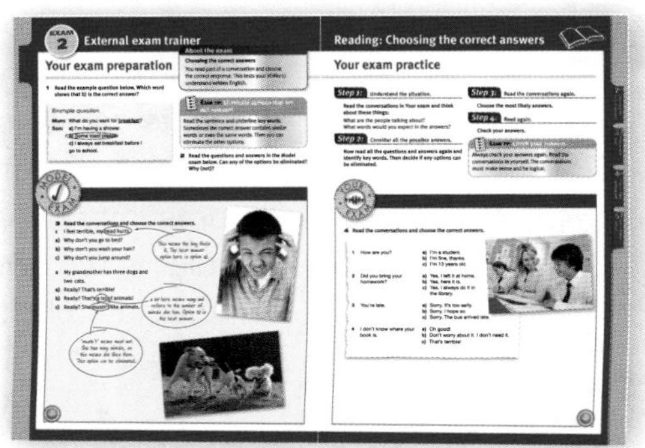

On the **Your exam practice** page students get the opportunity to put their exam strategies into action.

Exam tips give students advice and techniques to help them answer exam questions successfully.

Pulse Live! Digital Course

The *Pulse Live! Digital Course* is available in both teacher and student versions, providing tailored digital solutions which suit the technology available in all teaching environments. The *Digital Course* is compatible with all devices including interactive whiteboards.

The Teacher's *Digital Course* is a complete resource which groups digital versions of all *Pulse* teaching materials in one place for ease.

The course contains:

- Fully-interactive digital version of the ***Student's Book*** with integrated audio and video. Includes **answers** to help correction in class
- Fully-interactive digital version of the ***Workbook*** with integrated audio. Includes **answers** to help correction in class
- **Markbook** to keep track of students' marks and progress throughout the year
- **Interactive video** versions of the *Student's Book* mode dialogues from the Integrated skills pages, which allow students to see and hear real-life functional speaking situations
- **Culture videos and worksheets** to accompany each unit of the *Student's Book*
- **Vocabulary trainer** to help students learn and practise core vocabulary from the *Student's Book*
- *Teacher's Resource File* materials
- *Tests & Exams Pack* materials
- Teacher's Notes
- Audioscripts for all components

Digital student versions of both the *Student's Book* and *Workbook* are also available. All students using the print *Workbook* also have access to **interactive digital materials**.

All of the *Pulse Live! Digital Courses* link to the teacher's markbook to make correction and evaluation easier.

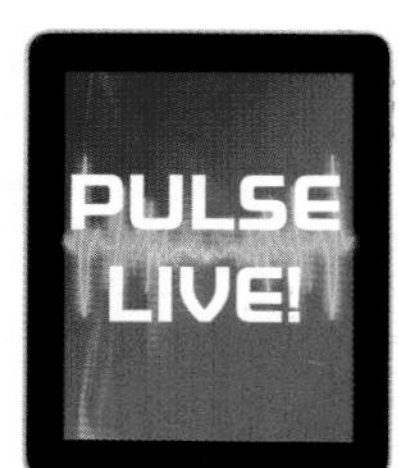

Additional resources for students

Macmillan Secondary Student's Website

The *Secondary Student's Website* provides learners with hundreds of additional activities to practise the language presented in the *Student's Book*. These exercises cover grammar, vocabulary, reading, writing and listening. Students can work at home or at school, and their results will always be recorded in the teacher's markbook. The website allows both students and teachers to monitor online work. www.macmillansecondary.com

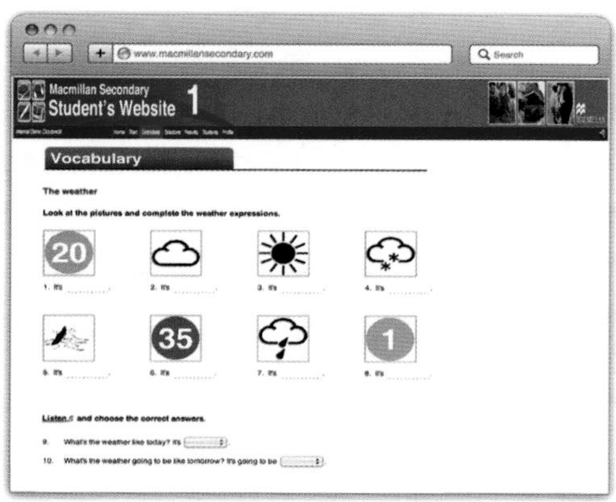

Macmillan Dictionary Online

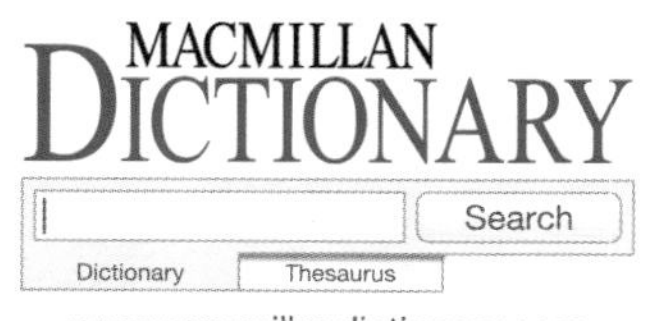

The Macmillan Dictionary Online is a free dictionary and thesaurus. The website presents users with clear definitions, word sets and useful synonym boxes in addition to grammar information, example sentences, common phrases and recorded British and American pronunciations.

The Macmillan Dictionary Online also offers innovative tools and resources for teachers to use in class, including e-lessons and language games.

Students can also use the website for self-study to become more confident users of English. The website features interactive language games to practise irregular verbs and phrasal verbs which can be used to complement classroom learning.

www.macmillandictionary.com

Pulse resources for teachers

Teacher's Book

The *Teacher's Book* contains everything you need to successfully work with *Pulse* in class.

Each unit features a clear overview of the contents and objectives with full teaching notes, answer keys and audioscripts. There are lesson objectives, language and culture notes, and extra activities for fast finishers. The *Teacher's Book* also includes all *Student's Book* reference materials and the *Workbook* answer key.

Teacher's Resource File

The *Teacher's Resource File* features a wealth of photocopiable worksheets and resources to recycle and practise language, develop skills and evaluate and assess your students. These include classroom diversity solutions, CLIL materials, evaluation rubrics and worksheets to help students develop digital competence.

Teacher's Resource File Multi-ROM

The Multi-ROM includes all the *Teacher's Resource File* materials in editable Word format. It also includes the accompanying audio recordings.

Class Audio CDs

All the audio recordings from the *Student's Book* are included on three audio CDs, which come with complete track listings.

Tests and Exams Pack

Tests and Exams Multi-ROM

The Tests and Exams Multi-ROM is available on disk in editable Word format as well as PDFs. The material includes:

- A Key competences diagnostic test which can be used to assess the language level of students
- Tests available at three levels: basic, standard and extra. Each level has:
  - one placement test
  - nine progress tests
  - three end-of-term tests
  - one end-of-year test
- Answer keys, audio and audioscripts for all the tests and exams.

CEFR Skills Exam Generator Multi-ROM

The *Pulse Tests and Exams Pack* includes the *CEFR Skills Exam Generator Multi-ROM,* which gives teachers the opportunity to generate their own skills-based exams. Covering CEFR levels A1+ /A2, A2, A2+ and B1/B1+, the exams include a range of reading, writing and speaking tasks typical of external exams.

Teacher's Book

The *Teacher's Book* contains a variety of different features and tasks to help teachers make the best use of all *Pulse* materials.

Each unit of the *Teacher's Book* begins with an extensive double-page **Overview** of the unit. The overview covers the following categories: Unit objectives and Key competences, Linguistic contents, Skills, Lifelong learning skills, Evaluation, External exam trainer, Digital material, Digital competence, Reinforcement material, Extension material and Teacher's Resource File.

Clear **Lesson objectives** are included at the start of each lesson. These provide a useful summary of the new language that will be presented in class and tasks that students will perform.

Optional **Warmer** tasks are short and practical, helping to prepare students for the lesson ahead.

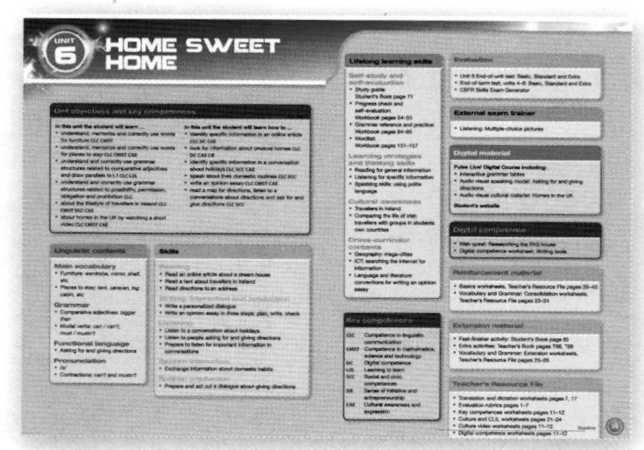
UNIT 6 HOME SWEET HOME

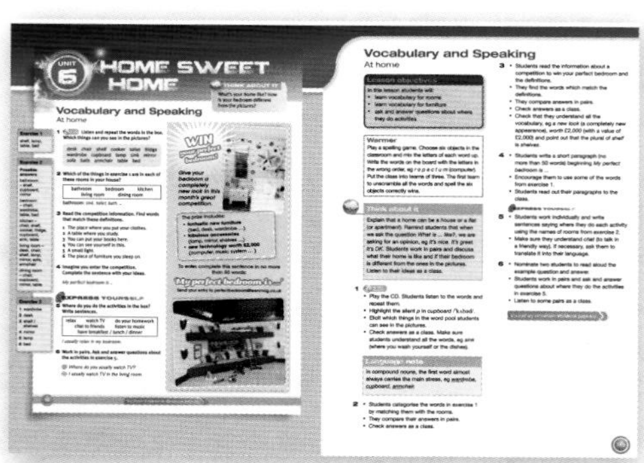
UNIT 6 HOME SWEET HOME

Vocabulary and Speaking

Language notes provide extra information about pronunciation, vocabulary or grammar for teachers. They may include a definition or the phonetic script of a difficult word or phrase, provide a more detailed grammar explanation or explain idiomatic use of English.

The **Culture note** feature provides additional cultural context for teachers. The boxes aim to give teachers useful information to answe questions that students might have about the people, places or events mentioned in the *Student's Book*.

The **Extra activity** boxes provide extra tasks for students who finish the *Student's Book* activities before their classmates. As such, this feature helps with classroom diversity.

Teacher's Resource File

With 290 pages of photocopiable material, complete answer keys and audioscripts, the *Teacher's Resource File* provides all the worksheets and extra materials you need to ensure your students have a meaningful and thorough learning experience with *Pulse*.

In addition, all materials are included on the *Teacher's Resource Multi-ROM* in both PDF and editable Word format, so that you can tailor them to the needs of your class.

The *Teacher's Resource File* is divided into different sections to ensure easy navigation. The relevant answer key is located after the worksheets at the end of the section.

Pulse Basics

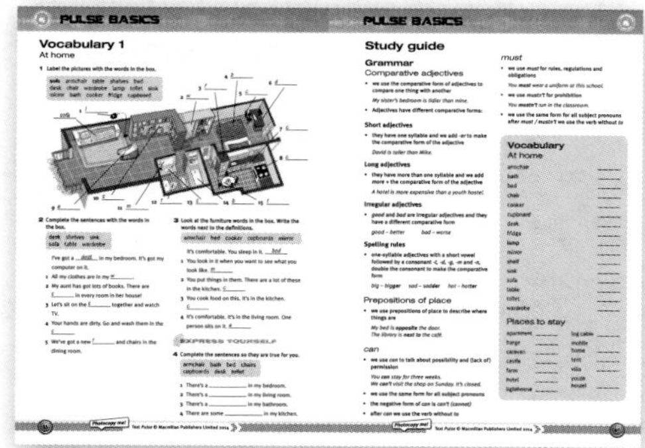
PULSE BASICS

Vocabulary 1

PULSE BASICS

Study guide

A 66-page photocopiable workbook tailored to lower-level students – an ideal solution for classroom diversity. It includes revision of key vocabulary and grammar in the *Student's Book*, reading and writing skills work, a language reference section and an answer key.

Vocabulary and Grammar Consolidation and Extension

VOCABULARY CONSOLIDATION

VOCABULARY EXTENSION

Each unit has two **Consolidation** worksheets and two **Extension** worksheets. These provide revision and extended practice of all vocabulary and grammar covered in the *Student's Book*.

Translation and Dictation

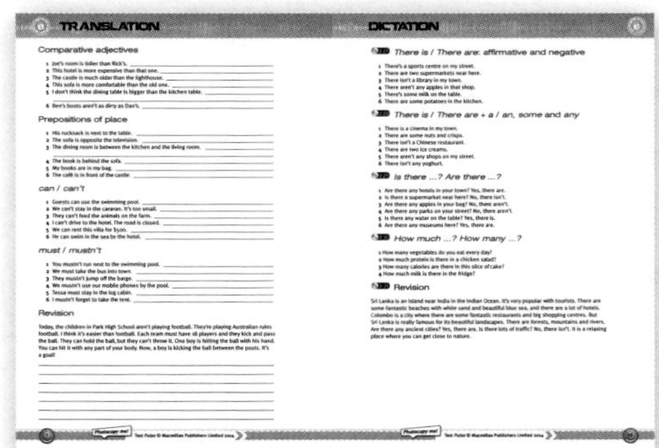

ranslation and **dictation** exercises are
nked to each unit.
ictation exercises are recorded on the
ictations Audio CD.

Evaluation rubrics

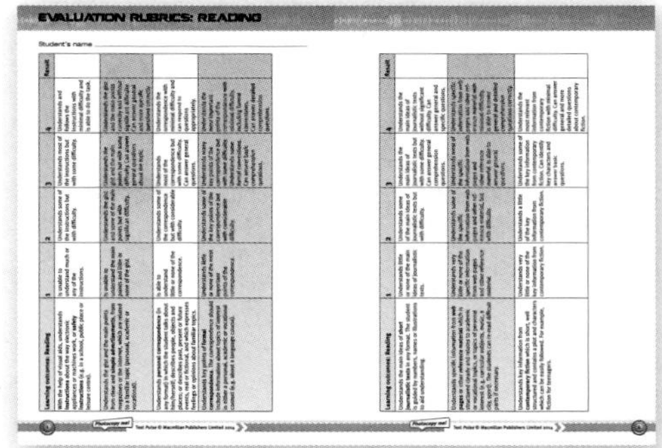

The **Evaluation rubrics** can be used to assess students' reading, writing, listening and speaking skills and their progress throughout the year. They focus on specific learning outcomes covered in class, such as writing a formal letter or giving a presentation, and include evaluation criteria which show what students are achieving successfully.

Key competences worksheets

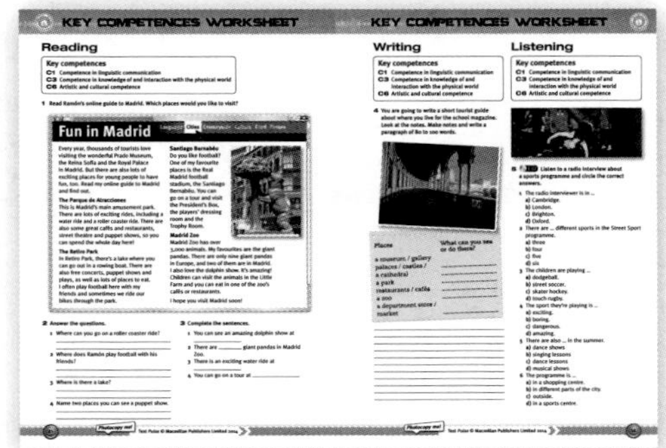

he **Key competences** worksheets provide further
vork on skills with reading, writing, listening and
peaking pairwork activities. Relevant competences
re clearly indicated on each worksheet.

Culture and CLIL worksheets

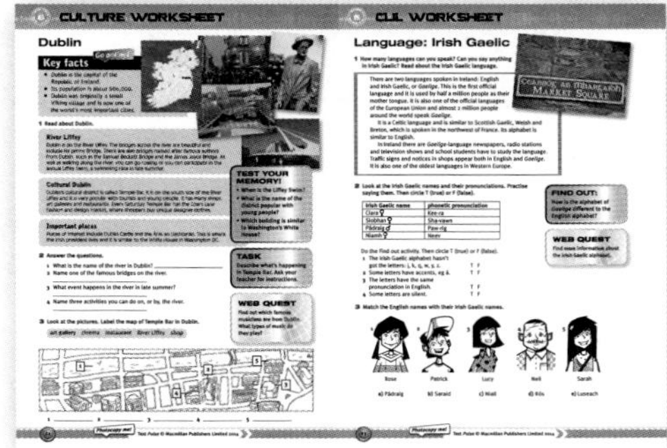

There is one Culture and one CLIL worksheet per unit. **Culture** worksheets are based around different cities in the English-speaking world, with activities focused on historical and cultural information. **CLIL** worksheets link cultural topics with other areas of the school curriculum. **Teacher's notes** provide ideas for using the material in class.

Culture video worksheets

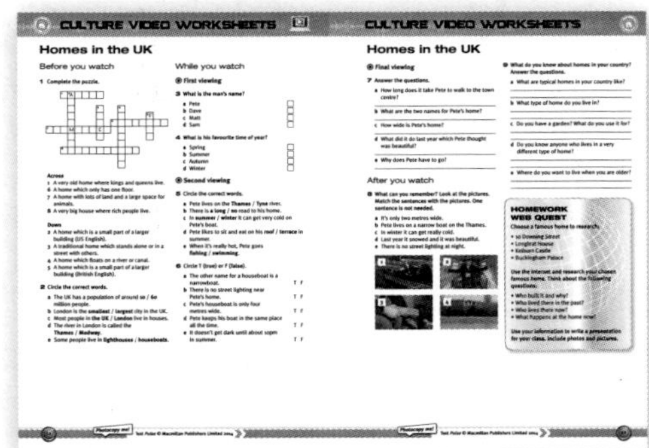

ach Cultural awareness page in the *Student's Book* is
nked to a related **culture video** with engaging footage
f real life in English-speaking countries. There are
vorksheets which test students' comprehension of the
udiovisual material during and after watching the videos,
nd **Teacher's notes** which explain how to make the
nost of the worksheets in class.

Digital competence worksheets

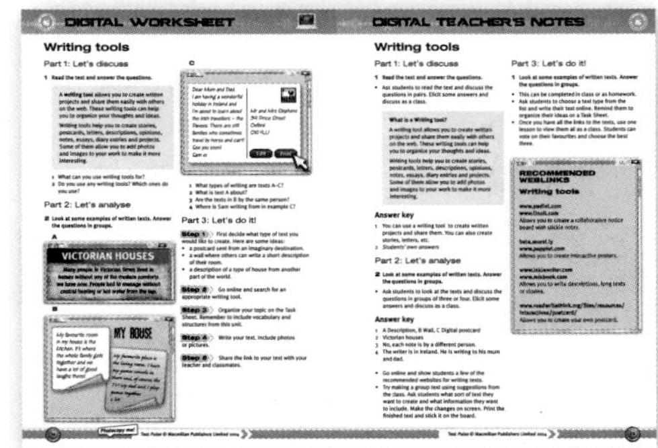

Students can develop their digital competence while learning English through the **Digital competence worksheets**, which teach them how to use web tools to create projects such as avatars, podcasts and online biographies. Worksheets come with **Teacher's notes** which provide more information about the web tools and explain how to carry out the tasks successfully in class.

STARTER WELCOME TO MY WORLD!

Vocabulary
Family

Exercise 1
1 dad
2 brother
3 mum
4 sister
Grandma and grandad aren't in the picture.

1 1.02 **Match the words in the box with the people in the picture. Which people aren't in the picture? Then listen and repeat.**

mum	dad	brother
sister	grandma	grandad

2 How many other family words can you write in one minute?

aunt, ...

Grammar 

Demonstrative pronouns

3 Read the sentences in the table. How do you say the words in blue in your language?

demonstrative pronouns	
This is my brother.	**These** are my parents.
That's my sister.	**Those** are my pets.

Exercise 4
1 That
2 This
3 Those
4 These

4 Copy and complete the sentences with *this*, *that*, *these* or *those*.

1 ...'s my cat.   2 ... is my dog.

3 ... are my rabbits.   
4 ... are my snakes!

Subject pronouns and possessive adjectives

Exercise 5
1 your
2 its
3 our
4 their

5 Copy and complete the table with the words in the box.

our	~~my~~	your	their	its

subject pronouns	possessive adjectives
I	*my*
you	(1) ...
he	his
she	her
it	(2) ...
we	(3) ...
you	your
they	(4) ...

Exercise 6
1 a my
b He's
2 a our
b Their
3 a my
b They
4 a She
b Her

6 Choose the correct words.

1 **a)** Andy is **my** / **you** best friend.
b) **His** / **He's** 13 years old.
2 **a)** These are **our** / **we** rabbits.
b) **They** / **Their** names are Honey and Bunny.
3 **a)** Bill and Joy are **they** / **my** grandparents.
b) **They** / **Their** are 72 years old.
4 **a)** Katy's my sister. **She** / **Her** is eight.
b) **She** / **Her** favourite colour is pink!

Vocabulary
Family

Lesson objectives

In this lesson students will:
- learn / revise words for family members
- learn / revise demonstrative pronouns
- learn / revise subject pronouns and possessive adjectives

Warmer

Play a game of Hangman to introduce the theme of family members in preparation for the next activity. Use the words *mother* and *father*.

1 1.02
- Students match the words in the word pool with the people and identify which people aren't in the picture.
- They compare their answers in pairs.
- Check answers as a class.
- Play the CD. Students listen and repeat.

2
- Highlight the example *aunt*.
- Students work individually and write down as many other words for family members as they can in one minute.
- They compare their answers in pairs.
- Check answers as a class. Possible answers include *uncle, son, daughter, cousin, grandchild.*

Extra activity

Students use the words from exercises 1 and 2 to draw a family tree in English.

Grammar
Digital

Demonstrative pronouns

3
- Show the class the difference between *this* and *that* by holding up something near to you and saying, eg *This is my pen*.
- Point to something in the class that is further away from you and say, eg *That's my coat*.
- Explain that *these* is the plural form of *this*, and *those* is the plural form of *that*.
- Students look at the table. Elicit how they say *this, that, these, those* in their language.

4
- Students work individually and complete the sentences using *this, that, these* or *those*.
- They compare their answers in pairs or small groups.
- Check answers as a class.

Subject pronouns and possessive adjectives

5
- Explain the concepts of a subject pronoun and a possessive adjective (give examples in the students' language if necessary).
- Students copy and complete the table using the words in the box.
- Check answers as a class. Make sure they pronounce *their* correctly as /ðeə/.

6
- Highlight the first sentence. Explain that *you* is not possible because it is a subject pronoun.
- Students work individually and choose the correct answer from each pair of words.
- They compare their answers in pairs.
- Check answers as a class. Point out that *He's* is the contracted form of *He is*.

Finished?

Ask fast finishers to write sentences like the ones in exercise 6 about their own friends, family and pets, eg *Luis is my best friend. He's 12 years old.*

Digital course: Interactive grammar table

Vocabulary

Days, months and dates

Lesson objectives

In this lesson students will:

- learn / revise days, months and dates
- learn / revise possessive *'s*
- write sentences about their family

Warmer

Write the days of the week on the board in random order. Write the numbers 1 to 7 in a column on another part of the board. Students work in pairs and put the days in the correct order beginning with *Monday*. Invite individual students to come to the board to write the correct day after each number.

1 1.03

- Students work individually and write down the months of the year in the correct order.
- They compare their answers in pairs.
- Play the CD. Students listen, check their answers and repeat.
- Invite students to the board to write the names of the months in the correct order.
- Check that the spelling and order are correct.

2

- Elicit today's date from the class, eg *the first of September*.
- Highlight that we use ordinal numbers when we say the date.
- Write the numbers 1 to 5 on the board and elicit their ordinal equivalents, *first, second, third, fourth, fifth*.
- Point out that the remaining ordinal numbers are like *fourth* and *fifth* and end in *-th* until 21, 22 and 23, which are like *first, second* and *third*. The same is true for 31 – *the thirty-first*.
- Students find Hazel's birthday on the calendar.
- Check the answer as a class. Make sure they say the date correctly with all the component words, *the twenty-fifth of September*.

3

- Nominate two students to read aloud the model dialogue to the class.
- Students work in groups of four and ask and answer the question.
- Listen to some example dialogues as a class.

Look!

Highlight that you can write dates in three ways: *3rd August, August 3rd* or *3 August*. Point out that you can say dates in two ways: *the third of August* or *August the third*. You don't need to write *the* or *of* when you write dates but you must use them when you say dates.

Grammar 

Possessive *'s*

4

- Students look at the grammar box.
- They match sentences 1–3 with grammar rules a or b.
- They compare their answers in pairs.
- Check answers as a class.

Language note

Although the rule is that names ending in *-s* are simply followed by an apostrophe, eg *Charles' birthday*, in spoken English many people add *'s*, eg *Charles's birthday, Carlos's sister*.

5

- Tell students there is one apostrophe missing in each sentence.
- Students work individually and put the apostrophes in the correct place.
- Check answers as a class.

EXPRESS YOURSELF

6

- Write two sentences about your family on the board as an example, eg *My mum's name is ... My sister's birthday is on ...*
- Students work individually to write at least three sentences.
- Ask students to swap notebooks and check each other's writing for the correct use of possessive adjectives, subject pronouns and the possessive *'s*.
- Check answers as a class.

7

- Put students into pairs. They ask and answer questions about their sentences in exercise 6.

Digital course: Interactive grammar table

Exercise 1
January
February
March
April
May
June
July
August
September
October
November
December

Exercise 2
25th September

Exercise 4
1 a
2 b
3 b

Exercise 5
1 mum's
2 sister's
3 brothers'
4 Chris'
5 John's
6 cat's

Vocabulary
Days, months and dates

1 1.03 **Write the 12 months of the year in the correct order. Then listen, check and repeat.**

January, ...

2 Look at the calendar. When is Hazel's birthday?

LOOK!

When we write dates, we omit *the* and *of*.
My birthday is on 7th August.
When we say dates, we say *the* and *of*.
*My birthday is on **the** seventh **of** August.*

3 When's your birthday? Ask your classmates.

Pablo, when's your birthday?
It's on the third of October.

Grammar

Possessive 's

4 Look at the table. Match sentences 1–3 with rules a) or b).

possessive 's
We use ***'s*** to show possession.
1 My brother**'s** name is Charles.
2 Charles**'** birthday is on Saturday.
3 My sisters**'** names are Katy and Agnes.

a) We use *'s* after a singular noun or a name that doesn't end in *-s*.
b) We use *'* after a plural noun or a name that ends in *-s*.

5 Correct the sentences. Add one apostrophe (') to each sentence.

My parents names are David and Patricia. ✗
My parents' names are David and Patricia. ✓

1 My mums birthday is on Wednesday. ✗
2 My sisters name is Vanessa. ✗
3 My brothers names are Chris and John. ✗
4 Chris birthday is on 4th February. ✗
5 Johns birthday is on 15th March. ✗
6 My cats name is Felix. ✗

EXPRESS YOURSELF

6 Write three sentences about your family. Use exercise 5 to help you.

My mum's name is...

Check Check your writing.

- ☑ possessive adjectives
- ☑ subject pronouns
- ☑ possessive *'s*

7 Work in pairs. Ask and answer questions about your sentences in exercise 6.

What's your mum's name?
My mum's name is Elena.

Exercise 1

Europe
Poland, Portugal, Spain, France
Asia
Japan, China
Africa
Morocco, South Africa
Australasia
Australia, New Zealand
North America
Canada, the USA
South America
Argentina, Brazil

Exercise 2

6 European countries
the UK, Poland, Portugal, Spain, France, Germany, Italy, Russia, Austria, Belgium, etc
5 countries where people speak English
the UK, Australia, South Africa, New Zealand, Canada, the USA, etc
4 European capitals
London, Madrid, Lisbon, Rome, Paris, Berlin, etc
3 countries in South America
Brazil, Argentina, Peru, Chile, Ecuador, etc
2 countries in North America
Canada, the USA
1 country in Africa
South Africa, etc

Vocabulary

Countries, nationalities and languages

1 1.04 **Copy and complete the table with the countries in the box. Then listen, check and repeat.**

the UK Australia Poland Portugal Japan Argentina Spain Morocco
New Zealand Brazil Canada China the USA South Africa France

Europe	Asia	Africa	Australasia	North America	South America
the UK, ...					

Exercise 3

Chinese – China
Polish – Poland
French – France
South African – South Africa
American – the USA
Portuguese – Portugal
New Zealander – New Zealand
Brazilian – Brazil
Canadian – Canada
Australian – Australia
Japanese – Japan
British – the UK
Spanish – Spain
Argentinian – Argentina
Moroccan – Morocco

2 Do the quiz in pairs. Can you finish first?

Quick Quiz!

Write the names of ...
6 European countries
5 countries where people speak Engl
4 European capitals
3 countries in South America
2 countries in North America
1 country in Africa

3 Match the nationalities in the box with countries from exercise 1. Write sentences.

Chinese Polish French South African American Portuguese New Zealander
Brazilian Canadian Australian Japanese British Spanish Argentinian Moroccan

Chinese people are from China.

Exercise 4

Spanish – Spain and Argentina
Mandarin – China
Arabic – Morocco
English – the UK, Australia, New Zealand, Canada, the USA, South Africa,
French – France

4 In which countries do people speak the languages in the box?

Portuguese Spanish Mandarin
Arabic English French

Portuguese – in Portugal and Brazil

LOOK!

***people* = plural**
~~British people is from the UK.~~ ✗
British people **are** from the UK. ✔

Vocabulary

Countries, nationalities and languages

Lesson objectives

In this lesson students will:

- learn the names of countries, nationalities and languages
- learn where certain countries are in the world
- learn where different languages are spoken

Warmer

Ask students to keep their books closed. Students work in pairs and write down the names of as many continents from the table in exercise 1 as they can. Invite individual students to the board to write the names of the continents. Make sure they spell them correctly (*Europe, Asia, Africa, Australasia, North America, South America*).

1 1.04

- Check students understand that they have to match the countries with the continents and write them in the correct column.
- Students compare their answers in pairs.
- Play the CD. Students listen, check their answers and repeat.

2

- Students answer the quiz questions in pairs.
- Check answers as a class.

3

- Point out that the nationality words are adjectives. Highlight the example sentence *Chinese people are from China*.
- Students match the nationalities with the countries from exercise 1.
- They compare their answers in pairs.
- Check answers as a class.
- You could point out that the nationality word for *New Zealand* is *New Zealander*.

Look!

The word *people* is plural, so British people are from the UK, French people are from France, etc. The definite article is always used with *UK* and *USA* – *the UK*, *the USA*.

Language note

Nationality words ending in *-ese* are stressed on the final syllable, eg *Chi'nese*, *Portu'guese*. Words ending in *-ish* are stressed on the first syllable, eg *'English*, *'Spanish*. *'Argentine* is an alternative to *Argen'tinian*.

4

- Point out that the words for languages are often the same as the words for nationalities but not always (eg *English*, *Mandarin* are different).
- Ask the students to use the countries from exercise 1. Students work individually and complete the exercise.
- They compare their answers in pairs.
- Check answers as a class.

Grammar 

be: affirmative, negative and interrogative

Lesson objectives

In this lesson students will:

- learn / revise the verb *be* in the affirmative, negative and question forms
- learn / revise short forms of *be* in the present simple tense
- learn / revise short answers

Warmer

Ask students to keep their books closed. Write an affirmative sentence with *be* from the previous lesson on the board in random order: *from people UK are British the*. Students work in pairs and write the sentence in the correct order (*British people are from the UK*).

1
- Students work individually and change the short forms to full forms using the words in the box.
- They compare their answers in pairs.
- Check answers as a class.

Language note

We normally use the short forms in speaking and the full forms in writing, especially in formal writing.

2
- Encourage the students to use short forms when completing this exercise.
- Students work individually using the table in exercise 1 to help them.
- Check answers as a class.

3
- Explain that all the sentences are factually incorrect.
- Nominate a student to read the example sentences aloud.
- Students write two sentences for each example, correcting the mistake.
- Check answers as a class.

4
- Complete the first gap with the class.
- Students fill the gaps using *is* or *are*.
- They compare answers in pairs.
- Check answers as a class.

5
- Students match the questions with the short answers.
- Check answers as a class.

Look!

Highlight that we do not use the short form in affirmative short answers. Point out that the short form is usually used in negative short answers.

Extra activity

Students work in pairs and ask and answer the questions in exercise 5. They make as many questions as possible with different subject pronouns and take it in turns to ask and answer them using short answers in both the affirmative and negative.

6
- Do one more example with the class first. Write *Rafael Nadal/French* on the board. Elicit the question *Is Rafael Nadal French?* and the answer *No, he isn't*.
- Students work in pairs and write questions and short answers using the prompts and the information in exercise 4.
- Check answers as a class.

Digital course: Interactive grammar table

Grammar 

be: affirmative, negative and interrogative

1 Copy the tables into your notebook. Change the short forms in blue for the full forms in the box.

are not	am	is not	am not	are	is

affirmative	
I'm You're He's / She's / It's We're / You're / They're	European. English. American. Spanish.

negative	
I'm **not** You **aren't** He / She / It **isn't** We / You / They **aren't**	Portuguese. Australian. South African. Japanese.

2 Copy and complete the sentences with the correct affirmative or negative form of *be*. Use short forms where possible.

1 I ... from Spain.
2 My parents ... from Brazil.
3 I ... Australian.
4 My teacher ... Spanish.
5 Morocco and South Africa ... in Europe.
6 Málaga ... the capital of Spain.

3 Correct the sentences. Write one negative and one affirmative sentence for each.

China is a small country. ✗

China isn't a small country. It's a big country.

1 London is the capital of France. ✗
2 Italy and Germany are in Africa. ✗
3 Luxembourg is a big country. ✗
4 China and Japan are in Europe. ✗
5 Portugal is next to France. ✗

4 Copy and complete the profile with *is* or *are*.

Steven Gerrard (1) ... a famous football player. His teams (2) ... Liverpool and England.

Steven (3) ... English. His parents (4) ... from Liverpool.

His wife's name (5) ... Alex. His daughters' names (6) ... Lilly-Ella, Lexie and Lourdes.

Steven's favourite number (7) ... four and his favourite colours (8) ... red and white!

Profile: Steven Gerrard

5 Match questions 1–3 with short answers a–c.

questions		
1 **Are**	you	a football fan?
2 **Is**	he / she / it	from Liverpool?
3 **Are**	we / you / they	English?

short answers
a) Yes, we **are**. / No, we **aren't**.
b) Yes, I **am**. / No, I'm **not**.
c) Yes, he **is**. / No, he **isn't**.

LOOK!

We don't use short forms in affirmative short answers.

~~Yes, I'm.~~ ✗ Yes, I am. ✔

6 Write questions with *Is* or *Are*. Use the information in exercise 4 to help you. Then write short answers.

Steven Gerrard / an actor?

Is Steven Gerrard an actor? No, he isn't.

1 he / English?
2 his parents / from London?
3 his wife's name / Victoria?
4 his children's names / Lilly-Ella, Lexie and Lourdes?
5 his favourite number / four?
6 his favourite colours / blue and yellow?

Exercise 1

affirmative
I am
You are
He is / She is / It is
We are / You are / They are
negative
I am not
You are not
He / She / It is not
We / You / They are not

Exercise 2

1 'm / 'm not
2 are / aren't
3 'm / 'm not
4 's / isn't
5 aren't
6 isn't

Exercise 3

1 London isn't the capital of France. It's the capital of the UK.
2 Italy and Germany aren't in Africa. They're in Europe.
3 Luxembourg isn't a big country. It's a small country.
4 China and Japan aren't in Europe. They're in Asia.
5 Portugal isn't next to France. It's next to Spain.

Exercise 4

1 is
2 are
3 is
4 are
5 is
6 are
7 is
8 are

Exercise 5

1 b
2 c
3 a

Exercise 6

1 Is he English? Yes, he is.
2 Are his parents from London? No, they aren't.
3 Is his wife's name Victoria? No, it isn't.
4 Are his children's names Lilly-Ella, Lexie and Lourdes? Yes, they are.
5 Is his favourite number four? Yes, it is.
6 Are his favourite colours blue and yellow? No, they aren't.

In the classroom

Exercise 1

1 pencil case
2 book
3 notebook
4 rubber
5 ruler
6 pencil sharpener
7 laptop
board
desk
schoolbag
Students' own answers

1 Match 1–7 with words in the box. Which things can you see in your classroom?

clock notebook book board laptop desk pen pencil rubber ruler pencil sharpener pencil case schoolbag dictionary

2 Look at questions a–e. How do you say them in your language?

a) How do you say 'cuaderno' in English?
b) Can you repeat that, please?
c) How do you spell that?
d) What does 'clock' mean?
e) What page are we on?

Exercise 3

1 e
2 d
3 a
4 b
5 c

3 1.05 Listen to five dialogues and write a–e from exercise 2 in the order you hear them. Then listen again and repeat.

4 1.06 Listen and repeat the alphabet.

a b c d e f g h i j k l m n
o p q r s t u v w x y z

5 1.07 Listen and write the three names.

Exercise 5

1 Rachel
2 William
3 Zoe

6 Choose objects from your classroom. In pairs, ask and answer the questions.

How do you say ... in English?
It's ... .
How do you spell that?

Integrated skills

In the classroom

Lesson objective

In this lesson students will:

- learn / revise classroom language

Warmer

Ask students to work in pairs and write down the English words for objects they can see in the classroom (eg *book*, *pen*). Set a time limit of two minutes for this. Elicit examples from the class and write them on the board.

1
- Ask students to read James' speech bubble.
- Students look at the words in the word pool and the picture.
- They work individually and write down the words in the word pool which are in the picture.
- They compare their answers in pairs and then write down the words in the word pool which are in the classroom.
- Check answers as a class.

2
- Ask students to look at question a *How do you say* cuaderno *in English?*
- Ask them how they say *How do you say … in English?* in their language.
- Students work in pairs and translate b–e.
- Check answers as a class.

3 1.05
- Ask students to copy the questions a–e from exercise 2 in their notebooks.
- Tell them they will hear five dialogues with one of the questions in each dialogue.
- They should write *1, 2, 3, 4* or *5* next to the questions depending on the order in which they hear them.
- Play the CD.
- Students compare answers in pairs.
- Check answers as a class.
- Play the CD again for students to listen and repeat.

4 1.06
- Play the CD. Students listen and repeat the letters of the alphabet.

5 1.07
- Play the CD. Students listen and write the three names.
- Check that they have spelt the names correctly.

Language note

Some problematic letters for many learners of English are *a* (pronounced as in *day*), *e* (pronounced as in *see*), *i* (pronounced as in *I*), *y* (pronounced as in *why*) and *r* (pronounced as in *are*). Write these words on the board as a memory aid for students to remember how to say these letters.

6
- Do one or two examples with the class first, eg *How do you say* ventana *in English? It's 'window'. How do you spell that? W-I-N-D-O-W.*
- Students work in pairs and ask and answer about other objects in the classroom.
- Monitor while they are working in pairs and give help with vocabulary when necessary.
- Listen to some examples as a class.

1.05 Audioscript, exercise 3

1 **A** What page are we on?
B We're on page 8.

2 **A** What does 'clock' mean?
B It means *reloj*.

3 **A** How do you say *cuaderno* in English?
B 'Notebook'.

4 **A** Can you repeat that, please?
B Yes – 'notebook'.

5 **A** How do you spell that?
B N-O-T-E-B-O-O-K.

1.07 Audioscript, exercise 5

1 **A** Hi. What's your name?
B My name's Rachel.
A How do you spell that?
B R-A-C-H-E-L.

2 **A** Hello. What's your name?
B My name's William.
A How do you spell that?
B It's W-I-L-L-I-A-M.

3 **A** Hi. What's your name?
B My name's Zoe.
A How do you spell that?
B Z-O-E.
A Can you repeat that, please?
B Yes – it's Z-O-E.
A Thanks!

Integrated skills – continued

Meeting and greeting

Lesson objective

In this lesson students will:
- practise the language of meeting and greeting

Warmer

Write on the board the question *Where are you from?* with the words in the wrong order, eg *you are Where from?*. Tell students to work in pairs and put the words into the correct order to form a question.

7 1.08
- Students read the dialogue.
- Tell them to listen to the dialogue and write the missing words 1–3.
- Play the CD.
- Ask if they have written all three words. If not, play the CD again.
- Students compare answers in pairs.
- Check answers as a class.
- Check students understand *next to*. Show the meaning using an example, eg *Luis is next to Jorge.*

8
- Play the CD again, pausing after each speaker's part for students to repeat as a class.
- Note the main stress on the questions: *What's your name? Where are you from? Where exactly?*
- Ask students to repeat these questions several times both chorally and individually.
- Students practise the dialogue in pairs. Then swap roles and practise the dialogue again.

9
- Students copy the three questions in bold from the dialogue in exercise 7 into their notebooks.
- They write their own answers to these questions, eg *What's your name? My name's ...*
- Check answers as a class.

10
- Ask students to look at the dialogue in exercise 7 again.
- Tell them to write a new dialogue like the one in exercise 7 but using their name, their town / country, etc. Tell them to use the Communication kit: Meeting and greeting for key phrases.

Skills builder

Speaking: Sounding enthusiastic

Ask students to look at the Skills builder and point out that when we meet someone for the first time, it's important to sound enthusiastic!

11
- Students work in pairs and practise their dialogues.
- Make sure they sound enthusiastic!

12
- Ask some of the pairs to act out their dialogues for the whole class.
- If time permits, all the pairs can act out their dialogues.

MEETING AND GREETING

Hello. **What's your name?**	Hi! My name's Rebecca.
Nice to meet you, Rebecca.	Nice to meet you too!
Where are you from?	I'm from (1) … .
Oh, really? **Where, exactly?**	Ballyboden, near (2) … .
Welcome to the class, Rebecca!	Thanks!
You can sit here, next to (3) … .	OK, great.

Exercise 7
1 Ireland
2 Dublin
3 James

7 1.08 **Listen to the dialogue. Copy and complete 1–3.**

8 Listen again and repeat. Practise your intonation.

9 Copy the questions in bold into your notebook. Then write answers that are true for you.

10 Write a new dialogue. Use the dialogue in exercise 7 to help you.

Hello. What's your name?
Hi! My name's …

SKILLS BUILDER

Speaking: Sounding enthusiastic
When we meet someone for the first time, it's important to sound enthusiastic.
Nice to meet you too!

11 Work in pairs. Take turns to practise your dialogues.

Hello. What's your name?
Hi! My name's …

12 Act your dialogue for the class.

COMMUNICATION KIT

Meeting and greeting
Hello. What's your name?
My name's … .
Nice to meet you, … .
Nice to meet you too!
Where are you from?
I'm from … .
Welcome to the class!
Thanks!

UNIT 1 SCREEN STORIES

Unit objectives and key competences

In this unit the student will learn …

- to understand and correctly use vocabulary to describe appearance and the body **CLC CMST SCC**
- to understand and correctly use have got and question words, draw parallels to L1 and produce them in a short speaking activity **CLC L2L**
- about the film industry in other countries and compare with the film industry in their country **CLC CMST CAE**
- about Bollywood film industry by watching a short video **CLC CMST CAE**

In this unit the student will learn how to …

- form questions with question words **CLC**
- identify specific information in a web article about motion capture films **CLC DC CAE**
- look online for information about a film actor and make a poster or glog (graphic blog) **CLC DC CAE SIE**
- identify specific information in a description of film characters **CLC CAE**
- read some cinema tickets, listen to people talking about their favourite films and buy tickets **CLC SCC CAE**
- write a description of a film character **CLC L2L**
- prepare for and do a speaking pairwork exam task **CLC L2L SIE**

Linguistic contents

Main vocabulary

- Adjectives to describe appearance: *tall, short, slim, wavy,* etc
- Vocabulary for parts of the body: *teeth, toes, arms, legs,* etc

Grammar

- Present simple of *have got* in affirmative, negative and interrogative
- Question words: *who, what,* etc

Useful language

- Phrases for buying tickets
- Phrases for asking for and giving personal information

Pronunciation

- /h/
- Rhythm and intonation

Skills

Reading

- Read a web article about motion capture films
- Read a magazine quiz about films
- Read some cinema tickets
- Read a description of film characters

Writing: Interaction and production

- Write a personalized dialogue about buying tickets
- Write a description in three steps: plan, write, check
- Learn how to use *'s* correctly

Listening

- Listen to someone describing film characters
- Listen to people talking about their favourite films
- Listen to someone buying cinema tickets

Spoken interaction

- Ask and answer questions about appearance
- Exchange information about likes and dislikes related to films and actors

Spoken production

- Prepare and act out a dialogue about buying cinema tickets
- Prepare and do a speaking pairwork exam

Lifelong learning skills

Self-study and self-evaluation

- Study guide: Student's Book page 19
- Progress check and self-evaluation: Workbook pages 14–15
- Grammar reference and practice: Workbook pages 82–83
- Wordlist: Workbook pages 151–157

Learning strategies and thinking skills

- Learning how to guess meaning when reading

Cultural awareness

- The film industry in countries around the world, including India and the USA
- Comparing the film industry in students' own country with the film industry around the world

Cross-curricular contents

- Language and literature: comic books, writing a description
- ICT: searching the internet for information, making a glog (graphic blog)

Key competences

CLC	Competence in linguistic communication
CMST	Competence in mathematics, science and technology
DC	Digital competence
L2L	Learning to learn
SCC	Social and civic competences
SIE	Sense of initiative and entrepreneurship
CAE	Cultural awareness and expression

Evaluation

- Unit 1 End-of-unit test: Basic, Standard and Extra
- CEFR Skills Exam Generator

External exam trainer

- Speaking: Giving personal information

Digital material

Pulse Live! Digital Course including:

- Interactive grammar tables
- Audio visual speaking model: Buying tickets
- Audio visual cultural material: The Bollywood film industry

Student's website

Digital competence

- Web quest: Make a glog (graphic blog) or poster
- Digital competence worksheet: Making avatars

Reinforcement material

- Basics worksheets, Teacher's Resource File pages 5–10
- Vocabulary and Grammar: Consolidation worksheets, Teacher's Resource File pages 3–4

Extension material

- Fast-finisher activity: Student's Book page 11
- Extra activities: Teacher's Book pages T10, T15
- Vocabulary and Grammar: Extension worksheets, Teacher's Resource File pages 5–6

Teacher's Resource File

- Translation and dictation worksheets pages 2, 12
- Evaluation rubrics pages 1–7
- Key competences worksheets pages 1–2
- Culture and CLIL worksheets pages 1–4
- Culture video worksheets pages 1–2
- Digital competence worksheets pages 1–2
- Macmillan Readers worksheets pages 1–2

UNIT 1

SCREEN STORIES

THINK ABOUT IT

What are your favourite films?

Vocabulary and Speaking

Describing people

Exercise 1

1 *The Hobbit*
2 *The Chronicles of Narnia*
3 *The Amazing Spider-Man*
4 *Alice in Wonderland*

1 Look at the cards. Copy and complete 1–4 with the films in the box.

Alice in Wonderland *The Hobbit* *The Chronicles of Narnia* *The Amazing Spider-Man*

2 1.09 Listen and repeat the words in blue.

Gandalf

Character: wizard
Film: (1) ...
Height: **average**
Build: average
Hair: **long**, **grey**
Eyes: blue
Other features: **beard** and **moustache**

Jadis

Character: witch
Film: (2) ...
Height: **tall**
Build: **slim**
Hair: **curly**, **fair**
Eyes: brown
Other features: ice crown

Peter Parker

Character: superhero
Film: (3) ...
Height: average
Build: slim
Hair: **short**, **dark**
Eyes: brown
Other features: none

The Red Queen

Character: queen
Film: (4) ...
Height: short
Build: slim
Hair: **wavy**, red
Eyes: brown
Other features: red **lips**, painted **eyebrows**

Exercise 3

Height
average
short
Build
average
Hair: colour
grey
fair
dark
Hair: length
short
Hair: type
curly
wavy
Other features
moustache
lips
eyebrows

3 Copy and complete the table with the blue words from exercise 2.

Height	Build	Hair: colour	Hair: length	Hair: type	Other features
tall	*slim*	*red*	*long*	*curly*	*beard*

EXPRESS YOURSELF

4 Choose a character from exercise 2. Write three sentences about him or her.

Jadis is a witch in The Chronicles of Narnia. She's tall and slim. Her hair is curly and fair.

5 Write two questions about each of the characters in exercise 2 with *Is* or *Are*.

Is her hair red?
Are her eyes blue?

6 Work in pairs. Ask and answer questions about your partner's character from exercise 4. Guess the character.

Is her hair red?
No, it isn't.
Is it Jadis?
Yes, it is!

Vocabulary extension: Workbook page 102

Vocabulary and Speaking

Describing people

Lesson objectives

In this lesson students will:
- learn adjectives to describe appearance
- describe the appearance of film characters

Warmer

Focus students on the question *What are your favourite films?* in the Think about it box. Students work individually and write down their favourite films (in English or in their own language if the film is not an English-language one). They work in pairs and compare their answers. Listen to their ideas as a class.

1
- Students look at the pictures and the information about the film characters.
- They write the names of the films in the gaps 1–4.
- Check answers as a class.

Culture note

The Hobbit is a series of films based on a book written in the 1930s by the English author J R R Tolkien. The first film was released in 2012. *The Chronicles of Narnia* is a series of films based on the novels by the English writer C S Lewis. *The Amazing Spider-Man* was released in 2012 and is based on the Marvel Comics Spider-Man character. *Alice in Wonderland* was written by the English writer and mathematician Lewis Carroll in 1865. There have been many film versions of the book. The computer-animated version was released in 2010.

2 1.09
- Play the CD. Students listen to the words in blue and repeat them.
- Make sure they pronounce *average* /'ævrɪdʒ/ correctly with only two syllables and that they stress the second syllable of *moustache* /mə'stæʃ/.

3
- Students copy the table into their books.
- They add the blue words from exercise 2.
- Check answers as a class.

EXPRESS YOURSELF

4
- Read aloud the three example sentences to the class.
- Students choose another character from the cards in exercise 2 and write three sentences, following the example.
- They compare their answers in pairs.
- Check answers as a class.

5
- Write the example questions on the board. Elicit two or three more examples, eg *Is he tall? Is she short?*
- The students work individually and write at least five more questions beginning with *Is ...?* or *Are ...?*
- Monitor while students are writing and give help if necessary.

6
- Do one example of the guessing game as an open-class activity.
- Think of one of the characters from the cards in exercise 2.
- Students ask questions beginning with *Is ...?* or *Are ...?* You can only answer *Yes* or *No*.
- Continue until they guess the character.
- Students work in pairs and play the guessing game using their questions from exercise 5.

Extra activity

Play a game of Twenty Questions in the same way as exercise 6 using famous men and women from the world of entertainment or sport. Do one example with the whole class first. Then students play the game in pairs.

Vocabulary extension: Workbook page 102

Reading

Text type: A web article

Lesson objectives

In this lesson students will:

- read a web article about films
- describe the difference between an actor and his characters

Recommended web links

www.serkis.com
www.avatarmovie.com
www.bfi.org.uk

Warmer

Write on the board *Who is your favourite actor?* Students work in pairs and compare their answers. Listen to their ideas as a class.

1 1.10

- Students read the question.
- Play the CD. Students follow the article in their books.
- They write the answer to the question.
- They compare their answers in pairs.
- Check the answer as a class.

Word check

Check students understand all the new words.

Culture note

Andy Serkis was born in London in 1964. He began his acting career in the theatre and moved to television in the early 1990s. He acted in his first film in 1994. He became famous for playing the part of Gollum in *The Lord of the Rings* trilogy.
Highlight the Did you know? box. The film *The Polar Express* (2004) was based on the children's book of the same name by Chris Van Allsburg.

2

- Write the words in the box on the board and check students understand their meaning. Ask them to translate the words into their language to check.
- Students look in the article and find the opposites to the adjectives.
- They write the words in pairs in their notebooks, eg *ugly ≠ good-looking*.

3

- Students read the sentences and fill the gaps by finding the words in the article.
- They compare their answers in pairs.
- Check answers as a class.

4

- Read the example sentence aloud to the class.
- Students work individually to find three differences and write their sentences.
- Check answers as a class.

Finished?

Ask fast finishers to make a list of other films with interesting special effects or computer animation.

Web quest

If your classroom has internet facilities for the class, students can be asked to do the Web quest activities in class. If not, set them as homework tasks and ask them to compare their answers at the start of the next lesson. These activities help to develop competence in processing information and use of ICT.

Students make a poster or glog (graphic blog) about a famous actor. Highlight the Web quest tip.

1 • Students choose a famous actor that they like.

2 • Ask students to open an internet web browser such as Internet Explorer.
• Students open a search engine (eg Google) and type in the name of their actor.
• They use the Images option to search for pictures and find pictures of the actor in three different films.

3 • They show their classmates the pictures and describe the different characters.

Acting the part

Many modern films use a technology called motion capture. Actors wear special body-suits with sensors. They can have hundreds of sensors on their faces too. The British actor Andy Serkis is one of the stars of motion capture films. He's Gollum in *The Hobbit* films and Caesar in *Rise of the Planet of the Apes*.

In real life, Andy Serkis is 1.73 metres tall. He's got blue eyes and dark, curly hair. He's also got a beard and a moustache. He's from London.

In *The Hobbit*, he isn't good-looking at all! Gollum is small and very thin. He's got white skin and big ears and he hasn't got much hair. In *The Lord of the Rings*, Gollum is very old – probably about 600 years old.

In *Rise of the Planet of the Apes*, Caesar is the leader of all the apes. He's very intelligent and he can speak English. Caesar's eyes are green and he's got a lot more hair than Andy Serkis!

Word check

body-suit sensor star ape leader

DID YOU KNOW?

The Polar Express was the first film made completely with motion capture technology.

Reading

A web article

1 1.10 **Read and listen to the article. Who are Gollum and Caesar?**

2 Check the meaning of the adjectives in the box. Then find opposite adjectives in the article.

ugly	big	fat	young	stupid

ugly ≠ good-looking

3 Read the article again and complete the sentences.

1 Andy Serkis has got ... hair.
2 Andy's eyes are ... .
3 Gollum's skin is ... .
4 Gollum has got ... ears.
5 Caesar has got ... eyes.
6 Caesar can ... .

4 Write three sentences about the differences between the actor and his characters.

Gollum is small, but Andy Serkis is 1.73m tall.

FINISHED?

Which other films have got interesting special effects or computer animation? Write a list.

Avatar, Mission Impossible, ...

WEB QUEST

Make a glog (graphic blog) or poster about a famous actor.

1 Choose a famous actor that you like.
2 Find pictures of the actor in three different films.
3 Show your classmates the pictures and tell them about the different characters.

Web Quest tip!

Use the *Images* option in your search engine to search for pictures.

Exercise 1

Gollum is a character in *The Hobbit* films and Caesar is a character in *Rise of the Planet of the Apes*.

Exercise 2

big ≠ small
fat ≠ thin
young ≠ old
stupid ≠ intelligent

Exercise 3

1 dark, curly
2 blue
3 white
4 big
5 green
6 speak English

Exercise 4

Possible answers

Gollum is very thin, but Andy isn't.

Gollum hasn't got much hair, but Andy has got dark, curly hair.

Caesar has got green eyes, but Andy has got blue eyes.

Grammar 

have got

1 Copy and complete the tables with *have*, *haven't*, *has* or *hasn't*.

affirmative	
I / You	**have got** dark hair.
He / She / It	(1) ... **got** blue eyes.
We / You / They	(2) ... **got** blue skin.

negative	
I / You	**haven't got** a beard.
He / She / It	(3) ... **got** much hair.
We / You / They	(4) ... **got** big ears.

Exercise 1
1 has
2 have
3 hasn't
4 haven't

LOOK!
have got = 've got   has got = 's got

2 Complete the sentences with the affirmative or negative form of *have got* so they are true for you.

1 I ... brown eyes.
2 Our teacher ... a moustache.
3 I ... long hair.
4 My best friend ... a sister.

Exercise 2
1 have got / haven't got
2 has got / hasn't got
3 have got / haven't got
4 has got / hasn't got

3 Correct the sentences with the information in brackets. Write one negative and one affirmative sentence.

Kristen Stewart has got curly hair. (straight)
She hasn't got curly hair. She's got straight hair.

1 Maxi Iglesias has got grey eyes. (brown)
2 Selena Gómez has got blonde hair. (dark)
3 Zac Efron has got one sister. (brother)
4 Daniel Radcliffe has got two cats. (dogs)

Exercise 3
1 He hasn't got grey eyes. He's got brown eyes.
2 She hasn't got blonde hair. She's got dark hair.
3 He hasn't got one sister. He's got one brother.
4 He hasn't got two cats. He's got two dogs.

4 Copy and complete the text with the correct form of *be* or *have got*.

Jennifer Lawrence is an American actor. She (1) ... long, fair hair and her eyes (2) ... blue. She's slim and she (3) ... 1.75m tall. Her birthday (4) ... on 15th August. Jennifer (5) ... two brothers, Ben and Blaine, but she (6) ... any sisters. She (7) ... an Oscar® for her role in *Silver Linings Playbook*. Jennifer is Katniss Everdeen in the film *The Hunger Games*.

Exercise 4
1 has got
2 are
3 is
4 is
5 has got
6 hasn't got
7 has got

5 Look at the questions and short answers table. Then choose the correct answers.

questions	**short answers**
Have I / you **got** curly hair?	Yes, I / you **have**. No, I / you **haven't**.
Has he / she / it **got** blue skin?	Yes, he / she / it **has**. No, he / she / it **hasn't**.
Have we / you / they **got** green eyes?	Yes, we / you / they **have**. No, we / you / they **haven't**.

1 The **first** / **third** person form is different.
2 We **use** / **don't use** *got* in questions.
3 We **use** / **don't use** *got* in short answers.

Exercise 5
1 third
2 use
3 don't use

LOOK!
~~Yes, I have got.~~ ✗   Yes, I have. ✔

6 Complete the questions. Then write short answers that are true for you.

Have you *got* brown eyes? *Yes, I have.*

1 ... you ... red hair?
2 ... you ... a brother?
3 ... your best friend ... a pet?
4 ... your friends ... mobile phones?

Exercise 6
1 Have you got red hair?
2 Have you got a brother?
3 Has your best friend got a pet?
4 Have your friends got mobile phones?

EXPRESS YOURSELF

7 Choose a classmate. Write a short description but don't write the name.

She's got dark hair and brown eyes. She's tall and ... .

8 Work in pairs. Ask and answer questions about the classmate in exercise 7. Guess the name.

Has she got dark hair?
Yes, she has.
Is she tall?
Yes, she is.
Is it Sara?

ANALYSE

In English, we don't use *have got* to talk about age or to say how we feel. How do you say these expressions in your language?

~~I've got 12 years.~~ ✗ I'm 12. ✔
~~I've got tired.~~ ✗ I'm tired. ✔

1.11–1.12 Pronunciation lab: /h/, page 124 

Digital course: Interactive grammar table    Study guide: page 19

Grammar 

have got

Lesson objectives

In this lesson students will:

- learn and use *have got* in the affirmative, negative, question forms and short answers
- use *have got* to write about themselves and speak about other people

Warmer

Write this sentence on the board with the words in the wrong order: *got he hair has brown*. Students work in pairs and write the sentence in the correct order. Write the correct form on the board (*He has got brown hair*).

1
- Ask students to complete the table with *have, haven't, has* or *hasn't*.
- Check answers as a class.
- Highlight the fact that in the affirmative only the *he / she / it* form changes – from *have* to *has*.

Look!

In the affirmative, short forms can also be used, eg *I've got blue eyes, She's got brown hair.*

2
- Students complete the sentences using the affirmative or negative form of *have got* so that they are true for them.
- They compare answers in pairs.
- Check answers as a class.

3
- Read the example sentences aloud to the class.
- Students complete the exercise individually.
- They compare answers in pairs.
- Check answers as a class.

4
- Students read the text first.
- They work individually and fill the gaps using the correct forms of *be* or *have got*.
- They compare their answers in pairs.
- Check answers as a class.

5
- Students read sentences 1–3.
- They look at the information in the table and choose the correct answers.
- They compare answers in pairs.
- Check answers as a class.

Look!

Highlight that fact that *got* is never used in short answers.

6
- Read the example question and short answer aloud to the class.
- Students complete the questions individually.
- Check the questions are correct.
- Students write true answers to the questions.
- Check answers as a class.

EXPRESS YOURSELF

7
- Students write a short description of a classmate.
- Monitor while they are writing and give help if necessary.

8
- Demonstrate the activity by doing an example with the whole class.
- Think of one student in the class. The students have to guess who it is by asking questions. You can only answer with short answers using *Yes* or *No*.
- Put students into pairs. They ask and answer questions to guess the student their partner wrote about in exercise 7.

Analyse

Students read the examples. Highlight the fact that we use the verb *be* with ages in English and with adjectives. We never use *have got* with ages or with adjectives.

Pronunciation lab: /h/, page 124

Digital course: Interactive grammar table

Study guide: page 19

Vocabulary and Listening

The body

Lesson objectives

In this lesson students will:

- learn some vocabulary for parts of human and animal bodies
- listen for specific information

Warmer

Play a game of Simon Says. Students stand up. Give instructions, eg *Simon says, wave your right hand*. Demonstrate the action by doing it yourself. Students follow your instructions. If you give an instruction without saying *Simon says* first (eg *Brush your teeth*), any students who do the action are out of the game and sit down. Continue until only one student is left – he or she is the winner.

1 1.13

- Play the CD. Students listen and repeat the words in the word pool.
- They say which words are not part of the human body.
- Check answers as a class.
- Check students understand all the words by asking them to translate them into their language.

2

- Students work individually and choose the correct words.
- They compare answers in pairs.
- Check answers as a class.

Look!

Foot – feet and *tooth – teeth* are examples of common irregular plurals in English. Other examples include *man – men, woman – women, child – children, mouse – mice*.

3

- Students look at the pictures from *Percy Jackson and the Olympians.*
- They read the three topics a–c and decide what the film is about.
- Check the answer as a class.

4 1.14

- Students read the descriptions.
- They match the descriptions with the characters in the pictures.
- They compare answers in pairs.
- Play the CD. Students listen and check their answers.

5 1.15

- Ask students to read the descriptions carefully first. Check that they understand them.
- Play the CD. Students fill the gaps. Note that you may need to play the CD more than once.
- Students compare their answers in pairs.
- Check answers as a class.

6 1.15

- Ask students to read the questions carefully first. Check that they understand all the vocabulary.
- Play the CD again. Students write short answers.
- Check answers as a class.

1.15 Audioscript, exercises 5 and 6

I like the Percy Jackson stories. They're by the American author Rick Riordan. I've got all five of the books! In the books, there are some different characters – they aren't all in the film.
For example, there's the Cyclops. The Cyclops is a giant. He's got a big head, big hands and big feet. He hasn't got two eyes – he's only got one eye. In the story, the Cyclops' name is Tyson. Tyson isn't a bad character – he's Percy's friend.
Then, there are the Sirens. The Sirens are very beautiful creatures. They've got human faces, with long, dark hair – but they've got birds' bodies, with wings and feathers. They've got beautiful voices – they can sing like birds – but they are very dangerous.
I also like the Minotaur – this character's in the film too. The Minotaur has got a bull's head and a man's body, with arms and legs. It's got two horns and a bull's tail. The Minotaur is Percy's enemy!

Vocabulary and Listening

The body

Exercise 1
wings, horns, tail

1 1.13 **Listen and repeat the words in the box. Which words are not parts of the human body?**

legs feet toes arms wings hands fingers head neck tail teeth horns

LOOK!

Irregular plurals
foot – feet tooth – teeth

Exercise 2
1 wings
2 teeth
3 legs
4 toes
5 horn

2 Choose the correct words.

1 Dragons have got two **wings** / **fingers**.
2 Vampires have got big **horns** / **teeth**.
3 Horses have got four **arms** / **legs** and a tail.
4 Humans have got ten **hands** / **toes**.
5 Unicorns have got one **leg** / **horn**.

The Hydra

The Centaur

Medusa

Exercise 3
c

3 Look at the characters in the photos. What do you think the film is about?

a) The legend of Robin Hood
b) Latin American folklore
c) Greek mythology

Exercise 4
1 The Centaur
2 Medusa
3 The Hydra

4 1.14 **Read the descriptions. Match them to the characters in the pictures. Then listen and check.**

1 This character has got a man's head and arms and a horse's body, legs and tail.
2 This character hasn't got normal hair. She's got snakes instead. She's also got blue eyes.
3 This horrible creature is a monster with many heads. It's got long necks and big teeth.

Exercise 5
1 head
2 eye
3 hair
4 wings
5 horns
6 tail

5 1.15 **Listen to the descriptions of three other characters from the *Percy Jackson* stories. Copy and complete the notes.**

The Cyclops has got a big (1) … , big hands and big feet. He's only got one (2) … .

The Sirens have got long, dark (3) … . They've got birds' bodies with (4) … and feathers.

The Minotaur has got a bull's head and a man's body. It's got two (5) … and a bull's (6) … .

6 Listen again. Write short answers to the questions.

Is the Cyclops a giant?
Yes, he is.

1 Is the Cyclops Percy's enemy?
2 Are the Sirens beautiful?
3 Have the Sirens got human faces?
4 Has the Minotaur got a man's body?
5 Is the Minotaur Percy's friend?

Exercise 6
1 No, he isn't.
2 Yes, they are.
3 Yes, they have.
4 Yes, it has.
5 No, it isn't.

Cultural awareness

The film industry

Exercise 1

six countries
India, Canada, Ireland, New Zealand, Australia, South Africa

four cities
Bombay, Ottawa, Toronto, Vancouver

three adjectives of nationality
American, Indian, British

Exercise 2

1 b
2 b
3 a
4 b
5 b
6 a

1 Read the quiz quickly and find:

a) six countries
b) four cities
c) three adjectives of nationality

Fact box

English around the world

People speak English in many countries around the world, including the UK, Ireland, the USA, Canada, Australia, New Zealand, South Africa and India.

2 1.16 Read and listen to the quiz. Then choose the correct answers.

Quiz: Are you a film fan?

Try our quiz about films around the world!

1 **Hollywood is the centre of the American film industry. How many film studios has the city got?**
a) Two – Disney and Dreamworks **b)** More than ten

2 **India has got a big film industry. Why is it called Bollywood?**
a) Because Bollywood is an Indian film director.
b) Because it's a combination of Bombay and Hollywood.

3 **There are film festivals in Ottawa, Toronto and Vancouver. What country are these cities in?**
a) Canada **b)** Ireland

4 **They filmed *The Hobbit* films in New Zealand. Who is the director?**
a) Pedro Almodóvar **b)** Peter Jackson

5 **The seven Harry Potter books are by the British writer J.K. Rowling. How many *Harry Potter*™ films are there?**
a) six **b)** eight

6 **Nicole Kidman, Russell Crowe and Sam Worthington are famous actors. Where are they from?**
a) Australia **b)** South Africa

Word check

film industry | film studio | film director | film festival

3 1.17 Listen and check your answers.

CULTURAL COMPARISON

4 Answer the questions.

1 Has your country got any film studios? Where?
2 Who are the most famous actors in your country?
3 When and where are the film festivals in your country?

Culture video: Bollywood film industry

Cultural awareness

The film industry

Lesson objectives

In this lesson students will:

- read a quiz from a film magazine
- practise reading to find specific information
- talk about the film industry in their country

Warmer

Books closed. Write the word *English* on the board. Students work in pairs and write down countries where people speak English. Listen to their ideas as a class. They open their books and check their answers by reading the *English around the world* Fact box.

1
- Check students understand the task.
- They look in the quiz and find six countries, four cities and three adjectives of nationality.
- They compare their answers in pairs.
- Check answers as a class.

2 1.16
- Play the CD. Students read and listen to the quiz.
- They work individually and answer the questions.
- They compare their answers in pairs.

3 1.17
- Play the CD. Students listen and check their answers.

Word check

Check students understand all the new words. Ask them to translate them into their language.

Culture note

The Indian film industry, known as Bollywood and based in Mumbai, India, makes more films than any other country in the world. Hollywood in California produces 500 films a year with a worldwide audience of 2.6 billion, while Bollywood produces 1,000 films a year and has a worldwide audience of 3 billion.

Finished?

Fast finishers can write two more quiz questions about films in their country with two possible answers, one correct and one incorrect. They work in pairs and ask and answer each other's questions.

CULTURAL  COMPARISON

4
- Students work individually and write answers to the questions.
- They compare their answers in pairs.
- Listen to their ideas as a class.

Culture video: Bollywood film industry

1.17 Audioscript, exercise 3

1 b There are more than ten film studios in Hollywood.
2 b Bollywood is a combination of Bombay and Hollywood.
3 a Ottawa, Toronto and Vancouver are in Canada.
4 b Peter Jackson is the director of *The Hobbit* films.
5 b There are eight Harry Potter films.
6 a Nicole Kidman, Russell Crowe and Sam Worthington are from Australia.

Grammar 

Question words

Lesson objectives

In this lesson students will:

- learn and use question words
- make questions

Warmer

Write the letter *w* on the board. Students work in pairs and write as many English words as possible beginning with this letter (eg *write, white, wing, with, what*). Set a time limit of two minutes for this. The pair with the most correct words wins. It is likely that students will include some question words in their list so this will help to prepare them for the next activity.

1
- Students read the questions in the table and translate the words in blue into their language.
- Highlight the difference in pronunciation between *who* /huː/ and *how* /haʊ/ as these are words that learners often confuse.
- Point out the different uses of *where* in *Where is the actor?* and *Where is the actor from?* Ask students to translate these two sentences into their language.
- Students try and answer the questions.
- Check answers as a class.

Look!

Highlight the fact that when someone asks a question beginning with *Why ...?*, we usually answer with *Because ...* Read the example question and answer aloud to the class.

2
- Check students understand the task. They can refer to the table in exercise 1 to help them.
- Students work individually to complete the questions and match them with the answers.
- They compare their answers in pairs.
- Check answers as a class.
- Ask who the character is (Mortadelo).

EXPRESS YOURSELF

3
- Students read the example question.
- Students work individually to write the questions.
- Check answers as a class.

4
- Students work individually and write their answers to the questions in exercise 3.
- Students work in pairs and ask and answer the questions.
- Listen to some pairs as a class.

 Grammar in context: Literature

Culture note

The first comic book appeared in the USA in 1933. The term *comic book* is used because the first comic books reprinted humour comic strips from newspapers. Despite their name, comic books are not necessarily funny. Modern comic books tell stories in a variety of genres, eg horror, science fiction, adventure.

5
- This activity practises the present simple tense of *be* and *have got*.
- Ask students to read the text.
- Students choose the correct word.
- They compare their answers in pairs.

6 
- Play the CD. Students listen and check their answers to exercise 5.

Extra activity

Use the first four sentences of the text in exercise 5 as a dictation. Put students into pairs. One student dictates the first two sentences while the other writes. Then they swap roles for the remaining two sentences.

CLIL task

Students choose one of the three superheroes. They use the internet to make a list of films based on their chosen comic book character.

Pronunciation lab: Rhythm and intonation, page 124

Digital course: Interactive grammar table

Study guide: page 19

Grammar

Question words

1 Look at the table. Translate the blue words into your language. Can you answer the questions?

question words
Who is the director of *The Hobbit* films?
What is *The Hobbit* about?
Which country is Ottawa in?
Where is the actor Sam Worthington from?
When is the San Sebastián film festival?
Why is Zac Efron famous?
How many *Harry Potter*™ films are there?
How old is Harry Potter in the final film?

Exercise 1
Who – Peter Jackson
What – Hobbits
Which – Canada
Where – Australia
When – September
Why – He's an actor and singer.
How – eight
How – seventeen

LOOK!

Why is India's film industry called Bollywood?
Because it's a combination of Bombay and Hollywood.

2 Complete the questions with question words from exercise 1. Then match them with answers a–e. Who is it?

1 ... is he from?
2 ... colour hair has he got?
3 ... old is he?
4 ... is he famous?
5 ... is his best friend?

a) Because he's a comic character.
b) He's from Spain.
c) His best friend is Filemón.
d) He hasn't got any hair!
e) He is over 50.

Exercise 2
1 Where, b
2 What, d
3 How, e
4 Why, a
5 Who, c
The character is Mortadelo.

EXPRESS YOURSELF

3 Order the words to make questions.

old / you / are / How ?
How old are you?

1 you / from / Where / are ?
2 got / What / colour / have / eyes / you ?
3 birthday / When / your / is ?
4 your / are / Who / favourite / actors ?
5 cousins / got / you / have / many / How ?
6 country / is / Which / in / Manchester ?

Exercise 3
1 Where are you from?
2 What colour eyes have you got?
3 When is your birthday?
4 Who are your favourite actors?
5 How many cousins have you got?
6 Which country is Manchester in?

4 Work in pairs. Ask and answer the questions in exercise 3.

How old are you?
I'm twelve years old.

CLIL Grammar in context: Literature

5 Read the text and choose the correct answers.

6 1.18 Listen and check your answers.

Exercise 5
1 are
2 aren't
3 haven't
4 is
5 has
6 are
7 are
8 Who

FROM COMICS TO FILMS

Comic books (1) **is** / **are** very popular around the world. They (2) **isn't** / **aren't** difficult to read because they (3) **hasn't** / **haven't** got many words. Today, many films are based on comic book characters, such as Spider-Man™, Batman and the X-Men. Superman (4) **is** / **are** the original superhero from the 1930s. Japan (5) **is** / **has** got a lot of comic book characters on screen too. Anime film heroes like Akira and Astroboy (6) **am** / **are** from Japanese Manga comics. In Spain, the most famous comic-book characters (7) **is** / **are** probably Mortadelo and Filemón. (8) **When** / **Who** are your favourite comic characters?

CLIL TASK
Choose a superhero:
• Superman • Wonder Woman • Batman
Find out about all the films based on the comic books.

1.19 Pronunciation lab: Rhythm and intonation, page 124

At the cinema

Hi! I'm going to see *Star Trek* with my family. Which film do you want to see?

MOVIE CINEMA PRESENTS...
STAR TREK 3D
SCREEN 4 ROW N SEAT 12
DATE: 23/09 TIME: 18.30 PRICE: £7.00

PARADISE CINEMA PRESENTS...
DESPICABLE ME 2D
SCREEN 6 ROW M SEAT 15
DATE 28/09 TIME 17.30 PRICE £6.50

MOVIE CINEMA PRESENTS...
THE AMAZING SPIDER-MAN 3D
SCREEN 1 ROW E SEAT 19
DATE: 18/10 TIME: 16.00 PRICE: £7.00

Step 1: Read

1 **Look at the cinema tickets. Guess the meaning of the words in the box. How do you say them in your language?**

screen row seat

SKILLS BUILDER

Reading: Guessing meaning
Don't worry if you can't understand every word. You can often guess the meaning from the context.

2 **Read the information on the tickets again. Answer the questions.**

Where is *Star Trek* on?
It's on at Movie Cinema.

1 When is *The Amazing Spider-Man* on?
2 Is *Star Trek* in 2D or 3D?
3 What time is *Star Trek* on?
4 How much are the tickets at Paradise Cinema?
5 What screen is *Despicable Me* on?

Exercise 2
1 October 18th at 16.00
2 3D
3 18.30
4 £6.50
5 six

Step 2: Listen

3 1.20 **Listen to three people talking about the films in exercise 1. Write the names of the films in the order you hear them.**

4 **Listen again. Choose the correct answers.**

Speaker 1
1 In his opinion, this film is **funny** / **terrible**.
2 Most of the characters are **monkeys** / **yellow**.
Speaker 2
3 There are **aliens** / **wizards** in this film.
4 The film has got great **special effects** / **music**.
Speaker 3
5 This is **an action** / **a science fiction** film.
6 The film is in **2D** / **3D**.

Exercise 3
1 *Despicable Me*
2 *Star Trek*
3 *The Amazing Spider-Man*

Exercise 4
1 funny
2 yellow
3 aliens
4 special effects
5 action
6 3D

Integrated skills

At the cinema

Lesson objectives

In this lesson students will:

- work on all four skills
- read information on cinema tickets
- listen to people talking about films
- write a personalized dialogue
- act out their dialogue

Warmer

Ask students to read Hazel's speech bubble. Then write the question *Which film do you want to see?* on the board. Students answer the question in pairs. Listen to answers as a class.

Step 1: Read

1
- Students look at the cinema tickets and find the three words.
- They guess the meaning of the words.
- They work in pairs and translate them into their language.
- Check answers as a class.

Skills builder

Reading: Guessing meaning

Explain to students that they do not need to understand every word when they read. Sometimes, they can guess the meaning of a new word from the context. For example, if they don't know the word *umbrella* and they read the sentence *It's raining today so John has got his umbrella*, they should be able to guess the meaning.

2
- Read the example question and answer aloud to the class.
- Students read the questions carefully.
- They read the cinema tickets and find the answers to the questions.
- They compare their answers in pairs.
- Check answers as a class. Note that we can either say *Six pounds fifty* or simply *six fifty*.

Step 2: Listen

3 1.20
- Check students understand the task. They should listen and identify the three films the people talk about.
- Play the CD. Students write the names of the films.
- They compare their answers in pairs.
- Check answers as a class.

4
- Ask students to read the statements and the different possible answers carefully first.
- Play the CD again. Students choose the correct answers.
- Check answers as a class.

1.20 Audioscript, exercises 3 and 4

1 It's a really funny film! The main characters are Gru and all the little yellow creatures... some of them have only got one eye! Gru is big and fat. He's the villain. It's a really original film, I recommend it!

2 I really enjoyed it ... it's a science-fiction film. It's based on the old *Star Trek* films, but the story is new. Chris Pine is the main actor. There are lots of different characters, including aliens! They're cool but they're a bit scary. The film has got great special effects too...

3 ... yes, it's an action film, it's based on the comic. My favourite character is Peter Parker – the boy who becomes Spider-Man, of course! The actor Andrew Garfield plays him in this film. It's such an exciting film and it's in 3D too ...

Integrated skills – continued

Buying tickets

5 1.21

- Students work in pairs and read the dialogue aloud to each other.
- Highlight the four alternatives (1–4).
- Play the CD. Students choose the correct answers.
- Check answers as a class. Highlight the different pronunciation of the letters *g* /dʒiː/ and *j* /dʒeɪ/.

6
- Play the CD again, pausing after each speaker's part for students to repeat as a class.
- Note the main stress on the questions: *What time? How many people? How much is it?*
- Ask students to repeat these questions several times both chorally and individually with the correct stress and intonation.
- Students practise the dialogue in pairs. Then swap roles and practise the dialogue again.

Step 3: Write

7
- Students choose one of the films on page 16 (or another film they like).
- They write notes to answer the questions.

8
- Students work individually and write their dialogue, using the dialogue in the book as a model and Communications kit: Buying tickets for key phrases.
- Monitor while they are writing and give help if necessary.

Step 4: Communicate

9
- Students practise their dialogues in pairs.
- For extra practice, they swap roles in both dialogues.

10
- Choose some pairs to act out their dialogue for the class.
- Students raise their hand if another pair has the same film, time, number of people or ticket price as they do. This will encourage them to listen carefully to their classmates.

Integrated skills: Workbook page 111

Next, please!	Hello, have you got tickets for *Star Trek* in (1) **2D** / **3D** please?
What time?	At (2) **half past six** / **eight o'clock**.
Yes, no problem. How many people?	Four, please – two adults and two children.
OK. I've got four seats in row (3) **G** / **J**.	That's fine. How much is it?
Have you got 3D glasses?	Yes, we have.
OK. So that's (4) **£18** / **£28** please.	Here you are.
Thanks. Here's your change.	Thanks. Bye!

Exercise 5
1 3D
2 half past six
3 J
4 £28

5 1.21 **Listen to the dialogue and choose the correct answers for 1–4.**

6 Listen again and repeat. Practise your intonation.

Step 3: Write

7 Choose one of the films on page 16, or use your own ideas. Copy and complete the notes.

Film: ...
2D or 3D?
What time?
How many people?
Ticket prices?

8 Prepare a new dialogue. Write both parts. Use the model dialogue in exercise 5 and your notes from exercise 7 to help you.

Next, please!
Hello, have you got tickets for ... ?

Step 4: Communicate

9 Work in pairs. Take turns to practise your dialogues.

Next, please!
Hello, have you got tickets for ... ?

10 Act your dialogue for the class.

COMMUNICATION KIT

Buying tickets

Next, please!
Have you got tickets for ... ?
What time?
How many people?
I've got ... seats in row ... .
How much is it?
Have you got 3D glasses?
Here's your change.

Writing
A description

Exercise 1
1 the planet Pandora
2 blue
3 no
4 Neytiri's best friend
5 yes
6 yes

Exercise 3
is
Neytiri's a warrior princess; She's three metres tall; He's green; He's like a dragon
has
she's got bue skin; she's got long, black hair; she's got a long tail; he's got four wings; it's got fantastic special effects
possession
Neytiri's eyes are green; Seze is Neytiri's best friend

Exercise 4
1 Her character's name is Neytiri. (possession)
2 Zoë's got brown eyes. (has)
3 Her hair's long and dark. (is)
4 Zoë's from the USA. (is)
5 Zoë's mother is from Puerto Rico. (possession)

Neytiri and Seze

Neytiri and Seze are my favourite characters from the first *Avatar* film.

Neytiri's a warrior princess from the planet Pandora. She's three metres tall and she's got blue skin. Neytiri's eyes are green and she's got long, black hair. Her ears are big and she's got a long tail like a lion.

Seze is Neytiri's best friend. He's green, and he's got four wings and a tail. Neytiri flies on Seze. He's like a dragon and a bird combined.

This film is in 3D and it's got fantastic special effects. I can't wait for the next *Avatar* film!

1 1.22 **Read and listen to the description. Then answer the questions.**

1 Where is Neytiri from?
2 What colour is her skin?
3 Has Neytiri got wings?
4 Who is Seze?
5 Has Seze got a tail?
6 Can Seze fly?

2 Read the Writing focus. Translate the sentences into your language.

WRITING FOCUS
's = *is*, *has*, or possession

's = is	Neytiri's (= Neytiri is) a warrior princess.
's = has	She's (= She has) got blue skin.
's = possession	Neytiri's eyes are green. (= possession)

3 Look at the description in exercise 1 again. Are the examples in blue *is*, *has* or possession?

4 Rewrite the sentences with an apostrophe ('). Are they *is*, *has* or possession?

Zoë Saldanas an actor. ✗
Zoë Saldana's an actor. = is

1 Her characters name is Neytiri. ✗
2 Zoës got brown eyes. ✗
3 Her hairs long and dark. ✗
4 Zoës from the USA. ✗
5 Zoës mother is from Puerto Rico. ✗

Writing task
Describe a character in one of your favourite films.

Plan Choose your character and make notes.

Name of character?
Which film is he / she / it in?
Where is he / she / it from?
Physical description (hair, eyes, body, other characteristics)
Special abilities?

Write Write your description. Use your notes and the description in exercise 1 to help you. Give your description a title.

Check Check your writing.

- ✔ 's for *is*, *has* or possession
- ✔ the correct forms of *be* and *have got*
- ✔ vocabulary for the body and describing people

Build your confidence: Writing reference and practice. Workbook page 120

Writing

A description

Lesson objectives

In this lesson students will:

- read a description of two film characters
- use *'s* to mean *is* or *has* or to indicate possession
- write a description of a film character

Warmer

Think of a film character that will be familiar to the students (one of the ones from this unit or one very popular with students of their age in their country). Students ask questions to guess who it is (eg *Is she young? Has she got black hair?*). You can only answer using short answers with *Yes* or *No*. Continue until they guess the name of the character.

1 1.22

- Students read the questions carefully first.
- Play the CD. Students listen and follow the description in their books. They write the answers.
- They compare their answers in pairs.
- Check answers as a class.

2

- Write *'s* on the board.
- Tell students this is used in three different ways in English.
- They read the example sentences in the Writing focus and translate them into their language.
- Check answers as a class. Point out that in the first two sentence we can also use the long versions of *'s* (*is* and *has*) but we cannot change the third sentence in any way.

3

- Students find the examples of *'s* in blue in the description.
- They decide if each *'s* = *is*, *has* or possession.
- Students compare their answers in pairs.
- Check answers as a class.

4

- Highlight the example and point out where we put the apostrophe in *Zoë Saldanas an actor*.
- Students work individually and rewrite the sentences with the apostrophe in the correct place.
- Students compare their answers in pairs.
- Check answers as a class. Ask students which *'s* replace *is*, which replace *has* and which are for possession.

Writing task

The aim of this activity is for students to produce a piece of guided writing that includes the correct use of *'s*. It also gives them practice in using *be* and *have got* correctly and in using vocabulary for the body and describing people. Ask the students to follow the stages in the Student's Book. At the Check stage, ask them to swap notebooks and check each other's writing.

Writing reference and practice: Workbook page 120

Study guide

Grammar, Vocabulary and Speaking

Tell the students the Study guide is an important page which provides a useful reference for the main language of the unit: the grammar, the vocabulary and the functional language from the Integrated skills pages. Explain that they should refer to this page when studying for a test or exam.

Grammar

- Tell the students to look at the example sentences of *have got* and make sure they know how to form the verb correctly.
- Then tell students to look at the example sentences of question words and ensure they understand the meaning. Get students to translate into their own language if necessary.
- Refer students to the Grammar reference on pages 84–85 of the Workbook for further revision.

Vocabulary

- Tell students to look at the list of vocabulary and check understanding.
- Refer students to the Wordlist on page 151 of the Workbook where they can look up any words they can't remember.

Speaking

- Check that students understand the phrases to use for buying tickets.
- Tell students to act out a conversation between a ticket sales assistant and a customer.

Additional material

Workbook

- Progress check page 14
- Self-evaluation page 15
- Grammar reference and practice page 84
- Vocabulary extension page 102
- Integrated skills page 111
- Writing reference and task page 120

Teacher's Resource File

- Pulse Basics worksheets pages 5–10
- Vocabulary and grammar consolidation worksheets pages 3–6
- Translation and dictation worksheets pages 2, 12
- Evaluation rubrics pages 1–7
- Key competences worksheets pages 1–2
- Culture and CLIL worksheets pages 1–4
- Culture video worksheets pages 1–2
- Digital competence worksheets pages 1–2
- Macmillan Readers worksheets pages 1–2

Tests and Exams

- Unit 1 End-of-unit test: Basic, Standard and Extra
- CEFR Skills Exam Generator

Study guide

Grammar
have got

affirmative		
I / You	**have got**	dark hair.
He / She / It	**has got**	
We / You / They	**have got**	

negative		
I / You	**haven't got**	fair hair.
He / She / It	**hasn't got**	
We / You / They	**haven't got**	

questions	short answers
Have I / you **got** red hair?	Yes, I / you **have**. No, I / you **haven't**.
Has he / she / it **got** red hair?	Yes, he / she / it **has**. No, he / she / it **hasn't**.
Have we / you / they **got** red hair?	Yes, we / you / they **have**. No, we / you / they **haven't**.

Question words

question words
Who is the director of *Avatar*?
Which actors are in the film?
What is the story about?
Where is Zoë Saldana from?
When is Zoë's birthday?
Why is Zoë Saldana famous?
How many *Avatar* films are there?
How old is Zoë?

Vocabulary
Describing people

average
beard
curly
dark
eyebrows
fair
grey
lips
long
moustache
short
slim
tall
wavy

The body

arms
feet
fingers
hands
head
horns
legs
neck
tail
teeth
toes
wings

Speaking
Buying tickets

Next, please!
Have you got tickets for ... ?
What time?
How many people?
I've got ... seats in row ... .
How much is it?
Have you got 3D glasses?
Here's your change.

LEARNING TO LEARN

Think of people you know and write sentences to describe them. You can remember things better if you write something that is true for you.

UNIT 2

SCHOOL DAYS

Unit objectives and key competences

In this unit the student will learn ...

- to understand, memorize and correctly use words for school subjects **CLC CMST**
- to understand, memorize and correctly use phrases for everyday activities **CLC SCC**
- understand and correctly use grammar structures related to the present and draw parallels to L1 **CLC L2L**
- about private schools and after-school activities in the UK **CLC CMST CAE**
- about asking for information **CLC SCC**
- about a typical day at a UK school by watching a short video **CLC CMST CAE**

In this unit the student will learn how to ...

- identify specific information in a magazine article about a school for performing arts **CLC CMST CAE**
- look for information about well-known musicians **CLC DC CAE CIE**
- identify specific information in a radio extract about a ballet school **CLC CAE**
- speak about differences between their school and the schools they read about **CLC CMST CAE**
- write a questionnaire **CLC CMST**
- read a school noticeboard and sign up for an after-school activity **CLC SCC**

Linguistic contents

Main vocabulary

- School subjects: *maths, art, history,* etc
- Everyday activities: *have a shower, go to school, have dinner,* etc

Grammar

- Present simple: affirmative and negative
- Present simple: questions and short answers

Functional language

- Asking for information

Pronunciation

- Syllables and word stress
- Third person verb endings

Skills

Reading

- Read a magazine article about a school for the performing arts
- Read a text about life at a private school
- Read a noticeboard

Writing: Interaction and production

- Write a personalized dialogue
- Write a questionnaire in three steps: plan, write, check

Listening

- Listen to a radio programme about life at a ballet school
- Listen to someone describing a typical school day
- Prepare for a True / False listening activity

Spoken interaction

- Exchange information about school timetables

Spoken production

- Prepare and act out a dialogue about after-school activities

Lifelong learning skills

Self-study and self-evaluation

- Study guide: Student's Book page 29
- Progress check and self-evaluation: Workbook pages 22–23
- Grammar reference and practice: Workbook pages 86–87
- Wordlist: Workbook pages 151–157

Learning strategies and thinking skills

- Reading quickly to get the general idea
- Learning to read options thoroughly before listening

Cultural awareness

- State schools and boarding schools in the UK
- Comparing a UK boarding school with students' own school

Cross-curricular contents

- Maths: numerical information
- ICT: searching the internet for information
- Language and literature: reading timetables, conventions for answering a questionnaire

Key competences

CLC	Competence in linguistic communication
CMST	Competence in mathematics, science and technology
DC	Digital competence
L2L	Learning to learn
SCC	Social and civic competences
SIE	Sense of initiative and entrepreneurship
CAE	Cultural awareness and expression

Evaluation

- Unit 2 End-of-unit test: Basic, Standard and Extra
- CEFR Skills Exam Generator

External exam trainer

- Listening: True / False activity

Digital material

Pulse Live! Digital Course including:

- Interactive grammar tables
- Audio visual speaking model: Asking for information
- Audio visual cultural material: A typical day at a UK school

Student's website

Digital competence

- Web quest: find out information about a famous singer
- Digital worksheet: Making a podcast

Reinforcement material

- Basics worksheets, Teacher's Resource File pages 11–16
- Vocabulary and Grammar: Consolidation worksheets, Teacher's Resource File pages 7–8

Extension material

- Fast-finisher activity: Student's Book page 21–22
- Extra activities: Teacher's Book pages T22
- Vocabulary and Grammar: Extension worksheets, Teacher's Resource File pages 9–10

Teacher's Resource File

- Translation and dictation worksheets pages 3, 13
- Evaluation rubrics pages 1–7
- Key competences worksheets pages 3–4
- Culture and video clip worksheets pages 3–4
- Digital competence worksheets pages 3–4
- Macmillan Readers worksheets pages 1–2

UNIT 2 SCHOOL DAYS

THINK ABOUT IT

What's your favourite school subject? And your least favourite?

Vocabulary and Speaking

School subjects

1 1.23 **Look at the poster. Listen and repeat the subjects in blue.**

2 Look at pictures a–f. Which subjects can you see?

Exercise 2
- **a** music
- **b** art
- **c** dance
- **d** ICT
- **e** PE
- **f** drama

3 Copy and complete the sentences to make them true for you.

1. On Mondays I've got ... and ... .
2. I study English on ... and ... .
3. I'm good at ... and ... .
4. ... isn't my favourite subject.

LOOK!

on Tuesday(s)
in the morning / afternoon
at the weekend

EXPRESS YOURSELF

4 In your notebook, design your perfect Friday. Choose your favourite subjects.

Friday	
10–11	*Drama*
11–12	
12–	

5 Work in pairs. Ask and answer questions about your timetables. Who has got the best Friday?

What have you got on Friday morning?
I've got drama at 10 o'clock and then ... .

THE SCHOOL OF PERFORMING ARTS

Welcome!

IN YEAR 1, YOU STUDY:
Nine obligatory subjects and one option

OBLIGATORY SUBJECTS: English, maths, science, ICT, history, PE, technology, citizenship and one foreign language (French, Spanish or German)

OPTIONS: art, drama, music, dance

ICT = Information and Communication Technology
PE = Physical Education

Vocabulary extension: Workbook page 103

Vocabulary and Speaking

School subjects

Lesson objectives

In this lesson students will:

- learn / revise school subjects
- revise days
- learn / revise times of day
- design the perfect school day

Warmer

Set a time limit of two minutes. Students work in pairs and write down as many school subjects as they can (eg *English, maths, science*). Elicit examples from the class and write them on the board in preparation for the next activity.

Think about it

Students work individually and decide on their favourite and least favourite school subject. Then they work in pairs and compare their answers. Check answers as a class.

1 1.23

- Students look at the poster.
- Play the CD. Students listen and repeat the subjects in blue.
- Make sure they pronounce these words with the correct stress: *ICT, technology, citizenship*.

Culture note

In the UK, *citizenship* is a school subject in which students learn about the rights and obligations people have as citizens and study concepts such as democracy, justice, identities and diversity.

2

- Students look at the six pictures and write down the subjects illustrated in each one.
- They compare their answers in pairs.
- Check answers as a class.

3

- Students work individually to make true sentences.
- Be prepared to give help with words for extra subjects if they are not in the list in the school information.
- They compare their answers in pairs or small groups.
- Check answers as a class.

Look!

Highlight the different prepositions we use with days (*on Tuesday(s)*, etc), parts of the day (also *in the evening*) and with the word *weekend* (*at the weekend)*. Point out that we also use *at* with times (*at ten o'clock, at half past four,* etc).

Language note

Explain that we add an *-s* when we mean *every Monday, every Tuesday,* etc – *on Mondays*. If we use it without an *-s*, it means a specific day, eg *This term finishes on Friday*.

4

- Explain the concept of a perfect day (a day when everything you do is interesting and fun).
- The students write their timetable for their perfect Friday in their notebooks. Ask them to write at least five subjects.
- Check answers as a class. Correct any errors in the pronunciation of the school subjects.

5

- Nominate two students to read aloud the example question and answer.
- Students work in pairs.
- They ask and answer questions to find out about each other's perfect Friday and decide which timetable they prefer.

Vocabulary extension: Workbook page 103

Reading

Text type: A magazine article

Lesson objectives

In this lesson students will:

- read a magazine article about a school for performing arts and technology
- compare their school with the school in the article

Recommended web links

www.brit.croydon.sch.uk

Warmer

Revise the school subjects from the previous lesson. Write the first and last letters of six subjects on the board with dashes for the other letters, eg *h _ _ _ _ _ y* (*history*). Students complete the spelling of each word. They compare answers in pairs. Individual students come to the board to write the correct letters in the spaces to complete the words.

1 1.24

- Students look at the pictures and say if they know the singers (Jessie J and Rizzle Kicks – Jordan 'Rizzle' Stephens and Harley 'Sylvester' Alexander-Sule).
- Play the CD. Students listen and follow the article in their books.

Word check

Check students understand the new words. Ask students to translate them into their own language. Also check students understand *gym* (the room at school where students do PE).

Culture note

Highlight the pictures of the singers and the Did you know? box. Tell students that Jessie J was born in London in 1988. She is a singer and songwriter who has won a number of awards. Rizzle Kicks was formed by Jordan 'Rizzle' Stephens and Harley 'Sylvester' Alexander-Sule in 2008. Leona Lewis was born in London in 1985. She became famous on the TV programme *The X Factor*. The Kooks are an Indie rock band from Brighton, England.

2

- Write the verbs *cost, perform, wear* and *study* on the board and check students understand their meaning.
- Check students understand all the sentences.
- Students read the sentences and decide if they are true or false.
- They correct the false sentences using the information in the article.
- Check answers as a class.

3

- Students read the questions and find the answers in the article.
- They compare their answers in pairs.
- Check answers as a class.

EXPRESS YOURSELF

4

- Students read the example sentence. Ask them if this sentence is true for their school.
- They work individually to find three differences and write their sentences.
- Check their answers as a class.

Finished?

Ask fast finishers to write two or three reasons why they would or wouldn't like to go to the BRIT School.

Web quest

Students find out about a famous singer from the BRIT School. Highlight the Web quest tip.

1. Students choose one of the singers in the text.
2. They write three questions they would like to know about that person, eg *How old is she? What is her home town?*
3. They swap their questions with another student.
   - Ask students to open an internet web browser such as Internet Explorer.
   - Students open a search engine (eg Google) and type in the name of the famous person.
   - They find the answers to their partner's three questions.

Welcome to the BRIT SCHOOL

The BRIT School in London is a very special place. It's a school for performing arts and technology and many of its past students are famous.

Students go to the BRIT School when they're 14 years old. It's free – it doesn't cost anything – but there are only about 140 places each year. The school has got excellent facilities. It's got a gym, a recording studio and a theatre. In the theatre, students perform concerts and musicals.

BRIT School students don't wear a uniform. They study obligatory subjects like English, maths, science and PE. They also do a special course in art, technology, media or performing arts.

Jessie J is a past student of the BRIT School. She's a very popular singer.

DID YOU KNOW?

Other famous past students include Rizzle Kicks, Leona Lewis and The Kooks!

Word check

performing arts facilities
recording studio media

Reading

A magazine article

1 1.24 **Look at the pictures. Do you know these singers? Then read and listen to the article.**

2 Check the meaning of the verbs in bold. Are the sentences true or false? Correct the false sentences.

1. Students **go** to the school when they're 12.
2. The school **costs** a lot of money.
3. Students **perform** concerts in the gym.
4. Students **wear** a blue and grey uniform.
5. All students **study** English and maths.

Exercise 2

1. False They go to the school when they're 14.
2. False The school is free – it doesn't cost anything.
3. False They perform concerts in the theatre.
4. False Students don't wear a uniform.
5. True

3 Read the article again and answer the questions.

1. Where is the BRIT School?
2. Is it a normal school? Why (not)?
3. What facilities has the school got?
4. What are the obligatory subjects?
5. What are the special courses?

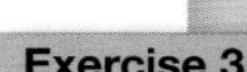

Exercise 3

1. In London.
2. No. It's a school for performing arts and technology.
3. A gym, a recording studio and a theatre.
4. English, maths, science and PE.
5. Art, technology, media and performing arts.

4 Is your school similar to the BRIT School? Write three differences.

Students go to my school when they are 12 years old.

WEB QUEST

Find out about a famous singer from the BRIT School.

1. **Choose one of the famous singers in the text about the BRIT School.**
2. **Write three things you want to know about this person.**
3. **Pairwork: swap your questions with another student. Search the internet for answers.**

Web Quest tip!

Before you search the internet, decide exactly what information you're looking for.

FINISHED?

Do you want to go to the BRIT School? Why (not)?

I want / don't want to go there because ...

Grammar 

Present simple: affirmative and negative

Exercise 1
1 sings
2 study
3 doesn't
4 don't

1 Copy and complete the table with *study*, *sings*, *don't* and *doesn't*.

affirmative		
I / You	**like**	the BRIT School.
He / She/ It	(1) ...	with The Kooks.
We / You / They	(2) ...	science and PE.
negative		
I / You	**don't study**	performing arts.
He / She / It	(3) ... **live**	at school.
We / You / They	(4) ... **wear**	a uniform.

LOOK!

word order
subject + verb + other words.
They (don't) wear a uniform.

Exercise 2
starts
studies
has
finishes
performs
goes

2 Read the spelling rules on page 29. Then write the third person form of the verbs in the box.

start study have finish perform go

Exercise 3
1 goes
2 studies
3 start
4 like
5 sings
6 loves

3 Copy and complete the sentences with the correct form of the verbs in brackets.

1 Anna ... (go) to the BRIT School.
2 She ... (study) performing arts.
3 Classes ... (start) at 8.45 in the morning.
4 Anna and her classmates ... (like) music.
5 Anna ... (sing) and she plays the guitar.
6 She ... (love) her school!

4 Change the words in bold to make the sentences true for you. Write one negative and one affirmative sentence.

I study English on **Sundays**.
I don't study English on Sundays. I study English on Mondays.

1 I go to **the BRIT School**.
2 My teacher lives in **England**.
3 My classes start at **ten o'clock**.
4 My school day finishes at **six o'clock**.
5 We study **20** subjects.

5 1.25 Complete the text with the correct form of the verbs in brackets. Then listen and check.

Exercise 5
2 goes
3 costs
4 don't pay
5 doesn't live
6 says
7 think
8 studies
9 dances

FROM SKATEBOARDING TO BALLET

Louis Moore (1) *loves* (love) skateboarding, but now he's got a new passion – ballet! Louis (2) ... (go) to The Royal Ballet School in London. The school is very prestigious. It (3) ... (cost) over £20,000 a year, but Louis' parents (4) ... (not pay) because he's got a scholarship.

Louis' parents live in Birmingham, but he (5) ... (not live) with them now. He only goes home at the weekends. His mum misses him! And what about his friends? Louis (6) ... (say) they're very happy for him and they (7) ... (think) it's great!

At ballet school, Louis (8) ... (study) normal subjects like English, maths and science. But he also (9) ... (dance) every day. He's very good at ballet because he's got perfect balance. The skateboarding is good practice!

ANALYSE

In the present simple in English, the third person verb is different. What about in your language?

1.26–1.27 **Pronunciation lab: Syllables and word stress, page 124**

Study guide: page 29

Grammar 

Present simple: affirmative and negative

Lesson objectives

In this lesson students will:

- learn the form of the present simple tense affirmative and negative
- use the present simple tense to write about people in the third person singular
- use the present simple tense to write about themselves

Recommended web links

www.royal-ballet-school.org.uk

Warmer

Write the sentence *The BRIT School is in London* on the board in random order: *London is School in The BRIT*. Students work in pairs and write the sentence in the correct order.

1
- Students copy and complete the table with *study, sings, don't* and *doesn't*.
- Check answers as a class.
- Highlight the fact that in the affirmative only *he / she / it* changes by adding an *-s*. In all the other persons, the verb remains the same. Point out that in the negative *don't* is the same for all the persons except *he/she/it* where it changes to *doesn't*.

Look!

Highlight the word order in the present simple affirmative and negative (subject + verb + other words) and the example.

2
- Students read the third person spelling rules on page 29. They write the third person forms of the verbs.
- They compare their answers in pairs.
- Check answers as a class.
- Highlight the fact that verbs that end in *-s, -sh*, *-ch* and *-x* add *-es*, *go* and *do* add *-es*,verbs that end in a consonant + *-y* remove the *-y* and add *-ies*, and that verbs that end in vowel + *-y* keep the *-y* and add *-s* in the third person.
- Point out that *have* is an irregular verb and that the third person is *has*.

3
- Ask the students to look at the picture and tell them that this is Anna.
- Students complete the exercise individually.
- Check answers as a class.

Finished?

Ask fast finishers to write the six sentences in the negative about another student (Petra) who doesn't go to the BRIT School.

4
- Students read the example sentences. Make sure they understand what they have to do with the words in bold. If necessary, do one more example with the class.
- Students work individually and complete the sentences. They compare their answers in pairs.
- Check answers as a class.

5 
- Ask the students to look at the picture and tell them that this is Louis.
- Make sure students understand what they have to do.
- Students work in pairs to complete the text.
- Play the CD. Students listen and check their answers.

Extra activity

Write these verbs on the board: *have, play, go, study, dance*. Put students in teams of three and ask them to work together and write down the third person form of each verb. The first team to write all five correctly wins the grammar race.

Analyse

Students read about the present simple in English and answer the question. Point out that in English an *-s* is added to form the third person of the verb. This is only one small change but it is very important!

Pronunciation lab: Syllables and word stress, page 124

Digital course: Interactive grammar table

Study guide: page 29

Vocabulary and Listening
Everyday activities

Lesson objectives
In this lesson students will:
- learn vocabulary for some everyday activities
- listen for specific information
- write about their school day

Warmer
Write *breakfast, lunch, dinner* and the question *Which is your favourite meal?* on the board. Students work in pairs and compare their answers. Listen to their ideas as a class.

1 1.28
- Students work in pairs. They write the words in the word pool in their notebooks with the meaning in their language. Give help if necessary.
- Play the CD. Students listen and repeat the everyday activities.
- Students look at the pictures and identify which everyday activities in the word pool are shown in the pictures.

2
- Students work individually and use the words in the word pool to fill the gaps in the information.

3 1.29
- Play the CD. Students listen and check their answers to exercise 2.
- Tell students that you will play the CD again. This time they listen and write down the time for each activity.
- Check answers as a class.

4
- Students write about their school day using the everyday activities in exercise 1.
- Monitor while they are writing and give help if necessary.
- Check answers as a class.

5 1.30
- Ask students to read the sentences carefully first. Check they understand them.
- Play the CD. Students listen and decide if the sentences are true or false.
- They correct the false sentences.
- Check answers as a class.

6
- Play the CD again. Students complete the notes.
- Check answers as a class.

1.29 Audioscript, exercise 3
At 7 o'clock, you get up and you get dressed.
At half past seven, you have breakfast – cereal or bacon and eggs!
At half past eight, you go to school. You study for two hours and you dance for two hours.
At one o'clock, you have lunch. Then you study or dance for another two hours.
At four o'clock, free time! You can do sport, watch TV or meet friends.
At six o'clock, you have dinner with your classmates.
At quarter past seven, you do your homework – in the classroom!
At quarter past nine, you have a shower and then go to bed. You're so tired after all that dancing!

1.30 Audioscript, exercises 5 and 6
Hello and welcome to Youth Focus! I'm Paul Turner and today we're bringing you the latest programme in our series 'Schools around the World'.
Are you a dance fan? Well, today we're looking at The Royal Ballet School. This is a very prestigious dance school in Richmond Park, London. Both girls and boys can go to The Royal Ballet School – they start at the age of 11 and stay until they're 16. Some students live at the school, but some live at home with their family. So, what is life like at The Royal Ballet School? Well, the students get up early and have breakfast. Then they dance for two to four hours every day. They don't just do ballet – they also learn other traditional dance styles, like Irish dancing and Scottish dancing. But it isn't all dancing! Students also study 12 subjects, including English, maths, science and ICT. And they all learn one foreign language – French. A lot of ballet words are in French! After dinner, students can do extra activities like art, sport, singing or playing in the orchestra.
The Royal Ballet School has got great facilities – obviously, it's got great dance studios! – and a gym and a swimming pool! There's also a big library and a theatre. If you love ballet, being a student at The Royal Ballet School is a fabulous opportunity. But life isn't easy! You get up early, work hard and go to bed early! Now we're going to talk to Louise Moor, who's a student at the Royal Ballet School. He can tell us more about life there. Hello, Louise…

Vocabulary and Listening

Everyday activities

Exercise 1
get dressed
have breakfast
go to school
watch TV
have dinner
do your homework
go to bed

Exercise 2
1 dressed
2 have
3 go
4 lunch
5 watch
6 have
7 do
8 bed

1 1.28 **Listen and repeat the everyday activities in the box. Which ones can you see in the pictures?**

2 Copy and complete the typical day with words from exercise 1.

meet friends get dressed go to bed do your homework tidy your room have lunch have breakfast go to school have a shower watch TV get up do sport have dinner

A typical day at ballet school

a *You get up, and you get (1) … .*

b *You (2) … breakfast – cereal or bacon and eggs!*

c *You (3) … to school. You study for two hours and you dance for two hours.*

d *You have (4) … . Then you study or dance for another two hours.*

e *Free time! You can do sport, (5) … TV or meet friends.*

f *You (6) … dinner with your classmates.*

g *You (7) … your homework in the classroom!*

h *You have a shower and then go to (8) … . You're so tired after all that dancing!*

Exercise 3
2 7.30
4 1.00
6 6.00
8 9.15

3 1.29 **Listen and check your answers to exercise 2. Then listen again and write the times in your notebook.**

4 Write about your school day. Use words from exercise 1.

I get up at half past seven. Then I …

Exercise 5
1 False The Royal Ballet School is for girls and boys.
2 False Some students live at the school.
3 True
4 True
5 False Life isn't easy for students at The Royal Ballet School.
6 True

5 1.30 **Listen to a radio programme about The Royal Ballet School. Are the sentences true or false? Correct the false sentences.**

1 The Royal Ballet School is only for girls.
2 All the students live at the school.
3 Students also learn Irish and Scottish dancing.
4 French is a useful language for ballet dancers.
5 Life is easy for students at The Royal Ballet School.
6 Students get up early in the morning.

6 Listen again. Copy and complete the notes about The Royal Ballet School.

THE ROYAL BALLET SCHOOL

WHERE?
Richmond Park in ***London****.*

STUDENTS
age (1) … to 16

SCHOOL LIFE:
· dance for 2-4 hours a day
· study (2) … subjects, including one foreign language: (3) … .

EXTRA ACTIVITIES
(4) … , sport, singing, orchestra practice

FACILITIES
dance studios, (5) … , swimming pool, library, (6) … .

Exercise 6
1 11
2 12
3 French
4 art
5 gym
6 theatre

Exercise 1
Eton College

Exercise 2
16

Cultural awareness
Boarding schools in the UK

Fact box

In the UK, only 7% of students go to private schools. Private schools can cost £30,000 a year, but some students receive a scholarship. State schools are free.

1 Read the first paragraph. What is the name of the school in the picture?

2 1.31 Read and listen. How many subjects does David study?

Life at boarding school

Some private schools are boarding schools – students eat, sleep and study there. Eton College is a famous boarding school for 13–18 year olds. It's near Windsor Castle and the River Thames. It's a very old school with a lot of traditions. Past students include Prince William, Prince Harry and several British prime ministers. Eton College is only for boys – girls can't go there!

What is life like for students at boarding school? David, 13, answers our questions ...

Do you go home at the weekend?
No, I don't. We can't go home at the weekend because we have classes on Saturdays!

Do you miss your family?
Yes, I do – but I see them in the holidays.

Do you share a bedroom?
No, I don't. All students have their own bedroom.

Do you like your school?
Yes, I do. The teachers are very good and the classes are small – there are only ten boys in my class. And I love the sports. My favourites are cricket and rowing.

What's a typical day like?
I get up at 7.30 and I get dressed. After breakfast, we have classes from 9 o'clock until 1.30. After lunch, we do sport and other activities. In the evening I do my homework and then we have dinner at 7.45. We go to church at 8.20. Then I have a shower and I go to bed at ten o'clock.

What subjects do you study?
I study English, maths, biology, chemistry, physics, Latin, French, Japanese, divinity, history, geography, PE, ICT, art, music and drama. We have 35 classes every week!

Word check

boarding school | prime minister | cricket | rowing | church | divinity

Exercise 3
1 b
2 b
3 a
4 b

3 Read the text again and choose the correct answers.

1 Is Eton College for boys and girls?
a) Yes, it is. **b)** No, it isn't.
2 Do students go home at the weekend?
a) Yes, they do. **b)** No, they don't.
3 Does David miss his family?
a) Yes, he does. **b)** No, he doesn't.
4 Do students share a bedroom?
a) Yes, they do. **b)** No, they don't.

CULTURAL COMPARISON

4 Compare your school and David's school. Write three sentences. Think about the things in the box.

class size	sports	subjects	uniform	weekends	everyday life	teachers

There are ten students in David's class.
In my class, there are 28 students.

Culture video: A typical day at a UK school

Cultural awareness

Boarding schools in the UK

Lesson objectives

In this lesson students will:

- read a text about a private school in England
- practise reading to find specific information
- compare their school with the English private school in the text

Recommended web links

www.etoncollege.com

Warmer

Ask students to read the Fact box about private schools and state schools in the UK. Ask if the percentage of students going to private schools is the same in their country.

1 • Ask students to read the first paragraph and answer the question.

2 1.31

- Write the question *How many subjects does David study?* on the board.
- Play the CD. Students listen and follow the text in their books.
- Check the answer as a class.

Word check

Check students understand all the new words. If necessary, illustrate *rowing* by miming the action.

3

- Ask the students to read the questions and the possible answers carefully first. Check they understand *miss* (if you *miss* someone you feel sad because they are not with you; if you *miss* something you feel sad because you no longer have it) and *share a bedroom* (a situation where two students sleep in the same bedroom).
- Students read the text again and choose the correct answers.
- They compare their answers in pairs.
- Check answers as a class.

CULTURAL  **COMPARISON**

4

- Nominate one student to read aloud the example sentences. Make sure students understand the task.
- Students work in pairs. They write at least three sentences about the differences between David's school and their school.
- Check their answers as a class.

Culture note

Eton College is about 25 miles west of London. It was founded in 1440. There are 1,300 boys at the school and approximately 130 teachers. To date, nineteen British prime ministers have attended Eton College.

Culture video: A typical day at a UK school

Grammar 

Present simple: questions and short answers

Lesson objectives

In this lesson students will:

- learn how to form questions in the present simple
- learn how to give short answers to questions in the present simple
- practise listening for specific information

Warmer

Write on the board two simple questions in the present simple with the words in the wrong order, eg *speak do English you* (*Do you speak English?*); *she school does like* (*Does she like school?*). Students work in pairs and put the words in the correct order to form questions. Check answers as a class and write the correct sentences on the board.

1
- Students copy the table into their notebooks.
- Highlight the fact that we use *Do* to ask questions for all persons except the third person where we use *Does*. Point out that with short answers we use *do / don't* for all persons except the third person where we use *does / doesn't*.
- Give students some practice in giving short answers. Ask them the questions in the table and elicit answers from individual students, eg *Do you like David's school? No, I don't.*

2
- Check students understand the task.
- Students work in pairs to complete the questions and write true short answers.
- Check answers as a class.

EXPRESS YOURSELF

3
- Do the first question with the class as an example. Point out that they don't have to add anything or change the rest of the sentence but simply add *Do* or *Does*.
- Students work individually to write the questions.
- Check answers as a class.

4
- Nominate two students to read aloud the example dialogue.
- Students work in pairs and ask and answer the questions from exercise 3.
- Listen to students' answers as a class.

 Grammar in context: PSHE

5
- This activity practises the use of the present simple tense in the affirmative, negative and question forms.
- Ask students to read the information before they look at the possible answers on the right.
- Students choose the correct word or phrase to fill each gap.
- They compare answers in pairs.

6  1.32
- Play the CD. Students listen and check their answers to exercise 5.

Extra activity

Put students into pairs. One student reads the introduction and asks the questions, and the other student answers them. Play the CD again and ask students to read the dialogue aloud in time with the recording. Then ask them to change roles. Play the CD again and repeat the activity.

Culture note

PSHE (Personal, Social, Health and Economic Education) has been part of the national curriculum for schools in England since 2000. PSHE helps children and young people develop as individuals and as members of families and social and economic communities. PSHE gives young people the knowledge, understanding and practical skills to live healthily, safely, productively and responsibly.

CLIL task

Listen to students' answers to the questions as a class.

Pronunciation lab: Third person verb endings, page 124

Digital course: Interactive grammar table

Study guide: page 29

Grammar

Present simple: questions and short answers

1 Study the table. When do we use *does* / *doesn't*?

questions	short answers
Do I / you **like** David's school?	Yes, I / you **do**. No, I / you **don't**.
Does he / she **study** Japanese?	Yes, he / she **does**. No, he / she **doesn't**.
Do we / you / they **go** home at weekends?	Yes, we/ you / they **do**. No, we / you / they **don't**.

2 Complete the questions with *Do* or *Does*. Then write true short answers. Find the information in the text on page 24.

Do students sleep at boarding school? *Yes, they do.*

1 ... girls go to David's school?
2 ... David have classes on Saturdays?
3 ... David live with his parents during school holidays?
4 ... David's classmates study Latin?
5 ... David go to bed at ten o'clock?

Exercise 2
1 Do; No, they don't.
2 Does; Yes, he does.
3 Does; Yes, he does.
4 Do; Yes, they do.
5 Does; Yes, he does.

EXPRESS YOURSELF

3 Write questions. Use *Do* or *Does* and the information in 1–6.

1 you / share a bedroom?
2 your friends / play cricket at school?
3 your best friend / live near you?
4 you / have classes on Saturdays?
5 you / study Japanese?
6 your English teacher / give you a lot of homework?

Exercise 3
1 Do you share a bedroom?
2 Do your friends play cricket at school?
3 Does your best friend live near you?
4 Do you have classes on Saturdays?
5 Do you study Japanese?
6 Does your English teacher give you a lot of homework?

4 In pairs, ask and answer the questions in exercise 3. Use short answers and then give extra information.

Do you share a bedroom?
Yes, I do. I share a bedroom with my brother.

CLIL Grammar in context: PSHE

PSHE is one of Sarah's school subjects. Here, she tells us more about it.

What does PSHE mean?
It (1) ... Personal, Social, Health and Economic Education.

What (2) ... in PSHE?
We (3) ... about things like health, relationships, diversity and personal finance.

Who is your teacher?
Our teacher's name is Mrs Evans. She (4) ... us interesting things and she (5) ... us much homework.

Do you have classes every day?
No, we (6) .... We (7) ... lessons twice a month.

(8) ... PSHE?
Yes, (9) .... We (10) ... exams and the classes are never boring!

5 Read the text and choose the correct answers.

	A	B	C
1	mean	means	does mean
2	do you study	you study	studies
3	learns	learn	do learn
4	teach	teaching	teaches
5	not give	doesn't give	don't give
6	not	don't	do
7	have	has	haven't
8	You like	Like you	Do you like
9	I do	I like	do I
10	no do	don't do	doesn't do

Exercise 5
1 B
2 A
3 B
4 C
5 B
6 B
7 A
8 C
9 A
10 B

6 1.32 Listen and check your answers.

CLIL TASK
Do you study a subject like PSHE? Who teaches you about health, relationships, diversity and personal finance?

1.33–1.34 Pronunciation lab: Third person verb endings, page 124

INTEGRATED SKILLS

At an after-school club

Hi! I'm Rebecca. I go to after-school clubs on Mondays and Thursdays. I do drama and football. Do you do any after-school activities?

Sign up for your after-school activity!

ORCHESTRA PRACTICE
Tuesday 4.00–5.00
The hall

Choir practice
Wednesday
3.45–5.00
Music room

ART CLUB
Friday 3.30–4.15
Art room

DRAMA CLUB
Monday 3.30–4.30
Room 2

Football training
Thursday
3.45–5.00
Football pitch

Step 1: Read

1 **Look at the noticeboard and answer the questions.**

1 What day is choir practice on?
2 What time does drama club start?
3 What time does football training finish?
4 Where is the orchestra practice?
5 Which activity can you do on Fridays?

Exercise 1
1 Wednesday(s)
2 3.30
3 5.00
4 the hall
5 art

2 **Which activities do you like? Which don't you like? Copy and complete the sentences.**

I like ... and ... .
I don't like ... or ... .

Step 2: Listen

SKILLS BUILDER

Listening: Multiple-choice answers
Before you listen, read all the options carefully.

3 1.35 **Listen to Rebecca talking about her typical school day. Choose the correct answers.**

1 Rebecca gets up at ... .
a) 6.30 **b)** 7.00 **c)** 7.15
2 She goes to school by ... .
a) car **b)** bike **c)** bus
3 Rebecca doesn't like ... .
a) maths **b)** French **c)** science
4 She does drama on ... .
a) Mondays **b)** Tuesdays **c)** Wednesdays
5 Rebecca wants to sign up for the ... .
a) orchestra **b)** chess club **c)** choir

Exercise 3
1 b
2 c
3 a
4 a
5 c

4 **Listen again. Complete the times.**

1 Rebecca's school starts at ... .
2 Her school finishes at ... .
3 Rebecca has dinner at ... .
4 She goes to bed at ... on school nights.

Exercise 4
1 9 o'clock
2 half past three
3 6 o'clock
4 half past nine on school nights

Integrated skills

At an after-school club

Lesson objectives

In this lesson students will:

- work on all four skills
- read posters about after-school activities on a noticeboard
- listen to someone talking about a school day
- write a personalized dialogue
- act out their dialogue

Warmer

Ask students to read the information about Rebecca in the speech bubble. Then write the question *Do you do any after-school activities?* on the board. Students answer the question in pairs. Listen to answers as a class.

Step 1: Read

1
- Ask students to read the questions carefully first. They then read the posters and find the answers.
- Check answers as a class.

2
- Students write their sentences individually and then compare with a partner.
- Check answers as a class.

Step 2: Listen

Skills builder

Listening: Multiple-choice answers
Encourage students to read all the options carefully because this will help to make the listening task easier.

3 1.35
- Play the CD. Students choose the correct answer for each question.
- They compare their answers in pairs.
- Check answers as a class.

4 1.35
- Ask students to read the beginnings of the sentences carefully first.
- Play the CD again. Students write the times.
- Check answers as a class. For further practice of the third person endings, ask students to give a full sentence when giving their answers, eg *Rebecca's school starts at 9 o'clock*.
- Write the complete sentences on the board. Students copy them into their notebooks.

1.35 Audioscript, exercises 3 and 4

Hi! I'm Rebecca and I'm going to tell you about my typical school day.
I get up at seven o'clock and I get dressed. Then I have breakfast and after that I go to school by bus. My sister gets the school bus too. School starts at 9 o'clock. Today is Monday, so my first class is maths. I don't like maths!
School finishes at half past three. On Mondays I stay for drama and on Thursdays I've got football training. I want to sign up for the choir, too – I love singing!
When I get home after school, I watch TV for a bit and then I have dinner at six o'clock. Then I do my homework and meet my friends or go out on my bike. On school nights, I go to bed at half past nine. I go to bed later at the weekend!

Integrated skills - continued

Asking for information

5 1.36

- Students work in pairs and read the dialogue on page 27 aloud to each other.
- Highlight the four gaps (1–4). Ask students what kind of word they expect to see after *on* (a day), *at* (a time) and *in* (a room).
- Ask students to look at the Communication kit: Asking for information box. Point out that *I'd like to* means the same as *I want to* but is more polite and formal.
- Play the CD. Students note down the answers for gaps 1–4.
- Check answers as a class.

6
- Play the CD again, pausing after each speaker's part for students to repeat as a class.
- Note the main stress on the questions: *What day is it on? What time does it start? What time does it finish? Where is it?*
- Ask students to repeat these questions several times both chorally and individually with the correct stress and intonation.
- Students practise the dialogue in pairs. Then swap roles and practise the dialogue again.

Step 3: Write

7
- Students write the four questions in bold in the dialogues in their notebooks. Ask them to mark the main stress on each question (see the teaching notes for exercise 6 above).
- Ask students to choose a different activity from the noticeboard on page 26 so that they write a different day, times and place from the original dialogue when they answer the questions.

8
- Students work individually and write their dialogue about the activity they chose in exercise 7, using the dialogue in the book as a model and the Communication kit: Asking for information for key phrases.
- Monitor while they are writing and give help if necessary.

Step 4: Communicate

9
- Students practise their dialogues in pairs.
- For extra practice, they swap roles in both dialogues.

10
- Choose some pairs to act out their dialogue for the class.
- Students raise their hand if another pair has the same activity, day, times and place as they do. This will encourage them to listen carefully to their classmates.

Integrated skills: Workbook page 112

ASKING FOR INFORMATION

Watch!

Hello! I'd like to find out about the choir.	The choir? Yes, of course.
What day is it on?	It's on (1) … .
What time does it start?	It starts at (2) … .
And **what time does it finish?**	It finishes at (3) … .
OK. I'd like to sign up, please.	Great! You're on the list. Enjoy it!
Thanks! Oh, one last question – **where is it?**	It's in the (4) … .

Exercise 5
1 Wednesdays
2 quarter to four
3 five o'clock
4 music room

5 1.36 **Listen to Rebecca asking about an after-school activity. Complete 1–4 in your notebook.**

6 **Listen again and repeat. Practise your intonation.**

Step 3: Write

7 **Copy the questions in bold. Choose an activity from the noticeboard on page 26 and write answers.**

8 **Write a new dialogue about your activity. Write both parts. Use the dialogue in exercise 5 to help you.**

Hello! I'd like to find out about the art club.
The art club? Yes, of course.

Step 4: Communicate

9 **Work in pairs. Take turns to practise your dialogues.**

Hello! I'd like to find out about the art club.
The art club? Yes, of course.

10 **Act your dialogue for the class.**

COMMUNICATION KIT

Asking for information

I'd like to find out about … .
What day is it on?
What time does it start?
What time does it finish?
Where is it?
I'd like to sign up, please.

Writing
A questionnaire

1 1.37 **Read and listen to the questionnaire. Copy and complete 1–5 with school subjects.**

Exercise 1
1 French
2 art
3 history
4 geography
5 maths

Questionnaire: School life

Name *Angela Carter* Class *8B* School *King James Secondary School*

1 What time do your classes start and finish?

Our classes start at 9.15 and school finishes at 3.30.

2 Do you wear a school uniform?

Yes, we do. We wear black trousers or skirts (for girls!), white shirts and blue and red ties and red sweatshirts.

3 Do you study languages?

Yes, I do. I study (1) ... and Spanish. Some students study German.

4 Which subjects do you like and which don't you like?

My favourite subjects are (2) ... and PE. I don't like (3) ... or maths.

5 Please describe a typical Monday.

After breakfast, I walk to school with my sister. In the morning, I've got history, (4) ... and science. I have lunch with my friends at half past twelve. In the afternoon, I've got (5) ... , English and ICT. Monday is not my favourite day!

Exercise 2
1 full stop, question mark, exclamation mark
2 comma
3 exclamation mark
4 question mark
5 brackets

2 Read the Writing focus and answer the questions.

WRITING FOCUS
Punctuation
. full stop , comma () brackets
? question mark ! exclamation mark

1 Which three punctuation marks always go at the end of a sentence?
2 Which one separates parts of a sentence or words in a list?
3 Which punctuation mark is used to show strong feelings?
4 Which one is only used in questions?
5 Which ones are used to give extra information?

Exercise 3
12 full stops
8 commas
4 question marks
2 exclamation marks
1 set of brackets

3 Read the questionnaire again. How many examples of each type of punctuation can you find?

4 Add punctuation to these sentences.

1 Do you wear a school uniform
2 School is great
3 I like maths science and ICT
4 Saturday is my favourite day
5 Do you study French

Exercise 4
1 Do you wear a school uniform?
2 School is great!
3 I like maths, science and ICT.
4 Saturday is my favourite day.
5 Do you study French?

Writing task
Complete a questionnaire.

Plan Prepare your answers to the questions in the questionnaire.

Write Copy questions 1–5 and write your own answers.

Check Check your writing.

✔ punctuation
✔ present simple verb forms
✔ question forms

Build your confidence: Writing reference and practice. Workbook page 122

Writing

A questionnaire

Lesson objectives

In this lesson students will:

- read a questionnaire
- understand and use basic punctuation
- answer a questionnaire

Warmer

Play a spelling game. Choose six school subjects and mix the letters of each word up. Write the words on the board with the letters in the wrong order, eg *s u c i m* (*music*). Put the class into teams of three. The first team to unscramble all the words and spell the six subjects correctly wins.

1 1.37

- Students look at the questionnaire and note where the five gaps are. Explain the task.
- Play the CD. Students listen and follow the text at the same time.
- Students write the missing school subjects.
- They compare answers in pairs.
- Check answers as a class.

2

- Write a full stop, comma, brackets, question mark and exclamation mark on the board.
- Ask students what these are examples of. Elicit that they are all types of punctuation.
- Students read the Writing focus and questions.
- They work in pairs and answer the questions with the different types of punctuation.
- Check answers as a class. Point out that in English there is never any punctuation at the beginning of a sentence.

3

- Students note down examples of each type of punctuation in the questionnaire. Tell them not to count the numbered gaps. They count the total number of each type.
- Students compare their total numbers in pairs.
- Check answers as a class.

Finished?

You can ask fast finishers to note down examples of each type of punctuation in the dialogue on Student's Book page 27.

4

- Do an example sentence with the class first. Write *Do you like school* on the board. Ask the class what the problem is (no punctuation). Ask what is missing (a question mark). Students now complete the punctuation of the five sentences using the punctuation types in the Writing Focus.
- Students compare their answers in pairs.
- Check answers as a class.

Writing task

The aim of this activity is for students to produce a piece of guided writing that gives them practice in using punctuation correctly. It also includes the correct use of the present simple in affirmative, negative and question forms. Ask the students to follow the stages in the Student's Book. At the Check stage, ask them to swap notebooks and check each other's writing.

Writing reference and practice: Workbook page 122

Study guide
Grammar, Vocabulary and Speaking

Tell the students the Study guide is an important page which provides a useful reference for the main language of the unit: the grammar, the vocabulary and the functional language from the Integrated skills pages. Explain that they should refer to this page when studying for a test or exam.

Grammar
- Tell the students to look at the example sentences of the present simple and make sure they know how to form the present simple correctly in the affirmative, negative and question forms.
- Refer students to the Grammar reference on pages 86–87 of the Workbook for further revision.

Vocabulary
- Tell students to look at the list of vocabulary and check understanding.
- Refer students to the Wordlist on page 151 of the Workbook where they can look up any words they can't remember.

Speaking
- Check that students understand the phrases to use for asking for information.
- Tell students to act out a conversation between a teacher and student asking for information.

Additional material

Workbook
- Progress check page 22
- Self-evaluation page 23
- Grammar reference and practice page 86
- Vocabulary extension page 103
- Integrated skills page 112
- Writing reference and task page 122

Teacher's Resource File
- Pulse Basics worksheets pages 11–17
- Vocabulary and grammar consolidation worksheets pages 7–10
- Translation and dictation worksheets pages 3, 13
- Evaluation rubrics pages 1–7
- Key competences worksheets pages 3–4
- Culture and CLIL worksheets pages 5–8
- Culture video worksheets pages 3–4
- Digital competence worksheets pages 3–4
- Macmillan Readers worksheets pages 1–2

Tests and Exams
- Unit 2 End-of-unit test: Basic, Standard and Extra
- CEFR Skills Exam Generator

Study guide

Grammar

Present simple

affirmative	
I / You	**study** history.
He / She / It	**studies** history.
We / You / They	**study** history.

negative	
I / You	**don't study** French.
He / She / It	**doesn't study** French.
We / You / They	**don't study** French.

questions	short answers
Do I / you **study** music?	Yes, I / you **do**. No, I / you **don't**.
Does he / she / it **study** music?	Yes, he / she / it **does**. No, he / she / it **doesn't**.
Do we / you / they **study** music?	Yes, we/ you / they **do**. No, we / you / they **don't**.

Third person spelling rules

- For most verbs, add *-s* to the infinitive
  read → reads   play → plays
- For verbs that end in *-s*, *-sh*, *-ss*, *-ch*, *-x*, or *-o* add *-es*
  teach → teaches   go → goes
- For verbs that end in consonant *+y*, omit the *-y* and add *-ies*
  study → studies   tidy → tidies
- Some verbs are irregular – they don't follow the rules!
  be → is   have → has

LEARNING TO LEARN

Make a list of third person spellings in your notebook. Add new verbs to your list when you learn them.

Vocabulary

School subjects

art
citizenship
dance
drama
English
French
German
history
maths
music
science
Spanish
technology
ICT (Information and Communication Technology)
PE (Physical Education)

Everyday activities

get up
have a shower
get dressed
have breakfast / lunch / dinner
go to school
do your homework
meet friends
watch TV
do sport
tidy your room
go to bed

Speaking

Asking for information

I'd like to find out about ...
What day is it on?
What time does it start?
What time does it finish?
Where is it?
I'd like to sign up, please.

UNIT 3 ACTIVE

Unit objectives and key competences

In this unit the student will learn ...

- to understand, memorize and correctly use vocabulary related to sports and action verbs **CLC SCC**
- to understand and correctly use adverbs of frequency, the verbs love, hate, (don't) like, don't mind + -ing, draw parallels to L1 and produce them in a short speaking activity **CLC L2L**
- about winter sports in Canada and compare against winter sports in their country **CLC CMST SCC CAE**
- about sport in the UK by watching a short video **CAE**

In this unit the student will learn how to ...

- form questions in the present simple with have got, be and other verbs **CLC**
- identify specific information in a magazine article about sporting activities **CLC CMST SCC**
- look online for information about Olympic sports and write a short profile of an Olympic athlete **CLC DC CAE CIE**
- identify specific information in a presentation about a sportswoman **CLC SCC CAE**
- read a survey about sporting activities, listen to people talking about sports and ask about routines **CLC SCC**
- write the results of a survey **CLC CMST CMST**
- prepare for and do a speaking pairwork activity exam **CLC L2L CIE**

Linguistic contents

Main vocabulary

- Sports: *surfing, swimming*, etc
- Verbs that go with different sports: *play, do, go*
- Action verbs: *lift, jump*, etc

Grammar

- Adverbs of frequency: *often, sometimes*
- *love, hate*, (*don't*) *like, don't mind + -ing*
- Questions with *be, have got* and other verbs

Functional language

- Phrases for asking about routines
- Phrases for asking for clarification in an exam
- Phrases for giving yourself time to think in an exam

Pronunciation

- *can*

Skills

Reading

- Read a magazine article about sporting activities
- Read a text about winter sports in Canada
- Read a survey about a swimming pool
- Read a survey questionnaire

Writing: Interaction and production

- Write a personalized dialogue about routines
- Write a questionnaire in three steps: plan, write, check
- Learn how to order your sentences correctly

Listening

- Listen to a presentation about an athlete
- Listen to people buying tickets and booking lessons

Spoken interaction

- Exchange information about sports and activities
- Ask and answer questions about what you like doing
- Ask and answer questions about sports you can / can't do

Spoken production

- Prepare and act out a dialogue about sports routines
- Prepare and do a speaking pairwork exam

Lifelong learning skills

Self-study and self-evaluation

- Study guide: Student's Book page 39
- Progress check and self-evaluation: Workbook pages 30–31
- Grammar reference and practice: Workbook pages 88–89
- Wordlist: Workbook pages 151–157

Learning strategies and thinking skills

- Using correct intonation in questions

Cultural awareness

- Winter sports in Canada
- Comparing winter sports in Canada with winter sports in students' own country

Cross-curricular contents

- PE: the heptathlon, winter sports
- Language and literature: reading and carrying out a survey
- ICT: searching the internet for information

Key competences

CLC	Competence in linguistic communication
CMST	Competence in mathematics, science and technology
DC	Digital competence
L2L	Learning to learn
SCC	Social and civic competences
SIE	Sense of initiative and entrepreneurship
CAE	Cultural awareness and expression

Evaluation

- Unit 3 End-of-unit test: Basic, Standard and Extra
- End-of-term test, Units 1–3: Basic, Standard and Extra
- CEFR Skills Exam Generator

External exam trainer

- Speaking: Pairwork activity

Digital material

Pulse Live! Digital Course including:

- Interactive grammar tables
- Audio visual speaking model: Asking about routines
- Audio visual cultural material: Sport in the UK

Student's website

Digital competence

- Web quest: A profile of an Olympic athlete
- Digital competence worksheet: Polls

Reinforcement material

- Basics worksheets, Teacher's Resource File pages 17-22
- Vocabulary and Grammar: Consolidation worksheets, Teacher's Resource File pages 11–12

Extension material

- Fast-finisher activity: Student's Book page 31
- Extra activities: Teacher's Book pages T35
- Vocabulary and Grammar: Extension worksheets, Teacher's Resource File pages 13–14

Teacher's Resource File

- Translation and dictation worksheets pages 4, 14
- Evaluation rubrics pages 1–7
- Key competences worksheets pages 5–6
- Culture and CLIL worksheets pages 9–12
- Culture video worksheets pages 5–6
- Digital competence worksheets pages 5–6
- Macmillan Readers worksheets pages 1–2

THINK ABOUT IT

How active are you? What sports and activities do you do ...
a) in PE at school?
b) in your free time?

Vocabulary and Speaking

Sports and activities

1 1.38 Look at the poster. Listen and repeat the sports and activities in blue. Which Activity Day do you prefer?

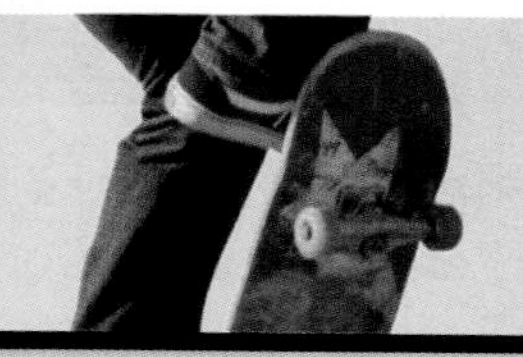

Activity Days

Sign up for a Saturday full of exercise and adventure! Choose from ...

ADRENALINE RUSH
- horse-riding
- mountain-biking
- surfing

URBAN SPORTS
- skateboarding
- cycling
- roller-skating

OLYMPIC FAVOURITES
- athletics
- gymnastics
- judo

RELAX AND RE-ENERGIZE
- swimming
- yoga
- aerobics

Exercise 2
1 judo, aerobics, yoga
2 surfing, swimming
3 horse-riding, mountain-biking, skateboarding, cycling, roller-skating, athletics

2 Put the sports in exercise 1 into categories 1–3.
1 indoor sports: *gymnastics* ...
2 water sports: ...
3 outdoor sports: ...

3 1.39 Listen and match sounds 1–5 to the sports in the box. What other ball sports do you know?

table tennis	tennis	golf	basketball	football

Exercise 3
a tennis
b football
c basketball
d golf
e table tennis

4 Read the rules for *play*, *do* and *go* on page 39. Which verb do we use for ball sports?

Exercise 4
play

5 Copy and complete the table with sports from exercises 1 and 3.

play	do	go
tennis	*athletics*	*horse-riding*

EXPRESS YOURSELF

6 Work in pairs. Ask questions about sports and activities. Use *play*, *do* and *go*.

Do you do judo?
No, I don't. But I do karate!

Exercise 5

play	do	go
football	gymnastics	mountain-biking
basketball	judo	surfing
golf	aerobics	skateboarding
table tennis	yoga	cycling
		roller-skating
		swimming

Vocabulary extension: Workbook page 104

Vocabulary and Speaking

Sports and activities

Lesson objectives

In this lesson students will:

- learn vocabulary for sports
- learn which sports go with *play, do* and *go*
- ask and answer questions about sports and activities

Warmer

Set a time limit of two minutes. Students work in pairs and write down as many sports as they can (eg *football, basketball, tennis*). Elicit examples from the class and write them on the board in preparation for the next activity.

Think about it

Students work individually and write down the sports and activities they do in PE (*physical education*) at school and the ones they do in their free time. Then they work in pairs and compare their answers. Check answers as a class. Help with vocabulary if necessary.

1 1.38

- Students look at the poster about Activity Days.
- Play the CD. Students listen to the blue words and repeat them.
- Students choose the Activity Day they prefer and compare their choices in pairs.
- Listen to their ideas as a class. Ask them to give reasons for their choice, eg *I like getting an adrenaline rush; I prefer relaxing activities like swimming and yoga*.
- Make sure they pronounce the two-word activities with the stress on the first word, eg *horse-riding, mountain-biking, roller-skating.*

2

- Check that students understand the activity – they sort the sports in exercise 1 into three different categories. Point out that some of these sports can be in more than one category.
- Students complete the activity individually.
- They compare answers in pairs.
- Check answers as a class.

Culture note

At indoor athletics championships the running track is shorter (200 m instead of 400 m) and the shortest sprint event is the 60 m. Cycling races are also held indoors in special arenas called *velodromes*.

3 1.39

- Play the CD. Students listen to the sounds and match them to the sports in the box.
- They compare their answers in pairs.
- Check answers as a class.

4

- Students read the rules for *play, do* and *go* on page 39.
- Ask which verb we use with ball sports. Elicit the answer (*play*).

5

- Students copy the table into their notebooks with the three example activities in the correct columns.
- They look again at the sports and activities from exercises 1 and 3 and put them into the correct columns.
- They compare their answers in pairs.
- Check answers as a class.

Language note

Highlight that we *play football* (*play* goes with all ball sports), we *do* martial arts and activities in a gym (eg *judo*, *aerobics*), and we *go swimming* (*go* goes with all *-ing* activities).

EXPRESS YOURSELF

6

- Nominate two students to read aloud the example dialogue.
- Students work in pairs and ask and answer questions about sports and activities.
- Students report back to the class which sports their partner does or does not do.
- Correct any errors in the use of *play, do* and *go*.

Vocabulary extension: Workbook page 104

Reading

Text type: A magazine profile

Lesson objectives

In this lesson students will:

- read a magazine article about sporting activities
- say which sporting activity they find more interesting and why
- use adjectives to describe sporting activities

Recommended web links

www.cheerleading.org.uk

Warmer

Mime *rowing* and ask students to guess the sport or activity. The student who guesses correctly then mimes another sport or activity. Write each word on the board.

1 1.40

- Read the question *What sports and activities do Paige and Joe do?* aloud to the class.
- Play the CD. Students read and listen to the profiles.
- Students work individually and write the answers to the question.
- They compare answers in pairs.
- Check answers as a class.

Word check

Check that students understand all the new words. Use the pictures to help clarify meaning. Note that *squad* is very similar to *team* and that the singular of *trophies* is *trophy*.

2

- Students complete the sentences individually by looking back at the profiles.
- They compare answers in pairs.
- Check answers as a class.

Culture note

Highlight the Did you know? box and point out that the first official drag race took place in 1950 on an unused runway at Santa Ana in California. Cheerleading began at Princeton University in New York in 1877, when students chanted *Hurrah* when watching their baseball and American football teams compete against other colleges.

3

- Students read the questions carefully first. Make sure they understand all the questions.
- They look for the answers in the profiles.
- They compare their answers in pairs.
- Check answers as a class. Point out that we say *twice* and not *two times*. Make sure students understand *fun*.

EXPRESS YOURSELF

4

- Highlight the words in the box. Make sure students understand them all.
- Students write answers to the question, giving reasons for their choice and using the words in the box or their own ideas.
- They compare answers in pairs.
- Check answers as a class.

Finished?

Ask fast finishers to write three questions to ask either Paige or Joe. Put them into pairs. They ask and answer the questions (students answering the questions can imagine the answers).

Web quest

Students write profiles of Olympic athletes from their country. Highlight the Web quest tip.

1
- Students work in groups of four and write a list of all the Olympic sports.
- Listen to their ideas as a class and make a list on the board.
- Give each student one of the sports.

2
- Students choose an Olympic athlete from their country that does their allocated sport.
- They write at least three questions they would like to know about that person (eg *How old is she? What is her home town?*).
- Ask students to open an internet web browser such as Internet Explorer.
- Students open a search engine (eg Google) and type in the name of their athlete.
- They find answers to their questions.

3
- Students write a short profile of their athlete and share their information with the group.

ACTIVE! PROFILES

This week, *Active!* magazine presents two fantastic young sports stars …

Paige Wheeler (12) is the European Finals Event Winner in drag racing.

Paige never drives on normal roads because she's only 12, but she often drives at 100 km/hr at the racetrack. Her dragster is faster than a Ferrari! 'I love it,' she says. 'It's so cool!' When she leaves school, Paige wants to be a full-time drag racer.

Lives in: Wellingborough, England

Hobbies: swimming, cycling, cheerleading

Favourite school subject: Spanish

Favourite colour: turquoise

Joe English (13) is the captain of the DAZL Boys, the only all-boy cheerleading squad in Europe.

The DAZL Boys usually train twice a week. They learn new cheerleading moves, dance hip hop and do gymnastics. Before a competition, they train every day. Joe likes being the captain because he always collects the trophies! People sometimes tease Joe because he's a boy cheerleader, but he doesn't mind. 'I love cheerleading,' he says. 'It's really energetic and fun.'

Lives in: Leeds, England

Family: two brothers and one sister

Favourite sports: rugby and football

Cheerleading uniform: red and black

Word check

drag racing | drive | captain | cheerleading | squad | trophies | tease

Exercise 1
Paige
drag-racing
Joe
cheerleading

Exercise 2
1 swimming, cycling and cheerleading
2 Spanish
3 turquoise
4 two brothers
5 football
6 red and black

Exercise 3
1 Because she is only 12 years old.
2 She wants to be a full-time drag-racer.
3 She lives in Wellingborough, England
4 Twice a week.
5 Every day.
6 Because it's really energetic and fun.

Reading
A magazine profile

1 1.40 **Read and listen to the profiles. What sport or activity do Paige and Joe do?**

2 Read and listen again. Copy and complete the sentences.

1 Paige's hobbies are …
2 Paige studies …
3 Her favourite colour is …
4 Joe has got one sister and …
5 Joe likes rugby and …
6 His cheerleading uniform is …

3 Read the profiles again and answer the questions.

1 Why can't Paige drive on normal roads?
2 What does Paige want to do when she leaves school?
3 Where does Paige live?
4 How often do the DAZL Boys usually train?
5 How often do they train before a competition?
6 Why does Joe love cheerleading?

DID YOU KNOW?

Drag racing is Europe's fastest motorsport.
Before 1923, cheerleading was just for men.

4 Which is more interesting, drag racing or cheerleading? Why? Use the words in the box or your own ideas.

exciting dangerous creative energetic fun

Drag racing is more interesting because it's exciting.

FINISHED?

Imagine you can interview Paige or Joe. Write three questions.

How many trophies have you got?

WEB QUEST

Work as a class. Write profiles of Olympic® athletes from your country.

1 Class work: write a list of all Olympic® sports. Allocate one to each student.
2 Find out about an Olympic® athlete from your country in your allocated sport.
3 Write a short profile. Then share what you find out with the class.

Web Quest tip!

Make sure you use official websites that you trust. Some websites contain false information.

Grammar 

Adverbs of frequency

1 Read the table and choose the correct words in rules a) and b).

adverbs of frequency
Paige **never** drives on normal roads. She **rarely** loses a race. Drag racing is **sometimes** dangerous. Paige **often** drives at 100 km/hr at the racetrack. The DAZL Boys **usually** train twice a week. Joe **always** collects the trophies.

a) Adverbs of frequency go **before** / **after** *be*.
b) Adverbs of frequency go **before** / **after** other verbs.

2 Rewrite the sentences with the adverbs of frequency in the correct place.

China wins Olympic® medals for football. (rarely)
China rarely wins Olympic medals for football.

1 The Olympic® Games are in summer. (usually)
2 I watch them on television. (often)
3 The Paralympics are after the Olympics®. (always)
4 Britain wins medals for diving. (sometimes)
5 The Winter Olympics® are in Brazil. (never)

3 Write questions with *How often ...* ?

1 drive a dragster?
2 play football?
3 go swimming?
4 watch sport on television?
5 do exercise?
6 walk to school?

4 Work in pairs. Ask and answer the questions in exercise 3. Use adverbs of frequency or the time expressions in the box.

every day / weekend   from time to time once / twice / three times a week

How often do you drive a dragster?
I never drive a dragster!

love, hate, (don't) like, don't mind + -ing

5 Copy and complete the table. Use the correct form of the words in the box. Then translate the sentences into your language.

~~don't mind~~   like   hate   love   don't like

love, hate, (don't) like, don't mind + -ing	
☺☺	I ... studying English!
☺	She ... swimming.
😐	He *doesn't mind* training every day.
☹	We ... doing exams.
☹☹	They ... getting up early.

6 Choose the correct answers in the dialogues.

Ann: What do you want to play?
Ben: I (1) **like** / **hate** playing golf. It's fun!
Ann: I (2) **love** / **don't like** golf. What about tennis?

Cath: Why don't we go to the gym at 8 o'clock?
Dave: At 8 o'clock?! I (3) **don't mind** / **don't like** going to the gym, but I (4) **love** / **hate** getting up early!

EXPRESS YOURSELF

7 Write questions. Use *like* and words from A and B.

A	B
you	(get up) early?
your friends	(speak) English?
your teacher	(play) tennis?
your brother / sister	(watch) football?

Does your teacher like speaking English?

8 Work in pairs. Ask and answer your questions from exercise 7.

ANALYSE

In English, we use *Do* / *Does* before the subject in questions with *love*, *hate*, *like* + *-ing*. How do you say these questions in your language?

~~You like play football?~~ ✗
Do you like playing football? ✔

Exercise 1
a Adverbs of frequency go after *be*.
b Adverbs of frequency go before other verbs.

Exercise 2
1 The Olympic Games are usually in summer.
2 I often watch them on television.
3 The Paralympics are always after the Olympics.
4 Britain sometimes win medals for diving.
5 The Winter Olympics are never in Brazil.

Exercise 3
1 How often do you drive a dragster?
2 How often do you play football?
3 How often do you go swimming?
4 How often do you watch sport on television?
5 How often do you do exercise?
6 How often do you walk to school?

Exercise 5
I love studying English!
She likes swimming.
We don't like doing exams.
They hate getting up early.

Exercise 6
1 like
2 don't like
3 don't mind
4 hate

Grammar

Digital

Adverbs of frequency

Lesson objectives

In this lesson students will:

- learn and use adverbs of frequency
- ask and answer questions using *How often ...?*
- use the verbs *love, hate, (don't) like* and *don't mind* plus the gerund (+ *-ing*) to describe activities

Warmer

Books closed. Write a sentence from the previous lesson on the board in random order: *on roads Paige drives never normal*. Students work in pairs and write the sentence in the correct order (*Paige never drives on normal roads*).

1
- Check students understand the term *adverbs of frequency* by giving them examples in their language (eg the equivalent of *always*).
- Ask students to read the two rules carefully.
- They look at the example sentences in the table and choose the correct words.
- Check answers as a class.

2
- Highlight the example sentence and show that *rarely* comes before the verb *wins*.
- Remind students that adverbs of frequency come after *be* and before other verbs.
- Students work individually to rewrite the sentences with the adverbs of frequency.
- They compare their answers in pairs.
- Check answers as a class.

3
- Do one example with the whole class first. Use a different example, eg *go cycling? How often do you go cycling?*
- Remind students to use *do you* in their questions.
- Students complete the exercise individually.
- Check answers as a class.

4
- Students work in pairs and ask and answer the questions from exercise 3.
- Point out that they can use the adverbs of frequency from exercise 1 or the time expressions in the box (see the Language note).
- Listen to some examples as a class.
- Make sure they put the adverbs of frequency in the correct place in the sentence.

Language note

The time expressions in the box do not follow the rules for adverbs of frequency. They are usually used at the end of the sentence, eg *I play football every weekend.*

love, hate, (don't) like, don't mind + -ing

5
- Students copy and complete the sentences using the correct form of the words in the box. Make sure they understand they may need to change the endings in the third person.
- They compare answers in pairs.
- Check answers as a class. Ask them to translate the verbs into their language.

Language note

Highlight the use of the *-ing* form after these verbs, eg *I like playing football*. Point out that in the sentence *He doesn't mind training every day, doesn't mind* means that he doesn't like it but he also doesn't not like it. He can do it and it isn't a problem for him.

6
- Students read the dialogues individually and choose the correct answers.
- They compare answers in pairs.
- Check answers as a class.

7
- Highlight the example question.
- Students work individually and write at least four questions.

8
- Students work in pairs and ask and answer their questions from exercise 7.
- Listen to some examples as a class.

Analyse

Ask students to look at the correct and incorrect questions and answers. Which are more similar to their language?

Digital course: Interactive grammar table

Study guide: page 39

Vocabulary and Listening

Action verbs

Lesson objectives

In this lesson students will:

- learn some action verbs
- listen for specific information
- ask and answer questions with *can*

Recommended web links

www.uka.org.uk
www.jessicaennis.net

Warmer

Students work in pairs and write down all the Olympic athletic events they can think of. Set a time limit of two minutes for this. Write their suggestions on the board. The pair with the most correct answers wins.

1 1.41

- Play the CD. Students listen to the verbs and repeat them.
- Students look at the pictures.
- They work in pairs and match the words in the word pool with the pictures.
- Check answers as a class.

2

- Ask students to work individually and use the verbs from exercise 1 to complete the phrases.
- They compare answers in pairs.
- Check answers as a class.

Look!

Ask students to look at the example sentences in the Look! box and highlight the fact that we never use *to* after *can* / *can't*.

3 EXPRESS YOURSELF

- Students write questions using *Can you ...?* and the prompts shown.

4

- In pairs students ask and answer the questions they wrote in exercise 3.
- Monitor while they are working and make sure their questions and answers are correct.
- Listen to some pairs as a class.

5 1.42

- Students read the questions and look at the information and pictures in the profile.
- They answer the questions.
- Play the CD. Students check their answers.
- They compare answers in pairs.
- Check answers as a class.

6

- Ask students to read the five sentences carefully first.
- Play the CD again.
- Students complete the sentences.
- Students compare answers in pairs.
- Check answers as a class.

Pronunciation lab: *can*, **page 124**

1.42 Audioscript, exercises 5 and 6

A Hello! My presentation today is about the British athlete Jessica Ennis. She's one of my favourite athletes because she's from my home city, Sheffield. She lives in Sheffield with her husband and her pet dog, Myla. Jessica is a heptathlete. The heptathlon event has got seven different parts: high jump, long jump, javelin, shot put, and three running events: hurdles, a 200-metre race and an 800-metre race. Jessica's favourite parts are the high jump and the hurdles. She loves running and jumping! She can run 200 metres in just 23 seconds! And she can jump more than six metres in the long jump.

Jessica usually trains for six hours a day, six days a week. She only has one day off a week – she doesn't usually train on Thursdays. In her free time, Jessica likes listening to music and watching TV. She also likes going for a walk with her dog. Jessica doesn't mind all the hard work because she loves her sport. She loves the adrenaline and she loves winning!

Thank you! Has anyone got any questions?

B How many gold medals has she got?

A Well, she won a gold medal in the 2012 Olympic Games in London. I watched it on TV. It was so exciting!

Vocabulary and Listening

Action verbs

1 1.41 **Match pictures 1–6 with verbs from the box. Which verbs can't you see? Then listen and repeat.**

run ride jump throw catch hit score kick lift ski dive skate

2 Copy and complete the phrases with verbs from exercise 1.

ski down a mountain

1 ... a marathon
2 ... a horse
3 ... a goal
4 ... a javelin
5 ... a football
6 ... 50 kg

LOOK!

can / can't

He can ~~to~~ lift 20 kg. I can't ~~to~~ lift 100 kg!

EXPRESS YOURSELF

3 Write questions with *Can you ...* ? and these ideas.

- ride (a horse / a bike)?
- run (10 km / a marathon)?
- play (rugby / hockey)?
- skate (on ice / in the park)?

4 Work in pairs. Ask and answer your questions from exercise 3.

Can you ride a horse?
No, I can't. But I can ride a bike!

5 1.42 **Look at the profile of the heptathlete Jessica Ennis and answer the questions. Then listen and check.**

1 Where is Jessica Ennis from?
2 How many events are there in a heptathlon?
3 How many running events are in the heptathlon?

6 Listen again and complete the sentences.

1 Jessica's pet ... is called Myla.
2 Her favourite events are the ... and the hurdles.
3 Jessica trains ... days a week.
4 ... is usually her free day.
5 In her free time, Jessica likes ... .
6 Jessica ... a gold medal.

ATHLETE PROFILE: JESSICA ENNIS

Date of birth: 28/01/1986 **Sport:** Heptathlon **From:** Sheffield

1.43 **Pronunciation lab: *can*, page 124**

Cultural awareness

Winter sports

Exercise 1
1 are
2 Where
3 is
4 do

1  1.44 Copy and complete questions 1–4 with the words in the box. Then read, listen and check.

Where	do	is	are

Fact box

Some parts of Canada are in the Arctic Circle. The temperature in winter can be -40°C!

Winter sports in Canada

Canada is a fantastic place for winter sports. Ice hockey is the official national sport – it's more popular than football! Skiing, snowboarding and ice skating are also popular.

Where (1) ... the best ski resorts?
Canada has got hundreds of mountains. The most popular ski resort is in Whistler, near Vancouver. More than two million people go there every year. It's enormous – there are 200 ski runs and 39 ski lifts.

(2) ... do people go dog-sledding?
Dog-sled racing is popular in northern Canada. The famous Canadian Challenge race is 500 km. Dog-sled racers are called 'mushers' and their teams have got nine dogs.

What (3) ... 'icebiking'?
Icebiking is cycling on ice! Icebikes have got special tyres so they can travel on ice. In winter, you can watch icebike races in many Canadian towns.

How (4) ... you play ice hockey?
There are two teams of six players. Players skate on the ice and hit the puck with their sticks. You can kick the puck, but you can't throw it. The aim is to score more goals than the other team.

Word check
ski resort · ski run · ski lift · tyre · puck · stick

2 Read the text again and answer the questions. Use short answers.

1 Is football Canada's national winter sport?
2 Do Canadians like skiing?
3 Is the Whistler ski resort near Vancouver?
4 Have dog-sled teams got 12 dogs?
5 Do icebikers cycle on ice?
6 Have ice-hockey teams got six players?

Exercise 2
1 No, it isn't.
2 Yes, they do.
3 Yes, it is.
4 No, they haven't.
5 Yes, they do.
6 Yes, they have.

3 Read the rules for ice hockey again. Choose the correct words.

1 Players **run** / **skate** on the ice.
2 Players **catch** / **hit** the puck with a stick.
3 You can **kick** / **throw** the puck.
4 The objective is to score **points** / **goals**.

Exercise 3
1 skate
2 hit
3 kick
4 goals

CULTURAL  COMPARISON

4 Answer the questions.

1 Can people go skiing in your country? Where?
2 What other winter sports do people do in your country?
3 Do you do winter sports?

Culture video: Sport in the UK

Cultural awareness

Winter sports

Lesson objectives

In this lesson students will:

- read a text about winter sports in Canada
- practise reading to find specific information
- talk about winter sports in their country

Warmer

Write the word *Canada* on the board. Highlight the Fact box. Students work in pairs and write down what else they know about Canada. Check ideas a class. Write relevant points on the board (eg *They speak English*; *They play ice hockey*; *The flag is red and white*, etc).

Culture note

Canada is by area the second largest country in the world after Russia. Its border with the USA is the longest land border in the world. It has a population of about 35 million and two official languages – English and French. The largest city in Canada is Toronto but the capital city is Ottawa.

1 1.44

- Ask students to look at the words in the box.
- They copy the questions into their notebooks and use these words to complete the four gaps.
- Play the CD so that they can check their answers.
- Check answers as a class.

Word check

Check students understand all the words. Use the pictures to clarify *tyre* and *stick.*

2

- Students read the questions carefully first.
- They look back in the text to find the answers if necessary. They write short answers to each question.
- They compare answers in pairs.
- Check answers as a class.

3

- Students work in pairs and choose the correct words.
- They check their answers by looking in the text again.
- Check answers as a class.

CULTURAL  **COMPARISON**

4

- Students work individually and answer the three questions.
- They compare their answers in pairs or small groups.
- Listen to their ideas as a class.

Culture video: Sport in the UK

Grammar 

Question forms: word order

Lesson objectives

In this lesson students will:

- learn how to form questions in the present simple with *be, have got* and other verbs
- practise the word order of different question forms
- ask and answer questions about themselves

Warmer

Write on the board two simple questions in the present simple with the words in the wrong order (eg *Do you like playing football? – football like Do playing you; Have you got a pet? – pet got a you Have*). Students work in pairs and put the words in the right order to form questions. They come to the board and write the questions.

1
- Students copy the tables into their notebooks.
- Explain that they should put the three questions in the correct place in the table.
- Check that they have the correct section for each question and ask them to write the questions in the table.

2
- Students write the words in the correct order to form questions. Tell them to refer to the table if necessary.
- They compare answers in pairs.
- Check answers as a class.
- Students then look at the fact file and write answers to the questions.
- Check answers as a class.

EXPRESS YOURSELF

3
- Do the first question with the class as an example.
- Students work individually to write the questions.
- Check answers as a class.

4
- Students work in pairs and ask and answer the questions from exercise 3.
- Listen to some pairs with the class. Correct any errors if necessary.

Extra activity

Students stand up and walk around the class, asking and answering their questions, noting down the names of the people they speak to and their answers. They report back to the whole class, eg *Pablo's favourite sports are basketball and swimming. His birthday is 15th June.*

Grammar in context: PE

5  1.45
- This activity practises the use of adverbs of frequency, verb forms in the present simple and *love / don't mind / don't like + -ing.*
- Ask students to read the whole text carefully first.
- Students choose the correct answers.
- They compare their answers in pairs.
- Play the CD. Students check their answers.

CLIL task

Students find three questions about PE in the text. They write true answers. They compare answers in pairs. Listen to some of their questions and answers as a class.

Extra activity

Put students into pairs. They discuss and write down the differences between PE in UK schools and in their school or in schools in general in their country. Listen to their ideas as a class.

Digital course: Interactive grammar table

Study guide: page 39

Grammar

Question forms: word order

Exercise 1

***be* questions**
b Where is the Whistler ski resort?
***have got* questions**
c Has Canada got a lot of mountains?
questions with other present simple verbs
a Does it snow in Canada?

1 Copy the tables into your notebook. Then add questions a–c.

***be* questions**			
question word	***am / is / are***	**subject**	
	Is	Canada	in the Arctic Circle?
Where	are	the ski resorts?	

***have got* questions**				
question word	***have / has***	**subject**	**got**	
	Have	hockey teams	got	eight players?
Why	has	he	got	a new snowboard?

questions with other present simple verbs				
question word	***do / does***	**subject**	**verb**	
	Do	Canadians	like	snowboarding?
Where	do	people	go	skiing?

a) Does it snow in Canada? **b)** Where is the Whistler ski resort? **c)** Has Canada got a lot of mountains?

Exercise 2

1 When is Rose's birthday? 24th January.
2 How fast do skeleton athletes go? More than 100 km/h.
3 Where does Rose live? Bath, England.
4 Has she got special equipment? Yes, she has.

2 Read the fact file. Then write the questions in the correct order.

1 is / Rose's / When / birthday ?
2 go / How fast / do / skeleton athletes ?
3 live / does / Rose / Where ?
4 got / she / special equipment / Has ?

FACT FILE

Name: Rose McGrandle
Sport: skeleton
Lives in: Bath, England
Birthday: 24th January

Did you know?
Skeleton athletes travel at more than 100 km/hr on a metal sled. They wear special clothes, goggles and a helmet.

EXPRESS YOURSELF

Exercise 3

1 What are your favourite sports?
2 Do you watch sport on TV?
3 When is your birthday?
4 Have you got any brothers and sisters?
5 Does your teacher do any sport?

3 Write questions. Use *is, are, do, does* and *have got*.

1 What / your favourite sports?
2 you / watch / sport on TV?
3 When / your birthday?
4 you / any brothers and sisters?
5 your teacher / do any sport?

4 Work in pairs. Ask and answer your questions from exercise 3.

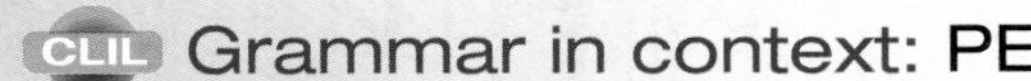

CLIL Grammar in context: PE

5 1.45 Read the text and choose the correct answers. Then listen and check.

Exercise 5

1 usually have
2 do you do
3 playing
4 often play
5 Are you
6 running
7 don't
8 's often
9 never wins
10 Does

PE is my favourite subject! We (1) ***have usually / usually have*** *three classes a week. How often (2)* ***do you do / you do*** *PE at school?*

In PE we play team sports like football, cricket and hockey. I love (3) ***playing / play*** *football. I'm in the school team. We (4)* ***play often / often play*** *matches after school. (5)* ***Are you / You are*** *in a school team?*

We also do something called cross-country running. We usually run about 5 km. I don't mind (6) ***to run / running*** *in the summer, but I (7)* ***don't / not*** *like it in winter. It (8)* ***'s often / often is*** *cold and wet!*

In June, my school has a sports day. My class (9) ***never wins / wins never****! (10)* ***Do / Does*** *your school have a sports day?*

CLIL TASK
Find three questions about PE in the text. Write answers that are true for you.

At the sports centre

I usually go to the sports centre twice a week. I play badminton on Thursday evenings and I go swimming at the weekend. How often do you go to the sports centre?

SURVEY: SUNNYSIDE SWIMMING POOL

Name: *Hazel Green* **Age:** *13* **Email address:** *hazelgreen@email.com*

1 How often do you go to the swimming pool?	2 When do you usually go to the pool?	3 Do you do any of these activities?	4 What other sports do you do?
☐ less than once a week	☐ Monday–Friday	☐ aqua-aerobics	☑ badminton
☑ once a week	☑ At the weekend	☑ swimming classes	☐ cycling
☐ twice a week or more		☐ snorkelling	☐ gymnastics
		☐ diving	

Step 1: Read

1 Read the survey and answer the questions.

1 How old is Hazel?
2 How often does Hazel go to the pool?
3 When does she usually go to the pool?
4 Does Hazel do aqua-aerobics?
5 What activity does Hazel do at the pool?
6 What other sport does she do?

2 Answer the survey questions for you. Are your answers different or similar to Hazel's?

3 Which activity do you want to try? Why?

I want to try aqua-aerobics because ...

Exercise 1

1 13
2 once a week
3 at the weekend
4 no
5 swimming classes
6 badminton

Step 2: Listen

4 1.46 **Listen to three short conversations. Which three activities do they talk about?**

a) yoga **b)** judo **c)** swimming **d)** badminton **e)** aqua-aerobics **f)** diving

5 Listen again. Are the sentences true or false? Correct the false sentences.

Conversation 1

1 He buys tickets for two adults and one child.
2 They've got ten hours in the pool.

Conversation 2

3 The classes are twice a week.
4 She books a place for next Thursday.

Conversation 3

5 The lessons are on Wednesday mornings.
6 He can swim, but he can't dive.

Exercise 4

c swimming
e aqua-aerobics
f diving

Exercise 5

1 False one adult and two children.
2 False two hours
3 True
4 False next Tuesday.
5 False Wednesday evenings.
6 True

Integrated skills

At the sports centre

Lesson objectives

In this lesson students will:
- work on all four skills
- read a survey
- listen to a phone conversation
- write a personalized dialogue
- act out their dialogue

Warmer

Play an alphabet game. Write the letter *a* on the board. Ask students to tell you a sport beginning with *a*. Elicit, for example, *athletics* and write it on the board. Continue for other letters. If no one can think of a sport for a particular letter, skip that letter and go to the next one.

Step 1: Read

1
- Ask students to read the information about Hazel in her speech bubble.
- Write the question *How often do you go to the sports centre?* on the board. Listen to answers as a class.
- Check that students understand the task.
- Ask students to read the questions first. Then they read the survey and find the answers.
- They compare answers in pairs.
- Check answers as a class.

2
- Students answer the questions by ticking the appropriate boxes.
- They compare answers in pairs and find out it their partner's answers are different or similar to Hazel's.
- Check answers as a class.

3
- Students answer the questions.
- They compare answers in pairs.
- Check answers as a class.

Step 2: Listen

4 1.46
- Students listen and tick the three activities the people are talking about.
- Play the CD. Students tick the three activities they hear.
- They compare answers in pairs.
- Check answers as a class.

5
- Ask students to read the sentences carefully first.
- Play the CD again. Students decide if the sentences are true or false.
- Play the CD again. They correct the false sentences.
- Check answers as a class.

1.46 Audioscript, exercises 4 and 5

1 Dad Hello! Three people for the swimming pool, please.
Receptionist Adults or children?
Dad One adult and two children, please.
Receptionist That's ten pounds, please.
Dad Ten pounds? Here you are.
Receptionist Thanks!
Dad How much time have we got in the pool?
Receptionist You've got two hours.
Dad OK, great. Thanks!

2 Receptionist Hello, Sunnyside Swimming pool. Can I help you?
Girl Oh, hello. Yes – I'd like to know if you have aqua-aerobics classes at the pool?
Receptionist Yes, we have. The classes are twice a week, on Tuesday and Thursday evenings.
Girl Oh, great.
Receptionist They're very popular, so it's a good idea to book if you want to come.
Girl Oh, OK. Can I book a place for next Tuesday then?
Receptionist Yes, of course. What name is it, please?
Girl It's Vanessa Brown ...

3 Receptionist Hello, can I help you?
Boy Yes – do you have diving lessons here?
Receptionist Yes, we do. They're once a week, every Wednesday evening.
Boy Ah, OK. And do you have different levels?
Receptionist Yes, we do – can you dive already?
Boy No, I can't. I can swim, though! I want to learn to dive as well.
Receptionist Great idea! The beginners' lesson is at 6 o'clock ...

Integrated skills - continued

Asking about routines

6  1.47

- Students read the three questions carefully first.
- They put the questions in the correct place in the dialogue.
- Play the CD. Students check their answers.

7

- Play the CD again, pausing after each speaker's part for students to repeat as a class.
- Note the main stress on the questions: *Can I ask you a few questions? How often do you use the sports centre? What activities do you usually do at the sports centre? And what other sports do you like doing?*
- Ask students to repeat these questions several times both chorally and individually with the correct stress and intonation.
- Students practise the dialogue in pairs. Then swap roles and practise the dialogue again.

Step 3: Write

8

- Students write questions a–c from exercise 6 in their notebooks. Ask them to mark the main stress on each question (see the notes for exercise 7 above).
- They write answers to the questions that are true for them. Note that if they don't actually use a sports centre, they should invent the answers.

9

- Students work individually and write their dialogue, using their answers to questions a–c from exercise 6 and the dialogue in the book as a model. Highlight the key phrases in the Communication kit: Asking about routines.
- Monitor while they are writing and give help if necessary.

Step 4: Communicate

Skills builder

Speaking: Intonation in questions
Highlight that when we ask *wh-* questions, the intonation usually goes down at the end.

10

- Students practise their dialogues in pairs using the correct intonation for questions.
- For extra practice, they swap roles in both dialogues.

11

- Choose some pairs to act out their dialogue for the class.
- Students raise their hand if another pair has the same answers as they do. This will encourage them to listen carefully to their classmates.

Integrated skills: Workbook page 113

Excuse me, (1) ...	Sure. Go ahead!
Thanks! It's for a survey about the sports centre.	Oh, OK.
(2) ...	I usually come here twice a week.
What activities do you usually do at the sports centre?	I go swimming once a week with school and I do judo once a week.
(3) ...	I like cycling and I love playing tennis!
OK, great. That's all. Thanks for your time!	No problem. Bye!

Exercise 5
1 c
2 b
3 a

6 1.47 **Copy and complete the dialogue with questions a–c. Then listen and check.**

a) And what other sports do you like doing?
b) How often do you use the sports centre?
c) Can I ask you a few questions?

7 **Listen again and repeat. Practise your intonation.**

Step 3: Write

8 **Imagine you're at the sports centre and Hazel asks you to complete the survey. Write your answers to the questions in exercise 6.**

9 **Prepare a new dialogue. Write both parts. Use your notes from exercise 8 and the dialogue in exercise 6 to help you.**

Excuse me, can I ask you a few questions?
Sure. Go ahead!

Step 4: Communicate

SKILLS BUILDER

Speaking: Intonation in questions
When we ask *wh-* questions, the intonation usually goes down at the end. →
What activities do you usually do?

10 **Work in pairs. Take turns to practise your dialogues. Use the correct intonation for questions.**

Excuse me, can I ask you a few questions?
Sure. Go ahead!

11 **Act your dialogue for the class.**

COMMUNICATION KIT

Asking about routines
Excuse me, can I ask you a few questions?
Sure. Go ahead!
How often do you ... ?
I usually ... once / twice a week.
That's all. Thanks for your time!

Writing
A class survey

Exercise 1
ten – basketball, swimming, walking, football, dancing, tennis, aerobics, cycling, skateboarding, athletics

1 1.48 **Read and listen to the survey and the results. How many sports and activities can you find?**

CLASS SURVEY:
Physical activity out of school

Name: *James Williams*

1 Do you do physical activity out of school?
Yes ☑ No ☐

2 How often do you do physical activity out of school?
3 times a week

3 What activities do you like doing?
Basketball, swimming and walking

4 Are you in a team or club out of school?
Yes ☑ No ☐

5 Which team or club are you in?
Basketball

Results

There are 31 students in my class. 28 students do regular physical activity out of school.

Most students usually do physical activity once or twice a week. Nine students often exercise more than twice a week.

My classmates' favourite activities are football, dancing and tennis. Other popular activities are swimming, aerobics, basketball, cycling and skateboarding.

14 students in my class are in a team or club out of school. These include football and basketball teams, and swimming and athletics clubs.

10% Never
30% More than twice a week
60% Once or twice a week

Exercise 2
a always
b before

2 Read the Writing focus. Then choose the correct words in rules a) and b).

a) In English we **usually** / **always** use a subject.
b) The subject goes **before** / **after** the verb.

WRITING FOCUS

Word order		
subject	**+ verb**	**+ other words**
Most students	do	physical activity.
14 students	are	in a team or club.

Remember!
Adverbs of frequency go after *be* and before other verbs.
Most students usually do physical activity once or twice a week.

Exercise 3
b football, dancing and tennis

3 Find phrases a–d in the Results. Which one is not a subject?

a) 28 students
b) football, dancing and tennis
c) Most students
d) My classmates' favourite activities

4 Order the words to make sentences.

1 every / day / physical / activity / do / I .
2 has / got / My / town / a / park .
3 the / football / team / Henry / is / in .
4 usually / go / We / swimming / on / Saturdays .
5 plays / football / and basketball / My brother .

Exercise 4
1 I do physical activity every day.
2 My town has got a park.
3 Henry is in the football team.
4 We usually go swimming on Saturdays.
5 My brother plays football and basketball.

Writing task
Write the results of a class survey

Plan First, write your own answers to the questions in the survey. Then, find out your classmates' answers.

Write Write the results. Use the text in exercise 1 to help you.

Check Check your writing.

☑ word order: subject + verb + other words
☑ word order: adverbs of frequency
☑ vocabulary for sports and activities

Build your confidence: Writing reference and practice. Workbook page 124

Writing

A class survey

Lesson objectives

In this lesson students will:

- gather information for the results of a survey
- write the results of a survey

Warmer

Play a game of Twenty Questions. Think of a sport or activity from this unit (eg *ice hockey*). Students have to guess what it is by asking *yes / no* questions (eg *Do you use a ball? Do you play this sport in a team?*)

1
- Students work individually and find sports and activities in the survey and results.
- They compare answers in pairs.
- Check answers as a class.

2
- Students read the Writing focus.
- They read rules a and b and work in pairs to choose the correct answers.
- Check answers as a class.
- If necessary, explain that the subject of a sentence is the person or object that performs the action.

3
- Students find the subjects of the sentences in the results and decide which phrase is not a subject.
- Check the answer as a class.

4
- Do an example on the board with the class first. Write *like the all football students* on the board. Ask the class to put the words in the correct order (*All the students like football*).
- They rewrite the four sentences in the correct order.
- Students compare their answers in pairs.
- Check answers as a class.

Writing task

The aim of this activity is for students to produce a piece of guided writing that includes the correct use of the present simple in affirmative, negative and question forms. It also gives them practice in using adverbs of frequency and vocabulary for sports and activities. Ask the students to follow the stages in the Student's Book. At the Check stage, ask them to swap notebooks and check each other's writing.

Writing reference and practice: Workbook page 124

Study guide

Grammar, Vocabulary and Speaking

Tell the students the Study guide is an important page which provides a useful reference for the main language of the unit: the grammar, the vocabulary and the functional language from the Integrated skills pages. Explain that they should refer to this page when studying for a test or exam.

Grammar

- Tell the students to look at the example sentences of adverbs of frequency and make sure they know how to use the adverbs correctly.
- Tell the students to look at the example sentences with *love*, *hate*, *(don't) like* and *don't mind +ing*. Make sure they understand each example. Get students to translate into their own language if necessary.
- Then tell students to look at the example sentences of question forms and word order. Ensure they understand how to form questions. Get students to translate into their own language if necessary.
- Refer students to the Grammar reference on pages 88–89 of the Workbook for further revision.

Vocabulary

- Tell students to look at the list of vocabulary and check understanding.
- Refer students to the Wordlist on page 152 of the Workbook where they can look up any words they can't remember.

Speaking

- Check that students understand the phrases to use for asking about routines.
- Tell students to act out a conversation where one person is asking questions and the other person is answering them.

Additional material

Workbook

- Progress check page 30
- Self evaluation page 31
- Grammar reference and practice page 88
- Vocabulary extension page 104
- Integrated skills page 113
- Writing reference and task page 124

Teacher's Resource File

- Pulse Basics worksheets pages 18–22
- Vocabulary and grammar consolidation worksheets pages 11–14
- Translation and dictation worksheets pages 4, 14
- Evaluation rubrics pages 1–7
- Key competences pages 5–6
- Culture and CLIL worksheets pages 9–12
- Culture video worksheets pages 5–6
- Digital competence worksheets pages 5–6
- Macmillan Readers worksheets pages 1–2

Tests and Exams

- Unit 3 End-of-unit test: Basic, Standard and Extra
- CEFR Skills Exam Generator
- End-of-term test: Basic, Standard and Extra

Study guide

Grammar

Adverbs of frequency

adverbs of frequency
I **never** ride my bike in the snow.
He **rarely** goes skiing.
Icebiking is **sometimes** dangerous.
Ice hockey is **often** exciting.
I **usually** play tennis on Sundays.
They **always** go swimming at the weekend.

love, hate, (don't) like, don't mind + -ing

love, hate, (don't) like, don't mind + -ing	
☺☺	I **love** doing judo!
☺	He **likes** playing football.
😐	She **doesn't mind** watching films.
☹	We **don't like** studying maths.
☹☹	They **hate** going to the gym.

Question forms: word order

***be* questions**			
question word	***am/is/are***	**subject**	
	Is	Vancouver	in Canada?
Where	are	my skis?	

***have got* questions**				
question word	***have/has***	**subject**	***got***	
	Have	you	got	a football?
When	has	the team	got	training?

questions with other present simple verbs				
question word	***do/does***	**subject**	**verb**	
	Do	you	like	PE?
Where	do	they	do	judo?

Rules for *play*, *do* and *go*

play + ball sports: play football / tennis / basketball
do + other activities: do judo / archery / karate
go + *-ing*: go swimming / running / climbing

Vocabulary

Sports and activities

aerobics
athletics
cycling
gymnastics
horse-riding
judo
mountain-biking
roller-skating
skateboarding
surfing
swimming
yoga

Action verbs

catch
dive
hit
jump
kick
lift
ride
run
score
skate
ski
throw

LEARNING TO LEARN

In vocabulary exercises, don't forget your grammar! Make sure you use the correct form of the verbs.

Speaking

Asking about routines

Excuse me, can I ask you a few questions?
Sure. Go ahead!
How often do you ... ?
I usually ... once / twice a week.
That's all. Thanks for your time!

COLLABORATIVE PROJECT 1

Step 1: Think — Step 2: Listen and plan — Step 3: Create — Step 4: Evaluate

Making a wall

TASK

Work in groups of three to create a 'wall' about a famous sports star from your country.

DIGITAL LITERACY

When you make a wall, remember to:

- write the information in your own words – don't copy and paste!
- use ICT and web resources in a responsible way.
- include different types of information – text, photos, video clips, links ...

Step 1: Think

1 Look at the wall below. Find an example of:

1. a video clip
2. facts about the person
3. a description of the person
4. a photo of the person
5. a link for more information
6. a quote by the person
7. an introduction

Tom Daley
Olympic diver

Sara
Tom Daley is a British diver. He specializes in the 10 metre platform event – he dives from 10 metres above the water!

7 an introduction

3 a description of the person

Pablo
Tom has got short, straight dark hair and brown eyes.

4 a photo of the person

Pablo
Tom trains every day. In fact, he usually trains twice a day! First, he goes to the gym for an hour to get strong. Then he practises in the pool for an hour.

2 facts about the person

Bea
In this video Tom Daley talks about diving. You can also see him training and diving in the pool!

1 a video clip

5 a link for more information

Bea
On this website, you can find more information about Tom:
www.tomdaley.tv

Sara
'I'm a diver not a swimmer!' Tom Daley

6 a quote by the person

Pablo
Born:
21 May 1994
From:
Plymouth, England
Medals / prizes:
Tom has got one Olympic® bronze medal (2012) and two Commonwealth gold medals (2010).

Collaborative project 1

Creating a wall

Lesson objectives

In this lesson students will:

- create a wall in groups about a famous sports star
- identify features of a wall
- listen to a group planning a wall
- read and complete a conversation extract

Recommended web links

www.padlet.com

Warmer

Play Hangman with the words *sports stars*. Write _ _ _ _ _ _   _ _ _ _ _ on the board. Students suggest letters and try to guess the words. Draw a part of the Hangman for each incorrect letter.

TASK

Read the task with the class and check students understand. NOTE: If students do not have access to computers, they can create a poster instead.

Step 1: Think

1
- Discuss walls with the class. Have they read any? Have they ever made one?
- Read the list of items students have to identify and help with any vocabulary. Point out that a link is a web address, and that *a quote* is something a person says.
- Ask students to read the wall and find an example of each item.
- Check answers as a class.
- Read the Digital literacy box with the class and check students understand.

Step 2: Listen and plan

2 1.49

- Ask students to read the questions carefully.
- Play the CD. Students listen and answer the questions.
- Check answers as a class.

3

- Read the Useful language box with the class and help with any vocabulary. Elicit other examples of each phrase, eg *We can write about David Beckham. We can do a wall about Rafa Nadal. I'd like to find the links.*
- Students read the conversation extract and complete it in pairs.
- Play the CD again. Students listen and check their answers.
- Check answers as a class. Students practise the conversation in groups.

4

- Explain to the class that they are going to plan a wall in groups.
- Ask students to read the list of things they need to do to plan their walls.
- Students work in groups of three and plan their walls. Ask one or two groups to report back to the class to explain their plans.

Step 3: Create

5

- Read the steps with the class to give students a clear idea of what they have to do.
- Monitor while they are writing and give help if necessary.

Share information

Students share their information in their groups. They discuss their work and how to improve it. They check for errors.

Create a wall

Each group creates their wall. Encourage them to be creative and to try to make the wall as attractive as possible. Remind them to use their own words and to check for errors.

Show and tell

Each group presents their wall and tells the class about it. Allow time for the other students to read the walls and comment on them. If you like, the class can vote for their favourite wall.

Step 4: Evaluate

6

- Look at the evaluation grids with the class.
- Read through the different options and help with any vocabulary as necessary.
- Students complete their self-evaluation. Give help if necessary.

Extra activity

Individually, in pairs or in small groups, students create another wall about a different sport or international sports star.

1.49 Audioscript, exercises 2 and 3

Mario OK, let's choose a sports star. We can write about Miguel Indurain or Fernando Alonso.
David They're OK, but I'd like to write about a young sports star.
Ana That's a good idea. What about Borja González? He's a footballer. He's only seventeen. What do you think?
Mario Yes, I agree. So what information can we include?
David Lets give some facts about him, for example where he's from and what he likes doing in his free time.
Silvia Yes, and we can include some photos and a video clip.
Mario OK. Can we add a quote or a link?
David A link is a good idea, but a quote is too difficult. All his quotes are in Spanish.
Ana OK. Look, there's some information on this website. Let's read it and then choose the interesting facts.
Mario Yes, and then write them in our own words.

Exercise 2

1 c Borja González
2 They decide to include facts about the person, photos and a video clip.
3 No. They decide to read the information, choose the interesting facts and then write them in their own words.

Exercise 3

1 choose
2 like
3 think
4 agree
5 Let's
6 can

Step 2: Listen and plan

2 1.49 **Listen to Mario, Ana, Silvia and David doing the task and answer the questions.**

1 Who do they decide to do the wall about?
a) Miguel Indurain **b)** Fernando Alonso
c) Borja González
2 Which things from Step 1 do they decide to include?
3 Do they copy the information from a website?

3 Complete the conversation extract with the words in the box. Listen again and check your answers.

like can choose Let's agree think

Mario: OK, let's (1) ... a sports star. We can write about Miguel Indurain or Fernando Alonso.
David: They're OK, but I'd (2) ... to write about a young sports star.
Ana: That's a good idea. What about Borja González? He's a footballer. He's only 17. What do you (3) ... ?
Mario: Yes, I (4) ... . So what information can we include?
David: (5) ... give some facts about him, for example where he's from and what he likes doing in his free time.
Silvia: Yes, and we (6) ... include some photos and a video clip.

4 Work in groups. Plan your wall. Use the Useful language box to help you.

- Choose a person to write about.
- Decide what information to include.
- Decide how to share the work. Make sure everyone contributes.
- Decide when to meet again to share your information.

Step 3: Create

5 Follow the steps to create your wall.

Share information
Read and listen to each other's work. Discuss your work. Check these things:

- Is it in your own words?
- Have you got all the information you need?
- Have you got photos, video clips and links?
- Is the grammar and vocabulary correct?
- Is the spelling and punctuation correct?

Create the wall
Put the information on the wall. Add your photos and video clips. Decide the final design. Then, check the grammar, vocabulary, spelling and punctuation again.

Show and tell
Present your wall to your class.

Step 4: Evaluate

6 Now ask your teacher for the group and individual assessment grids. Then complete the grids.

USEFUL LANGUAGE

We can write about a famous tennis player.
What information can we include?
Let's write about ... .
I'd like to find the photos.
Do you agree?
Yes, I agree. / No, I don't agree.
That's a good idea.
That's very difficult.
I can find some facts.

Unit objectives and key competences

In this unit the student will learn …

- understand, memorize and correctly use words for clothes **CLC SCC**
- understand, memorize and correctly use adjectives describing character **CLC**
- understand and correctly use grammar structures related to the present continuous and present simple and draw parallels to L1 **CLC L2L**
- about festivals and traditional costumes in the UK **CLC CMST CAE**
- about traditional clothes around the world by watching a short video **CLC CMST CAE**

In this unit the student will learn how to …

- identify specific information in a text about prom dances **CLC CAE**
- look for information about prom dances **CLC DC CAE CIE**
- identify specific information in an extract from a TV programme **CLC SCC CAE**
- speak about what people are wearing **CLC SCC**
- write a description of a photo **CLC SCC**
- listen for specific information in an exam **CLC L2L**
- read a web page for specific information, listen to a telephone conversation and buy and try on clothes in a shop **CLC DC SCC**

Linguistic contents

Main vocabulary

- Clothes and shoes: *jumper, coat, trainers,* etc
- Adjectives of character: *cheerful, friendly, proud,* etc

Grammar

- Present continuous: affirmative, negative, questions and short answers
- Present continuous and present simple

Functional language

- Trying on clothes

Pronunciation

- *-ing* endings

Skills

Reading

- Read an article about prom dances
- Read a text about festivals and costumes in the UK
- Read a web page

Writing: Interaction and production

- Write a personalized dialogue
- Write a description in three steps: plan, write, check

Listening

- Listen to an extract from a TV programme about the psychology of colours
- Listen to people buying clothes
- Prepare to listen for specific information in an exam

Spoken interaction

- Describe what someone is wearing
- Ask and answer questions about what's happening now

Spoken production

- Prepare and act out a dialogue about buying clothes

Lifelong learning skills

Self-study and self-evaluation

- Study guide: Student's Book page 51
- Progress check and self-evaluation: Workbook pages 38–39
- Grammar reference and practice: Workbook pages 90–91
- Wordlist: Workbook pages 151–157

Learning strategies and thinking skills

- Skimming a text for specific information

Cultural awareness

- Prom dances at high schools in the USA
- Traditional clothing in England, Scotland and Wales
- Comparing traditional costumes in England, Scotland and Wales with traditional costumes in students' own countries or regions

Cross-curricular contents

- Design and technology: textiles
- ICT: searching the internet for information
- Language and literature: conventions for writing a description

Key competences

CLC	Competence in linguistic communication
CMST	Competence in mathematics, science and technology
DC	Digital competence
L2L	Learning to learn
SCC	Social and civic competences
SIE	Sense of initiative and entrepreneurship
CAE	Cultural awareness and expression

Evaluation

- Unit 4 End-of-unit test: Basic, Standard and Extra
- CEFR Skills Exam Generator

External exam trainer

- Listening: Gap-fill activity

Digital material

Pulse Live! Digital Course including:

- Interactive grammar tables
- Audio visual speaking model: Trying on clothes
- Audio visual cultural material: Clothing and appearance

Student's website

Digital competence

- Web quest: History of prom in the USA
- Digital competence worksheet: Web-based image editing tools

Reinforcement material

- Basics worksheets, Teacher's Resource File pages 23–28
- Vocabulary and Grammar: Consolidation worksheets, Teacher's Resource File pages 15–16

Extension material

- Fast-finisher activity: Student's Book page 43
- Extra activities: Teacher's Book pages T42, T47
- Vocabulary and Grammar: Extension worksheets, Teacher's Resource File pages 17–18

Teacher's Resource File

- Translation and dictation worksheets pages 5, 15
- Evaluation rubrics pages 1–7
- Key competences worksheets pages 7–8
- Culture and CLIL worksheets pages 13–16
- Culture video worksheets pages 7–8
- Digital competence worksheets pages 7–8
- Macmillan Readers worksheets pages 3–4

THINK ABOUT IT

When is looking good important? Think about ...

school parties special occasions

Vocabulary and Speaking

Clothes and shoes

1 2.02 Listen and repeat the words in blue in the quiz. Which things are you wearing today?

2 Do the quiz. Do you agree with your result?

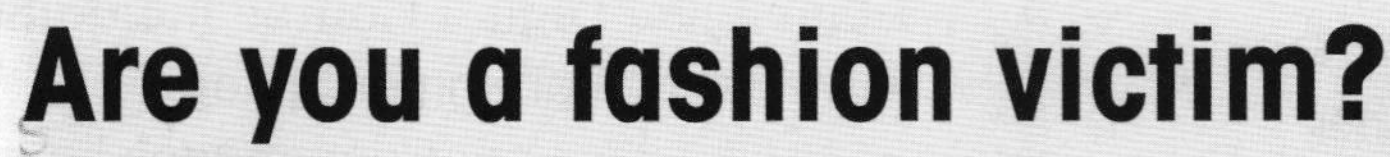

Are you a fashion victim?

START HERE

It's the school disco. What are you wearing?

- A fabulous **dress** or **skirt** and some new **shoes**.
- Some nice **trousers**, with a **jacket**, **shirt** and maybe a **tie**.
- Something casual: **jeans**, **T-shirt** and maybe a **jumper**.

You're at the shopping centre. What do you buy?

- All the new fashions! I need to get the new style of **coat** or **boots**.
- Something from a sports shop ... maybe some football **shorts** or **socks** or a baseball **cap**.

When you meet somebody new, what do you remember about them?

- Their **trainers** or the colour of their T-shirt.
- The music they like ... maybe their interests. Definitely not their clothes!

Clothes and fashion are important to you and you're prepared to pay for it!

You prefer a sporty look, but you like to dress up for a party!

You're definitely not a fashion victim. Personality is more important for you!

EXPRESS YOURSELF

3 Choose a classmate. Write a list of what he or she is wearing, including the colours.

She's wearing blue jeans and a white T-shirt, ...

4 Work in pairs. Describe the classmate. Guess who it is.

- *She's wearing blue jeans and a white T-shirt.*
- *Is it Julia?*
- *No, it isn't. It's Sara!*

LOOK!

adjective + noun

I usually wear a ~~shirt white~~. ✗

I usually wear a white shirt. ✔

Vocabulary extension: Workbook page 105

Vocabulary and Speaking

Clothes and shoes

Lesson objectives

In this lesson students will:

- learn vocabulary for clothes
- describe what someone is wearing
- learn / revise words for colours

Warmer

Students work in pairs and write down as many words for colours as they can (eg *red, blue, black*). Elicit examples from the class and write them on the board in preparation for exercise 3.

Think about it

Explain the meaning of *looking good* (having attractive or nice clothes, nice hair, etc). Students work in pairs and decide when it is important to look good and why, using the three categories to help them. Check ideas as a class.

1 2.02

- Play the CD. Students listen to the words and repeat them.
- Students identify which of the things they are wearing today.
- Check answers as a class.
- Make sure students understand all the words. Ask them to translate into their language if necessary.

2

- Explain how the quiz works – the answer you give to the first question takes you to the next question, and so on.
- Students answer the questions in the quiz.
- They compare their results in pairs (eg *I prefer a sporty look. How about you?*).
- Check ideas as a class. Explain *fashion victim* (someone who is easily influenced by the latest trends in fashion).

3

- Students choose a classmate and write a list of what he or she is wearing, using colours and the clothes words from exercise 2.
- Check answers as a class.

4

- Students work in pairs.
- They use *he's / she's wearing* and the words for colours and clothes to describe one of the students in the class.
- Their partner guesses which student he or she is describing.

Look!

Remind students that in English adjectives go before nouns.

Extra activity

Students write a sentence beginning *I'm wearing* ... and describe the clothes they are wearing today, using colours and the clothes vocabulary from exercise 2.

Vocabulary extension: Workbook page 105

Reading

Text type: A web article

Lesson objectives

In this lesson students will:
- read a web article about clothes
- say which clothes they prefer and why

Recommended web links

www.duckbrand.com/promotions/stuck-at-prom

Warmer

Revise some of the clothes vocabulary from the previous lesson. Write the first and last letters of six to eight words on the board with dashes for the other letters, eg *t _ _ _ _ _ _ s* (*trainers*). Students work in pairs and write the words. Individual students come to the board to write the words. If the spelling is incorrect, ask other students to correct it.

1 2.03
- Students look at the pictures.
- Read the question aloud to the class and elicit student's ideas.
- Play the CD. Students listen and follow the article in their books to check their ideas.
- They compare answers in pairs.
- Check the answer as a class.

Word check

Check that students understand all the new words. Use the pictures to help clarify meaning. Note that a *limousine* is a large, expensive car with a chauffeur.

Language note

Point out that *tuxedo* (or *tux*) is American English for *dinner jacket*.

Culture note

Highlight the Did you know? box and point out that a prom (short for *promenade*) is usually held near the end of students' final year at high school and is a major event. Proms are also held in Canada and are becoming increasingly popular in the UK.

2
- Students complete the sentences individually by looking back at the information in the article.
- They compare answers in pairs.
- Check answers as a class.

3
- Students read the questions carefully first. Make sure they understand all the questions.
- They look for the answers in the article.
- They compare their answers in pairs.
- Check answers as a class.

4
- Students write answers to the question, giving reasons for their choice.
- They compare answers in pairs.
- Check answers as a class.

Finished?

Ask fast finishers to design clothes for the Stuck at Prom® competition. Remind them to use colours and clothes from this lesson and encourage them to be imaginative.

Web quest

Students research the history of prom in the USA. Highilght the Web quest tip.

1
- Students write three things they would like to know about prom dances, eg *How old are students at prom dances?*
- They work in pairs and write a list of keywords to research prom in the USA.

2
- Students work together and open an internet web browser such as Internet Explorer.
- They open a search engine (eg Google) and type in their questions.
- They find the answers to their three questions.

3
- Students share their information with the rest of the class.

Stuck at Prom!

The annual prom dance is a very important event for high school students in the USA. They sometimes travel to the prom in limousines, and they dance all evening with their friends. Every year, two popular students become the Prom King and Queen.

Students always wear special clothes for prom. Girls usually wear beautiful, formal dresses and they carry flowers. Boys usually wear tuxedos. But some students' prom clothes are more unusual – they're trying to win a competition called *Stuck at Prom®*. This competition is organized by Duck Tape® and students can win college scholarships of $5,000 each.

As you can see in the picture, Lara and Cole aren't wearing traditional prom clothes. They're *Stuck at Prom®* winners and everything except their shoes is made of Duck Tape®! Cole isn't wearing a normal tuxedo – he's wearing a black and purple jacket, black trousers, a purple waistcoat and a black tie. And it's all made of tape! Of course Lara's dress is made of the special tape too. And that isn't real jewellery – it's also made of tape.

If your school has an end-of-year party, why not try making your own clothes? There are more than 20 colours of Duck Tape®, so the only limit is your imagination!

a

Cole

Lara

b

c

Word check

stuck high school carry competition tape scholarship waistcoat

DID YOU KNOW?

Every year, Americans spend more th[an] $6 billion on high school proms.

Reading

A web article

1 2.03 **Look at the pictures. Where do you think these people are going? Read, listen and check.**

2 Copy and complete the sentences with information from the text.

1 High school proms are very important in ...
2 In the competition, students can win ...
3 Cole is wearing a purple ...
4 Lara's dress is made of ...

3 Read the article again and answer the questions.

1 What do students usually wear for prom?
2 Are Lara and Cole wearing traditional prom clothes?
3 What is Cole wearing?
4 Is Lara's dress made of tape?
5 Why are they wearing unusual clothes?

4 Do you prefer the clothes in picture a), b) or c)? Why?

Exercise 1

They are going to a prom dance.

Exercise 2

1 the USA
2 college scholarships of $5,000
3 waistcoat
4 is made of Duck Tape®

Exercise 3

1 special clothes – girls usually wear beautiful, formal dresses and boys, tuxedos
2 no
3 a black and purple jacket, black trousers, a purple waistcoat and a black tie
4 yes
5 because they're Stuck at Prom® winners

WEB QUEST

Research the history of prom in the USA.

1 **Keywords: In pairs, make a list of the keywords you need to research prom in the USA.**
2 **Collaboration: work together to find out about the history of prom in the USA.**
3 **Share your knowledge with the rest of the class.**

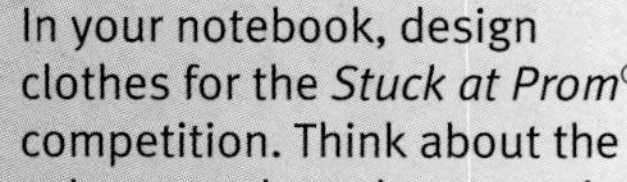

Remember to use more than one website to check your facts.

FINISHED?

In your notebook, design clothes for the *Stuck at Prom®* competition. Think about the colours, style and accessories.

Grammar 

Present continuous

Exercise 1
now; today; at the moment

1 **Look at the tables. Which time expressions do we use with the present continuous?**

affirmative
I'**m** study**ing** English now.
He / She / It'**s** wear**ing** new clothes today.
We / You / They'**re** sing**ing** a song.

negative
I'**m not** watch**ing** television.
He / She / It **isn't** wear**ing** jeans at the moment.
We / You / They **aren't** danc**ing** now.

Exercise 2
1 swimming
2 having
3 sitting
4 winning
5 going
6 diving

2 **Write the *-ing* form of verbs 1–6. Use the spelling rules in the Study guide on page 51.**

1 swim 2 have 3 sit 4 win 5 go 6 dive

ANALYSE

In English, present continuous sentences always have a subject, the verb *be* and an *-ing* form. Is this the same in your language?

Exercise 3
1 Rufus and Jack aren't walking. They're running.
2 Jack isn't wearing pyjamas. He's wearing sports clothes.
3 Beth and Amy aren't going to school. They're going to a party.
4 Amy isn't carrying flowers. She's carrying a present.
5 June and Jane aren't riding a horse. They're riding a bike.

3 **Look at the picture. Write affirmative and negative sentences.**

Beth (not wear trousers / wear a dress)
Beth isn't wearing trousers. She's wearing a dress.

1 Jack and Rufus (not walk / run)
2 Jack (not wear pyjamas / wear sports clothes)
3 Amy and Beth (not go to school / go to a party)
4 Amy (not carry flowers / carry a present)
5 Jane and June (not ride a horse / ride a bike)

Exercise 4
a -ing
b be

4 **Look at the table. Complete rules a) and b) with *be* and *-ing*.**

questions and short answers	
Are you study**ing**?	Yes, I **am**. No, I**'m not**.
Is he / she / it sing**ing** a song?	Yes, he / she / it **is**. No, he / she / it **isn't**.
Are we / you / they watch**ing** television?	Yes, we / you / they **are**. No, we / you / they **aren't**.

a) The word order for questions is:
be + subject + verb + ... + other words + ?
b) We use the affirmative or negative form of ... in short answers.

Exercise 5
1 Are they wearing school uniform?
2 Is he walking?
3 Are they riding a bike?
4 Are you wearing a dress?
5 Are you studying?

5 **Write present continuous questions for these answers.**

(speak) English? Yes, we are.
Are we speaking English?

1 (wear) school uniform? No, they aren't.
2 (walk)? No, he isn't.
3 (ride) a bike? Yes, they are.
4 (wear) a dress? No, I'm not.
5 (study)? Yes, I am.

EXPRESS YOURSELF

Exercise 6
1 Are you using a computer now?
2 Is it raining at the moment?
3 Is your teacher speaking English now?
4 Are your friends wearing jeans?
5 Are your parents working today?

6 **Write present continuous questions for 1–5.**

1 you / use a computer / now?
2 it / rain / at the moment?
3 your teacher / speak English / now?
4 your friends / wear / jeans?
5 your parents / work / today?

7 **Work in pairs. Ask and answer your questions from exercise 6.**

2.04–2.05 **Pronunciation lab: *-ing* endings, page 124**

Grammar 

Present continuous

Lesson objectives

In this lesson students will:

- learn and use the present continuous in the affirmative and negative
- ask questions in the present continuous and give short answers

Warmer

Write this sentence from the previous lesson on the board in random order: *and jacket black 's wearing a he purple*. Students work in pairs and write the sentence in the correct order (*He's wearing a black and purple jacket*).

1
- Point out the blue short forms (*'m*, etc).
- Point out that we use the verb *be* plus the *-ing* form of the verb (*studying*, etc) to form the present continuous tense. Highlight the blue *-ing* forms.
- Point out that we use the present continuous tense to talk about things that are happening now. Write *He usually wears a blue jacket* and *He's wearing a black and purple jacket today* on the board and check that students understand the difference.
- Elicit the time expressions used with the present continuous in the table.

2
- Ask students to read the present continuous spelling rules on page 51.
- Students complete the exercise individually.
- They compare answers in pairs.
- Check answers as a class.

Analyse

Ask students to read the information about the present continuous in English and compare it with their own language. Ask if the sentence *I am eating* is formed in the same way in their language.

3
- Students look at the picture and read the example sentences. Highlight the use of short forms.
- They write affirmative and negative sentences individually.
- They compare their answers in pairs.
- Check answers as a class.

4
- Students look at the table and rules a–b.
- They complete the rules with *be* and *-ing* using the information in the table.
- Check answers as a class.

Language note

Highlight the use of short forms in the negative short answers – *No, I'm not, No, he isn't, No, they aren't*. Point out that we never use short forms in affirmative short answers.

5
- Read the example prompt, answer and question aloud to the class.
- Students write the questions individually.
- They compare answers in pairs.
- Check answers as a class.

EXPRESS YOURSELF

6
- Do question 1 with the whole class. Elicit the question and write it on the board – *Is it raining at the moment?*
- Students write the remaining questions individually.
- They compare answers in pairs.
- Check answers as a class. Highlight the use of *at the moment, now* and *today* with the present continuous.

7
- Students work in pairs and take it in turns to ask and answer the questions from exercise 6.
- Listen to some examples as a class.

Pronunciation lab: *-ing* endings, page 124

Digital course: Interactive grammar table

Study guide: page 51

Vocabulary and Listening

Adjectives of character

Lesson objectives

In this lesson students will:

- learn some adjectives to describe character
- listen for specific information

Warmer

Elicit words for colours in English and write them on the board in random order. Students work in pairs and rank the colours from favourite to least favourite.

1
- Check students understand the word *character* in this context (the kind of person you are).
- Students look at the pictures and discuss the question in pairs.
- Listen to their ideas as a class.

2 2.06
- Ask students to read the text.
- Play the CD. Students listen and repeat the words in blue.
- Elicit the translation for each word from the class.

Look!

Check that students understand *quite / a bit shy* (as opposed to *very shy*) and *very confident*.

3
- Make sure students understand how a Venn diagram works.
- They complete the diagram by putting the words in the correct sections.
- They compare their answers in pairs.
- Check answers as a class.

4
- Students say what their favourite colour is.
- They look at the part of the text that describes the character of people who like that colour.
- They tell the class whether they agree or disagree with the text and why.

5 2.07
- Tell students they will hear the first part of a radio programme. An expert is talking about two of the people in the pictures a–c.
- Play the CD. Students identify the two people.
- They compare their answers in pairs.
- Check answers as a class.

6 2.08
- Ask students to read the beginnings and alternative endings of the sentences first.
- Play the CD.
- Students choose the correct answers.
- They compare answers in pairs.
- Check answers as a class.

2.07 Audioscript, exercise 5

Man Hello! Today in *Popular Science* we're looking at the psychology of colour theory – can you guess a person's personality from the colours they're wearing? Here to help us with our experiment is Doctor Ella Browning. Hello, Ella.
Ella Hello!
Man So, here we've got photos of two people – can you give us your opinion about their personality?
Ella OK - let's see! In this photo, the girl's wearing a black jumper and covering her face. In my opinion, this means that she's quite shy. Also, she isn't wearing any bright colours. I think this means she's quite serious. I also think she's probably quite creative.
Man OK, and what about this other photo?
Ella Well, this girl looks very energetic! In my opinion, she's very sporty. And her body language is very open – she's smiling and wearing bright colours – so I think she's a confident and cheerful person.
Man OK. Thanks, Ella – now let's see if these opinions match the reality of the person …

2.08 Audioscript, exercise 6

Man OK. Thanks, Ella – now let's see if these opinions match the reality! Please welcome Lucy and Amanda …
Lucy Hi!
Amanda Hello.
Host So, Lucy, what do you think of Ella's analysis?
Lucy Well, it's true that I'm covering my face – but it's because I'm feeling cold! So, actually I'm not shy – in fact, I'm quite sociable. I love talking to people! And I do like to wear bright colours usually. So, in general, the analysis is not correct. But I am quite creative – that part's true!
Host I see. So, the reality is quite different! What about you, Amanda?
Amanda Yeah, I look so happy in this photo! I'm smiling because it's a lovely sunny day and I'm having fun with my friends. In general, I agree with the analysis – I'm quite confident and I often wear bright colours. But I'm definitely not a sporty person, so that part isn't correct!
Host Great! Thanks, both of you. Well, I think we can conclude that there's some truth in the analsys …

Vocabulary and Listening

Adjectives of character

1 Look at the people in the pictures. Can you guess their character from the colours they're wearing?

2 2.06 Read the text. Listen and repeat the words in blue. How do you say them in your language?

What does colour say about YOU?

What colours are you wearing today? Read our guide to see what they say about your character.

- People who like red are often **confident**, but they can also be a bit **selfish**.
- Yellow is the colour of sunshine. If you prefer yellow, you're probably **cheerful** and **friendly**.
- If you love blue, you're probably **clever** and **proud**. But you can also be a bit **unfriendly**.
- Green is the colour of nature. If you like green, you're probably **quiet**, but you can also be **jealous**.
- Orange is a mix of red and yellow. If you love orange, you're probably **adventurous** and **funny**, but a bit **lazy**!
- If black is your favourite colour you're probably **shy**, but your friends know that you're a **nice** person underneath!

Exercise 3
positive
cheerful
friendly
clever
adventurous
funny
nice
negative
unfriendly
jealous
lazy
neutral
quiet
shy

3 Copy and complete the diagram with the adjectives from the text.

4 What's your favourite colour? Do you agree or disagree with the text?

My favourite colour is red. I'm quite confident, but I'm not selfish!

LOOK!

adverbs of degree

He's **quite** / **a bit** shy. He isn't **very** confident.

5 2.07 Listen to the first part of a radio interview. Which two people from pictures a–c does the expert talk about?

Exercise 5
a and b

6 2.08 Listen to the second part of the interview. Choose the correct answers.

1 In the photo, Lucy is ...
  a) thinking about her exams.
  b) feeling cold.
2 In reality, Lucy is ...
  a) sociable and creative.
  b) shy and serious.
3 In the photo, Amanda is smiling because ...
  a) it's a lovely sunny day.
  b) it's the weekend.
4 In general, Amanda ...
  a) agrees with the analysis.
  b) doesn't agree with the analysis.

Exercise 6
1 b
2 a
3 a
4 a

Cultural awareness

Traditional costume

Fact box

The United Kingdom includes England, Wales, Scotland and Northern Ireland.

Exercise 1

a The girl is wearing a white cap, a black hat, black gloves, a long black skirt, a white blouse and the Welsh flag over her skirt.
She's from Wales.

b The man is wearing a tartan kilt, a black jacket, black socks and a sporran.
He's from Scotland.

c The dancer is wearing a white shirt, black trousers, white socks, a hat with flowers and bells on his socks.
He's from England.

1 Look at pictures a–c. What are the people wearing? Are they from England, Scotland or Wales?

DAILY LIFE | FESTIVALS | COSTUMES | FOOD | SPORT | HOMES

Like 420 | +1 0 | Tag

Project UK: Traditional British costume

In Wales, women and girls sometimes wear their traditional costume on special occasions. This girl is wearing a black hat and black gloves. She's got a long skirt and a white blouse. She's also wearing the Welsh flag over her skirt. Welsh men and boys don't have a traditional costume. They just wear smart clothes on special occasions.

Scotland's national costume is famous around the world. Scottish men often wear kilts at weddings and other celebrations. This man is wearing a tartan kilt, a black jacket and black socks. He's also got a sporran – that's Gaelic for purse. Each Scottish family, or clan, has got a different tartan. There are more than 2,000 types of tartan!

There isn't really a national costume in England, but Morris dancers' clothes are very traditional. This Morris dancer is wearing a white shirt, black trousers and white socks. He's also got a funny hat with flowers on. You often see Morris dancers at spring festivals in May. You can hear them immediately, because they always wear bells on their socks!

Word check

blouse flag wedding tartan bell

Exercise 3

1 no
2 the Welsh flag
3 a tartan kilt, a black jacket, black socks, a sporran
4 at weddings and other celebrations
5 at spring festivals in May
6 bells

2  2.09 Read and listen to the text. Check your answers to exercise 1.

3 Read the text again and answer the questions.

1 Do Welsh women wear traditional clothes every day?
2 What's the Welsh girl wearing over her skirt?
3 What is this Scottish man wearing?
4 When do Scottish men usually wear kilts?
5 When do you usually see Morris dancers?
6 What do Morris dancers always wear on their socks?

CULTURAL COMPARISON

4 Copy and complete the sentences.

1 The traditional costume in my region / country is ...
2 Women and girls wear ...
3 Men and boys wear ...
4 People often wear traditional costume when ...
5 I sometimes / never wear traditional clothes when ...

Culture video: Clothing and appearance

Cultural awareness

Traditional costume

Lesson objectives

In this lesson students will:

- read a text about traditional costumes in Wales, Scotland and England
- practise reading to find specific information
- describe traditional costumes in their country

Warmer

Write the word *Wales* on the board. Students work in pairs and write down what they know about Wales. Listen to their ideas a class. Write relevant points on the board, eg *They speak English and Welsh, Cardiff is the capital,* etc.

1
- Focus students on the Fact box and write the names of three of the countries on the board – *England, Scotland, Wales*.
- Students look at the pictures. They describe what the people are wearing and say where they are from.

2 2.09
- Play the CD. Students listen and read to check their answers.

Word check

Check students understand all the new words. Use picture b to clarify *tartan*.

3
- Students read the questions carefully first.
- Make sure students understand all the questions.
- They find the answers by reading the text again.
- Students compare answers in pairs.
- Check answers as a class.

Culture note

England, Scotland and Wales are all situated on the largest island of the British Isles – Great Britain. England has the largest population (about 52 million). Scotland has a population of about 5.5 million and Wales 3 million. About 20% of the population of Wales speak Welsh, a Celtic language, and there are about 60,000 speakers of another Celtic language, Gaelic, in Scotland.

CULTURAL  COMPARISON

4
- Students work individually and complete the five sentences.
- Give help with clothes vocabulary if necessary.
- They compare their answers in pairs or small groups.
- Check ideas as a class.

Culture video: Clothing and appearance

Grammar 

Present continuous and present simple

Lesson objectives

In this lesson students will:

- learn and practise the difference between the present continuous and the present simple
- learn and practise common time expressions used with the present continuous and the present simple

Recommended web links

www.britishfashioncouncil.com

Warmer

Write a present simple sentence and a present continuous sentence on the board, with the words in the wrong order, eg *wears trousers usually he* (*He usually wears trousers*); *'s kilt today wearing he a* (*He's wearing a kilt today*). Students work in pairs and put the words in the right order to form correct sentences. They come to the board and write the sentences.

1
- Students copy the tables into their notebooks.
- Explain that they should write sentences a–b in the correct place in the tables.
- Check that they have the correct section for each sentence and ask them to write the sentences in the tables.
- Highlight the fact that we use the present continuous to talk about things that are happening now or today and the present simple to talk about routines or habits (things that usually or always happen, or happen every day).

2
- Students look at the examples of time expressions in the table.
- They copy the table into their notebooks and add the expressions from the box to the table.
- They compare answers in pairs.
- Check answers as a class.

3
- Do the first sentence with the class as an example.
- Encourage students to refer to the time expressions in the table to help them decide whether to use the present continuous or the present simple.
- Students work individually to choose the correct answers and identify the time expressions.
- Check answers as a class and ask students to add *every weekend* to their list of present simple time expressions in their notebook.

EXPRESS YOURSELF

4
- Remind students that we form questions in the present simple with *do / does* and in the present continuous with *am / are / is*.
- Students work individually and write the questions and true answers.
- They compare answers in pairs.
- Check answers as a class.

Extra activity

Students work in groups of four. They ask and answer their questions, noting down students' answers. They report back to the whole class, eg *Luisa usually plays tennis at the weekend.*

CLIL Grammar in context: Design and Technology

5
- This activity practises the use of the present simple and present continuous with different time expressions.
- Ask students to read the whole text carefully first.
- Students choose the correct form of the verb in brackets to fill each gap.
- They compare their answers in pairs.

6  2.10
- Play the CD.
- Students check their answers to exercise 5.

CLIL task

Set this as a homework task. Students use an internet search engine (eg Google) to find the names of five fashion designers from their country. At the beginning of the next lesson, ask students to tell you the names they have found.

Digital course: Interactive grammar table

Study guide: page 51

Grammar

Present continuous and present simple

1 Copy and complete the tables. Add sentences a) and b).

present continuous: things that are happening now
What **is** the Scottish man **wearing**?
He**'s wearing** a kilt.

present simple: routines or habits
Do they always **wear** kilts?
They usually **wear** kilts at weddings.

a) Welsh girls sometimes wear traditional clothes.
b) This Welsh girl is wearing the Welsh flag.

2 Copy and complete the table with the time expressions in the box.

never now usually today once a week

Time expressions	
present continuous	**present simple**
at the moment	*every day*

3 Choose the correct words. What are the time expressions in 1–5?

1 Amy **doesn't usually wear** / **isn't usually wearing** a dress.
2 She **is wearing** / **wears** a dress at the moment.
3 She **goes** / **is going** to a wedding now.
4 She **wears** / **is wearing** jeans every weekend.
5 In this photo, she **smiles** / **is smiling**.

EXPRESS YOURSELF

4 Complete the questions with the present simple or present continuous. Then write true answers.

What ... you usually ... (wear) at weddings?
What do you usually wear at weddings?
I usually wear ...

1 What ... you ... (wear) today?
2 ... it usually ... (snow) in winter in your town?
3 ... it (snow) now?
4 What ... you ... (do) at the moment?
5 What ... you usually ... (do) at the weekend?

CLIL Grammar in context: Design and technology

5 Complete the text with the correct form of the verbs in brackets. Use the present simple or the present continuous.

6 2.10 Listen and check your answers.

(1) *Do you study* (study) textiles at school? We do! We (2) ... (not study) textiles all year – we do textiles in term 1, food technology in term 2, and woodwork in term 3. They're part of a subject called design and technology. I (3) ... (like) it because it's very practical.

Our textiles teacher (4) ... (not usually buy) her clothes – she (5) ... (make) them! She always (6) ... (wear) unusual and original things.

This is our first year in textiles. I (7) ... (make) a top, and my friend Lisa (8) ... (make) a skirt. The teacher (9) ... (help) me because my sewing machine (10) ... (not work) at the moment. Or perhaps the problem is me – I'm not exactly Stella McCartney!

CLIL TASK
Go online. Find the names of five fashion designers from your country.

Exercise 1
Present continuous
Present simple

Exercise 2
Present continuous
now, today
Present simple
never, usually, once a week

Exercise 3
1 doesn't usually wear
2 is wearing; at the moment
3 is going; now
4 wears; every weekend
5 is smiling

Exercise 4
1 What are you wearing today?
2 Does it usually snow in winter in your town?
3 Is it snowing now?
4 What are you doing at the moment?
5 What do you usually do at the weekend?

Exercise 5
2 don't study
3 like
4 doesn't usually buy
5 makes
6 wears
7 'm making
8 's making
9 's helping
10 isn't working

Shopping online

I'm looking on the internet – I want to buy a present for my friend Carlos. Do you or your family ever buy things on the internet?

4:42 PM

BEST of BRITISH

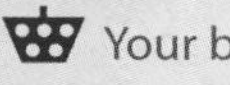

Your basket
Go to checkout

Product search

Search by category
Clothing
Accessories
Souvenirs

Log in **here**
or
Create a new account

Click on a picture for more information.

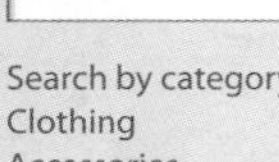

socks
red/white/blue only
S, M, L
£3.50

sweatshirt
pink/white/black
S, M, L
£16.99

mug
red/white/blue only
one size
£5.00

flip-flops
red/white/blue only
S, M, L
£8.50

sunglasses
red/white/blue only
child or adult
£6.99

hat
red/white/blue only
one size
£8.00

Step 1: Read

SKILLS BUILDER

Reading for specific information
When you read, you don't need to understand every word. Read quickly to find specific information.

1 Look at the web page. Complete the sentences with specific information.

1 The 'I ❤ Britain' mug costs … .
2 The 'I ❤ London' sweatshirt costs … .
3 You can buy the flip-flops in … different sizes.
4 The colour of the mug is … .
5 You can buy the sunglasses in … different sizes.

2 Imagine you have £20. You buy a pair of sunglasses and a hat. How much money do you have left?

Exercise 1
1 £5.00
2 £16.99
3 three
4 red/white/blue only
5 two

Exercise 2
£5.01

Step 2: Listen

3 2.11 **Listen to James' phone enquiry and complete information a–f.**

The Best of British shop is on the High Street in (a) … .
Its opening times are:
Monday – Saturday
from (b) … o'clock to (c) … o'clock.
Sundays
from (d) … o'clock to (e) … o'clock.
Student discount? Yes, (f) … %

4 Listen again. When does the sale start?

Exercise 3
a Manchester
b 9
c 6
d 11
e 5
f 10%

Exercise 4
on Saturday

Integrated skills

Shopping online

Lesson objectives

In this lesson students will:

- work on all four skills
- read a web page
- listen to a phone conversation
- write a personalized dialogue
- act out their dialogue

Warmer

Play a game of Hangman to revise clothes vocabulary. Choose four or five words from the beginning of this unit. Write dashes on the board to represent the number of letters in each word, eg *trousers*: _ _ _ _ _ _ _ _ . Ask students to suggest letters that could be in the word. Make sure they pronounce the letters correctly. Continue until they have guessed the word.

Step 1: Read

1
- Highlight James' speech bubble. Elicit answers to the question *Do you or your family ever buy things on the internet?* from the class.
- Ask students to read the sentences carefully first. Then they look at the web page and find the answers quickly.
- Check answers as a class.
- Ask students what *S*, *M* and *L* mean (*small, medium* and *large*).
- Check students understand the word *adult* (a person over 18 years old).

Skills builder

Reading for specific information

Explain to students that when we read, we normally do not need to understand every word. Ask them to think about what they read in their own language, eg TV listings. Elicit that they would look for what programme is on at a specific time or look to see what time a particular programme is on. Emphasise that to do this, they do not need to read everything. Encourage them to read quickly to find specific information.

2
- Check that students understand the task.
- Students answer the question by looking at the prices on the web page.
- Check answers as a class.

Step 2: Listen

3 2.11
- Make sure the students understand the task. Explain the word *discount* if necessary (a reduction in the price).
- Point out that the answer to question a is a place (a city), the answers to b–e are times, and the answer to f is a percentage.
- Tell them they will hear the information in a phone conversation.
- Play the CD. Students write the answers.
- They compare their answers in pairs.
- Check answers as a class.

4 2.11
- Write the question on the board. Check that students understand *sale* (a period of time when shops reduce their prices).
- Play the CD again. Students write the answer.
- Check the answer as a class.

2.11 Audioscript, exercises 3 and 4

Woman Hello, you're speaking to Linda at Best of British. How can I help you?
James Oh, hi. I'm looking at your website now, but I want to know if you've got a shop in Manchester.
Woman Yes, we have. Our Manchester store is on the High Street.
James Ah, OK. And is it open every day?
Woman Yes, it's open seven days a week.
James What are the opening times?
Woman From Monday to Saturday, 9 o'clock in the morning until 6 o'clock. And on Sundays from 11 o'clock until 5 in the afternoon.
James OK, thanks.
Woman No problem. Is there anything else I can help you with today?
James Oh – yes! Do you give a student discount?
Woman Yes, we do. There's 10% off all our products for students.
James Great, thanks!
Woman And our sale starts on Saturday, too!
James Oh, really? That's great!
Woman Thanks for calling. Have a good day!
James Thanks, bye!

Integrated skills - continued

Trying on clothes

5 2.12

- Students read the questions. Make sure they understand the verb *look for* (try to find something).
- Play the CD. Students write the answers.
- They compare answers in pairs.
- Check answers as a class.

6 2.12

- Play the CD again, pausing after each speaker's part for students to repeat as a class.
- Note the main stress on the questions: *Can I try it on? What size are you? Can I try the 'small'?*
- Ask students to repeat the questions and responses several times both chorally and individually with the correct stress and intonation.
- Students practise the dialogue in pairs. Then swap roles and practise the dialogue again.

Step 3: Write

Look!

Point out that we never say ~~*a jeans, a shorts, a trousers*~~, but *some jeans, some shorts, some trousers*. All kinds of trousers are plural in English (because they have two legs!).
If we want to refer specifically to one item, we use *a pair of*, eg *a pair of jeans, a pair of shorts, a pair of trousers.*

7

- Students choose the correct words.
- They compare answers in pairs.
- Check answers as a class.

8

- Students choose one of the items from the web page on page 48.
- They work individually and write their dialogue, using the dialogue in the book as a model and the Communication kit: Trying on clothes for key phrases.
- Monitor while they are writing and give help if necessary.

Step 4: Communicate

9

- Remind students about the main stress on questions.
- Students practise their dialogues in pairs.
- For extra practice, they swap roles in both dialogues.

10

- Choose some pairs to act out their dialogue for the class.
- Students raise their hand if another pair has the same items or sizes as they do. This will encourage them to listen carefully to their classmates.

Integrated skills: Workbook page 114

TRYING ON CLOTHES

Excuse me. I'm looking for a jacket like this, but in blue.	Oh, yes. They're over here.
Great! Can I try it on?	Sure. What size are you?
Probably medium.	There you are. There's a mirror here.
I think it's too big! Can I try the 'small'?	Yes, of course. There you are.
That's better!	Yes – it looks great!
I'll take it, thanks.	OK. You can pay over there.

Exercise 5
1 a blue jacket
2 small

5 2.12 **Listen to the dialogue and answer the questions.**

1 What is James looking for?
2 What size does he buy?

6 **Listen again and repeat. Practise your intonation.**

LOOK!

In English, all kinds of trousers are plural.
~~a jeans~~ ✗ some jeans ✓

Step 3: Write

Exercise 7
1 some
2 It looks
3 them
4 it

7 **Choose the correct words.**

1 I'm looking for **a** / **some** football shorts.
2 That T-shirt's nice. **It looks** / **They look** great!
3 I like these jeans. Can I try **it** / **them** on?
4 This bag's nice. I'll take **it** / **them**.

8 **Choose an item from page 48. Write a new dialogue. Write both parts. Use the dialogue in exercise 5 to help you.**

Excuse me. I'm looking for a / some ...

Step 4: Communicate

9 **Work in pairs. Take turns to practise your dialogues.**

Excuse me. I'm looking for a / some ...
Oh, yes. They're over there.

10 **Now act your dialogue for the class.**

COMMUNICATION KIT

Trying on clothes

Excuse me. I'm looking for a / some ...
Can I try it / them on?
What size are you?
Small / medium / large
It's / They're too big / small / long / short.
It looks / They look great!
I'll take it / them, thanks.
You can pay over there.

Harry Styles

Harry Styles is a singer. He's a member of my favourite band, One Direction.

In the first picture, Harry looks smart. He's wearing a grey jacket and a white shirt. I think he's going to an awards ceremony.

In the second picture, Harry is singing with the other members of One Direction. Their clothes are casual. Harry's wearing white trousers, a blue jacket and red shoes. I think they're competing in a talent show.

In the third picture, Harry is shopping. He's wearing a grey sweatshirt and white trainers, and he's carrying a bag. In this picture he looks serious.

Exercise 1

1 A grey jacket and a white shirt. He's going to an awards ceremony.
2 White trousers, a blue jacket and red shoes. He's competing in a talent show.
3 A grey sweatshirt and white trainers. He's shopping.

Exercise 2

1 before
2 after
3 haven't

Exercise 3

Rule 1 a grey sweatshirt
Rule 2 Harry looks smart.
Rule 3 red shoes white trainers.

Exercise 4

1 Harry's hair is curly.
2 They look very energetic.
3 Their songs are great.
4 He's wearing a grey sweatshirt.
5 These photos look nice.

Writing
Describing photos

1 2.13 **Read and listen to the description. Copy and complete the notes.**

Harry Styles	Picture 1	Picture 2	Picture 3
What's he wearing?	*A grey jacket and ...*	...	...
What's he doing?	*He's going to ...*	...	...

2 Read the examples in the Writing focus. Complete rules 1–3 with *after*, *before* or *have* / *haven't*.

WRITING FOCUS
Using adjectives

1 Adjectives go ... a noun.
He's wearing a grey jacket.
2 Adjectives go ... the verbs *be* and *look*.
Their clothes are casual. Harry looks serious.
3 Adjectives ... got plural forms.
~~*whites shorts*~~ ✗ *white shorts* ✔

3 Read the description in exercise 1 again. Find one more example for rules 1–3.

4 Order the words to make sentences.

1 is / Harry's / curly / hair .
2 look / They / energetic / very .
3 are / songs / great / Their .
4 sweatshirt / He's / wearing / grey / a .
5 nice / These / photos / look .

Writing task

Write a description of three pictures. Use pictures of a friend or choose a famous person.

Plan Find three pictures. Makes notes about them. Use the notes in exercise 1 to help you.

Write Write your description. Write one paragraph for each picture. Give your writing a title.

Check Check your writing.

- ✔ adjective + noun
- ✔ *is* / *are* or *look(s)* + adjective
- ✔ present continuous verb forms
- ✔ vocabulary for clothes and adjectives of character

Writing

Describing photos

Lesson objectives

In this lesson students will:

- learn how to use adjectives correctly
- write three short descriptions

Warmer

Write the words *shirt, trousers* and *shoes* on one piece of paper and *shirt, skirt* and *shoes* on another. Add colours to each of the words, eg *a blue shirt*. Tell students you have a picture of a boy and a girl and they have to guess what they are wearing. You can only answer with short answers using *Yes* or *No*, so they have to ask questions like this: *Is he wearing a red shirt? No, he isn't. Is he wearing a blue shirt? Yes, he is.* Continue until they have guessed the colours of all six items of clothing.

1 2.13

- Ask students to look at the notes about Harry Styles.
- Play the CD. Students listen and read the description.
- Students copy and complete the notes in their notebooks.
- They compare answers in pairs.
- Check answers as a class.

2

- Explain the task – students complete the rules about adjectives in the Writing focus using *after, before* or *have / haven't*.
- Students complete the rules individually.
- They compare answers in pairs.
- Check answers as a class.

3

- Students find one more example of rules 1–3 in the description of Harry Styles.
- Check answers as a class.

4

- Do the first question with the whole class as an example. Check students understand *curly hair* (not straight).
- Students order the words to make sentences individually.
- They compare answers in pairs.
- Check answers as a class.

Writing task

The aim of this activity is for students to produce a piece of guided writing that includes the correct use of adjectives + noun, *is / are* or *look(s)* + adjectives and present continuous forms. It also gives them practice in using vocabulary for clothes and adjectives of character, and in using punctuation correctly. Ask the students to follow the stages in the Student's Book. At the Check stage, ask them to swap notebooks and check each other's writing.

Writing reference and practice: Workbook page 126

Study guide

Grammar, Vocabulary and Speaking

Tell the students the Study guide is an important page which provides a useful reference for the main language of the unit: the grammar, the vocabulary and the functional language from the Integrated skills pages. Explain that they should refer to this page when studying for a test or exam.

Grammar

- Tell the students to look at the example sentences of the present continuous and make sure they know how to form the tense correctly.
- Then tell students to look at the example sentences of the present continuous and the present simple and ensure they understand when to use which tense. Get students to translate into their own language if necessary.
- Refer students to the Grammar reference on pages 90–91 of the Workbook for further revision.

Vocabulary

- Tell students to look at the list of vocabulary and check understanding.
- Refer students to the Wordlist on page 151 of the Workbook where they can look up any words they can't remember.

Speaking

- Check that students understand the phrases to use for trying on clothes.
- Tell students to act out a conversation between a shop assistant and a customer.

Additional material

Workbook

- Progress check page 38
- Self-evaluation page 39
- Grammar reference and practice page 90
- Vocabulary extension page 105
- Integrated skills page 114
- Writing reference and task page 126

Teacher's Resource File

- Pulse Basics worksheets pages 23–28
- Vocabulary and grammar consolidation worksheets pages 15–18
- Translation and dictation worksheets pages 5, 15
- Evaluation rubrics pages 1–7
- Key competences worksheets pages 7–8
- Culture and CLIL worksheets pages 13–16
- Culture video worksheets pages 7–8
- Digital competence worksheets pages 7–8
- Macmillan Readers worksheets pages 3–4

Tests and Exams

- Unit 4 End-of-unit test: Basic, Standard and Extra
- CEFR Skills Exam Generator

Study guide

Grammar

Present continuous

affirmative		
I	**'m**	**playing** the piano now.
He / She / It	**'s**	**wearing** a coat today.
We / You / They	**'re**	**playing** football.

negative		
I	**'m not**	**wearing** a dress.
He / She / It	**isn't**	**speaking** French now.
We / You / They	**aren't**	**singing** at the moment.

questions and short answers	
Are you **studying**?	Yes, I **am**.
	No, I**'m not**.
Is he / she / it **wearing** a hat?	Yes, he / she / it **is**.
	No, he / she / it **isn't**.
Are we / you / they **going** to a party?	Yes, we / you / they **are**.
	No, we / you / they **aren't**.

Present continuous and present simple

present continuous: things that are happening now
What **are** you **wearing** now?
I**'m wearing** a uniform.

present simple: routines or habits
Do you always **wear** a uniform?
I never **wear** a uniform at the weekend!

Present continuous spelling rules

- For most verbs, add *-ing* to the infinitive
  do → doing jump → jumping
- For verbs that end in *-e*, omit the *-e* and add *-ing*
  have → having ride → riding
- For one-syllable verbs that end in vowel + consonant (except *w*, *x* or *y*), double the consonant and add *-ing*
  run → running swim → swimming

Vocabulary

Clothes and shoes

boots, cap, coat, dress, jacket, jeans, jumper, shirt, shoes, shorts, skirt, socks, tie, trainers, trousers, T-shirt

Adjectives of character

adventurous, cheerful, clever, confident, friendly, funny, jealous, lazy, nice, proud, quiet, selfish, shy, unfriendly

Speaking

Trying on clothes

Excuse me. I'm looking for a / some ... .
Can I try it / them on?
What size are you?
Small / medium / large.
It's / They're too big / small / long / short.
It looks / They look great!
I'll take it / them, thanks.
You can pay over there.

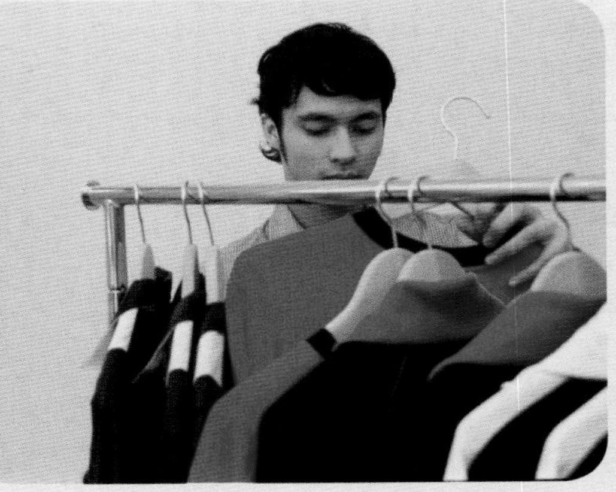

LEARNING TO LEARN

When you learn adjectives of character, list them under headings: positive, negative and neutral.

Progress check: Workbook page 38

Grammar reference: Workbook page 90

UNIT 5 FEELING GREAT!

Unit objectives and key competences

In this unit the student will learn …

- understand, memorize and correctly use words for places for leisure activities **CLC SCC**
- understand, memorize and correctly use words for different kinds of food **CLC CMST**
- understand and correctly use grammar structures related to the present and draw parallels to L1 **CLC L2L**
- about traditional food in Australia **CLC CMST SCC CAE**
- about typical food in the UK by watching a short video **CLC CMST SCC CAE**

In this unit the student will learn how to …

- identify specific information on an internet message board **CLC DC CAE**
- look for information about leisure facilities **CLC DC SCC CIE**
- identify specific information in interviews about food **CLC CMST SCC**
- speak about their leisure habits **CLC SCC**
- write a recipe **CLC CMST CAE**
- read a café menu, listen to a conversation in a café and order food **CLC SCC**
- describe a photo in an exam **CLC L2L**

Linguistic contents

Main vocabulary

- Places for leisure: *bowling alley, cinema,* etc
- Food and drink: *juice, cheese, biscuits,* etc

Grammar

- Present simple: *there is, there are* + *a/an*, *some* and *any*
- Countable and uncountable nouns; *How much? How many?*

Functional language

- Ordering food
- Phrases for describing where things are in a photo

Pronunciation

- Difficult sounds: /ɪ/ and /iː/

Skills

Reading

- Read a message board about feeling great
- Read a text about traditional foods in Australia
- Read a menu

Writing: Interaction and production

- Write a personalized dialogue
- Write a recipe in three steps: plan, write, check

Listening

- Listen to interviews about food
- Listen to people ordering food

Spoken interaction

- Exchange information about leisure habits

Spoken production

- Prepare and act out a dialogue about ordering food
- Prepare and describe a photo in a speaking exam

Lifelong learning skills

Self-study and self-evaluation

- Study guide: Student's Book page 61
- Progress check and self-evaluation: Workbook pages 46–47
- Grammar reference and practice: Workbook pages 92–93
- Wordlist: Workbook pages 151–157

Learning strategies and thinking skills

- Listening for and understanding price information

Cultural awareness

- Traditional food in Australia
- Comparing traditional food in students' own countries with traditional Australian food

Cross-curricular contents

- Science: nutrition
- ICT: searching the internet for information
- Maths: prices
- Food technology: recipes

Key competences

CLC	Competence in linguistic communication
CMST	Competence in mathematics, science and technology
DC	Digital competence
L2L	Learning to learn
SCC	Social and civic competences
SIE	Sense of initiative and entrepreneurship
CAE	Cultural awareness and expression

Evaluation

- Unit 5 End-of-unit test: Basic, Standard and Extra
- CEFR Skills Exam Generator

External exam trainer

- Speaking: Describing a photo

Digital material

Pulse Live! Digital Course including:

- Interactive grammar tables
- Audio visual speaking model: Ordering food
- Audio visual cultural material: Typical food in the UK

Student's website

Digital competence

- Web quest: Poster about places to visit in the UK
- Digital worksheet: Presentation tools

Reinforcement material

- Basics worksheets, Teacher's Resource File pages 29–34
- Vocabulary and Grammar: Consolidation worksheets, Teacher's Resource File pages 19–20

Extension material

- Fast-finisher activity: Student's Book page 53
- Extra activities: Teacher's Book pages T52, T57
- Vocabulary: Extension worksheet, Teacher's Resource File pages 21–22

Teacher's Resource File

- Translation and dictation worksheets pages 6, 16
- Evaluation rubrics pages 1–7
- Key competences worksheets pages 9–10
- Culture and CLIL worksheets pages 17–20
- Culture video worksheets pages 9–10
- Digital competence worksheets pages 9–10
- Macmillan Readers worksheets pages 3–4

UNIT 5 FEELING GREAT!

THINK ABOUT IT

What makes you feel great?
Think about ...

health relaxation sport holidays hobbies

Vocabulary and Speaking

Places to go

1 2.14 **Listen and repeat the words. Can you go to all these places in your town?**

park sports centre gym swimming pool café cinema library bowling alley shopping centre football stadium restaurant skate park

2 Look at the poster. Copy and complete 1–6 with words from exercise 1.

Exercise 2

1 park
2 swimming pool
3 bowling alley
4 café
5 gym
6 cinema

Relax with your friends in the (1) ...

Have fun at the (2) ...

Try your luck at the new (3) ...

Welcome to Newville!

There's lots to do to keep you feeling great ...

Meet your friends for a drink in a (4) ...

Get fit – sign up for the (5) ...

Watch a great film at the (6) ...

Exercise 3

Possible answers

You can relax in the park.
You can go skateboarding at the skate park.
You can do sport at the sports centre.
You can meet your friends at the café.

3 Where can you do the activities in the box? Write sentences.

go swimming relax go skateboarding do sport meet your friends

You can go swimming at the swimming pool.

EXPRESS YOURSELF

4 Choose four places from exercise 1. Write true sentences with expressions of frequency.

I go to the park once a week.

LOOK!

expressions of frequency

every day / weekend
once / twice / three times a week / month

5 Work in pairs. Ask and answer. Use *How often ...* ?

How often do you go to the skate park?
I never go to the skate park!

Vocabulary extension: Workbook page 106

Vocabulary and Speaking

Places to go

Lesson objectives

In this lesson students will:

- learn vocabulary for places
- learn vocabulary for activities
- write sentences about how often they do activities

Warmer

Write the words *free time* on the board. Students work in pairs and write down what they do in their free time, eg *play tennis, watch TV, go swimming*. Check ideas as a class.

Think about it

Explain the meaning of *feel great* (feel very healthy and happy). Students work in pairs and discuss what makes them feel great and why, using the five categories to help them. Check ideas as a class.

1  2.14

- Students look at the pictures.
- Play the CD. Students listen to the words and repeat them.
- Ask if they can go to all of these places in their town. If not, ask which places they can go to.

Language note

In two-word noun phrases, the first word almost always carries the main stress, eg *sports centre, swimming pool, bowling alley*.

2

- Demonstrate the activity by doing the first example with the class – *park*.
- Students use the words in the word pool from exercise 1 to complete the sentences.
- They compare their answers in pairs.
- Check answers as a class.

Extra activity

Focus on some of the expressions in the visitor information. Make sure students understand *relax, have fun, try your luck* and *get fit*. If necessary, ask them to translate the expressions into their language. Ask them to write the expressions in their notebooks.

3

- Nominate a student to read aloud the example sentence. Point out that we use the preposition *at* for places such as *swimming pool, bowling alley* and *gym*, *at* or *in* for places such as *restaurant, café* and *library*, but that we say *in the park*.
- Students write sentences beginning *You can* ... for the other activities, following the example sentence.
- Check answers as a class. Note that many different answers are possible.

Look!

Students read the expressions of frequency. Point out that we usually use these at the end of the sentence, eg *I go to the gym three times a week.*

4

- Read the example sentence aloud to the class.
- Students work individually. They choose four places from exercise 1.
- They write true sentences using expressions of frequency.

Language note

Remind students about questions beginning with *How often?*, eg *How often do you play football?* and the possible answers *I play football every day, I play football twice a week, I never play football,* etc. Ask them to look at the expressions of frequency in the Look! box and point out that we can say, *every day, every weekend, every Saturday*, etc. Remind them that we say *once* and *twice*, not *one time* and *two times.*

5

- Nominate two students to read aloud the example question and answer.
- Students work in pairs and ask and answer similar questions using the vocabulary from exercises 1 and 3.
- Listen to some pairs with the whole class.

Vocabulary extension: Workbook page 106

Reading

Text type: An online message board

Lesson objectives

In this lesson students will:

- read a message on an online message board
- say which activities they do

Recommended web links

www.visitbritain.com

Warmer

Revise some of the places and activities vocabulary from the previous lesson. Write these words on the board: *have fun, relax, get fit.* Students work in pairs and say where they can do these things. Listen to their ideas as a class, eg *You can get fit at the gym.*

1 2.15

- Read the question aloud to the class.
- Play the CD. Students read and listen to the messages on the online message board to find the answer.
- They compare their answers in pairs.
- Check the answer as a class.

Language note

Note that in English a *library* is a place where you can borrow books. If you want to buy books, you have to go to a *bookshop*.

2

- Focus students on the Word check. Check the meaning of any unknown words, eg *tips* (pieces of helpful advice).
- Ask students to translate the words into their language.

Culture note

In the UK, youth clubs are places where teenagers can go to relax and meet their friends. You have to be a member to go to a youth club. This usually means you pay a small amount of money to join and then you can use the facilities. Youth clubs often offer indoor sports such as table tennis and there are sometimes events like discos.

3

- Students read the questions carefully first. Make sure they understand all the sentences.
- They look for the information in the messages.
- They compare their answers in pairs.
- Check answers as a class.

4

- Students look at the messages and find the activities they do. They write sentences like the example sentences.
- They compare answers in pairs.
- Check answers as a class.

Finished?

Ask fast finishers to write their own top tips for NewGirl.

Web quest

Students make a class poster or do a project about places to visit in the UK. Highlight the Web quest tip.

1
- Students work in groups. They look at a map of the UK and allocate a different town or city to each student, eg Oxford, York, Cambridge, Liverpool, etc.
- They should not choose London because there will be too many facilities there.

2
- Ask students to open an internet web browser such as Internet Explorer. They open a search engine (eg Google) and type in *leisure facilities in ...*
- They find what facilities are available in their chosen town or city and also find pictures.

3
- Groups make their poster or do their project. They then share their information with the class.

MESSAGE BOARD

FAQs Register Login Search... Go

Top tips for feeling great?

Post reply 4 posts Page 1 of 1

NewGirl

Top tips for feeling great?
by **NewGirl** Wed 12/01 18.12
Hello there! I want to find out about ways to stay healthy and make friends at the same time. Any top tips for feeling great?

HealthFan

Re: Top tips for feeling great?
by **HealthFan** Wed 12/01 19.27
Hi NewGirl! If you want to meet new people, try joining the Scouts! There's a Scouts group where I live – they organize activities like trips to the bowling alley and the skate park. Is there a sports centre near you? There's a fantastic gym in my town – there are some great classes like zumba® and pilates. There's a swimming pool at the gym too – swimming's a great way to relax! Find out about your local facilities. There's usually an information board at the library.

Andy02

Re: Top tips for feeling great?
by **Andy02** Thurs 13/01 20.42
There aren't any gym classes in my village, but I don't mind – I'd rather be outside! Is there a park near your new house? Go for a walk – it's good to get fresh air! There are also lots of young people in my local park. Just relax and keep smiling! ☺

NewGirl

Re: Top tips for feeling great?
by **NewGirl** Thurs 13/01 20.57
Thanks for your tips – there are some great ideas! I want to try zumba – it looks fun. There isn't a Scout group here, but there's a youth club. I'm going there on Friday. Wish me luck! ☺

Word check
tips make friends outside relax youth club Wish me luck!

Reading
An online message board

Exercise 1
eight – bowling alley, skate park, sports centre, gym, swimming pool, library, park

Exercise 3
1 True
2 False There's a fantastic gym in HealthFan's town.
3 True
4 False Andy02 likes walking.
5 False There's a youth club in NewGirl's town.

1 2.15 **Read and listen to the messages. How many places are mentioned?**

2 Check the meaning of the words and expressions in the Word check. How do you say them in your language?

3 Are these sentences true or false? Correct the false sentences.

1 There's a Scout group in HealthFan's town.
2 There's isn't a gym in HealthFan's town.
3 There aren't any gym classes in Andy02's village.
4 Andy02 doesn't like walking.
5 There isn't a youth club in NewGirl's town.

4 Which of the activities in the messages do you do? Write sentences that are true for you.

I go to the bowling alley.
I don't go to a Scout group.

Write five of your own top tips for NewGirl.
Go to a yoga class!

WEB QUEST

Make a class poster or do a project about places to visit in the UK.
1 **Group work: look at a map of the UK. Allocate a different town or city to each student.**
2 **Find out about places to visit in the town or city. Think about parks, football stadiums, museums, etc.**
3 **Be creative! Find or draw pictures of places to visit in the town or city. Then share your information with the group.**

Web Quest tip!
Use very specific keywords when you search for information. This helps you to find information more quickly.

Grammar

There is / There are + *a / an*, *some* and *any*

Exercise 1
1 an
2 a
3 some
4 any

1 Copy the tables. Then complete 1–4 with *a*, *an*, *some* and *any*.

singular
There's a pool at the gym.
There's (1) ... information board at the library.
There isn't (2) ... Scout group here.

plural
There are three people on the message board.
There are (3) ... great classes.
There aren't (4) ... dance classes in my town.

Exercise 2
1 There are
2 There's
3 There are
4 There's
5 There are

2 Complete the sentences with *There's* or *There are*.

There's a swimming pool.

1 ... two tables.
2 ... a juice bar.
3 ... three restaurants.
4 ... an Indian restaurant.
5 ... five people.

Exercise 3
1 False There aren't two tables. There's one table.
2 True
3 False There aren't three restaurants. There are two restaurants.
4 False There isn't an Indian restaurant. There's an Italian restaurant and there's a Chinese restaurant.
5 False There aren't five people. There are four people.

3 Look at the picture. Are the sentences in exercise 2 true or false? Correct the false sentences.

There's a swimming pool.
False. There isn't a swimming pool. There's a gym.

Countable and uncountable nouns

4 Look at the tables. Then complete rules a) and b) with *Countable* or *Uncountable*.

countable nouns
We can count countable nouns.
There's **a** restaurant. ✔ There are **some** restaurants. ✔

uncountable nouns
We can't count uncountable nouns.
~~There's a food.~~ ✘ ~~There are some foods.~~ ✘ There's **some** food. ✔

a) ... nouns have got singular and plural forms.
b) ... nouns haven't got plural forms.

Exercise 4
a Countable
b Uncountable

5 Copy and complete the lists with the words in the box.

spinach bananas apples water fruit grapes oranges juice

COUNTABLE NOUNS	UNCOUNTABLE NOUNS
bananas	*spinach*

Exercise 5
countable nouns apples, grapes, oranges
uncountable nouns water, fruit, juice

6 Copy and complete the recipe with *a / an*, *some* or *any*.

Green smoothie

Fancy a healthy treat? Don't worry if there aren't (1) ... juice bars near you! Try making this delicious green smoothie in a smoothie machine. Put (2) ... apple, (3) ... kiwi and (4) ... green grapes in the smoothie machine. Add (5) ... banana, (6) ... spinach and (7) ... water. Mix it up, then serve in (8) ... glass.

Exercise 6
1 any
2 an
3 a
4 some
5 a
6 some
7 some
8 a

ANALYSE

In English, we use ***there is*** for singular nouns and ***there are*** for plural nouns. Translate sentences a) and b). Are the bold words different in your language?

a) There's one banana.
b) There are ten strawberries.

Digital course: Interactive grammar table
Study guide: page 61

Grammar Digital

There is / There are + *a / an*, *some* and *any*

Lesson objectives

In this lesson students will:

- learn and use *there is / there are* in the affirmative and negative
- use *a / an*, *some* and *any* with countable and uncountable nouns

Warmer

Ask students to tell you what facilities there are in their town. Elicit examples from the group and write them on the board (eg *cafés, sports centre, park*). Ask what facilities they don't have in their town but would like to have. Write these on the board too (eg *BMX track, bowling alley*).

1
- Students copy the tables into their notebooks.
- They work individually and complete the sentences using *a, an, some* and *any*.
- Check answers as a class.
- Point out that we use *there's / there isn't* for singular nouns and *there are / aren't* for plural nouns.
- All of the forms can use short forms except *there are*.
- Remind students that *an* is used in gap 1 because *information* begins with a vowel.

Language note

Highlight the fact that we use *some* in affirmative sentences (eg *There are some great classes*) and *any* in negative sentences (eg *There aren't any dance classes*) and questions (eg *Are there any sports centres in your town?*).

2
- Students complete the exercise individually.
- They compare their answers in pairs.
- Check answers as a class.
- Remind students that *people* is the plural form of *person*.

3
- Nominate two students to read aloud the example sentences.
- Students look at the picture and decide if the sentences in exercise 2 are true or false.
- They correct the false sentences individually.
- Check answers as a class.

Countable and uncountable nouns

4
- Explain the aim of the activity – to complete rules for countable and uncountable nouns.
- Students look at the tables and rules a–b.
- They complete the rules with *Countable* or *Uncountable* using the information in the tables.
- Check answers as a class.
- Point out that we don't use *a* with uncountable nouns.

5
- Students copy and complete the lists with the words in the box.
- They compare answers in pairs.
- Check answers as a class.

Language note

Point out that we can use *some* with both countable and uncountable nouns, eg *some restaurants, some water*. In the negative we can use *any* with both countable and uncountable nouns, eg *there aren't any restaurants, there isn't any water*.

6
- Ask students to read the whole recipe first.
- They work individually and fill the gaps using *a / an*, *some* or *any*.
- They compare answers in pairs.
- Check answers as a class.

Analyse

Ask students to translate sentences a and b into their language. Point out that there may only be one form in their language but there are singular and plural forms in English.

Digital course: Interactive grammar table

Study guide: page 61

Vocabulary and Listening

Food and drink

Lesson objectives

In this lesson students will:
- learn words for different kinds of food
- listen for specific information

Warmer

Write *breakfast, lunch* and *dinner* on the board. Ask students to work in pairs and compare their favourite foods for each meal. Check ideas as a class and write the foods they mention on the board.

1
- Students read the magazine article about school lunches in the UK and compare the food with the lunch they usually have.
- Listen to their ideas as a class.
- Highlight the information in the Top Tips box. Elicit answers to the questions *Do you eat breakfast?* and *How often do you eat fish?* from the class.

2 2.16
- Play the CD. Students listen and repeat the words in blue.
- Elicit the translation for each word from the class.

3
- Students work individually and copy the list into their notebooks.
- They complete the list with the blue words from exercise 2.
- They compare their answers in pairs.
- Check answers as a class.

4 2.17
- Play the CD. Students should listen and say which country each person is from.
- Check answers as a class.

5
- Students copy the table into their notebooks.
- Play the CD again. Students complete the table.
- Check answers as a class.

6
- Students decide if the sentences are true or false. They correct the false sentences.
- Check answers as a class.

Pronunciation lab: Difficult sounds: /ɪ/ and /iː/; page 125

2.17 Audioscript, exercises 4 and 5

1 Paul We're at Newton High School in London, England. Let's see what the students are having for lunch today ... Hi there, we're doing a programme about school lunches around the world. What are you having for lunch today?
Sara Well, I'm having chilli with rice and for dessert I've got some yoghurt.
Paul Right. And what are you having to drink?
Sara Apple juice.
Paul OK. Is there a choice of food here?
Sara Oh, yes. There are lots of different things you can have ...
Paul And do you always have lunch at this time?
Sara Yes – at half past twelve. The younger children have lunch at twelve o'clock and we come in at half past twelve.
Paul Thanks! Enjoy your lunch!

2 María We're at the Instituto Manuel Diego in Madrid. Hello. What are you having today?
David Well, for first course today there's salad, then fish for the main course. I've got fruit for dessert.
María And you're drinking ... water?
David Yes, water.
María Are there always three courses for lunch here?
David Yes, we always have three courses.
María Do all your friends have lunch at school?
David No, some of my friends go home for lunch.
María Thanks for talking to us. Enjoy the rest of your lunch!

3 Kevin I'm talking to students at the Santa Monica High School in California. Hi there, what are you having for lunch today?
Maya I've got pizza and fries and for dessert I'm having ice cream.
Kevin And to drink?
Maya Cola!
Kevin Do you always have lunch here in the school cafeteria?
Maya I do – but some of the older students leave school for lunch.
Kevin Is there much choice here at school?
Maya No, not really. I mean, there aren't a lot of healthy options. There's mostly pizza, burgers and fries ...
Kevin Well, thanks for talking to us! So, now back to the studio ...

Vocabulary and Listening

Food and drink

1 Read the article about school lunches. Are they similar to your lunches?

2 2.16 Listen and repeat the words in blue.

How healthy is your school lunch?

In the UK, about half of all students have a school lunch and half take a packed lunch.

Here's a typical school lunch. There's usually some **chicken**, meat or **fish** with **rice**, pasta or **potatoes** and bread. There's usually **salad** or vegetables like **peas**, broccoli or green beans. For dessert there's fruit, **yoghurt** or a piece of **cake**. And there's **milk**, **juice** or water to drink.

This is a typical packed lunch, but it isn't very healthy! There are sandwiches (usually with **cheese**, **ham** or tuna) and there's a bag of **crisps**. There's a chocolate bar, some **biscuits** and a fizzy drink. But there isn't any fruit! It's a good idea to have an apple, **orange** or some **nuts** for a snack.

Top Tips

If you want to study better:

- don't forget to have breakfast – it gives you energy to start the day.
- eat fish regularly – it contains Omega-3 which is good for concentration!

3 Copy and complete the list with the blue words from exercise 2.

Protein	*chicken, ...*
Carbohydrates	*rice, ...*
Fruit and vegetables	*peas, ...*
Dairy products	*yoghurt, ...*
Fat and sugar	*cake, ...*
Drinks	*juice, ...*

4 2.17 Listen to three conversations about food at school. Where are the students from?

5 Listen again. Write the answers to 1–6 in your notebook.

	Main meal	Dessert	Drink
Sara	chilli with (1) ...	(2) ...	apple juice
David	(3) ... , then fish	fruit	(4) ...
Maya	(5) ... and fries (chips)	(6) ...	cola

6 Are the sentences true or false? Correct the false sentences.

1 There's a choice of food at Sara's school.
2 Sara has lunch at 12 o'clock.
3 There are always three courses for lunch at David's school.
4 All of David's friends have lunch at school.
5 There isn't a cafeteria at Maya's school.
6 There are a lot of healthy options at Maya's school.

2.18–2.19 Pronunciation lab: Difficult sounds: /ɪ/ and /iː/, page 125

Exercise 3

Protein
fish, ham
Carbohydrates
rice, potatoes
Fruit and vegetables
salad, orange, nuts
Dairy products
milk, cheese, yoghurt
Fat and sugar
cake, biscuits, crisps
Drinks
milk, juice

Exercise 4

1 London, England
2 Madrid, Spain
3 California, the USA

Exercise 5

1 rice
2 yoghurt
3 salad
4 water
5 pizza
6 ice cream

Exercise 6

1 True
2 False She has lunch at half past twelve.
3 True
4 False Some of David's friends go home for lunch.
5 False There is a cafeteria at Maya's school.
6 False There aren't a lot of healthy options at Maya's school.

Cultural awareness

Traditional food

Fact box

In Australia, traditional food is called 'bush tucker' (bush = countryside; tucker = food). But this isn't the standard diet for most Australians!

1 Look at the pictures. Would you like to eat the insects? Why (not)?

Exercise 2

1 a
2 b
3 a
4 b

2 2.20 Guess the answers to 1–4. Then read, listen and check.

1 Are there any bush tucker restaurants in Australia?
a) Yes, there are. **b)** No, there aren't.

2 How much protein is there in a witchetty grub?
a) 1.5% **b)** 15%

3 Are there any vitamins and minerals in insects?
a) Yes, there are. **b)** No, there aren't.

4 How many people in the world eat insects?
a) 6% **b)** 60%

WORLD FOODS: **AUSTRALIA**

Bush Tucker | BBQs | Contemporary

FAQs

Q: What is bush tucker?
A: Bush tucker is native Australian food. It consists of all of Australia's native plants, animals, reptiles and insects. It includes proteins like kangaroo or crocodile meat, insects like witchetty grubs and other food like fruit, eggs and honey.

Q: Who eats bush tucker?
A: Traditionally, bush tucker is the food of Australian Aborigines. But now there are a lot of restaurants where you can eat bush tucker too.

Q: What are witchetty grubs?
A: Witchetty grubs are large, white larvae. They taste like almonds! They're about 15% protein and they also contain vitamin C.

Q: Is there much nutritional value in insects?
A: Yes! Insects contain a lot of protein, fibre, vitamins and minerals. They haven't got many calories, because they don't contain much fat.

Q: Are there any other countries where people eat insects?
A: Yes – more than 60% of people in the world eat insects regularly. There are toasted grasshoppers in Mexico and fried tarantulas in Cambodia!

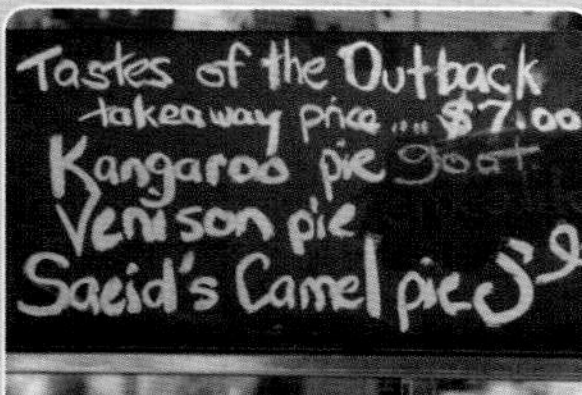

Word check

egg honey almond toasted grasshopper fried

CULTURAL COMPARISON

3 Answer the questions.

1 What traditional food is there in your country?
2 Are there any unusual food products?
3 What's your favourite regional food?
4 Can you cook any traditional food recipes?

Culture video: Typical food in the UK

Cultural awareness

Traditional food

Lesson objectives

In this lesson students will:

- read some frequently asked questions (FAQs) about traditional food in Australia
- practise reading to find specific information
- talk about traditional food in their country

Warmer

Write *Australia* on the board. Students work in pairs and write down what they know about Australia. Check ideas a class. Write relevant points on the board (eg *There are kangaroos there. The weather is very hot. It's a very large island*, etc).

1

- Students look at the pictures. They decide whether they would like to eat the insects and why or why not.
- They compare their answers in pairs.
- Listen to their ideas as a class.

Culture note

Highlight the Fact box. In Australia the bush is the name for the wild, uninhabited countryside outside the towns and cities, also known as the outback. Tucker is Australian slang for food, so bush tucker is food that can be found in the outback. Traditionally, bush tucker was the food of native Australians.

2 2.20

- Explain *witchetty grub* by asking students to look at the picture. It is the larva of a moth (an insect like a butterfly that usually flies at night).
- Make sure students understand all the questions.
- They choose an answer for each of the questions.
- Students compare answers in pairs.
- Play the CD. Students read, listen and check their answers.

Word check

Check that students understand all the new words. Ask them to translate them into their language.

Extra activity

Highlight some more of the vocabulary in the text. Ask students to find two words for animals (*kangaroo, crocodile*) and two words for types of insects (*grasshopper, tarantula*). Check students understand these words by asking them to say what the words for these creatures are in their language.

CULTURAL  COMPARISON

3

- Students work individually and answer the four questions.
- Give help with food vocabulary if necessary.
- They compare their answers in pairs or small groups.
- Check ideas as a class.

Culture video: Typical food in the UK

Grammar

Is there ...? Are there ...?

Lesson objectives

In this lesson students will:
- ask and answer questions with *Is there ...?* and *Are there ...?*
- make questions using *How much ...?* and *How many ...?*

Warmer

Play a word race game. Write *There's* and *There are* on the board and an example under each heading, eg *a table* under *There's* and *twenty desks* under *There are*. Put the students into pairs. Tell them they have two minutes to write down as many words as possible for objects they can see in the classroom. The pair with the most words in each column wins.

1
- Students copy the tables into their notebooks.
- Ask them to translate the questions.

Language note

In the short answers, only the negative answers have short forms. We never say ~~*Yes, there's*~~. Point out that the final word carries the strongest stress in the short answers, eg *Yes, there is*.

2
- Students work individually and complete the questions. They compare answers in pairs.
- Check answers as a class.
- Ask students whether we use *some* or *any* after *Are there?* (*any*).
- Elicit what word is used after *Is there?* (*a/an*).

EXPRESS YOURSELF

3
- Nominate two students to read aloud the example dialogue.
- Do the first question with the class as a further example. Use a short answer and give extra information, eg *Is there a library at your school? Yes, there is. It's next to the cafeteria.*
- Students work in pairs and ask and answer the questions.
- Listen to some pairs as a class.

How much ...? How many ...?

4
- Students look at the tables.
- Highlight that we use *How much* with uncountable nouns (eg *How much water?*) and *How many* with countable nouns (eg *How many students?*).
- Students work individually and complete the questions with *How much* or *How many*.
- They compare their answers in pairs.
- Check answers as a class.

5
- Students read the four answers and match them with the questions in exercise 4.
- They compare answers in pairs.
- Check answers as a class.

Extra activity

Write these questions on the board: *How often do you eat crisps? How many flavours of crisps are there in your country? What is your favourite flavour?* Students write their answers to the questions. They compare their answers in pairs. Listen to their ideas as a class.

Grammar in context: Science (nutrition)

6
- Ask students to read the whole text carefully first.
- Students work individually and choose the correct answer from the three possibilities.
- They compare their answers in pairs.

7

- Play the CD. Students check their answers.

CLIL task

Set this task as a homework task. Students choose their lunch or dinner. They make a list of everything they eat and match them with the different food groups (eg fruit and vegetables, protein, carbohydrates, etc). At the beginning of the next lesson, they present their results to the class.

Digital course: Interactive grammar table

Study guide: page 61

Grammar 

Is there ...? Are there ...?

1 Read the tables. Translate the questions into your language.

singular
Is there much nutritional value in insects?
Yes, **there is.** / No, **there isn't.**

plural
Are there any unusual meals in your country?
Yes, **there are.** / No, **there aren't.**

Exercise 2
1 Is there
2 Are there
3 Is there
4 Are there
5 Is there
We use any after Are there?

2 Copy and complete the questions with *Is there* or *Are there*. Do we use *some* or *any* after *Are there*?

1 ... a library at your school?
2 ... any cafés in your town?
3 ... a gym near your house?
4 ... any Italian restaurants in your town?
5 ... a bowling alley in your town?

EXPRESS YOURSELF

3 Work in pairs. Ask and answer the questions in exercise 2.

Are there any nice cafés in your town?
Yes, there are. I like Rainbow Café on Market Street.

How much ...? How many ...?

uncountable nouns	
How much protein is there in an insect?	There's **a lot.** There isn't **much.**

countable nouns	
How many calories are there in an insect?	There are **a lot.** There aren't **many.**

Exercise 4
1 How much
2 How much
3 How many
4 How many

4 Complete the questions with *How much* or *How many*.

1 ... fat is there in a bag of crisps?
2 ... salt is there?
3 ... children eat crisps every day?
4 ... bags of crisps do British people buy?

Exercise 5
1 b
2 d
3 a
4 c

5 Match answers a–d with the questions in exercise 4.

a) A lot! About 50% of children eat crisps every day.
b) There's a lot. There's 8.5 g of fat in every bag.
c) People buy more than 5 billion bags every year!
d) There's a lot. Crisps consist of about 8% salt.

CLIL Grammar in context: Science (nutrition)

6 Read the text and choose the correct answers.

Exercise 6
1 any
2 How much
3 some
4 There are
5 is
6 There are
7 There's
8 an

7 2.21 Listen and check your answers.

What's on your plate for lunch today?

Are there (1) **a** / **some** /**any** vegetables? (2) **How much** / **How many** / **Are there** protein is there? Is there any fruit for dessert? If there isn't a variety of food in your lunch, read this information and make (3) **a** / **some** / **any** changes to your menu!

The five food groups:

- **Fruit and vegetables**
  (4) **There's** / **There are** / **Is there** vitamins and minerals in fruit and vegetables. You should eat five portions every day.
- **Protein**
  There (5) **is** / **are** / **aren't** protein in meat, fish, eggs and beans. It helps your body grow.
- **Carbohydrates**
  (6) **Is there** / **There isn't** / **There are** carbohydrates in bread, rice, pasta and potatoes. They give you energy.
- **Dairy products**
  (7) **There are** / **There's** / **Is there** calcium in dairy products like milk and cheese. Calcium is necessary for healthy bones.
- **Fat and sugar**
  Don't eat too many things in this group – just (8) **a** / **an** / **any** occasional treat!

CLIL TASK

Analyse your lunch or dinner. Write a list of all the things you eat. Which food group are they in?

At a café

My friend Katy and I are going to the Health Café for lunch. Katy's vegetarian and she's very healthy! Are any of your friends vegetarian?

The Health Café menu

Salads

Tuna salad	£4.95
Pasta salad	£4.60

Soup

Vegetable soup	£2.50
Tomato soup (served with bread)	£2.25

Sandwiches

Cheese and tomato	£1.95
Ham	£1.95

Baked potatoes

With cheese and beans	£3.25
With vegetarian chilli	£3.60

Drinks

Juice (apple, orange, pineapple or mango)	£1.20
Mineral water (still or sparkling)	95p

Step 1: Read

Exercise 1
1 Yes, there is
2 two
3 £3.25
4 No, there aren't.
5 four

Exercise 2
1 tuna
2 still, sparkling
3 pasta, bread, potatoes
4 apple, orange, pineapple, mango

1 Look at the menu and answer the questions.

1 Is there any meat on the menu?
2 How many types of soup are there?
3 How much is a baked potato with cheese and beans?
4 Are there any pizzas on the menu?
5 How many types of juice are there?

2 Read the menu again. Find ...

a) one type of fish
b) two words to describe water
c) three types of carbohydrates
d) four types of fruit

SKILLS BUILDER

Listening: Understanding prices

p = pence We say pence or p.
95p = ninety-five p/pence

£ = pound(s) We say pound(s).
£2.00 = two pounds

When there are pounds and pence, we sometimes omit these words.
£1.95 = one ninety-five

Step 2: Listen

Exercise 3
1 a banana
2 a cookie

Exercise 4
1 40
2 2.40
3 95
4 1.50

3 2.22 **Listen to Hazel and Katy. Choose the correct answers.**

1 For dessert, Katy has **an apple** / **a banana**.
2 Hazel has **a cookie** / **some carrot cake**.

4 Copy the dessert menu into your notebook. Then listen again and complete the prices.

Dessert menu

Fresh fruit

Apple	30p
Banana	(1) ...p

Cakes and biscuits

Carrot cake	(2) £...
Cookie	(3) ...p

Ice cream

Vanilla or chocolate	(4) £...

Integrated skills

At a café

Lesson objectives

In this lesson students will:
- work on all four skills
- read a menu
- listen to conversation in a café
- write a personalized dialogue
- act out their dialogue

Warmer

Play an alphabet game to revise food vocabulary and prepare students for the next activity. Write the letter *a* on the board and elicit a food beginning with this letter (eg *apple*). Continue with the other letters.

Step 1: Read

1
- Highlight Hazel's speech bubble. Elicit answers to the question *Are any of your friends vegetarian?* from the class.
- Ask students to read the questions carefully first. Then they look at the menu and find the answers quickly.
- Check answers as a class. Ask why there isn't any meat or any pizza on the menu (because the menu is healthy).

2
- Check that students understand the task.
- Students work individually and find the answers.
- Check answers as a class. Make sure students understand the difference between *still water* (no gas) and *sparkling water* (with gas).

Skills builder

Listening: Understanding prices

Highlight the two ways to say 95p in English – *ninety-five p* or *ninety-five pence* – and that the £ symbol is used for *pounds*. When people say prices they sometimes omit these words, so £1.95 is *one ninety-five* rather than *one pound ninety-five pence*.

Step 2: Listen

3 2.22
- Make sure the students understand the task – to check what desserts the girls have.
- Tell them they will hear the answers in a conversation.
- Play the CD. Students choose the correct answers.
- Check answers as a class.

4 2.22
- Students copy the dessert menu into their notebooks.
- Check they understand the task.
- Play the CD again. Students write the answers.
- Check answers as a class.

Extra activity

Make a copy of the audioscript of the dialogue in exercise 3 and give each student a copy. Play the CD again. Students follow the audioscript. Play the CD again. This time students read the dialogue aloud in time with the recording. This will give them practice in rhythm and intonation. Note that this may seem difficult at first but students quickly get used to the activity.

2.22 Audioscript, exercises 3 and 4

Hazel Do you want a dessert?
Katy Er, I don't know – what is there?
Hazel Let's see, there's fresh fruit, carrot cake, cookies and ice cream.
Katy Mmm! I'm not sure. I haven't got much money.
Hazel Well, you can have an apple for 30p! Or a banana for 40p?
Katy Hmm, how much is the carrot cake?
Hazel Er, The carrot cake ... two forty!
Katy Two forty? That's a lot! And the cookies?
Hazel The cookies are 95p each.
Katy Well, I've only got one sixty ...
Hazel One sixty? Well, you could have some ice cream? It's only one fifty.
Katy Nah, I'll have a banana!
Hazel A banana? Oh. I think I'll have a cookie ...

Integrated skills - continued

Ordering food

5 2.23

- Students read the dialogue.
- They copy Hazel's receipt into their notebooks.
- They fill in the gaps in the receipt, finding the prices in the menu on page 58.
- Play the CD. Students check the total price.
- They compare answers in pairs.
- Check answers as a class.

6
- Play the CD again, pausing after each speaker's part for students to repeat as a class.
- Note the main stress on the questions, eg *Can I help you? Anything else? Is that everything? How much is it?*
- Ask students to repeat the questions and responses several times both chorally and individually with the correct stress and intonation.
- Students practise the dialogue in pairs. Then swap roles and practise the dialogue again.

Step 3: Write

7
- Students look at the menu on page 58 again.
- They choose a meal and a drink for themselves and a friend and write their order.

8
- Students work individually and write their dialogue, using the dialogue in the book as a model and the Communication kit: Ordering food for key phrases.
- Monitor while they are writing and give help if necessary.

Step 4: Communicate

9
- Remind students about the main stress on questions.
- Students practise their dialogues in pairs.
- For extra practice, they swap roles in both dialogues.

10
- Choose some pairs to act out their dialogue for the class.
- Students raise their hand if another pair has the same food or drink as they do. This will encourage them to listen carefully to their classmates.

Integrated skills: Workbook page 115

Hi, can I help you?	Yes – I'd like a tuna salad, please.
OK. Anything else?	Yes – some vegetable soup for my friend, please.
Would you like anything to drink?	Oh, yes. Have you got any orange juice?
Yes, sure.	OK. One orange juice and one apple juice, please.
OK. Is that everything?	Yes, I think so. How much is it?
That's £ ... , please.	Here you are.
Thank you and enjoy your meal!	Thanks.

Exercise 5

1 vegetable soup 2.50
2 orange juice 1.20
3 apple juice 1.20
4 19.85

5 2.23 **Read the dialogue. Copy and complete Hazel's receipt. Use the menu on page 58 to help you. Then listen and check the total price.**

THE HEALTH CAFÉ
3 MAIN STREET, GREENTOWN

TUNA SALAD	£4.95
(1) ...	£ ...
(2) ...	£ ...
(3) ...	£ ...
TOTAL	**£ ...**

THANK YOU. HAVE A GOOD DAY!

6 Listen again and repeat. Practise your intonation.

Step 3: Write

7 Look at the menu on page 58 and write your order for you and your friend.

8 Write a new dialogue to order your food and drinks. Use the dialogue in exercise 5 to help you.

Hi, can I help you?
Yes – I'd like a ...

Step 4: Communicate

9 Work in pairs. Take turns to practise your dialogues.

Hi, can I help you?
Yes – I'd like a ...
Ok. Anything else?
Yes – ...

10 Act your dialogue for the class.

COMMUNICATION KIT

Ordering food

Can I help you?
I'd like a / an / some ... , please.
Would you like anything to drink?
Anything else? / Is that everything?
Have you got any ... ?
How much is it?
Enjoy your meal.

Writing
A recipe

Exercise 1
fry, boil

1 2.24 **Check the meaning of the verbs in the box. Then read and listen to the recipe. Which two verbs are not in the recipe?**

wash cook fry cut add boil prepare

Jacket potatoes

Jacket potatoes are very popular in the UK. They're easy to make and they're healthy and delicious. There's a lot of fibre in jacket potatoes because we eat the potato skin too. There are also a lot of vitamins and minerals. But be careful with the filling – there's a lot of fat in butter and cheese!
Here's the recipe ...

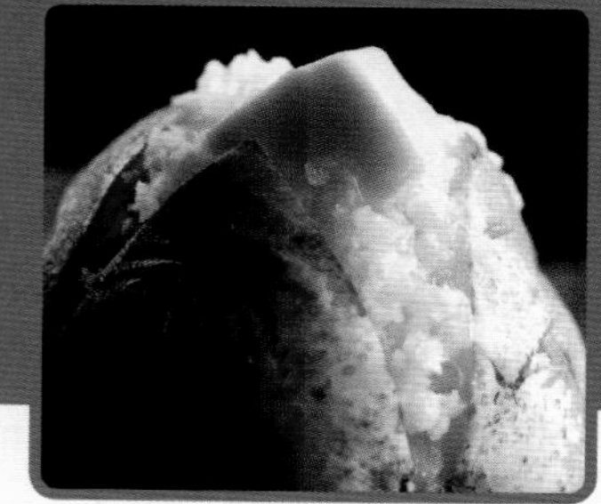

Ingredients

- a big potato for each person
- some butter
- your favourite filling (for example: cheese, tuna, baked beans, chilli, etc)

Method

First, wash the potatoes.
Then, cook the potatoes in the oven (200°C) for about 75 minutes.
Next, cut the potatoes and add some butter.
Finally, prepare the filling. My favourite is cheese and beans!

Exercise 2
a First
b Finally

2 Look at the Writing focus and answer questions a) and b).

a) Which connector do we use at the start of the sequence?
b) Which connector do we use at the end of the sequence?

WRITING FOCUS

Connectors of sequence

We use connectors of sequence to show the order of events or instructions.
First, wash the potatoes.
Then, put the potatoes in the oven.
Next, add some butter.
Finally, add your favourite filling.

Exercise 3
c First, cut the bread.
d Then, spread the butter.
a Next, add the cheese and ham.
b Finally, eat the sandwich!

3 Write the instructions in the correct order. Add connectors of sequence.

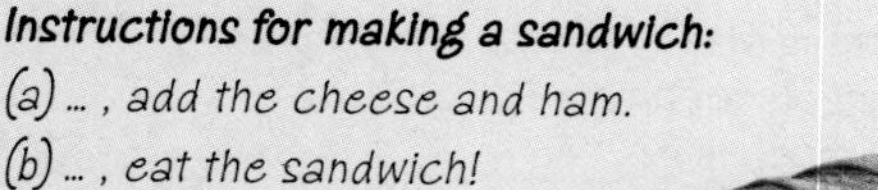

Instructions for making a sandwich:
(a) ... , add the cheese and ham.
(b) ... , eat the sandwich!
(c) ... , cut the bread.
(d) ..., spread the butter.

4 Write the instructions for making the jacket potato filling. Use the phrases in the box and connectors of sequence.

heat the beans ~~open a tin of beans~~ put the beans on the potato add some cheese

First, open a tin of beans. Then, ...

Exercise 4
Then, heat the beans.
Next, put the beans on the potato.
Finally, add some cheese.

Writing task

Write a recipe for a simple dish from your country.

Plan Choose a dish. Copy and complete the notes.

Ingredients	Method	
...	1 ...	3 ...
...	2 ...	4 ...

Write Write the recipe. Include three sentences about your recipe at the beginning. Use the text in exercise 1 to help you.

Check Check your writing.

☑ connectors of sequence
☑ *there's / there are* and *a / an / some*
☑ vocabulary for food

Build your confidence: Writing reference and practice. Workbook page 128

Writing

A recipe

Lesson objectives

In this lesson students will:

- learn some key verbs related to cooking
- write a short recipe

Warmer

Write five or six food words on the board with the letters in the wrong order, eg *t t s e o a p o* (*potatoes*); *e e e s c h* (*cheese*). Students work in pairs and put the letters in the correct order. The first pair to spell all the words correctly wins.

1 2.24

- Ask students to look at the verbs in the box.
- Check they understand all the verbs, especially *fry* (cook in hot oil) and *boil* (cook in very hot water). If necessary, ask them to translate the verbs into their language.
- Check students understand *recipe* (instructions for making food).
- Play the CD. Students read and listen and identify the two verbs that aren't in the recipe.
- Check answers as a class.

2

- Students look at the Writing focus and answer questions a–b.
- They compare answers in pairs.
- Check answers as a class.

Language note

Point out that *then* and *next* are interchangeable, so we could say *Next, put the potatoes in the oven* and *Then, add some butter* without changing the meaning.

3

- Explain the task.
- Students work individually. They write the instructions in the correct order and add the connectors of sequence from the Writing focus – *First, Then, Next* and *Finally*.
- They compare answers in pairs.
- Check answers as a class.

4

- Check students understand the verb *heat* (cook something until it is hot).
- Students look at the picture of the jacket potato.
- They write the instructions for making the filling by putting the phrases in the correct order and by adding connectors of sequence.
- They compare answers in pairs.
- Check answers as a class.

Writing task

The aim of this activity is for students to produce a piece of guided writing that includes the key verbs related to cooking and the correct use of connectors of sequence in a recipe. It also gives them practice in using *there's / there are* and *a / an / some* and food vocabulary. Ask the students to follow the stages in the Student's Book. Monitor while they are writing and give help with vocabulary if necessary. At the Check stage, ask them to swap notebooks and check each other's writing.

Writing reference and practice: Workbook page 128

Study guide

Grammar, Vocabulary and Speaking

Tell the students the Study guide is an important page which provides a useful reference for the main language of the unit: the grammar, the vocabulary and the functional language from the Integrated skills pages. Explain that they should refer to this page when studying for a test or exam.

Grammar

- Tell the students to look at the example sentences which present *There is, There are, a, an, some* and *any*. Make sure students know how to use the words within sentences correctly.
- Then tell students to look at the example sentences which present countable and uncountable nouns, *Is there ...? / Are there ...?, How much ...? / How many ...?* Get students to translate into their own language if necessary.
- Refer students to the Grammar reference on pages 92–93 of the Workbook for further revision.

Vocabulary

- Tell students to look at the list of vocabulary and check understanding.
- Refer students to the Wordlist on page 151 of the Workbook where they can look up any words they can't remember.

Speaking

- Check that students understand the phrases to use for ordering food.
- Tell students to act out a conversation between a café assistant and a customer.

Additional material

Workbook

- Progress check page 46
- Self-evaluation page 47
- Grammar reference and practice page 92
- Vocabulary extension page 106
- Integrated skills page 115
- Writing reference and task page 128

Teacher's Resource File

- Pulse Basics worksheets pages 29–34
- Vocabulary and grammar consolidation worksheets 19–22
- Translation and dictation worksheets pages 6, 16
- Evaluation rubrics pages 1–7
- Key competences worksheets pages 9–10
- Culture and CLIL worksheets pages 17–20
- Culture video worksheets pages 9–10
- Digital competence worksheets pages 9–10
- Macmillan Readers worksheets pages 3–4

Tests and Exams

- Unit 5 End-of-unit test: Basic, Standard and Extra
- CEFR Skills Exam Generator

Study guide

Grammar

There is / There are + a / an, some and any

singular	plural
There's a cake in the fridge.	**There are** some vitamins in potatoes.
There's a recipe in the magazine.	**There are** some recipes online.
There isn't a gym in town.	**There aren't** any biscuits in my lunch box.

Countable and uncountable nouns

countable nouns	uncountable nouns
There's **a** sandwich. There are **some** sandwiches.	There's **some** pasta.

Is there ...? Are there ...?

singular	plural
Is there a gym?	**Are there** any cafés?
Yes, **there is**. No, **there isn't**.	Yes, **there are**. No, **there aren't**.

How much ...? How many ...?

uncountable nouns	
How much protein is there in a chicken sandwich?	There is **a lot**. There isn't **much**.
countable nouns	
How many calories are there in a chicken sandwich?	There are **a lot**. There aren't **many**.

Vocabulary

Places to go

bowling alley
café
cinema
football stadium
gym
library
park
restaurant
shopping centre
skate park
sports centre
swimming pool

Food and drink

biscuits
cake
cheese
chicken
crisps
fish
ham
juice
milk
nuts
orange
peas
potatoes
rice
salad
yoghurt

Speaking

Ordering food

Can I help you?
I'd like a / an / some ... , please.
Anything else?
Would you like anything to drink?
Is that everything?
Have you got any ... ?
How much is it?
Enjoy your meal.

LEARNING TO LEARN

When learning new vocabulary, write in your notebook if the noun is countable (c) or uncountable (u).

sandwich (c)
pasta (u)

Progress check: Workbook page 46

Grammar reference: Workbook page 92

UNIT 6 HOME SWEET HOME

Unit objectives and key competences

In this unit the student will learn ...

- understand, memorize and correctly use words for furniture **CLC CMST**
- understand, memorize and correctly use words for places to stay **CLC CMST CAE**
- understand and correctly use grammar structures related to comparative adjectives and draw parallels to L1 **CLC L2L**
- understand and correctly use grammar structures related to possibility, permission, obligation and prohibition **CLC**
- about the lifestyle of travellers in Ireland **CLC CMST SCC CAE**
- about homes in the UK by watching a short video **CLC CMST CAE**

In this unit the student will learn how to ...

- identify specific information in an online article **CLC DC CAE**
- look for information about unusual homes **CLC DC CAE CIE**
- identify specific information in a conversation about holidays **CLC SCC CAE**
- speak about their domestic routines **CLC SCC**
- write an opinion essay **CLC CMST CAE**
- read a map for directions, listen to a conversations about directions and ask for and give directions **CLC SCC**

Linguistic contents

Main vocabulary

- Furniture: *wardrobe, mirror, shelf,* etc
- Places to stay: *tent, caravan, log cabin,* etc

Grammar

- Comparative adjectives: *bigger than*
- Modal verbs: *can / can't, must / mustn't*

Functional language

- Asking for and giving directions

Pronunciation

- /ə/
- Contractions: *can't* and *mustn't*

Skills

Reading

- Read an online article about a dream house
- Read a text about travellers in Ireland
- Read directions to an address

Writing: Interaction and production

- Write a personalized dialogue
- Write an opinion essay in three steps: plan, write, check

Listening

- Listen to a conversation about holidays
- Listen to people asking for and giving directions
- Prepare to listen for important information in conversations

Spoken interaction

- Exchange information about domestic habits

Spoken production

- Prepare and act out a dialogue about giving directions

Lifelong learning skills

Self-study and self-evaluation

- Study guide: Student's Book page 71
- Progress check and self-evaluation: Workbook pages 54–55
- Grammar reference and practice: Workbook pages 94–95
- Wordlist: Workbook pages 151–157

Learning strategies and thinking skills

- Reading for general information
- Listening for specific information
- Speaking skills: using polite language

Cultural awareness

- Travellers in Ireland
- Comparing the life of Irish travellers with groups in students own countries

Cross-curricular contents

- Geography: mega-cities
- ICT: searching the internet for information
- Language and literature: conventions for writing an opinion essay

Key competences

CLC	Competence in linguistic communication
CMST	Competence in mathematics, science and technology
DC	Digital competence
L2L	Learning to learn
SCC	Social and civic competences
SIE	Sense of initiative and entrepreneurship
CAE	Cultural awareness and expression

Evaluation

- Unit 6 End-of-unit test: Basic, Standard and Extra
- End-of-term test, units 4–6: Basic, Standard and Extra
- CEFR Skills Exam Generator

External exam trainer

- Listening: Multiple-choice pictures

Digital material

Pulse Live! Digital Course including:

- Interactive grammar tables
- Audio visual speaking model: Asking / giving directions
- Audio visual cultural material: Homes in the UK

Student's website

Digital competence

- Web quest: Researching the PAS house
- Digital competence worksheet: Writing tools

Reinforcement material

- Basics worksheets, Teacher's Resource File pages 35–40
- Vocabulary and Grammar: Consolidation worksheets, Teacher's Resource File pages 23–24

Extension material

- Fast-finisher activity: Student's Book page 63
- Extra activities: Teacher's Book pages T66, T68
- Vocabulary and Grammar: Extension worksheets, Teacher's Resource File pages 25–26

Teacher's Resource File

- Translation and dictation worksheets pages 7, 17
- Evaluation rubrics pages 1–7
- Key competences worksheets pages 11–12
- Culture and CLIL worksheets pages 21–24
- Culture video worksheets pages 11–12
- Digital competence worksheets pages 11–12
- Macmillan Readers worksheets pages 3–4

UNIT 6 HOME SWEET HOME

THINK ABOUT IT

What's your home like? How is your bedroom different from the pictures?

Vocabulary and Speaking

At home

Exercise 1

shelf, lamp, table, bed

Exercise 2

Possible answers

bathroom – shelf, cupboard, mirror

bedroom – chair, wardrobe, table, bed

kitchen – chair, shelf, cooker, fridge, cupboard, sink, table

living room – desk, chair, shelf, lamp, mirror, sofa, armchair

dining room – chair, cupboard, mirror, table

Exercise 3

1 wardrobe
2 desk
3 shelf / shelves
4 mirror
5 lamp
6 bed

1 2.25 **Listen and repeat the words in the box. Which things can you see in the pictures?**

desk chair shelf cooker toilet fridge
wardrobe cupboard lamp sink mirror
sofa bath armchair table bed

2 Which of the things in exercise 1 are in each of these rooms in your house?

bathroom bedroom kitchen
living room dining room

bathroom: *sink, toilet, bath, ...*

3 Read the competition information. Find words that match these definitions.

1 The place where you put your clothes.
2 A table where you study.
3 You can put your books here.
4 You can see yourself in this.
5 A small light.
6 The piece of furniture you sleep on.

4 Imagine you enter the competition. Complete the sentence with your ideas.

My perfect bedroom is ...

EXPRESS YOURSELF

5 Where do you do the activities in the box? Write sentences.

relax watch TV do your homework
chat to friends listen to music
have breakfast / lunch / dinner

I usually relax in my bedroom.

6 Work in pairs. Ask and answer questions about the activities in exercise 5.

Where do you usually watch TV?
I usually watch TV in the living room.

WIN your perfect bedroom!

Give your bedroom a completely new look in this month's great competition.

The prize includes:

- **fantastic new furniture** (bed, desk, wardrobe ...)
- **fabulous accessories** (lamp, mirror, shelves ...)
- **new technology worth £2,000** (computer, music system ...)

To enter, complete this sentence in no more than 50 words:

'My perfect bedroom is ...'

Send your entry to perfectbedroom@teenmag.co.uk

Vocabulary extension: Workbook page 107

Vocabulary and Speaking

At home

Lesson objectives

In this lesson students will:

- learn vocabulary for rooms
- learn vocabulary for furniture
- ask and answer questions about where they do activities

Warmer

Play a spelling game. Choose six objects in the classroom and mix the letters of each word up. Write the words on the board with the letters in the wrong order, eg *r o p e c t u m* (*computer*). Put the class into teams of three. The first team to unscramble all the words and spell the six objects correctly wins.

Think about it

Explain that a home can be a *house* or a *flat* (or *apartment*). Remind students that when we ask the question *What is ... like?*, we are asking for an opinion, eg *It's nice. It's great. It's OK.* Students work in pairs and discuss what their home is like and if their bedroom is different from the ones in the pictures. Listen to their ideas as a class.

1 2.25

- Play the CD. Students listen to the words and repeat them.
- Highlight the silent *p* in *cupboard* /ˈkʌbəd/.
- Elicit which things in the word pool students can see in the pictures.
- Check answers as a class. Make sure students understand all the words, eg *sink* (where you wash yourself or the dishes).

Language note

In compound nouns, the first word almost always carries the main stress, eg *wardrobe, cupboard, armchair.*

2

- Students categorise the words in exercise 1 by matching them with the rooms.
- They compare their answers in pairs.
- Check answers as a class.

3

- Students read the information about a competition to win your perfect bedroom and the definitions.
- They find the words which match the definitions.
- They compare answers in pairs.
- Check answers as a class.
- Check that they understand all the vocabulary, eg *a new look* (a completely new appearance), *worth £2,000* (with a value of £2,000) and point out that the plural of *shelf* is *shelves*.

4

- Students write a short paragraph (no more than 50 words) beginning *My perfect bedroom is ...*
- Encourage them to use some of the words from exercise 1.
- Students read out their paragraphs to the class.

EXPRESS YOURSELF

5

- Students work individually and write sentences saying where they do each activity using the names of rooms from exercise 2.
- Make sure they understand *chat* (to talk in a friendly way). If necessary, ask them to translate it into their language.

6

- Nominate two students to read aloud the example question and answer.
- Students work in pairs and ask and answer questions about where they do the activities in exercise 5.
- Listen to some pairs as a class.

Vocabulary extension: Workbook page 107

Reading

Text type: An online article

Lesson objectives

In this lesson students will:
- read an online article
- give their opinion about the house described in the article

Recommended web links

www.etnies.com/blog/2001/6/30/pas-house
www.skateboardingskateboards.com

Warmer

Write the words *living room* and *kitchen* on the board. Set a time limit of two minutes. Students work in pairs and write words for furniture you normally find in each room. The pair with the most correct words wins.

1
- Check the meaning of the words in the box.
- Check students understand *skateboarding* – use the pictures if necessary.
- Students work in pairs and decide which four words will be in the article.

2 

- Play the CD. Students listen and follow the article in their books.
- Students work individually and find the answers to the question in exercise 1.
- They compare answers in pairs.
- Check answers as a class.

Language note

Note that the letters *ch* in *architect* are pronounced as a /k/ sound /'ɑːkɪtekt/, while in *champion*, they are pronounced as a /ʧ/ sound /'ʧæmpɪən/.

Word check

Check the meaning of the new words.

Culture note

Focus students on the Did you know? information. Skateboarding was invented in California when bored surfers wanted something to do when the waves were flat. They attached roller-skate wheels to their surfboards.

3
- Check students understand the concept of the comparative. Give them an example from their own language but tell them that some comparatives are formed in a different way in English.
- Check the meaning of any unknown words (eg *expensive* – costing a lot of money).
- Students find the comparative form of the adjectives in the text and write them down.
- Check answers as a class.

4
- Students read the questions carefully first. Make sure they understand them.
- Students look for the answers in the article and comments.
- They compare their answers in pairs.
- Check answers as a class.

5
- Students work individually and say whether they would like to live in the PAS house or not.
- They write a comment to post on the website.
- They compare answers in pairs.
- Check answers as a class.

Finished?

Ask fast finishers to design a dream house. They draw pictures and write a short description in their notebooks.

Web quest

Students find articles, pictures and videos about the PAS house. Highlight the Web quest tip.

1 • Students write a list of keywords to search for information about the PAS house.

2 • Ask students to open an internet web browser such as Internet Explorer.
• Students open a search engine (eg Google) and type in their keywords.
• They find articles, pictures and videos.

3 • They list the URLs of their favourite websites and report back to the class.

THE PAS HOUSE

Imagine skateboarding all around the house – without getting in trouble! That's the case in this unusual house. You can skateboard across the floor and up the walls and on the ceiling. You can even skateboard over the table, the sofa and the fridge. It's better than going to a skate park!

For champion skateboarder Pierre André Senizergues, this dream is becoming a reality. Designer Gil Le Bon Delapointe and architect François Perrin are building his dream house in Malibu, California. This house is as big as a normal house, but its design is more unusual. There are three different 'spaces': one for the living room, dining room and kitchen; one for the bedroom and bathroom; and one for skateboard practice. There's all the usual furniture, but it's specially designed for skateboarding. And there are fabulous views over the ocean!

Is this your idea of a dream house? Tell us what you think!

Comments

James, 22nd May @ 19:46
It's fantastic! It's better than a skate park because you can practise indoors when it's raining! ☺

Hazel, 23rd May @ 14:22
It's interesting, but it isn't as cosy as my house. And I imagine it's more difficult to clean! ☺

Sonia, 23rd May @ 21:14
This house is cool! It's bigger than my apartment, but I'm sure it's more expensive too!

Word check
get in trouble view indoors cosy cool

DID YOU KNOW?
American surfers invented skateboarding in the 1950s.

Reading
An online article

1 **Check the meaning of the words in the box. Which four do you think are in the article?**

ceiling skate park windows champion architect garden

2  2.26 **Read and listen to the article and comments. Check your answers to exercise 1.**

3 **Read the article and the comments again. Then find the comparative form of the adjectives in the box.**

good unusual difficult big expensive

good – better

4 **Read the text again and answer the questions.**

1 Where is the PAS house?
2 Who is Pierre André Senizergues?
3 Is the furniture designed specially for the house?
4 Is the house near the sea?
5 Why does James like the house?
6 Does Hazel want to live in the PAS house?

5 **Would you like to live in this house? Why (not)? Write your comment.**

FINISHED?
In your notebook, design your dream house. Draw pictures and write a description.

Exercise 2
ceiling
skate park
champion
architect

Exercise 3
more unusual
more difficult
bigger
more expensive

Exercise 4
1 in Malibu, California
2 a champion skateboarder
3 yes
4 yes
5 Because you can practise indoors when it's raining.
6 no

WEB QUEST
Find articles, pictures and videos about the PAS house.
1 Write a list of keywords to search for information about the PAS house.
2 Look at different articles, pictures and videos. Choose your favourites.
3 Write the URLs of your favourite websites. Compare and share with your classmates.

Web Quest tip!
Remember to bookmark the websites you visit.

Grammar

Comparative adjectives

Exercise 1
1 smaller
2 more expensive
3 better

1 **Read the spelling rules in the Study guide on page 71. Then complete 1–3 in the table.**

short adjectives and adjectives ending in -y
It's **tidier** than my bedroom.
It's (1) ... (small) than my room.
long adjectives
It's **more unusual** than my house.
It's (2) ... (expensive) too.
irregular adjectives
good – **better** bad – **worse**
It's (3) ... (good) than a skate park!

Exercise 2
1 more expensive
2 richer
3 better / worse
4 faster
5 more difficult / easier

2 **Choose an adjective and complete the sentences with the correct comparative form.**

China is ... (big / small) than Spain.

China is bigger than Spain.

1 The royal palace is ... (cheap / expensive) than my house.
2 The king is ... (rich / poor) than me.
3 Real Madrid are ... (good / bad) than Real Betis.
4 Usain Bolt is ... (fast / slow) than me.
5 Japanese is ... (easy / difficult) than English.

3 **Look at pictures a) and b). Write comparative sentences with the adjectives in the box.**

big	small	colourful	tidy	clean	dirty

Rob's room is bigger than Kate's room.

Exercise 3
Possible answers
Kate's room is more colourful than Rob's room.
Kate's room is tidier than Rob's room.
Rob's room is bigger than Kate's room.
Kate's room is cleaner than Rob's room.
Rob's room is dirtier than Kate's room.

Prepositions of place

4 **Look at the prepositions in the box. How do you say them in your language?**

prepositions of place			
opposite	under	behind	on
in front of	in	between	next to

5 **Look at pictures a) and b) and choose the correct words.**

1 Kate's shelves are **between** / **opposite** the wardrobe and the bed.
2 Kate's bag is **in** / **on** the chair.
3 Kate's mirror is **behind** / **opposite** the bed.
4 Rob's rubbish bin is **next to** / **under** the desk.
5 Rob's chair is **in front of** / **behind** the desk.

Exercise 5
1 between
2 on
3 behind
4 under
5 in front of

EXPRESS YOURSELF

6 **Work in pairs. Ask and answer about these things in the pictures.**

Rob's sock / shorts / dog
Kate's dress / books / cat

Where's Rob's sock?
It's under the bed.

In English, comparatives are different when the adjectives are short, long or irregular. Are they the same or different in your language?

a) Rob's room

b) Kate's room

2.27–2.28 **Pronunciation lab: /ə/, page 125**

Grammar

Comparative adjectives

Lesson objectives

In this lesson students will:

- learn and use the different forms of comparative adjectives
- learn and use prepositions of place

Warmer

Write the word *adjective* on the board. Put students into pairs. Set a time limit of two minutes. Students write as many adjectives as they can. Check answers as a class. The pair with the most correct adjectives wins.

1
- Students read the comparative adjective spelling rules on page 71.
- They copy the table into their notebooks and complete 1–3 using the information in the Study guide.
- Check answers as a class.
- Highlight the two common irregular comparatives in English – *better* and *worse*.
- Highlight the double *g* in *bigger* and point out that all one-syllable adjectives ending in vowel + consonant double the final consonant, eg *hot – hotter, fat – fatter, thin – thinner.*

Language note

Long adjectives are those of three syllables or more but some two-syllable adjectives also form their comparatives with *more*, eg *stupid, modern, crowded*. Two-syllable adjectives ending in *-y* normally form their comparative with *-er*, eg *healthier, prettier*.

2
- Students complete the sentences individually.
- They compare their answers in pairs.
- Check answers as a class. (Note that students' answers to questions 3 and 5 may depend on which team they support and their nationality.)

3
- Explain the aim of the activity – to compare the two rooms using adjectives.
- Students look at the pictures and complete the exercise individually.
- They compare their answers in pairs.
- Check answers as a class.

Prepositions of place

4
- Demonstrate, using a book or similar, *on the table* and *under the table*.
- Students match the prepositions with the pictures.
- They compare their answers in pairs.
- Check answers as a class.
- Ask students to translate the prepositions into their language.

5
- Students choose the correct words according to the pictures.
- They compare their answers in pairs.
- Check answers as a class.

EXPRESS YOURSELF

6
- Nominate two students to read aloud the question and answer.
- Students work in pairs and make further questions and answers from the prompts about the things in the pictures.
- Listen to some pairs as a class.

Analyse

Ask students to read the information about comparatives in English and compare it with their own language. Ask if short and long adjectives are formed in the same way in their language and if the same adjectives are irregular.

Pronunciation lab: /ə/ in *-er* forms; page 125

Digital course: Interactive grammar table

Study guide: page 71

Vocabulary and Listening

Places to stay

Lesson objectives

In this lesson students will:
- learn some words for different places to stay
- listen for specific information

Warmer

Write on the board the names of some countries that are well-known holiday destinations, eg Italy, Turkey, Egypt, Switzerland, the USA, South Africa. Ask students to choose the best place for a holiday and the worst place for a holiday. Ask them to give reasons for their choice.

1 2.29
- Ask students to look at the web page.
- Students look at the words in blue.
- Play the CD. Students listen and repeat the words in blue.
- Make sure they pronounce all the words correctly, especially *caravan* /ˈkærəvæn/ and *hotel* /həʊˈtel/.

2
- Students read the definitions.
- They match the definitions with words in the web page.
- Check answers as a class.

3
- Students put the places to stay in order from 1 (favourite) to 12 (least favourite).
- They compare answers in pairs.
- Listen to their ideas as a class. Ask them to give reasons for their choice.

Culture note

Camping holidays are very popular in the UK. Some families have their own mobile home and drive in it to a campsite or they have their own caravan and drive with it to the campsite. Staying in tents in also popular but usually only in the summer!

4 2.30
- Write the question on the board.
- Tell students they will hear a family conversation and should listen only for where they are going on holiday.
- Play the CD. Students write the answer.
- Check the answer as a class.

5
- Students read the words in the box.
- Point out that students need to listen for the place each person wants to go.
- Play the CD again. Students write the answers.
- They compare their answers in pairs.
- Check answers as a class.

2.30 Audioscript, exercises 4 and 5

Dad Hey, Alice! Ben! Come here a minute! Mum and I are thinking about our summer holiday ...
Ben Yay!! Can we go to the USA?!
Dad Er, no ... We're definitely staying in Europe. Look – here are some possibilities ...
Alice Let's see.
Dad 'A luxury family tent in France' – see? I'd like to stay in a tent like this! They're more luxurious than our little tent!
Ben Yeah!
Dad There are beds in the tent! There's even a fridge and a cooker!
Mum Yes, but there isn't a bathroom in the tent!
Dad No, that's true.
Alice I'd prefer to stay in a villa in Spain. Look – the villa has got a swimming pool! And it's directly opposite the beach!
Mum This Spanish campsite is near the beach, too. Why don't we stay there in a mobile home? It's nicer than a tent – there's a bathroom with a toilet and a shower ...
Alice Yeah, definitely better ...
Dad Yes, but the mobile homes are more expensive than the tents.
Mum Hmm. That's true ... What do you think, Ben? What do you prefer?
Ben I'd love to stay at a hotel in Barcelona! It's more exciting to stay in the city. And if we stay in Barcelona ... we can go to the Nou Camp football stadium!
Dad Good idea! But we can't stay at a hotel or a villa – sorry! It's too expensive.
Mum Let's stay at a campsite near Barcelona then. In a mobile home?
Dad OK, in a mobile home.
Alice And we can still go to the beach?
Mum Yeah, definitely.
Ben And the Nou Camp stadium?
Dad Yes!

Vocabulary and Listening

Places to stay

1 2.29 **Look at the web page. Listen and repeat the words in blue.**

Home from home!

Book your holiday now!

QUICK SEARCH Country ... Type ... Arrive: Depart: Pets? Y N

Rent a **caravan** for 2–5 people.

A family **tent** in France.

A **mobile home** – more space for all the family!

Family rooms at a **youth hostel.**

Rent a **log cabin** in the forest.

Holiday on water in a beautiful old **barge.**

Stay in a remote **lighthouse!**

A luxurious Scottish **castle.**

Choose a **hotel.**

Rent a self-catering **apartment.**

A **villa** with a pool in Spain.

Stay on a **farm!**

Click on a picture to see more details and prices.

Exercise 2
1 barge
2 villa
3 castle
4 log cabin
5 tent

2 Find words on the web page that match definitions 1–5.

1 It's a type of boat.
2 This place has got a swimming pool.
3 Kings and queens lived here.
4 This place is made of wood.
5 This place hasn't got solid walls.

3 Work in pairs. Which places do you prefer? Put them in order from best to worst. Number 1 is the best.

1 castle, 2 ...

4 2.30 **Listen to a family conversation. Are they going on holiday to France, Spain or the USA?**

5 Listen again. Which place does each person prefer?

hotel tent villa mobile home

1 Dad ...
2 Mum ...
3 Alice ...
4 Ben ...

Exercise 4
Spain

Exercise 5
1 tent
2 mobile home
3 villa
4 hotel

Cultural awareness

Different lifestyles

Exercise 1
b

1 Read the text quickly. What is it about?

a) People who go on holiday to Ireland.
b) An ethnic minority group called 'Irish travellers'.

Fact box

The population of Ireland is about 4.5 million, but more than 80 million people around the world have got Irish origins!

2 2.31 Read and listen to the text. Do you agree with Paul, Beth or David?

Irish travellers

Irish travellers have their own culture and language. They're originally from Ireland, but now many Irish travellers live in other countries, including the UK and the USA. There are about 30,000 travellers in Ireland today.

Traditionally, Irish travellers lived in small, old-fashioned caravans and they travelled from place to place with horses. Now, about half live in bigger caravans or mobile homes and half live in houses or flats. They still travel sometimes to go to horse fairs and family weddings.

Irish travellers are an ethnic minority. They sometimes suffer discrimination from people who don't understand their culture.

What do you think? Could you live a nomadic life?

Paul, 13

Yes, definitely! There are too many rules in society. People always say 'you must do this' and 'you mustn't do that'. I think you can have more freedom with a nomadic life.

Beth, 12

No, I wouldn't be happy. You can't stay in one place so you have to go to lots of different schools and make new friends all the time.

David, 14

I'm not sure. I think we must respect people from different cultures and we mustn't discriminate against them. But I love my house! ☺

Word check

ethnic minority · discrimination · rule · freedom · nomadic · respect

Exercise 3
1 caravans
2 bigger
3 independent
4 better
5 house

3 Read the text again and choose the correct words.

1 About 50% of Irish travellers live in mobile homes or **caravans** / **tents**.
2 Modern caravans are **bigger** / **smaller** than old-fashioned caravans.
3 Paul thinks there are lots of rules in society and a nomadic life is more **independent** / **boring**.
4 Beth thinks it's **better** / **worse** to live in one place.
5 David would be happier in a **caravan** / **house**.

CULTURAL COMPARISON

4 Answer the questions.

1 Are there any travellers in your country?
2 Would it be easy or difficult to live a nomadic life in your country?
3 Would you like to live a nomadic life?
4 Do many people from your country / region now live in other countries? Where?

Cultural awareness

Different lifestyles

Lesson objectives

In this lesson students will:

- read a website about travellers in Ireland
- practise reading for gist and specific information
- talk about travellers in their country

Warmer

Write *Ireland* on the board. Focus on the Fact box and ask if any students have Irish origins. Students work in pairs and write down what they know about Ireland. Listen to their ideas a class. Write relevant points on the board, eg *They speak English there. It often rains*, etc.

1
- Students read the two questions first.
- They read the text quickly to get a general idea of the content and choose the correct answer.
- Check the answer as a class.

2 2.31
- Explain that students will hear and read a text from a website about Irish travellers' lifestyle followed by some comments.
- They should listen and say which person they agree with most.
- Play the CD. Students follow in their books.
- Listen to their ideas as a class and take students' cultural sensitivities into account.

Word check

Ask students to read the list of new words. Check they understand by asking them to say what these words are in their language. Note that in *ethnic minority*, the second word carries the stronger stress because it is an adjective + noun combination.

Culture note

The number of Irish travellers in the UK is not known. Estimates vary from as few as 15,000 to as many as 300,000. Some still live on caravan sites but many now live in houses or flats.

3
- Students read the sentences and the different possible answers.
- They read the text again and choose the correct words.
- They compare their answers in pairs or small groups.
- Check answers as a class.

CULTURAL  COMPARISON

4
- Students answer the questions individually.
- They compare their answers in pairs.
- Listen to their ideas as a class again taking students' cultural sensitivities into account.

Extra activity

Books closed. Students write down as many new words from the lesson as they can remember. They compare their lists in pairs. Listen to their answers as a class and make a list of the words on the board. Students copy the new words into their notebooks.

Culture video: Homes in the UK

Grammar 

can / can't and *must / mustn't*

Lesson objectives

In this lesson students will:

- learn and use *can* for possibility and (lack of) permission
- learn and use *must* for obligation and prohibition
- use *must* and *mustn't* to write about their English class

Warmer

Draw a circular red road sign on the board with a large letter P in the middle and a diagonal red line across it. Elicit that this means *No parking*. Ask students to work in pairs and think of similar signs they might see in the street or in buildings. Listen to their ideas as a class and write relevant suggestions on the board, eg *No smoking, No dogs, No entry,* etc.

1
- Students copy the tables into their notebooks.
- They answer questions a–b.
- Check answers as a class.
- Point out that *You mustn't do that* (prohibition) is stronger than *You can't do that* (lack of permission).

Language note

Must forms its negative by adding the short form *n't*. In formal written notices the full form of the negative is used, eg *You must not run on the escalators*. As *must* is a modal auxiliary verb, the auxiliary verb *do / does* is never used with *must*.

2
- Make sure students understand that there is a mistake in the underlined part of each of these sentences.
- They read the sentences and correct the mistakes. Tell them to refer to the tables if necessary.
- They compare answers in pairs.
- Check answers as a class.

3
- Tell students the text is about a village where there are no children.
- They read the text and choose the correct words.
- They compare answers in pairs.
- Check answers as a class.

4
- Students read the example sentence.
- They write sentences using *must* or *mustn't* and ideas 1–6.
- Check answers as a class. Make sure they understand *shout* (to speak in a very loud voice).

CLIL Grammar in context: Geography

5
- This activity practises the use of comparatives, *can* and *must*.
- Ask students to read the whole text carefully first.
- Do the first example with the whole class to demonstrate the activity and elicit the correct answer (*in*).
- Students work individually and choose the correct answer from the three possibilities.
- They compare answers in pairs.

6 2.32
- Play the CD. Students listen and check their answers to exercise 5.

CLIL task

Students look at the information about the three biggest cities in the world. They use the internet to find the information to make a similar table about the three biggest cities in Europe.

Pronunciation lab:
Contractions: *can't* and *mustn't*, page 125

Digital course: Interactive grammar table

Study guide: page 71

Grammar

can / can't and *must / mustn't*

Exercise 1
1 no
2 no

1 Look at the tables and answer questions a) and b).

***can / can't*:** **possibility and (lack of) permission**	
I / You / He / She / It / We / You / They	**can** move house. **can't** stay here.

***must / mustn't*:** **obligation and prohibition**	
I / You / He / She / It / We / You / They	**must** do this. **mustn't** do that.

a) Does the form of *can* and *must* change with the different subject pronouns?
b) Do we use *to* after *can* and *must*?

Exercise 2
1 must change
2 can't stay
3 mustn't discriminate
4 must respect

2 Correct the mistakes.

1 Travellers must to change schools. ✗
2 A traveller can't stays at the same school all the time. ✗
3 We don't must discriminate against ethnic minorities. ✗
4 We must respecting people of all cultures. ✗

Exercise 3
1 can
2 can't
3 mustn't
4 can't
5 can't

3 Read the text and choose the correct words.

Welcome to Firhall!

Firhall is an unusual village in Scotland. To live there, you must be older than 45. Children (1) **must / can** visit Firhall, but they (2) **can't / must** stay for more than three weeks. They (3) **mustn't / must** be noisy and they (4) **must / can't** play football in the street. Residents can have a cat or a dog, but they (5) **can't / must** have birds or rabbits. There are a lot of rules in Firhall!

EXPRESS YOURSELF

Exercise 4
Possible answers
1 We mustn't use our mobile phones.
2 We must listen to the teacher.
3 We mustn't shout in class.
4 We must do our homework.
5 We mustn't forget our books.
6 We must respect people.

4 Write about your English class. Use *must / mustn't* and ideas 1–6.

speak English *We must speak English.*

1 use our mobile phones
2 listen to the teacher
3 shout in class
4 do our homework
5 forget our books
6 respect people

CLIL Grammar in context: Geography

5 Read the text and choose the correct answers.

6 2.32 Listen and check your answers.

Exercise 5
1 in
2 Can you
3 bigger
4 do
5 easier
6 are
7 better
8 live
9 worse
10 breathe

Mega-cities

- The biggest mega-city* in the world is Tokyo, (1) **on / in / at** Japan. It's got a population of more than 34 million people. (2) **Can you / You can / You must** imagine? That's like the population of Portugal, Ireland and Greece combined!
- In 1800, the world's urban population was only 3% and the rural population was 97%. Now the urban population is (3) **big / bigger / small** than the rural population.
- Why (4) **do / does / are** people move from villages to mega-cities? They think it's (5) **more / easier / than** to find work. They (6) **is / am / are** looking for a (7) **worse / better / bad** life for their families, but often the opposite is true.
- In mega-cities, many poor people (8) **live / to live / not live** in unhealthy areas called slums. The sanitation is terrible and the pollution is much (9) **more bad / better / worse** than in rural areas. When the pollution is very bad, you can't (10) **breathe / to breathe / breathing** without a mask.

The world's biggest cities

City	Population
Tokyo (Japan)	34,300,000
Guangzhou (China)	25,200,000
Seoul (South Korea)	25,100,000

*A mega-city is a city with more than 10 million inhabitants.

CLIL TASK
Go online. Find out about the three biggest cities in Europe. Are they mega-cities? Make a table like the one above.

2.33–2.34 Pronunciation lab: Contractions: *can't* and *mustn't*, page 125

Getting around town

My friend Michael is moving house today. His new house is near Green Park. Have you ever moved house?

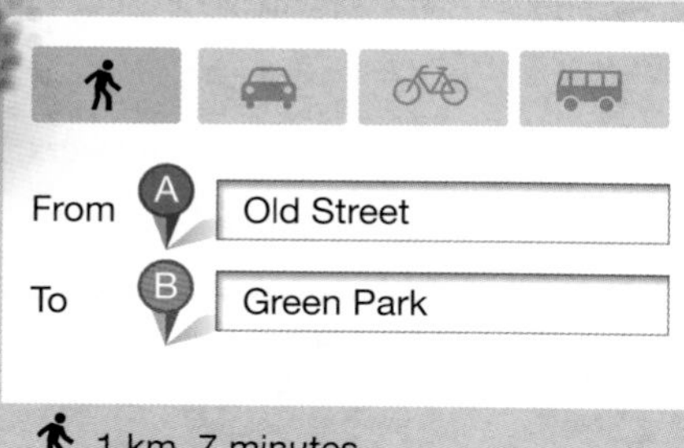

1 km 7 minutes

Walking directions

- Old Street
- Go straight along Old Street.
- Turn right onto Green Street.
- Turn left onto Castle Road.
- Your destination is on the right.
- Green Park

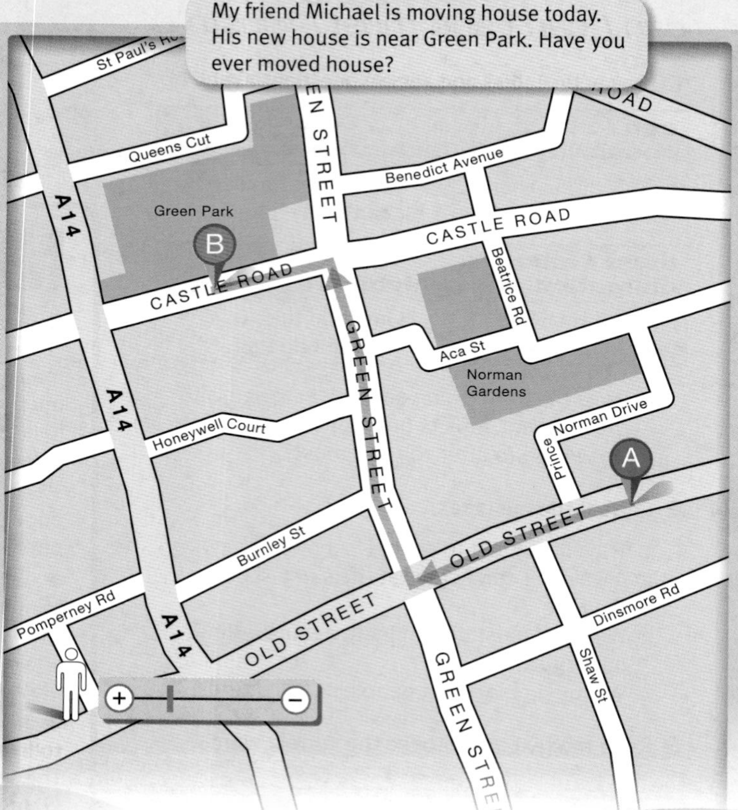

Step 1: Read

1 Look at the directions and the map. Then match 1–4 to symbols a–d.

1 turn left — a) ↱
2 turn right — b) ↰
3 go straight — c) ⊗
4 your destination — d) ↑

2 Read the directions again. Choose the correct answers.

1 The starting point is ...
a) Old Street. b) Castle Road.
2 The directions are for ...
a) going by car. b) walking.
3 The destination is ...
a) Green Street. b) Green Park.
4 It takes ... minutes.
a) five b) seven
5 It's about ... km.
a) 1 b) 7

Exercise 1
1 b
2 a
3 d
4 c

Exercise 2
1 a
2 b
3 b
4 b
5 a

Step 2: Listen

3 2.35 Copy the GPS instructions into your notebook. Then listen and number them in the order you hear them.

a) At the end of the road, turn right.
b) Depart.
c) After 300 metres, turn left.
d) Your destination is on the right.
e) Go straight along Magnolia Avenue.

4 Listen again. Are the sentences true or false? Correct the false sentences.

1 Michael's mum sets the GPS.
2 Their new house is at 25 Roman Street.
3 Their new house is in a different town.
4 The new house is bigger than the old house.

Exercise 3
1 b
2 a
3 e
4 c
5 d

Exercise 4
1 False Michael sets the GPS.
2 False Their new house is at 12 Roman Street.
3 False Their new house isn't in a different town. It's just round the corner.
4 True

Integrated skills

Getting around town

Lesson objectives

In this lesson students will:

- work on all four skills
- read a map
- listen to people asking for and giving directions
- write a personalized dialogue
- act out their dialogue

Warmer

Play a spelling game with words for places in town. Write on the board five or six words with the letters in the wrong order, eg *k a p r* (*park*), *r y b l a i r* (*library*), etc. Students work in pairs and write the words with the correct spelling. The first pair to write all the words correctly wins.

Step 1: Read

1
- Highlight James' speech bubble. Elicit answers to the question *Have you ever moved house?* from the class.
- Students match the directions with the symbols.
- They compare answers in pairs.
- Check answers as a class. Make sure students understand *destination* (the place you want to go to).

2
- Check that students understand the task.
- They read the directions and choose the correct answers.
- Check answers as a class.

Culture note

Miles are used for distance in both the UK and the USA. One mile is equivalent to approximately 1.6 km. 1 km is approximately 0.6 miles. The word *mile* comes from the Latin word for thousand as a mile was approximately one thousand steps in Roman times.

Step 2: Listen

3 2.35
- Make sure the students understand the task.
- They copy the GPS instructions into their notebooks.
- Play the CD. Students number the instructions 1–5 according to the order in which they hear them.
- Check answers as a class.

4
- Students read the sentences.
- Play the CD again. Students decide if the sentences are true or false and correct the false sentences.
- Check answers as a class.

Extra activity

Write these words and phrases on the board: *Off we go! Ready! Let's go! Here we are!* Play the CD again. Students raise their hands when they hear these words and phrases. Play the CD again, pausing after each of these words or phrases. Students repeat the words and phrases chorally and individually.

2.35 Audioscript, exercises 3 and 4

Mum OK, off we go! Can you set the GPS, Michael?
Michael OK – what's the name of the road?
Mum Roman Street, number 12.
Michael OK. Ready!
Mum Great – let's go!
Sat-nav Depart.
At the end of the road, turn right.
Go straight along Magnolia Avenue.
After 300 metres, turn left.
Your destination is on the right.
Mum Here we are!
Michael Great! It isn't very far!
Mum No, it's just round the corner. But this house is bigger – now you can have your own bedroom and you don't have to share with your brother!

Integrated skills - continued

Asking for and giving directions

5 2.36

- Students read the dialogue and the alternative answers.
- Play the CD. Students choose the correct answers.
- They compare answers in pairs.
- Check answers as a class.

6 2.36

- Play the CD again, pausing after each speaker's part for students to repeat as a class.
- Note the main stress and the falling tone in instructions, eg *Go straight on, then turn left*.
- Ask students to repeat the questions and responses several times both chorally and individually with the correct stress and intonation.
- Students practise the dialogue in pairs. Then swap roles and practise the dialogue again.

Step 3: Write

7

- Students choose one of the three places, *the park, the supermarket* or *the sports centre*.
- They write directions from their school to their chosen place.
- Check answers as a class.

8

- Students work individually and write their dialogue, using the dialogue in the book as a model and the Communication kit: Asking for and giving directions for key phrases.
- Monitor while they are writing and give help if necessary.

Step 4: Communicate

9

- Students practise their dialogues in pairs.
- For extra practice, they swap roles in both dialogues.

10

- Choose some pairs to act out their dialogue for the class.
- Students raise their hand if another pair has the same places and the same directions as they do. This will encourage them to listen carefully to their classmates.

Skills builder

Speaking: Being polite

Highlight that British people use *excuse me, please* and *thank you* a lot. It is important to use these words when you speak to someone you don't know because you will be considered impolite if you do not use them.

Integrated skills: Workbook page 116

Excuse me! Can you tell me how to get to Roman Street, please?	Roman Street? Let me think.
It's near (1) **Castle Park** / **the campsite**.	Ah, yes. I know where it is!
Which way is it?	Go straight on, then turn (2) **left** / **right**.
Straight on, then left?	Yes. Then cross the road and go past the park. Roman Street is on the (3) **left** / **right**.
OK. Is it far?	No – it's a (4) **five** / **ten** minute walk.
Thank you!	No problem. Bye!

Exercise 5
1 Castle Park
2 left
3 right
4 five

5  2.36 **Read and listen to the dialogue. Choose the correct answers for 1–4.**

6 Listen again and repeat. Practise your intonation.

Step 3: Write

7 Choose one of the places a–e. Then write directions from your school to the place.

a) the nearest café
b) the park
c) the supermarket
d) the sports centre
e) the library

8 Prepare a new dialogue. Write both parts. Use your notes from exercise 7 and the dialogue in exercise 5 to help you.

Excuse me! Can you tell me how to get to the nearest café, please?
The nearest café? Let me think.

Step 4: Communicate

9 Work in pairs. Take turns to practise your dialogues.

Excuse me! Can you tell me how to get to the nearest café, please?
The nearest café? Let me think.

10 Act your dialogue for the class.

SKILLS BUILDER

Speaking: Being polite
You must be polite when you speak to someone you don't know.
Remember to say *excuse me*, *please* and *thank you*!

COMMUNICATION KIT

Asking for and giving directions

Excuse me! Can you tell me how to get to ... , please?

Which way is it?	Go past ... .
Go straight on.	Is it far?
Turn left / right.	It's a five / ten minute walk.
Cross the road.	

Writing
An opinion essay

1 2.37 **Read and listen to the essay. Do you agree with Jane's opinion?**

IN YOUR OPINION, IS IT BETTER TO GO ON HOLIDAY TO A HOTEL OR ON A BARGE?

In my opinion, it's better to go on holiday on a barge. My family and I spend two weeks on a barge every summer. It's more interesting than staying in a hotel.

I like staying on a barge because you have more freedom - you can go wherever you want. I also like it because it's relaxing - you're always near the water.

Some people prefer hotels, but not me! I don't like staying in hotels because it's boring. It's more fun going on holiday on a barge.

By Jane, 13

2 **Look at the Writing focus. How do you say *because* in your language?**

Exercise 3

I don't like staying in hotels because it's boring.

WRITING FOCUS

because

We use *because* to give reasons.

*I like staying on a barge **because** you have more freedom.*

*I also like it **because** it's relaxing.*

3 **Read the essay again. Find one more example of *because*.**

4 **Match 1–4 with a–d. Then join the sentences with *because*.**

1 I like living in a city.
2 I prefer living in a village.
3 I'd like to live near the sea.
4 I can't live in a palace.

a) I love windsurfing.
b) There are more facilities.
c) It's very expensive!
d) It's quieter.

Exercise 4

1 b I like living in a city because there are more facilities.
2 d I prefer living in a village because it's quieter.
3 a I'd like to live near the sea because I love windsurfing.
4 c I can't live in a palace because it's very expensive!

Writing task

Write an essay with this title:
In your opinion, is it better to live in a city or a village?

Plan Decide which option you prefer. Then make notes.

I like ... because ...
I don't like ... because ...

Write Write three paragraphs using sentences 1–3. Use the essay in exercise 1 to help you.

1 In my opinion, it's better to ... .
2 I like ... because ... .
3 Some people prefer ... , but not me! I don't like ... .

Check Check your writing.

- ✔ using *because* to give reasons
- ✔ comparative adjectives
- ✔ vocabulary for places

Build your confidence: Writing reference and practice. Workbook page 130

Writing

An opinion essay

Lesson objectives

In this lesson students will:

- learn how to use *because* to give reasons
- write a short opinion essay

Warmer

Put students into pairs. Ask them to make a list of all the possible places to stay that they learnt earlier in this unit. Elicit their answers and write them on the board, eg *tent, caravan, castle, hotel*. This will prepare them for the next activity.

1 2.37

- Ask students to look at the pictures. Ask students what they show (people on holiday on barges).
- Play the CD. Students read the essay and listen.
- Ask if they agree with Jane's opinion or not. Ask why.

2
- Students read the Writing focus.
- Elicit the word or words for *because* in their language.

Language note

Because can be used at the beginning of a sentence (eg *Because I like swimming, I usually spend my holidays at the seaside*) but it is much more usual to place the *because* clause after the main clause (eg *I usually spend my holidays at the seaside because I like swimming*).

3
- Students find another example of *because* in the essay.
- They copy the sentence into their notebooks.
- Check the answer as a class.

Culture note

The United Kingdom has a huge network of canals that were built in the early days of the Industrial Revolution in the 18th century to transport raw materials and goods around the country. Canals were replaced by railways in the 19th century and were mostly disused for many years. Today canal boat holidays are extremely popular and many of the canals are in use again.

4
- Students match the statements 1–4 with the reasons a–d.
- They compare answers in pairs.
- Check answers as a class.

Writing task

The aim of this activity is for students to produce a piece of guided writing using *because* appropriately to give reasons. It also gives them practice in using comparative adjectives and vocabulary for places. Ask the students to follow the stages in the Student's Book. Monitor while they are writing and give help with vocabulary if necessary. At the Check stage, ask them to swap notebooks and check each other's writing.

Writing reference and practice: Workbook page 130

Study guide
Grammar, Vocabulary and Speaking

Tell the students the Study guide is an important page which provides a useful reference for the main language of the unit: the grammar, the vocabulary and the functional language from the Integrated skills pages. Explain that they should refer to this page when studying for a test or exam.

Grammar

- Tell the students to look at the example sentences of comparative adjectives and make sure they know how to form comparative adjectives correctly.
- Then tell students to look at the example sentences of *can* and *must*. Ensure they understand their meanings. Get students to translate into their own language if necessary.
- Refer students to the Grammar reference on pages 94–95 of the Workbook for further revision.

Vocabulary

- Tell students to look at the list of vocabulary and check understanding.
- Refer students to the Wordlist on page 151 of the Workbook where they can look up any words they can't remember.

Speaking

- Check that students understand the phrases to use for asking for and giving directions.
- Tell students to act out a conversation between someone asking for directions and the other person giving directions.

Additional material

Workbook

- Progress check page 54
- Self evaluation page 55
- Grammar reference and practice page 94
- Vocabulary extension page 107
- Integrated skills page 116
- Writing reference and task page 130

Teacher's Resource File

- Pulse Basics worksheets pages 35–40
- Vocabulary and grammar consolidation worksheets pages 23–26
- Translation and dictation worksheets pages 7, 17
- Evaluation rubrics pages 1–7
- Key competences worksheets pages 11–12
- Culture and CLIL worksheets pages 21–24
- Culture video worksheets pages 11–12
- Digital competence worksheets pages 11–12
- Macmillan Readers worksheets pages 3–4

Tests and Exams

- Unit 6 End-of-unit test: Basic, Standard and Extra
- CEFR Skills Exam Generator
- End-of-term test: Basic, Standard and Extra

Study guide

Grammar

Comparative adjectives

short adjectives and adjectives ending in *-y*
London is **smaller** than Tokyo. The city is **busier** than my home town.
long adjectives
Caravans are **more popular** than tents. Hotels are **more expensive** than youth hostels.
irregular adjectives
good – **better** bad – **worse** I think caravans are **better** than tents.

Prepositions of place

on
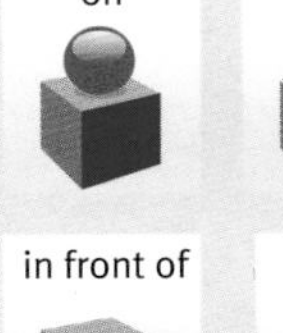

in

under

between

in front of

opposite

next to

behind

can / can't and *must / mustn't*

***can / can't*: possibility and (lack of) permission**	
I / You / He / She / It / We / You / They	**can** go on holiday. **can't** drive.
***must / mustn't*: obligation and prohibition**	
I / You / He / She / It / We / You / They	**must** listen to the teacher. **mustn't** skateboard inside.

Speaking

Asking for and giving directions

Excuse me! Can you tell me how to get to ... , please?

Which way is it? Go past ... .

Go straight on. Is it far?

Turn left / right. It's a five / ten minute walk.

Cross the road.

Comparative adjectives: spelling rules

- For short adjectives, add *-er*.

  small → smaller loud → louder

- For short adjectives that end in vowel + consonant, repeat the consonant and add *-er*.

  big → bigger hot → hotter

- For short adjectives that end in *-y*, remove the *-y* and add *-ier*.

  busy → busier tidy → tidier

- For long adjectives, do not change the word. Add *more* before the word.

  unusual → more unusual

  organized → more organized

- Some adjectives are irregular. They don't follow the rules!

  good → better bad → worse

Vocabulary

At home

armchair
bath
bed
chair
cooker
cupboard
desk
fridge
lamp
mirror
shelf
sink
sofa
table
toilet
wardrobe

Places to stay

apartment
barge
caravan
castle
farm
hotel
lighthouse
log cabin
mobile home
tent
villa
youth hostel

LEARNING TO LEARN

Label objects in your home. If you see the words every day, it's easier to remember them.

Progress check: Workbook page 54

Grammar reference: Workbook page 94

COLLABORATIVE PROJECT 

Step 1: Think — Step 2: Listen and plan — Step 3: Create — Step 4: Evaluate

Making a leaflet

TASK

Work in groups of four to create a leaflet about your town.

DIGITAL LITERACY

When you write a leaflet, remember to:

- include images to make your leaflet look attractive.
- use different fonts and colours.
- look up words in an online dictionary.

Step 1: Think

Exercise 1
adverts
activities for children

1 **Read the leaflet below. Use a dictionary to check the meaning of the words in the box. Which information is not included in the leaflet?**

opening times · adverts · places to visit · sports and leisure facilities · activities for children · restaurants · markets · a description of the town

All about Brighton

Brighton is a city on the south coast of England. Is has got wonderful beaches and lots of places to visit.

Famous local landmarks include the Royal Pavilion (a 19th century palace) and the pier. Other sights include Brighton Museum and Art Gallery and Queen's Park. The oldest aquarium in the world is also in Brighton. To find out more about places to visit, see page 2.

There is lots to do at night. Brighton has got about 400 restaurants – more than any other city outside London (see page 3)! The town is famous for musicians such as The Kooks, and there are a lot of live music events.

Brighton also has a famous festival in May – it's the second biggest in the UK. Go to their website: brightonfestival.org

Are you a sports fan? Brighton's got two football stadiums, a skate park and lots of swimming pools, gyms and sports centres (see page 4).

Come to Brighton! There's something for everyone!

Contents

Collaborative project 2

Making a leaflet

Lesson objectives

In this lesson students will:

- create a leaflet in groups about their town
- identify features of a leaflet
- listen to a group planning a leaflet
- read and complete a dialogue extract

Warmer

Play an alphabet game to revise places in a town. Write the letter *a* on the board and elicit a place in a town beginning with this letter e.g. *aquarium*, *art gallery* etc. In teams, ask students to write as many places in town as they can for each letter of the alphabet. Give students a time limit. The team with the most words for each letter comes to the board and writes the words. The other students say if they agree and if the spelling is correct. Give two points for each correct word with correct spelling and one point for a correct word with incorrect spelling. The team with the most points wins.

TASK

Read the task with the class and check students understand. NOTE: If students do not have access to computers, they can create the leaflet by hand.

Step 1: Think

1
- Discuss leaflets with the class. Have they read any? Have they ever made one? What kind of things do people write brochures about?
- Encourage students to use dictionaries to check the meaning of the words in the box.
- Check students understand that *leisure facilities* are places such as sports centres, gyms, cinemas, bowling alleys, etc and that *markets* are public places for selling things and are often not permanent.
- Students read the leaflet and choose which information is not mentioned.
- Check answers as a class.
- Read the Digital literacy box with the class and check students understand.

Step 2: Listen and plan

2 2.38

- Ask students to read the questions carefully.
- Play the CD. Students listen and answer the questions.
- Check answers as a class.

3
- Read the Useful language box with the class and help with any vocabulary.
- Students read the conversation extract and complete it in pairs.
- Play the CD again. Students listen and check their answers.
- Check answers as a class. Students practise the conversation in groups.

4
- Explain to the class that they are going to plan a leaflet in groups.
- Ask students to read the list of things they need to do to plan their leaflets.
- Students work in groups of four and plan their leaflets. Ask one or two groups to report back to the class to explain their plans.

Step 3: Create

5
- Read the steps with the class to give students a clear idea of what they have to do.
- Monitor while they are writing and give help if necessary.

Share information

Students share their information in groups. They discuss their work and how to improve it. They check for errors and try to make the vocabulary as interesting as possible.

Create the leaflet

Each group creates their leaflet. They decide what to include and what order to put the information in. Then they find pictures and organize the layout. Finally they check their work carefully before printing the finalized leaflets out.

Show and tell

Each group shows their leaflet and tells the class about it. Allow time for the other students to read the leaflets and comment on them. If you like, the class can vote for their favourite leaflet.

Step 4: Evaluate

6
- Look at the evaluation grids with the class.
- Read through the different options and help with any vocabulary as necessary.
- Students complete their self-evaluation. Give help if necessary.

Extra activity

Students work in teams to write a quiz about one of the leaflets. Collect in their questions. Ask the whole class the questions or give them out to another team to answer.

2.38 Audioscript, exercises 2 and 3

David OK, so our leaflet has got a description of our town, information about places to visit and things for teenagers to do. Let's put the description on the first page. We can start now.
Ana Wait a minute, David. We need to finish planning! Let's include information about shopping too.
Mario Shopping? I don't agree at all! I think shopping is really boring!
Ana Maybe you don't like shopping, Mario, but I think it's interesting for visitors. We can put information about the local markets.
Silvia I agree with Ana. It's a great idea.
Mario OK, let's include shopping. What about sport? What's the word for places like sports centres, gyms and swimming pools?
David Look it up in the dictionary!
Mario It's 'leisure facilities'. OK, let's have a page on leisure facilities.
Silvia Good idea! Now let's plan who is writing about each thing.
Ana Silvia and I can write about shopping and activities for teenagers.
David Who wants to write about places to visit?
Mario I can write about places to visit. Let's all find information for the description.
Ana OK, let's write about each thing and then decide on the order. We can …

Step 2: Listen and plan

Exercise 2
1 b
2 b
3 b
4 a
5 a

2 2.38 **Listen to Mario, Ana, Silvia and David doing the task and answer the questions.**

1 David wants to ... the leaflet.
a) finish planning **b)** start writing

2 Mario thinks including information about shopping is ...
a) a good idea. **b)** boring.

3 When there is a word they don't know, they ...
a) ask the teacher. **b)** use a dictionary.

4 Silvia wants to decide who is writing ...
a) each part of the brochure.
b) about shopping.

5 ... finding information for the description.
a) They are all **b)** Only Mario is

Exercise 3
1 has got
2 Wait
3 agree
4 think
5 with
6 for
7 up
8 about

3 Complete the conversation extract with the words in the box. Listen again and check your answers.

for think up has got agree with Wait about

David: OK, so our leaflet (1) ... a description of our town, information about places to visit and things for teenagers to do. Let's put the description on the first page. We can start now.
Ana: (2) ... a minute, David. We need to finish planning! Let's include information about shopping too.
Mario: Shopping? I don't (3) ... at all! I think shopping is really boring!
Ana: Maybe you don't like shopping, Mario, but I (4) ... it's interesting for visitors. We can add information about the local markets.
Silvia: I agree (5) ... Ana. It's a great idea.
Mario: OK, let's include shopping. What about sport? What's the word (6) ... places like sports centres, gyms and swimming pools?
David: Look it (7) ... in the dictionary!
Mario: It's ... 'leisure facilities'. OK, let's have a page on leisure facilities.
Silvia: Good idea! Now let's plan who is writing (8) ... each thing.

4 Work in groups. Plan your leaflet. Use the Useful language box to help you.

- Decide which things you want to include.
- Decide who is writing about each thing.
- Find the words you need.
- Decide when to meet again to look at each other's work.

Step 3: Create

5 Follow the steps to create your leaflet.

Share information
Read or listen to each other's work. Discuss your work. Check these things:

- What can you improve?
- Are the sentences clear?
- Is the vocabulary interesting?
- Can you use a wider variety of words?
- Are there any mistakes?

Create the leaflet
Decide what order the information should go in. Find photos and pictures and organize the layout. Check the grammar, vocabulary, spelling and punctuation.

Show and tell
Show the rest of the class your leaflet.

Step 4: Evaluate

6 Now ask your teacher for the group and individual assessment grids. Then complete the grids.

USEFUL LANGUAGE
Our leaflet has got a description.
What about sport?
Who wants to write about sport?
Wait a minute!
What's the word for ...?
Look it up in the dictionary!
I think it's a great idea/really boring.
We need to do the research first.
Let's find information about restaurants.

UNIT 7

FUN AND GAMES

Unit objectives and key competences

In this unit the student will learn…

- understand, memorize and correctly use words related to computer games **CLC DC**
- understand, memorize and correctly use words for different TV programmes **CLC SCC CAE**
- understand and correctly use grammar structures related to the past and draw parallels to L1 **CLC L2L**
- about the history of cartoons **CLC CAE**
- about TV technology **CLC CMST CAE**
- about soap operas in the UK by watching a short video **CLC SCC CAE**

In this unit the student will learn how to ...

- identify specific information in an exhibition guide **CLC DC CAE**
- look for information about computer games **CLC DC CIE**
- identify specific information in a conversation about TV programmes **CLC SCC CAE**
- speak about their favourite computer games **CLC DC SCC**
- write a review of a TV programme **CLC SCC CAE**
- read a game FAQs, listen to a conversation about a game and explain the rules of a game **CLC SCC**
- prepare for an exam role-play activity **CLC L2L**

Linguistic contents

Main vocabulary

- Computer games: *strategy, puzzle, trivia,* etc
- TV programmes: *documentary, cartoon, soap opera,* etc

Grammar

- Past simple: *was / were*
- Past simple affirmative of regular verbs

Functional language

- Explaining the rules of a game
- Phrases for making and responding to suggestions in a speaking exam

Pronunciation

- *was / were*
- Past simple endings

Skills

Reading

- Read an exhibition guide about computer games
- Read a text about the history of cartoons
- Read instructions for playing a computer game

Writing: Interaction and production

- Write a personalized dialogue
- Write a review of a TV programme in three steps: plan, write, check

Listening

- Listen to a conversation about television programmes
- Listen to people explaining the rules of a game

Spoken interaction

- Exchange information about favourite computer games
- Ask and answer questions about events in the past using *was* and *were*

Spoken production

- Prepare and act out a dialogue explaining the rules of a game
- Prepare and do a role-play activity in a speaking exam

Lifelong learning skills

Self-study and self-evaluation

- Study guide: Student's Book page 83
- Progress check and self-evaluation: Workbook pages 62–63
- Grammar reference and practice: Workbook pages 96–97
- Wordlist: Workbook pages 151–157

Learning strategies and thinking skills

- Using pictures and titles to predict the content of a text

Cultural awareness

- Animated TV in the USA
- Comparing animated cartoons from the USA with animated cartoons from students' own countries

Cross-curricular contents

- ICT: searching the internet for information
- Technology: televisions
- Language and literature: conventions for writing a review

Key competences

CLC	Competence in linguistic communication
CMST	Competence in mathematics, science and technology
DC	Digital competence
L2L	Learning to learn
SCC	Social and civic competences
SIE	Sense of initiative and entrepreneurship
CAE	Cultural awareness and expression

Evaluation

- Unit 7 End-of-unit test: Basic, Standard and Extra
- CEFR Skills Exam Generator

External exam trainer

- Speaking: Everyday interaction

Digital material

Pulse Live! Digital Course including:

- Interactive grammar tables
- Audio visual speaking model: Explaining the rules of a game
- Audio visual cultural material: Soap operas in the UK

Student's website

Digital competence

- Web quest: The development of a computer game
- Digital competence worksheet: Timelines

Reinforcement material

- Basics worksheets, Teacher's Resource File pages 41–46
- Vocabulary and Grammar: Consolidation worksheets, Teacher's Resource File pages 27–28

Extension material

- Fast-finisher activity: Student's Book page 75
- Extra activities: Teacher's Book page T78
- Vocabulary and Grammar: Extension worksheets, Teacher's Resource File pages 29–30

Teacher's Resource File

- Translation and dictation worksheets pages 8, 18
- Evaluation rubrics pages 1–7
- Key competences worksheets pages 13–14
- Culture and CLIL worksheets pages 25–28
- Culture video worksheets pages 13–14
- Digital competence worksheets pages 13–14
- Macmillan Readers worksheets pages 5–6

THINK ABOUT IT

What do you do for fun? Think about ...

games friends TV hobbies sport

Vocabulary and Speaking

Computer games

1 3.02 Listen and repeat the words in blue. Do you like computer games? What types do you play?

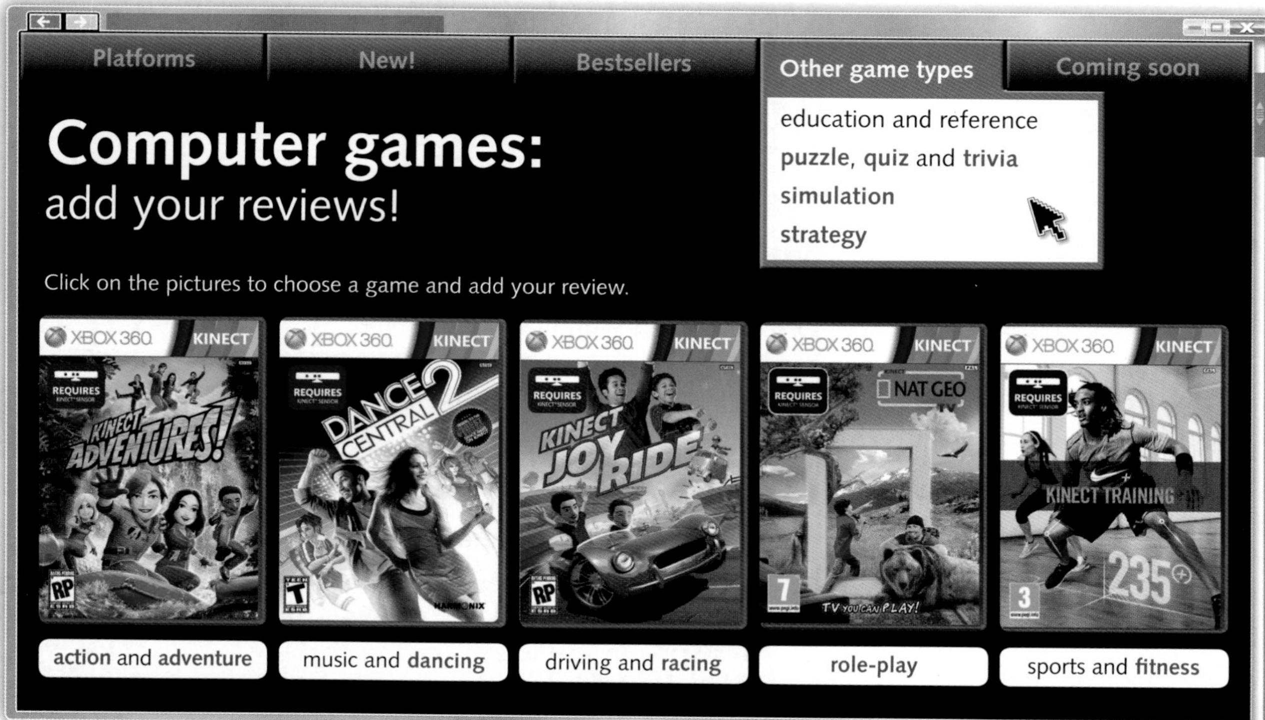

2 Work in pairs. Write examples of the types of computer games in exercise 1.

action and adventure – Prince of Persia, Sorcery, ...

LOOK!

fun* and *funny

It's fun = I enjoy it.

It's funny = It makes me laugh.

3 Check the meaning of the adjectives in the box. Then match the opposites.

easy funny slow difficult serious exciting fast boring

easy ≠ difficult

Exercise 3

funny ≠ serious
slow ≠ fast
exciting ≠ boring

EXPRESS YOURSELF

4 Complete the sentences. Use adjectives from exercise 3 or your own ideas.

1 My favourite game is ... . It's ... .

2 I don't like playing ... games. They're ... .

5 Work in pairs. Compare your choices.

My favourite game is Pro Evolution Soccer. It's fun!

Really? I prefer racing games. They're more exciting.

Do you like playing strategy games?

Yes – I think they're ...

Vocabulary extension: Workbook page 108

Vocabulary and Speaking

Computer games

Lesson objectives

In this lesson students will:

- learn vocabulary associated with computer games
- learn a set of adjectives
- compare choices

Warmer

Do a class survey. Write on the board *How often do you play computer games?* and *How many hours a week do you play computer games?* Students ask and answer the questions in pairs or small groups. Listen to their answers as a class. Find out which students play computer games the most and which the least.

Think about it

Write the word *fun* on the board. Ask students to look at the five categories. They work in pairs and tell their partner what they do for fun. Listen to their ideas as a class.

1 

- Play the CD. Students listen to the words in blue and repeat them.
- Highlight the pronunciation of *quiz* /kwɪz/.
- Ask students if they like computer games and which types of computer games they play.
- Listen to their answers as a class.

Language note

Remind students that in compound nouns, the first word almost always carries the main stress, eg *role-play*.

2
- Demonstrate the activity by highlighting the examples (Prince of Persia, Sorcery) and eliciting one or two further examples.
- Students work individually and write the names of games in the other categories.
- They compare their ideas in pairs.
- Listen to their ideas as a class. Write the names of the games on the board as these will be useful for exercise 4.

Look!

Elicit examples of things that are *fun* (eg going to parties, dancing at discos, meeting your friends) and things that are *funny* (jokes, comedy programmes on TV, comic films).

3
- Check the meaning of the adjectives by asking students to translate them into their language.
- Students work individually and match the adjectives with their opposites.
- They compare their answers in pairs.
- Check answers as a class.

Finished?

Ask fast finishers to write further examples of pairs of opposites (eg *good* ≠ *bad*, *big* ≠ *small*).

4
- Students work individually and complete the sentences using the adjectives from exercise 3 and the games / types of games from exercise 2 or their own ideas.
- Give help with further adjectives to describe the games if necessary (eg *scary, amazing, terrible*).

5
- Nominate two students to read aloud the example conversation.
- Students work in pairs and compare the games they wrote about in exercise 4 or their views on computer games.
- Listen to some pairs as a class.

Vocabulary extension: Workbook page 108

Reading

Text type: An exhibition guide

Lesson objectives

In this lesson students will:
- read an exhibition guide
- say which computer games were popular when they were younger and which are popular now

Recommended web links

www.computerhistory.org

Warmer

Write the word *computer* on the board. Ask students to work in pairs and write words associated with the word *computer*. Set a time limit of two minutes. Listen to their ideas and write correct examples on the board, eg *home computer, laptop, computer game, computer program, printer, mouse*, etc.

1 3.03
- Students look at the words in the box.
- Students read the exhibition guide. Ask them to guess the answers to gaps 1–4.
- Play the CD. Students follow the text in their books and check the answers.
- Check answers as a class.

Word check

Check students understand all the new words.

Culture note

Focus students on the Did you know? box. William Higinbotham was an American physicist. His video game Tennis for Two was a forerunner of Pong, a two-dimensional table-tennis game created by Atari in 1972.

2
- Read aloud to the class the example definition and word.
- Students read the four definitions.
- They work individually to find the words.
- They compare answers in pairs.
- Check answers as a class.

3
- Students read the questions and possible answers carefully first. Make sure they understand all the questions.
- They look for the answers in the exhibition guide.
- They compare their answers in pairs.
- Check answers as a class.

4
- Students work in pairs and answer the questions.
- Listen to their ideas as a class.

Finished?

Ask fast finishers to make a list of the advantages and disadvantages of computer games. Monitor while they are writing and give help if necessary.

Web quest

Students research the history and development of a computer game. Highlight the Web quest tip.

1 • Students work in pairs and choose a computer game to research.

2 • Ask students to open an internet web browser such as Internet Explorer. They open a search engine (eg Google) and type in the name of their game.
• They find as much information as they can about the history and development of their game, eg who designed it and when, etc.

3 • Pairs report back to the class.

Reading

An exhibition guide

xercise 1
Tetris
Sega Rally
Tomb Raider
Wii Sports

xercise 2
graphics
sound effects
smartphone
decade

xercise 3
b
a
a
b

1 3.03 **What do you know about the history of computer games? Complete the guide with the words in the box. Then listen and check.**

Tetris®	Sega® Rally
Wii™ Sports	Tomb Raider™

2 Find words in the exhibition guide that mean ...

games hardware *console*

1 the images on the screen
2 the noises and music in a game
3 a modern mobile telephone
4 a period of ten years

3 Read the guide again and choose the correct answers.

1 Were there home computers in the 1970s?
a) Yes, there were.
b) No, there weren't.
2 Was Tetris® popular in the 1980s?
a) Yes, it was.
b) No, it wasn't.
3 Were racing and adventure games popular in the 1990s?
a) Yes, they were.
b) No, they weren't.
4 Were there karaoke games in 1980?
a) Yes, there were.
b) No, there weren't.

4 Work in pairs. Ask and answer the questions.

1 Which computer games were popular when you were younger?
2 Which games are popular now? Why?

FINISHED?

In your opinion, what are the advantages and disadvantages of computer games? Write a list.

+ *They're fun!* - *You stay indoors.*

GAME STORY

THE HISTORY OF COMPUTER GAMES

Welcome to the exhibition. Enjoy playing the games!

1970s In the 1970s there weren't any home computers. People played arcade games like Pong. When Atari® invented the first home console, people loved it! It was big, the graphics were basic and the sound effects weren't realistic, but the games Space Invaders™ and PacMan™ were very popular.

1980s In the 1980s, games were more expensive than today. Nintendo® invented the first mini-console, and its Mario games were best-sellers. Fantasy and role-play games and the puzzle game (1) ... were all popular too.

1990s During the 1990s there were important technological developments, such as 3D animation and better sound effects. With consoles like Sony PlayStation®, games were more realistic. Racing games like (2) ... and adventure games like (3) ... were popular.

2000 After 2000, computer games were more sociable. They were fun for all the family: there were karaoke games, dance mats and even memory games. In 2006, Nintendo invented (4) ... .

2010 In the past, people usually played computer games at home because there weren't any smartphones or tablet computers. Today we can play computer games anywhere. Games are developing all the time – what will they be like in the next decade?

Word check

arcade game graphics sound effect development dance mat

DID YOU KNOW?

William Higinbotham created the first video game in 1958. It was called Tennis for Two.

WEB QUEST

Go online. Research the history and development of a computer game.

1 **Decision-making:** in pairs, choose a game.
2 **Collaboration:** work together to find out about the history and development of the game.
3 Share your knowledge with the rest of the class.

Web Quest tip!

Don't get distracted when you use the internet. Remember the aims of your research!

Grammar

was / were

Exercise 1
1 were
2 wasn't
3 Was
4 weren't

1 Copy and complete the tables with *was*, *were*, *wasn't* or *weren't*.

affirmative and negative
I **was** / **wasn't** happy.
You (1) ... / **weren't** happy.
He / She / It **was** / (2) ... popular.
We / You / They **were** / **weren't** popular.

questions and short answers	
Was I happy?	Yes, I **was**. No, I **wasn't**.
Were you happy?	Yes, you **were**. No, you **weren't**.
(3) ... he / she / it popular?	Yes, he / she / it **was**. No, he / she / it **wasn't**.
Were we / you / they popular?	Yes, we / you / they **were**. No, we / you / they (4) ... .

Exercise 2
1 The Pokémon game wasn't Spanish. It was Japanese.
2 In 1980, home consoles weren't cheap. They were expensive.
3 The Tetris game wasn't American. It was Russian.
4 The Atari graphics weren't sophisticated. They were basic.
5 Sega Rally wasn't a quiz game. It was a racing game.

2 Write affirmative and negative sentences. Use *was* / *wasn't* or *were* / *weren't*.

Pokémon characters (people / creatures)
The Pokémon characters weren't people. They were creatures.

1 The Pokémon® game (Spanish / Japanese)
2 In 1980, home consoles (cheap / expensive)
3 The Tetris® game (American / Russian)
4 The Atari® graphics (sophisticated / basic)
5 Sega® Rally (quiz game / racing game)

EXPRESS YOURSELF

Exercise 3
1 were
2 was
3 was
4 were
5 were

3 Complete the questions with *was* or *were*.

1 Where ... you born?
2 Who ... your first teacher?
3 When ... your last birthday?
4 What ... your favourite subjects last year?
5 Where ... you at 8 o'clock this morning?

4 Work in pairs. Ask and answer the questions in exercise 3.

ANALYSE

How many different ways are there to say *was* and *were* in your language?

there was / there were

5 Look at the tables and translate sentences a) and b). Are the singular and plural forms the same or different in your language?

affirmative and negative
a) **There was** a TV in my grandad's house, but **there wasn't** a computer.
b) **There were** game consoles in the 1980s, but **there weren't** smartphones.

questions and short answers	
Was there a computer at your grandad's school?	Yes, **there was**. No, **there wasn't**.
Were there tablet computers in the 1990s?	Yes, **there were**. No, **there weren't**.

Exercise 6
2 there weren't
3 there were
4 There weren't
5 There wasn't
6 there wasn't
7 there were

6 Complete the text with *there was* / *there were* or *there wasn't* / *there weren't*.

Victorian toys and games

Last weekend I was at the Museum of Childhood in London. (1) *There was* an exhibition about Victorian toys and games. In 1900 (2) ... any computer games, but (3) ... games like chess and cards. (4) ... any plastic toys, but there were wooden trains and porcelain dolls. (5) ... a garden in many Victorian houses, so children often played in the street. And (6) ... much space in the house, because (7) ... a lot of children in each family – sometimes 10 or 12!

Exercise 7
1 Were there; No, there weren't.
2 Were there; Yes, there were.
3 Was there; No, there wasn't.
4 Was there; No, there wasn't.
5 Were there; Yes, there were.

7 Copy and complete the questions with *Was there* or *Were there*. Then write short answers. Use the information in exercise 6.

Was there an exhibition about Victorian toys and games? *Yes, there was.*

1 ... computer games in 1900?
2 ... games like chess and cards?
3 ... a garden in all Victorian houses?
4 ... much space in the house?
5 ... a lot of children in each family?

3.04 Pronunciation lab: *was* and *were*, page 125

Digital course: Interactive grammar table

Study guide: page 83

Grammar 

was / were

Lesson objectives

In this lesson students will:

- learn and use the past simple form of *be*
- learn and use *there was / there were*

Warmer

Quickly revise the verb *be* in the present simple. Write a table on the board with the headings *affirmative* and *negative* and the subject pronouns *I, we/you/they* and *he/she/it*. Elicit the affirmative and negative short and full forms for each pronoun and complete the table.

	affirmative	negative
I	*'m / am*	*'m not / am not*
we / you / they	*'re / are*	*aren't / are not*
he / she / it	*'s / is*	*isn't / is not*

1
- Tell students the aim of the activity is to learn the past simple form of *be*.
- They copy the tables into their notebooks and complete gaps 1–4 using *was, were, wasn't* or *weren't*.
- Check answers as a class.

2
- Read the example sentences aloud to the class.
- Students complete the exercise individually.
- They compare their answers in pairs.
- Check answers as a class. Note the stress of *sophisticated* /sə'fɪstɪkeɪtɪd/.

EXPRESS YOURSELF

3
- Students complete the sentences individually using *was* or *were*.
- They compare their answers in pairs.
- Check answers as a class. Highlight that we say *Where / When were you born?* and answer *I was born in ...*

4
- Students work individually and write their answers to the questions in exercise 3.
- They work in pairs and ask and answer the questions.
- Listen to some pairs as a class.

Analyse

Ask students to look at the different ways of saying *was* and *were* in their language.

there was / there were

5
- Students look at the tables and translate sentences a–b into their language.
- Check answers as a class.
- Highlight the difference between *there was / there were* in their language and in English.
- Remind students that English has two words for *there was* and *there were* and that *there was* is used for the singular and *there were* for the plural.
- Students copy the tables into their notebooks.

6
- Students read the text carefully first.
- They fill the gaps using *there was / there were* or *there wasn't / there weren't.*
- They compare their answers in pairs.
- Check answers as a class.

Culture note

The Victoria and Albert Museum of Childhood in London was first designated as a specialist childhood museum in 1974. It is situated in a building that has been a museum since 1872. It displays artefacts associated with childhood (eg toys) dating from the 17th century to the present day. More than 400,000 people visit the museum each year.

7
- Read the example question and short answer aloud to the class.
- Do the first question and short answer with the whole class as an example.
- Students work individually and write the remaining questions and short answers.
- They compare their answers in pairs.
- Check answers as a class.

Pronunciation lab: *was* and *were*, page 125

Digital course: Interactive grammar table

Study guide: page 83

Vocabulary and Listening

TV programmes

Lesson objectives

In this lesson students will:

- learn some words for different types of TV programmes
- listen for specific information

Warmer

Write these two questions on the board: *How often do you watch television? What is your favourite programme?* Students work in pairs and ask and answer the questions. Listen to their ideas as a class.

1 3.05
- Play the CD. Students listen and repeat the words.
- They say which TV programmes they can see in the pictures in the TV guide.

2
- Students find one example of each of the six types of programmes in the TV guide.
- They compare answers in pairs.
- Check answers as a class.

3
- Complete the first two sentences yourself as an example, eg *I often watch documentaries. Last night I watched a film.*
- Students complete the sentences with information that is true for them using the words from exercise 1.
- They compare answers in pairs.
- Listen to their ideas as a class.

4 3.06
- Students look at the TV guide again and read the two gapped sentences carefully.
- Elicit that they need to listen for the type of programme, the number of the channel and the time.
- Play the CD. Students complete the sentences.
- They compare their answers in pairs.
- Check answers as a class.

5
- Students read the sentences and the alternative answers carefully first.
- Play the CD again. Students choose the correct answers.
- They compare answers in pairs.
- Check answers as a class.

Extra activity

Write the beginnings of the first two lines from the audioscript on the board. Dictate the first six lines of the dialogue to the class. Students write them in their notebooks. Students work in pairs, one taking the part of Hazel and the other the part of James. Play the CD again. Students read aloud in time with the recording. Swap roles and repeat the activity.

3.06 Audioscript, exercises 4 and 5

Hazel Hey James, how's it going?
James Everything's fine, thanks. How are you?
Hazel Great thanks! I'm just waiting for the bus ...
James Yeah, me too. Are you going home?
Hazel No, I'm going to my friend's house.
James Ah, right. I'm going home. It's my sister's birthday so we're having a special meal.
Hazel Yeah? Hey – did you watch *Life in the Wild* yesterday?
James *Life in the Wild*? No, I didn't. What time was it on?
Hazel About 5 o'clock, I think. On Channel 1.
James No ... What was it about?
Hazel It was a documentary about penguins in the Antarctic.
James Penguins? Was it any good?
Hazel Yeah, it was fantastic! Really interesting. It was about an expedition to study the penguins there. There were hundreds of penguins! It was so cold, but there were all these little baby penguins – they were so cute!
James That sounds nice. Well, I watched a film called *New Dawn.*
Hazel *New Dawn*? What was that like?
James It was terrible! The story was rubbish! It was really long and there were so many adverts ...
Hazel Were there any famous actors in it?
James No, I don't think so. I can't remember their names ...
Hazel Was it exciting?
James No, it wasn't – not at all! And the special effects were terrible!
Hazel Oh dear. Anyway – here's my bus. See you tomorrow!
James Yeah. See you later.
Hazel Say Happy birthday to your sister from me!
James Will do. Bye!

Vocabulary and Listening

TV programmes

1 3.05 **Listen and repeat the words in the box. Which TV programmes can you see in the pictures?**

reality show chat show soap opera the news weather forecast game show sports programme comedy cartoon documentary film drama advert music programme

Exercise 1
documentary
comedy
chat show
game show
sports programme
reality show

2 Read the TV guide. Find one example of each of these programmes.

a reality show *I'm a Celebrity ...*

1 a music programme
2 a soap opera
3 a film
4 a sports programme
5 a drama
6 a cartoon

Exercise 2
1 The Talk Show
2 Neighbours
3 New Dawn
4 Olympic Dreams
5 Law and order
6 Crazy Kids!

3 Complete the sentences with true information. Use words from exercise 1.

1 I often watch ... .
2 Last night I watched ... .
3 I don't like watching ... .
4 My parents like ... .
5 ... is on at 9 o'clock in the evening.

4 3.06 **Look at the TV guide. Then listen to the informal conversation and complete sentences a) and b).**

a) Hazel watched (1) ... on Channel (2) ... at (3) ... o'clock.
b) James watched (1) ... on Channel (2) ... at (3) ... o'clock.

Exercise 4
a documentary
1
5
a film
2
8

5 Listen again and choose the correct answers.

1 Hazel and James are chatting at the **bus stop** / **train station**.
2 Hazel is going **home** / **to her friend's house**.
3 It's James' **sister's** / **mum's** birthday today.
4 The programme that Hazel watched was **boring** / **fantastic**.
5 The programme that James watched was **terrible** / **scary**.

Exercise 5
1 bus stop
2 to her friend's house
3 sister's
4 fantastic
5 terrible

TV Guide

Channel 1

4.00 Crazy Kids!
All our favourite cartoon characters.

5.00 Life in the Wild
Documentary about penguins in the Antarctic.

5.45 The Big Bang Theory
Double comedy – two episodes.

7.15 Top of the Charts
The Friday night music programme.

8.00 Law and Order
Another exciting episode of this famous crime drama.

9.00 The Talk Show
Chat show guests include rap star Def Jim.

Channel 2

4.00 Neighbours
Sophie gets good news in today's episode of the Australian soap opera.

5.00 Who Wants To Be A Millionaire?
More difficult questions for the game show contestants.

6.00 The News at 6
National and regional news.

6.55 Weather Forecast

7.00 Olympic Stars
The sports programme that follows Britain's top athletes.

8.00 New Dawn
Film directed by Bart Samson. Amy Lee stars in this exciting drama.

10.30 I'm a Celebrity ...
The reality show where celebrities have to eat insects!

Cultural awareness

Animated TV

1 3.07 **Look at the title and the pictures. What do you think the article is about? Then read, listen and check.**

Fact box

The American Walt Disney is sometimes called 'the father of animation'. He was born in Chicago in 1901.

Cartoon crazy!

Are Mickey Mouse and Bart Simpson more famous than the president of the USA? Probably! Cartoons are an essential part of American culture. Millions of children watch them on 24-hour cartoon channels, and people love *The Simpsons*™ all over the world.

What's the origin of animated cartoons? Well, they started long before television. *Felix the Cat* arrived on the big screen during the 1920s, at the time of silent films. A few years later, in 1928, Walt Disney created Mickey Mouse.

When television arrived in the USA in the 1940s, people loved it. Lots of different programmes appeared – there were cooking shows, chat shows and game shows. Then, in the 1950s, the big animation studio Hanna-Barbera started to produce new cartoons especially for television. *Yogi Bear*, *The Flintstones* and *Scooby-Doo* were all popular, particularly when colour TV arrived in the 1960s.

Technology is changing all the time and animation is now becoming more sophisticated. But Americans still love cartoons. *Time* magazine voted *The Simpsons* 'best TV series of the 20th century'. The Simpsons even have a star on the Hollywood Walk of Fame … not far from Mickey Mouse!

Word check

the big screen | silent film | animation studio

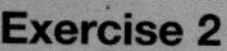

2 Check the meaning of the verbs in the box. Then find the past forms in the article.

start arrive create love appear vote

3 Read the article again. Find and correct one mistake in each sentence.

1. *Felix the Cat* was popular in the 1960s. ✗
2. Walt Disney created *The Simpsons* in 1928. ✗
3. Television arrived in the USA in the 1920s. ✗
4. Hanna-Barbera was a TV programme. ✗
5. Colour TV arrived in the USA in the 1980s. ✗

CULTURAL COMPARISON

4 Answer the questions.

In your country …

1. do they make animated films or cartoons?
2. are American cartoons popular?
3. what other American TV programmes do people watch?
4. who is the most famous cartoon character?

Culture video: Soap operas in the UK

Cultural awareness

Animated TV

Lesson objectives

In this lesson students will:

- read an article about cartoons
- practise reading for specific information
- talk about animated films or cartoons and other American TV programmes

Warmer

Write the word *cartoon* on the board. Then focus on the Fact box. Students work in pairs and write down the names of Walt Disney cartoons and other cartoons they know. Listen to their ideas as a class.

1 3.07

- Students read the question first.
- They look at the title and the pictures and say what they think the article is about.
- Play the CD. Students follow the text in their books.
- Check the answer as a class.

Word check

Check students understand the words. A *silent film* is one with no words. An *animation studio* is where cartoons are made. Ask students to translate the words into their language.

2
- Students translate the verbs into their language.
- They look in the article and find the past forms of these verbs.
- Check answers as a class.
- Point out that verbs add *-ed* to form the past tense. Verbs ending in *-e* (eg *love*) just add *-d*.

3
- Explain the task. Each sentence contains a mistake. Students should find the mistakes and correct them.
- They look in the article and correct the mistakes.
- They compare their answers in pairs or small groups.
- Check answers as a class.

CULTURAL  COMPARISON

4
- Students answer the questions individually.
- They compare their answers in pairs.
- Listen to their ideas as a class.

Culture note

Cartoons are now produced using digital technology but before the arrival of modern-day computers, each frame had to be drawn manually. This meant that thousands of pictures had to be drawn even for a short 10-minute cartoon like *Tom and Jerry*.

Extra activity

Students work in teams to write a quiz about one of the brochures. Collect in their questions and ask them to the whole class or compile them and give them out to the teams to answer.

Culture video: Soap operas in the UK

Grammar 

Past simple affirmative: regular verbs

Lesson objectives

In this lesson students will:

- learn and use the past simple of regular verbs in the affirmative
- use past time expressions

Recommended web links

www.tvhistory.tv

Warmer

Write the first and last letters of some of the past tense affirmative forms of the verbs from the previous lesson on the board with dashes for the remaining letters, eg *a _ _ _ _ _ d* (*arrived*), *s _ _ _ _ _ d* (*started*), *v _ _ _ d* (*voted*). Students work in pairs and write the full forms of the verbs. This will help to prepare them for the next activity.

1
- Students read questions a–b.
- They look at the table and answer the questions.
- Check answers as a class.
- Highlight the fact that the ending is the same for all subject pronouns.

2
- Students read the past simple affirmative spelling rules on page 83.
- They write the past simple affirmative forms of the verbs, referring to the spelling rules if necessary.
- They compare answers in pairs.
- Check answers as a class.

3
- Students look at the picture. Ask them if they know these characters.
- They read the text and complete the sentences with the past simple forms of the verbs in brackets.
- They compare answers in pairs.
- Check answers as a class.

EXPRESS YOURSELF

4
- Read the example sentence to the class.
- Do the first sentence with the class as an example – *I arrived at school at 8 o'clock this morning.*
- Students work individually and write true sentences in the past.
- Check answers as a class. Make sure they use the past simple and the past time expressions correctly.

Look!

Students read the past time expressions. Note that we say *last night* and not *yesterday evening*. Point out that we can also use days and months with *last*, eg *last Tuesday, last September*. Highlight that all of these expressions are used with the past simple tense.

 Grammar in context: Technology

5
- Ask students to read the whole text carefully first.
- Students work individually and choose the correct word or words from the three possibilities.
- They compare their answers in pairs.

6 3.08
- Play the CD.
- Students check their answers to exercise 5.

Culture note

John Logie Baird (1888–1946) was a Scottish engineer who invented the world's first practical publicly demonstrated television system. He also invented the world's first electronic colour television tube and is credited with the invention of a video recording device.

CLIL task

Students make a list of flat-screen technology. Encourage them to use the internet to research further examples. They compare their answers at the beginning of the next lesson.

Pronunciation lab: Past simple endings, page 125

Digital course: Interactive grammar table

Study guide: page 83

Grammar

Past simple affirmative: regular verbs

Exercise 1
1 -ed (verbs ending in -e just add -d)
2 no

1 Read the table. Then answer questions a) and b).

regular verbs
Animated cartoons **started** before television.
Television **arrived** in the USA in the 1940s.
They **watched** cartoons last night.

a) What is the past simple ending for regular verbs?
b) Does the verb form change for different subject pronouns?

Exercise 2
played
studied
watched
arrived
stopped
tidied
helped
started

2 Read the spelling rules on page 83. Then write the past simple affirmative form of the verbs in the box.

play study watch arrive stop tidy help start

3 Copy and complete the text with the past simple form of the verbs in brackets.

Exercise 3
1 appeared
2 studied
3 helped
4 created
5 watched

Wallace and Gromit

The UK's most famous animated characters are probably Wallace and Gromit. Recently, they (1) … (appear) in the science programme *World of Invention*. In this programme, Wallace (2) … (study) a lot of different inventions and Gromit (3) … (help) him.

The animator Nick Park (4) … (create) Wallace and Gromit in 1989 and millions of people (5) … (watch) their first film, *A Grand Day Out*.

EXPRESS YOURSELF

4 Write true sentences for you. Use past time expressions.

(watch) TV — *I watched TV last night.*

1 (arrive) at school
2 (study) maths
3 (play) a computer game
4 (listen) to music

LOOK!

past time expressions

yesterday   last week / month / year
last night   at … o'clock   this morning

CLIL Grammar in context: Technology

5 Read the text and choose the correct answers.

6 3.08 Listen and check.

Exercise 5
1 it was
2 there weren't
3 started
4 wasn't
5 arrived
6 were
7 They were
8 was

TV technology

When the Scottish engineer John Logie Baird invented the first television in 1925, (1) **it was / there was / it were** very different from today's technology. Of course, (2) **there wasn't / there weren't / they weren't** any flat-screen televisions then!

Technology developed and televisions (3) **starts / starting / started** to use technology called CRT*. These early televisions were much heavier than modern screens and the picture quality (4) **wasn't / weren't / there wasn't** as good.

LCD* technology (5) **arrive / arrived / arriving** in the late 20th century. The new flat-screen televisions (6) **was / they were / were** much thinner. (7) **They were / Were / There were** also better for the environment because they used less energy. Flat-screen technology (8) **was / were / there was** also important for the development of computers and mobile phones.

*CRT: cathode ray tube
*LCD: liquid crystal display

CLIL TASK

Find examples of flat-screen technology at your school, at home and in public places. Write a list.

3.09–3.10 Pronunciation lab: Past simple endings, page 125

Playing games

I like playing Topple the Tower and Sevens. What are your favourite games?

TOPPLE THE TOWER

FAQs

* **What is Topple the Tower?**
  Topple the Tower is a strategy game.
* **Where can you play it?**
  You can play it on a smartphone or on Facebook.
* **Who are the characters?**
  There are kings and knights. The kings with crowns are stronger than normal kings. Some knights have got special powers.
* **How do you play Topple the Tower?**
  First you must use the cannon to shoot the knights through the air. Then you must avoid the kings and find the tower. Don't forget to use the knights' special powers!
* **How do you win?**
  To win, you must destroy the tower.

Step 1: Read

SKILLS BUILDER

Reading: Using context to help understanding
Before you read a text, look at the pictures and the titles to help you understand the context.

1 Read the information about Topple the Tower. Then check the meaning of the words in the box.

tower cannon kings knights crown

2 Read the information again and answer the questions.

1 Is Topple the Tower a trivia game?
2 Where can you play Topple the Tower?
3 What's the special characteristic of the kings with crowns?
4 What must you find?
5 How do you win the game?

Exercise 2
1 No, it isn't. It's a strategy game.
2 On a smartphone or on Facebook.
3 They are stronger than normal kings.
4 The tower.
5 You must destroy the tower.

Step 2: Listen

3 3.11 **Listen to a radio programme. Which three subjects do they talk about?**

a) The history and origin of the game.
b) The names of the designers.
c) The different versions of the game.
d) The price of the game.

Exercise 3
a
c
d

4 Listen again and choose the correct answers.

1 Topple the Tower was released in ...
a) 2007. **b)** 2010. **c)** 2013.
2 Designers from ... created the game.
a) the UK **b)** the USA **c)** France
3 Topple the Tower appeared on Facebook in ...
a) 2010. **b)** 2011. **c)** 2012.
4 The first special version of the game was for...
a) Easter. **b)** Halloween. **c)** Christmas.
5 Topple the Tower costs ...
a) 69p. **b)** 89p. **c)** 99p.

Exercise 4
1 b
2 a
3 b
4 c
5 c

Integrated skills

Playing games

Lesson objectives

In this lesson students will:

- work on all four skills
- read some frequently asked questions (FAQs) about a computer game
- listen to a person explaining the rules of a game
- write a personalized dialogue
- act out their dialogue

Warmer

Write the word *game* on the board. Ask students what games they know (not computer games). Elicit examples such as *dominoes, chess*, different card games, etc. Find out which students play these games.

Step 1: Read

Skills builder

Reading: Using context to help understanding
Highlight that students should look at the pictures and titles before they read to help them understand the context.

1
- Highlight Hazel's speech bubble. Elicit answers to the question *What are your favourite games?* from the class.
- Students look at the information about Topple the Tower.
- Ask the students to check the meaning of the words in the box in pairs and to identify the words in the pictures.
- Check the meaning of the words as a class by getting students to translate the words into their own language. Elicit that all the words are illustrated in the picture.

2
- Students read the questions carefully first.
- They read the information again and find the answers.
- Check answers as a class.

Step 2: Listen

3 3.11
- Make sure the students understand the task.
- They read the multiple-choice questions in exercise 4 and guess which three subjects are mentioned in a talk about Topple the Tower.
- Play the CD. Students check their guesses.
- Check answers as a class.

4 3.11
- Students read the sentences and the three possible answers.
- Play the CD again. Students choose the correct answers.
- They compare their answers in pairs.
- Check answers as a class.

3.11 Audioscript, exercises 3 and 4

So, are you a fan of Topple the Tower? Which knight is your favourite? I love the red ones with their green shields!
Seriously though, millions of people around the world are playing the game! It's an app phenomenon! But how much do you know about the origins of the game?
Well, Topple the Tower was released in 2010. In a small studio in London, two game designers created the first knights (the heroes) and their enemies, the fat kings in their towers.
A year later, in 2011, the game appeared on Facebook. Soon there were different versions of the game: first they produced Topple the Tower for Christmas by replacing the kings with Santa Clauses. Then they created a Halloween version and even one for Valentine's Day!
What's the secret of this game's success? Well, it's funny, it's addictive ... and it only costs 99p! What's not to like?! And now for ...

Integrated skills - continued

Explaining the rules of a game

5 3.12

- Students read the questions.
- Play the CD. Students follow the text of the dialogue in their books and then answer the questions.
- They compare answers in pairs.
- Check answers as a class.

6 3.12

- Play the CD again, pausing after each speaker's part for students to repeat as a class.
- Note the main stress on the questions, eg *Are you ready to play Sevens? Can you explain the rules?*
- Ask students to repeat the questions and responses several times both chorally and individually with the correct stress and intonation.
- Students practise the dialogue in pairs. Then swap roles and practise the dialogue again.

Step 3: Write

7
- Students read the information on page 80.
- They copy and complete the rules for Topple the Tower.
- Check answers as a class.

8
- Students work individually and write their dialogue, using the dialogue in the book as a model and the Communication kit: Explaining the rules of the game for key phrases.
- Monitor while they are writing and give help if necessary.

Step 4: Communicate

9
- Students practise their dialogues in pairs.
- For extra practice, they swap roles in both dialogues.

10
- Choose some pairs to act out their dialogue for the class.

Integrated skills: Workbook page 117

Are you ready to play Sevens?	No – wait a minute! Can you explain the rules?
Well, first you must put down a card the same colour or number as this.	OK. Then what?
Then you must take another card from the pile.	I see. And how do you win?
To win, you must put down all your cards first.	Is that it?
Yes! Oh, and don't forget to shout 'last card' when you've only got one card left!	All right. I think I'm ready now!
Good luck!	Thanks!

Exercise 5

No, he doesn't.
You must put down all your cards first.
When you've only got one card left.

5 3.12 **Read and listen to the dialogue. Answer the questions.**

1 Does James know the rules of Sevens?
2 How do you win the game?
3 When must you shout 'last card'?

6 Listen again and repeat. Practise your intonation.

Step 3: Write

Exercise 7

First you must use the cannon to shoot the knights through the air.
2 Then you must avoid the kings and find the tower.
3 To win, you must destroy the tower.
4 Don't forget to use the knights' special powers!

7 Look at the information on page 80. Then copy and complete the rules for Topple the Tower.

Topple the Tower: the rules
First you must (1) … .
Then you must (2) … .
To win, you must (3) … .
Don't forget to (4) …!

8 Imagine you're explaining the rules of Topple the Tower to a friend. Prepare a new dialogue. Write both parts. Use your notes from exercise 7 and the dialogue in exercise 5 to help you.

Are you ready to play?
No – wait a minute! Can you explain the rules?

Step 4: Communicate

9 Work in pairs. Take turns to practise your dialogues.

Are you ready to play?
No – wait a minute! Can you explain the rules?

10 Act your dialogue for the class.

COMMUNICATION KIT

Explaining the rules of a game

Are you ready to play … ?
No – wait a minute! / Yes, I'm ready now.
Can you explain the rules?
First you must … .
Then you must … .
Don't forget to … .
How do you win?
To win, you must … .
Good luck!

Writing

A review

Exercise 1
1 comedy
2 science
3 funny

1 3.13 **Read the review and choose the correct answers for 1–3. Then listen and check.**

LAST NIGHT I WATCHED ...

Last night I watched *The Big Bang Theory*. It's an American (1) **comedy / sports** programme. It was on at 8 o'clock.

I enjoyed the programme because it was very entertaining. It was also interesting because it's about (2) **history / science**. The main characters, Sheldon and Leonard, are physicists.

The Big Bang Theory was very (3) **funny / boring** last night. There was a good story about Sheldon and his neighbour, Penny. There were also some great jokes.

Last night I also watched the soap opera *Hollyoaks*, but it wasn't as good as *The Big Bang Theory*.

By Sam, 14

2 **Read the Writing focus. How do you say *also* in your language?**

WRITING FOCUS

also

We use *also* to add information.

be + *also*	*It **was also** interesting.*
also + other verbs	*I **also watched** a soap opera.*

Exercise 3
There were also some great jokes.
Also is after the verb.

3 **Read the review again. Find another example of *also*. Is it before or after the verb?**

4 **Add *also* to each of the second sentences.**

It was boring. It was *also* very long.

1. I watched *Glee*. I did my homework.
2. There were some funny parts. There was some great music.
3. I watched *Friends*. My mum watched it.
4. The characters were rich. They were stupid!
5. We watched a film. We watched the news.

Exercise 4
1 I also did my homework.
2 There was also some great music.
3 My mum also watched it.
4 They were also stupid!
5 We also watched the news.

Writing task

Write a review of a TV programme you watched recently.

Plan Choose a programme to review. Complete the notes about the programme.

Last night / weekend I watched ... .
It's a ... .
It was on Channel ... at ... o'clock.
I enjoyed this programme because it was ... . It was also ... .
There was ... . There were also ... .

Write Write your review. Use your notes and the text in exercise 1 to help you.

Check Check your writing.

- ☑ use *also* correctly
- ☑ *was / were* and *there was / there were*
- ☑ past simple verbs
- ☑ vocabulary for TV programmes

Build your confidence: Writing reference and practice. Workbook page 132

Writing

A review

Lesson objectives

In this lesson students will:

- learn how to use *also* to add information
- write a review of a TV programme

Warmer

Elicit words for different types of TV programmes and write them on the board (eg *cartoon, soap opera, news, sports programme*). Students work in pairs and rank them in order from favourite to least favourite. Listen to their ideas as a class.

1 3.13

- Ask students to look at the picture. Ask if they know this programme.
- They read the review.
- They choose the correct answers for 1–3.
- Play the CD. Students listen and check their answers.

Culture note

The Big Bang Theory is a comedy series set in the California Institute of Technology. The first episode was broadcast in the USA in September 2007 and since then more than 120 episodes have been broadcast. The show is not only popular in the United States. It has been shown on TV in more than 80 countries around the world.

2
- Students read the Writing focus.
- Elicit the word or words for *also* in their language.
- Highlight the position of *also* after the verb *be* but before other verbs.

3
- Students find another example of *also* in the review.
- They copy the sentence into their notebooks.
- Check the answer as a class. Elicit that *also* comes after the verb because it is the verb *be*.

4
- Students add *also* to each of the second sentences.
- They compare answers in pairs.
- Check answers as a class.

Writing task

The aim of this activity is for students to produce a piece of guided writing using *also* correctly and to write a review of a TV programme. It also gives them practice in using *was / were*, *there was / there were,* past simple verbs and vocabulary for TV programmes. Ask the students to follow the stages in the Student's Book. Monitor while they are writing and give help with vocabulary if necessary. At the Check stage, ask them to swap notebooks and check each other's writing.

Writing reference and practice: Workbook page 132

Study guide

Grammar, Vocabulary and Speaking

Tell the students the Study guide is an important page which provides a useful reference for the main language of the unit: the grammar, the vocabulary and the functional language from the Integrated skills pages. Explain that they should refer to this page when studying for a test or exam.

Grammar

- Tell the students to look at the example sentences using *was / were* and *there was / there were* and make sure they know how to use the form correctly in affirmative, negative and question forms.
- Then tell students to look at the example sentences of the past simple affirmative of regular verbs and ensure they understand how to form the tense correctly. Get students to translate into their own language if necessary.
- Refer students to the Grammar reference on pages 96–97 of the Workbook for further revision.

Vocabulary

- Tell students to look at the list of vocabulary and check understanding.
- Refer students to the Wordlist on page 151 of the Workbook where they can look up any words they can't remember.

Speaking

- Check that students understand the phrases to use for explaining the rules of a game.
- Tell students to act out a conversation between a two people. One person explains the rules of a game to the other person.

Additional material

Workbook

- Progress check page 62
- Self evaluation page 63
- Grammar reference and practice page 96
- Vocabulary extension page 108
- Integrated skills page 117
- Writing reference and task page 132

Teacher's Resource File

- Pulse Basics worksheets pages 41–46
- Vocabulary and grammar consolidation worksheets pages 27–30
- Translation and dictation worksheets pages 8, 18
- Evaluation rubrics pages 1–7
- Key competences worksheets pages 13–14
- Culture and CLIL worksheets pages 25–28
- Culture video worksheets pages 13–14
- Digital competence worksheets pages 13–14
- Macmillan Readers worksheets pages 5–6

Tests and Exams

- Unit 7 End-of-unit test: Basic, Standard and Extra
- CEFR Skills Exam Generator

Study guide

Grammar

was / were

affirmative and negative	
I **was** / **wasn't** You **were** / **weren't** He / She / It **was** / **wasn't** We / You / They **were** / **weren't**	good at Tetris®.

questions and short answers	
Was I good at the game?	Yes, I **was**. No, I **wasn't**.
Were you good at the game?	Yes, you **were**. No, you **weren't**.
Was he / she / it good at the game?	Yes, he / she / it **was**. No, he / she / it **wasn't**.
Were we / you / they good at the game?	Yes, we / you / they **were**. No we / you / they **weren't**.

there was / there were

affirmative and negative
There was a funny film on TV last night.
There were cartoons in the 1950s.

questions and short answers	
Was there a comedy on TV last night?	Yes, **there was**. No, **there wasn't**.
Were there any good films on TV on Sunday?	Yes, **there were**. No, **there weren't**.

Past simple affirmative: regular verbs

regular verbs
John Logie Baird **invented** the television.
Colour TV **arrived** in the 1960s.
Hanna-Barbera **produced** new cartoons.

LEARNING TO LEARN

Write the titles of different games and TV programmes next to the types. Examples help you remember new vocabulary.

Past simple affirmative spelling rules

- For most regular verbs, add *-ed*.
  watch → watched
- For verbs that end in *-e*, add *-d*.
  like → liked
- For verbs that end in consonant + *y*, change *-y* to *-i* and add *-ed*.
  carry → carried tidy → tidied
- For verbs that end in consonant + vowel + consonant (except *w*, *x* or *z*), double the final consonant and add *-ed*.
  stop → stopped permit → permitted

Vocabulary

Computer games

action
adventure
dancing
fitness
puzzle
quiz
racing
role-play
simulation
strategy
trivia

TV programmes

advert
cartoon
chat show
comedy
documentary
drama
film
game show
music programme
news
reality show
soap opera
sports programme
weather forecast

Speaking

Explaining the rules of a game

Are you ready to play?
No – wait a minute! / Yes, I'm ready now.
Can you explain the rules?
First you must … . Then you must … .
Don't forget to … .
How do you win?
To win, you must … .
Good luck!

UNIT 8

SONG AND DANCE

Unit objectives and key competences

In this unit the student will learn…
- understand, memorize and correctly use words related to music **CLC CAE**
- understand, memorize and correctly use adjectives of opinion **CLC**
- understand and correctly use grammar structures related to the past and draw parallels to L1 **CLC L2L**
- about music in the UK by watching a short video **CLC CAE**

In this unit the student will learn how to ...
- identify specific information in a feature article **CLC CMST SCC CAE**
- look for information about a composer or musician **CLC DC CAE**
- dentify specific information in a radio extract **CLC CMST CAE**
- learn about Scottish traditions in music and dance **CLC CMST CAE**
- speak about their musical likes and dislikes **CLC SCC CAE**
- write a personal profile **CLC CMST**
- read a web page for a festival, listen to announcements at a festival and talk about past events **CLC DC SCC CAE**

Linguistic contents

Main vocabulary
- Instruments and musicians: *guitar, guitarist, piano, pianist,* etc
- Adjectives of opinion: *boring, lively, fun,* etc

Grammar
- Past simple regular and irregular verbs affirmative and negative
- Past simple questions and short answers

Functional language
- Phrases for talking about past events

Pronunciation
- Diphthongs

Skills

Reading
- Read a feature article about an unusual orchestra
- Read a text about Scotland
- Read a web page about a music festival

Writing
- Write a personalized dialogue
- Write a personal profile in three steps: plan, write, check

Listening
- Listen to a radio extract about music
- Listen to people talking about a past event
- Prepare to understand a conversation and select the important information

Spoken interaction
- Exchange information about musical preferences
- Ask and answer questions about events in the past

Spoken production
- Prepare and act out a dialogue about a past event

Lifelong learning skills

Self-study and self-evaluation

- Study guide: Student's Book page 93
- Progress check and self-evaluation: Workbook pages 70–71
- Grammar reference and practice: Workbook pages 98–99
- Wordlist: Workbook pages 151–157

Learning strategies and thinking skills

- Using the questions on the page to help identify key words when listening

Cultural awareness

- Traditional music and dance in Scotland
- Comparing traditional Scottish music and dance with music and dance from students' own countries or regions

Cross-curricular contents

- Music: composers, genres and instruments
- ICT: searching the internet for information
- Language and literature: conventions for writing a personal profile

Key competences

CLC Competence in linguistic communication
CMST Competence in mathematics, science and technology
DC Digital competence
L2L Learning to learn
SCC Social and civic competences
SIE Sense of initiative and entrepreneurship
CAE Cultural awareness and expression

Evaluation

- Unit 8 End-of-unit test: Basic, Standard and Extra
- CEFR Skills Exam Generator

External exam trainer

- Listening: Multiple-choice answers

Digital material

Pulse Live! Digital Course including:

- Interactive grammar tables
- Audio visual speaking model: Talking about past events
- Audio visual cultural material: Music in the UK

Student's website

Digital competence

- Web quest: Watch the Liverpool Signing Choir
- Digital competence worksheet: Digital stories

Reinforcement material

- Basics worksheets, Teacher's Resource File pages 47–52
- Vocabulary and Grammar: Consolidation worksheets, Teacher's Resource File pages 31–32

Extension material

- Fast-finisher activity: Student's Book page 85
- Extra activities: Teacher's Book pages T84, T91
- Vocabulary and Grammar: Extension worksheets, Teacher's Resource File pages 33–34

Teacher's Resource File

- Translation and dictation worksheets pages 9, 19
- Evaluation rubrics pages 1–7
- Key competences worksheets pages 15–16
- Culture and CLIL worksheets pages 29–32
- Culture video worksheets pages 15–16
- Digital competence worksheets pages 15–16
- Macmillan Readers worksheets pages 5–6

UNIT 8 SONG AND DANCE

THINK ABOUT IT

How many types of music and dance do you know? Write a list from A to Z.

African, ballet, country, ...

Vocabulary and Speaking

Instruments and musicians

1 3.14 **Read the *What's on?* guide. Listen and repeat the blue words. Which concert do you prefer?**

2 3.15 **Match the musicians with instruments from the guide. Then listen and repeat.**

pianist – piano

pianist guitarist drummer bass player singer keyboard player

LOOK!

Suffixes: *-ist* / *-er*

violin → violinist drum → drummer

3 Describe the band in picture a). Use words from exercise 2.

Adam is the singer. James is ...

4 3.16 **Listen to five short music extracts. Match them with the types of music in the box.**

classical	country	rock	jazz	Latin

EXPRESS YOURSELF

5 Order the words to make questions. Then write answers that are true for you.

1 favourite / What's / **pop** / song / your ?
2 you / the / Can / play / **guitar** ?
3 like / **country** / Do / music / you ?
4 **rock** / your / singer / Who's / favourite ?
5 band / your / **Latin** / favourite / What's ?

6 Work in pairs. Ask and answer the questions in exercise 5. You can change the bold words.

What's your favourite rap song?
I like ...

What's on?

SATURDAY 14TH MAY

Maroon 5

The American pop-rock band in concert. With Adam on **vocals**, James on **guitar**, Mickey on **bass**, Matt on **drums** and PJ on **keyboards**.

a

THURSDAY 19TH MAY

Simón Bolívar Youth Orchestra

Conductor Gustav Dudamel brings Venezuela's famous **orchestra** to London. With Vilma Sánchez on **piano** and special guests: Britain's National Youth **Choir**.

b

Exercise 2

pianist – piano
guitarist – guitar
drummer – drums
bass player – bass
singer – vocals
keyboard player – keyboards

Exercise 3

James is the guitarist.
Mickey is the bass player / bassist.
Matt is the drummer.
PJ is the keyboard player.

Exercise 4

1 country
2 classical
3 Latin
4 jazz
5 rock

Exercise 5

1 What's your favourite pop song?
2 Can you play the guitar?
3 Do you like country music?
4 Who's your favourite rock singer?
5 What's your favourite Latin band?

Vocabulary extension: Workbook page 109

Vocabulary and Speaking

Instruments and musicians

Lesson objectives

In this lesson students will:

- learn vocabulary for instruments and musicians
- learn vocabulary for different types of music
- talk about their musical tastes

Warmer

Focus students on the Think about it box. Students work in pairs and write a music or dance word for each letter of the alphabet, as shown in the examples. If they can't think of a music or dance word for a particular letter (eg *q* or *x*), they should move on to the next letter. The pair with the most correct words wins.

1 3.14

- Students read the What's on? guide.
- Play the CD. Students listen to the blue words and repeat them.
- Highlight the pronunciation and stress of *orchestra* /'ɔ:kɪstrə/ and the pronunciation of *choir* /kwaɪə/.
- Ask which concert students prefer – the pop-rock band or the classical concert.

2 3.15

- Students work individually and match the musician words in the word pool to the instruments in the What's on? guide.
- Play the CD. Students listen and repeat.
- Check answers as a class.

Look!

Highlight that we add either *-ist* or *-er* to instruments to make the words for musicians. Point out that *bass player* and *singer* are more common, but we can also say *bassist* and *vocalist*.

Culture note

The Simón Bolívar Youth Orchestra was founded in Caracas, Venezuela in 1975. The orchestra made its debut in London at a BBC concert in August 2007 which was broadcast live on BBC television. Its conductor, Gustavo Dudamel, is well known for encouraging young people to take up music.

3

- Students write a description of the five members of the band in picture a continuing the example.
- They compare their answers in pairs.
- Check answers as a class.

4 3.16

- Tell students they will hear five short pieces of music.
- They should match them with the words for different types of music.
- Play the CD.
- Students compare their answers in pairs.
- Check answers as a class.

EXPRESS YOURSELF

5

- Do the first question with the whole class as an example. Elicit the question from the students – *What's your favourite pop song?*
- Students work individually and write the questions.
- They write their answers to the questions.
- Check that the questions have been formed correctly as a class.

6

- Students work in pairs and ask and answer the questions from exercise 5.
- Focus on the example question and check students understand that they can change the bold words.
- Listen to some pairs as a class.

Extra activity

Students write a short paragraph about the types of music they like and the types they don't like. Encourage them to use the words in exercise 4.

Vocabulary extension: Workbook page 109

Reading

Text type: A feature article

Lesson objectives

In this lesson students will:

- read a short text
- talk about their musical experiences

Recommended web links

www.theliverpoolsigningchoir.co.uk
www.rpo.co.uk
www.vegetableorchestra.org

Warmer

Write the words for different musical instruments from the previous lesson on the board, eg *drums, guitar, piano, bass, keyboards*. Students work in pairs and write the words for the musicians who play these instruments – *drummer, guitarist, pianist, bass player / bassist, keyboard player*.

1 3.17

- Students look at the picture of the choir.
- They say what they think is special about it.
- Play the CD. Students follow the text in their books and check the answer to the question.
- Check the answer as a class.

Word check

Check students understand the meaning of the new words. A *deaf* person cannot hear. Ask them to translate the words into their language.

Culture note

There are Deaf Youth Orchestras in the UK in Yorkshire, Manchester, Peterborough and London. Members are aged between 6 and 16 and they play many different instruments including drums, harp and piano.

2

- Point out that some common verbs in English have irregular past tense forms.
- Students find the past tenses of the verbs by looking in the article.
- Check answers as a class and ask students to write the four irregular past forms in their notebooks.

3

- Students read the sentences carefully first. Make sure they understand them.
- They read the article again and check whether the sentences are true or false.
- They correct the false sentences.
- They compare their answers in pairs.
- Check answers as a class.

4  EXPRESS YOURSELF

- Students work individually and answer the questions.
- They then work in pairs and ask and answer the questions.
- Listen to some pairs as a class.

Finished?

Ask fast finishers to make a list of famous composers.

Web quest

Students watch the Liverpool Signing Choir online. Highlight the Web quest tip.

1. Ask students to open an internet web browser such as Internet Explorer. Students open a search engine (eg Google) and type in *Liverpool Signing Choir.*
2. Students search for videos of the choir's performances.
3. Students make a note of the URLs and report back to the class.

Reading
A feature article

Exercise 1
The members of the choir 'sing' with sign language.

1 3.17 **Look at the picture. What do you think is special about this choir? Read, listen and check.**

The Liverpool Signing Choir

In the Liverpool Signing Choir, they don't sing – they sign. Some members of the choir can hear, but many of them are deaf. In the choir, they don't use their voices – they use their hands. They 'sing' with sign language!

The Liverpool Signing Choir began several years ago. The conductor Catherine Hegarty started it as an after-school club and then it grew much bigger. Now there are about 100 young people in the choir, aged 6–24. They perform different kinds of music, including pop songs, opera and football songs.

A few years ago, they performed for the Queen when she visited Liverpool. In 2009, they went to London and performed at Wembley Stadium. Then, in 2012, they became famous when they returned to London to perform at the Olympic closing ceremony.

This choir shows that there's more to music than sound. A choir is also a great opportunity to make new friends and to express yourself … singing *or* signing!

DID YOU KNOW?
Deaf people around the world don't all use the same sign language. There are around 200 different sign languages! In the UK, people use British Sign Language.

Word check
sign deaf sign language closing ceremony

Exercise 2
became
started
began
grew
performed
visited
went
returned
The four irregular past forms are *became*, *began*, *grew* and *went*.

2 Find the past form of the verbs in the box in the text. Which four are irregular?

become	start	begin	grow
perform	visit	go	return

Exercise 3
1 True
2 False Some members of the choir can hear.
3 False The choir performs different kinds of music.
4 False The choir performed for the Queen in Liverpool.
5 True

3 Read the article again. Are the sentences true or false? Correct the false sentences.

1 The Liverpool Signing Choir uses sign language.
2 All the members of the choir are deaf.
3 The choir only performs classical music.
4 The choir performed for the Queen in London.
5 The choir became famous in 2012.

4 In pairs, ask and answer the questions.

1 Do you like singing? Why (not)?
2 Are you in a choir?
3 Do you play a musical instrument?
4 Are you in an orchestra?

FINISHED?
How many famous orchestras do you know? Write a list.
London Symphony Orchestra, …

WEB QUEST
Watch the Liverpool Signing Choir online.
1 Use the keywords 'Liverpool Signing Choir' in your search engine.
2 Can you find any videos of their performances?
3 Make a note of the URLs and share your information with the class.

Web Quest tip!
The spelling of your keywords is very important. Make sure you type *signing* not *singing*.

Grammar 

Past simple: affirmative and negative

1 Study the table. Then answer questions a–c.

affirmative	
I / You / He / She / It / We / You / They	**performed** in London. **went** to London.
negative	
I / You / He / She / It / We / You / They	**didn't perform** in Madrid. **didn't go** to Madrid.

a) Which verb is irregular, *perform* or *go*?
b) How do we form the past simple of regular verbs?
c) Is the negative form different for regular and irregular verbs?

2 Copy and complete the table with the past simple form of the verbs in the box. Then check your answers with the Irregular verbs list on page 126.

listen have begin watch wear buy continue give exist download

Regular verbs	Irregular verbs
listen – *listened*	have – *had*

3 Write affirmative and negative sentences about teenagers in the 1950s.

watch DVDs / go to the cinema
They didn't watch DVDs. They went to the cinema.

1 have MP3 players / have record players
2 download music / buy records
3 listen to hip hop / listen to rock 'n' roll
4 watch colour TV / watch black and white TV
5 wear trainers / wear shoes

4 Read the Look! box and translate the sentences. What is the position of *ago*?

LOOK!

ago

The Liverpool Signing Choir began several years **ago**.
A few years **ago**, they performed for the Queen.

5 Write true sentences with the words in the box and *ago*.

minutes hours days months years

This class (start) ...
This class started forty minutes ago.

1 I (have) breakfast ... .
2 I (celebrate) my birthday ... .
3 I (begin) this exercise ... .
4 Our teacher (give) us homework ... .
5 I (start) school ... .

6 Complete the text with the past simple form of the verbs in brackets.

MUSIC ON THE MOVE!

Not long ago, people (1) *didn't listen* (not listen) to portable music. They (2) ... (not have) MP3 players – they (3) ... (have) old-fashioned gramophones and they (4) ... (buy) records. Portable music players (5) ... (not exist) until the 1980s, when Sony® (6) ... (invent) the Walkman®. After that, CDs (7) ... (become) very popular. Then, in 2001, Apple® (8) ... (create) their first MP3 player, the iPod. People (9) ... (love) it – Apple (10) ... (sell) more than half a million iPods in the first year.

ANALYSE

In English there are more than 150 irregular verbs. Are there any irregular verbs in your language?

Exercise 1
a go
b we add -ed (see Language Note)
c no

Exercise 2
regular verbs
listen – listened
watch – watched
continue – continued
exist – existed
download – downloaded
irregular verbs
have – had
begin – began
wear – wore
buy – bought
give – gave

Exercise 3
1 They didn't have MP3 players. They had record players.
2 They didn't download music. They bought records.
3 They didn't listen to hip hop. They listened to rock 'n' roll.
4 They didn't watch colour TV. They watched black and white TV.
5 They didn't wear trainers. They wore shoes.

Exercise 4
ago comes at the end of the time phrase

Exercise 5
students' own answers in the gaps
1 I had breakfast ... ago.
2 I celebrated my birthday ... ago.
3 I began this exercise ... ago.
4 Our teacher gave us homework ... ago.
5 I started school ... ago.

Exercise 6
2 didn't have
3 had
4 bought
5 didn't exist
6 invented
7 became
8 created
9 loved
10 sold

Grammar 

Past simple: affirmative and negative

Lesson objectives

In this lesson students will:

- learn and use the past simple affirmative and negative of regular and irregular verbs
- write sentences using *ago*

Warmer

Write *study, love, tidy, visit, appear, arrive, begin*, *create* on the board. They work in pairs and write the past tense forms of these verbs. Check answers as a class and highlight the irregular verb *begin* - *began*.

1
- Students copy the table into their notebooks.
- They answer questions a–c.
- Check answers as a class.
- Highlight that regular and irregular verbs do not change in the negative form – we simply use *didn't* (eg *didn't perform, didn't go*).

Language note

Point out that irregular past tenses is that they do not add *-ed*. They form their past tenses in different ways, often by changing a vowel in the final syllable, eg *begin – began, become – became*. It is important for students to know irregular past simple forms because these verbs are among the most widely used in English.

2
- Students copy the table into their notebooks.
- They write the past simple form of the verbs in the correct column.
- They check their answers in the Irregular Verb List on page 126.
- Check answers as a class. Note the pronunciation of *bought* /bɔ:t/.

3
- Read aloud the example sentences to the whole class.
- Point out the first sentence is in the past simple negative and the second in the past simple affirmative.
- Students work individually and write about teenagers in the 1950s using the prompts.
- They compare their answers in pairs.
- Check answers as a class.

4
- Focus students on the Look! box and the example sentences with *ago*.
- Students work individually and translate the sentences.
- Check answers as a class.
- Highlight the position of *ago* at the end of the time phrase. Compare it with the position in the students' language.

5
- Read the example sentence aloud to the class.
- Point out that we can use *ago* with all the words in the box, eg *three hours ago, ten years ago.*
- Students work individually to write sentences using the past simple of the verbs in brackets and the words in the box with *ago*.
- Check answers as a class. Point out that time expressions with *ago* usually come at the end of the sentence.

6
- Students read the text carefully first.
- They fill the gaps using the past simple affirmative or negative of the verbs in brackets.
- They compare their answers in pairs.
- Check answers as a class. Point out that *sell* has an irregular past tense form – *sold*.

7
- Nominate two students to read the example question and answer aloud to the class.
- Students look at the Irregular Verb List on page 126 and choose five irregular verbs. They write down the past simple forms.
- They work in pairs and test their partner following the model in the example question and answer.
- Listen to some pairs as a class.

Analyse

Ask students to think about irregular verbs in their language. How many are there? Are there more in English or in their language?

Digital course: Interactive grammar table

Study guide: page 93

Vocabulary and Listening

Adjectives of opinion

Lesson objectives

In this lesson students will:

- learn some adjectives of opinion
- listen for specific information

Warmer

Students work in pairs and write down as many different kinds of music as they can. Set a time limit of two minutes. Listen to their ideas as a class and write the different music genres on the board, eg *Latin, pop, heavy rock, hip hop,* etc.

1 3.18

- Ask students to look at the word pool.
- Check they understand the words by asking them to translate them into their language.
- Explain that a *catchy song* catches your attention and is easy to remember.
- Play the CD. Students listen and repeat the words.

2
- Students look in the reviews and underline all the adjectives they can find.
- Students compare answers in pairs.
- Check answers as a class.

3
- Students copy the Venn diagram into their notebooks.
- They put the adjectives from exercise 1 in the sections for positive or negative adjectives, or in the overlapping section for adjectives that could be either positive or negative.
- They compare answers in pairs.
- Check answers as a class.

4
- Give your own opinion of one or two songs to illustrate this activity. Tell the class a song you like and one you don't like with an adjective from exercise 1 to describe each one.
- Students complete the sentences with information that is true for them.
- They compare answers in pairs.
- Listen to their ideas as a class.

5 3.19

- Play the CD. Students write the answer to the question.
- Check the answer as a class.

6
- Play the CD again. Students tick the adjectives they hear.
- Note that you may need to play the CD more than once.
- Students compare answers in pairs.
- Check answers as a class.

7
- Students read the sentences carefully.
- Students decide which sentences are true and which are false.
- They correct the false sentences.
- Students compare answers in pairs.
- Check answers as a class.

3.19 Audioscript, exercises 5 and 6

Hello and welcome to this week's *Chart Show!* I'm Dale Evans and I'm going to start off today's show with this week's new songs.
First up today, there's very exciting news: there's a new song by Sophie Styles. This one's quite surprising for Sophie ... there's just a piano and amazing vocals. It's totally original! Apparently she wrote the lyrics to this song about a relationship she had. It's so emotional – I absolutely loved it!
The second new song of the week is from the Australian singer Ben Miller. Now, I'm a big fan of Ben Miller so I went out and bought this immediately. I put it on my MP3 player and I listened to it this morning on the train, and I just love it! I thought: 'Yeah, it's so catchy. It's lively ... it's unusual' Basically, it's just a great song'
Also this week, there's Yo-yo's new song, Monday. I'm sorry but I can't recommend this one! When I first listened to it, I thought it was rubbish! Now, every time I hear it on the radio, I find it more and more annoying. As you can imagine, I didn't buy this song! Also, out this week there's the new single from ...

Vocabulary and Listening
Adjectives of opinion

1 3.18 **Check the meaning of the words in the box. Then listen and repeat.**

great traditional boring terrible amazing rubbish surprising
annoying unusual original loud quiet lively catchy

Exercise 2
great
amazing
fantastic
favourite
unusual
original
lively
catchy
annoying
interesting
rubbish
boring
terrible

2 **Read the reviews. How many adjectives can you find?**

This week's song reviews

HOT

NOT

BILLY JEAN
★★★★★

New York Girls

Great lyrics and an amazing guitar solo. A fantastic pop song – my favourite song this week!

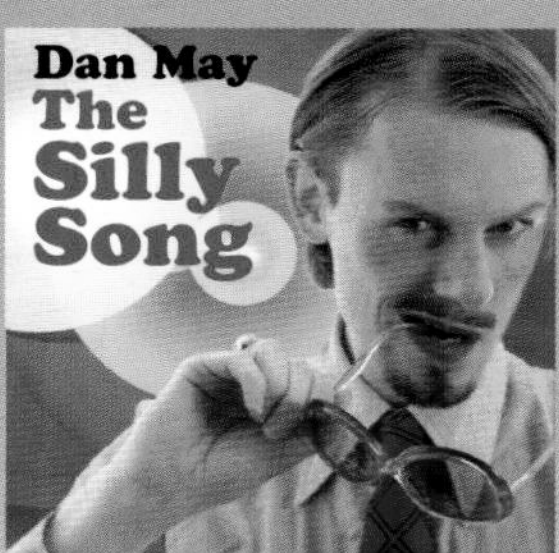

DAN MAY
★

The Silly Song

Catchy or annoying, depending on your opinion. Interesting lyrics, but a rubbish video!

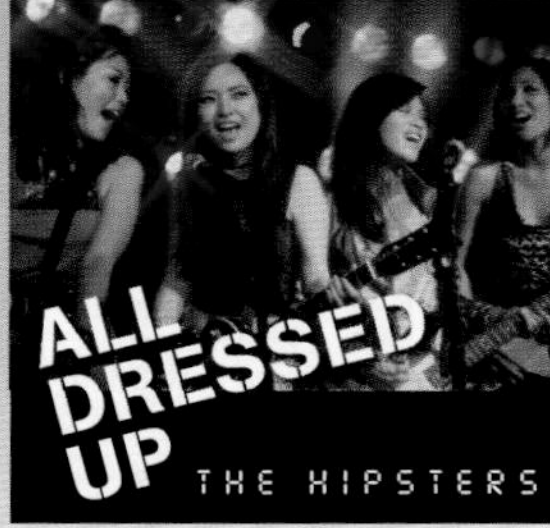

THE HIPSTERS
★★★

All Dressed Up

This is quite an unusual song. It's original and lively, but not my favourite Hipsters song.

YO-YO

Monday

What can we say about this internet sensation? Boring lyrics and a terrible song!

Exercise 5
Monday
(by Yo-yo)

Exercise 6
original
emotional
lively
unusual
rubbish
annoying

Exercise 3
positive
amazing
original
lively
catchy
negative
terrible
rubbish
annoying
neutral
surprising
unusual
loud
quiet

3 **Copy and complete the diagram with the adjectives from exercise 1.**

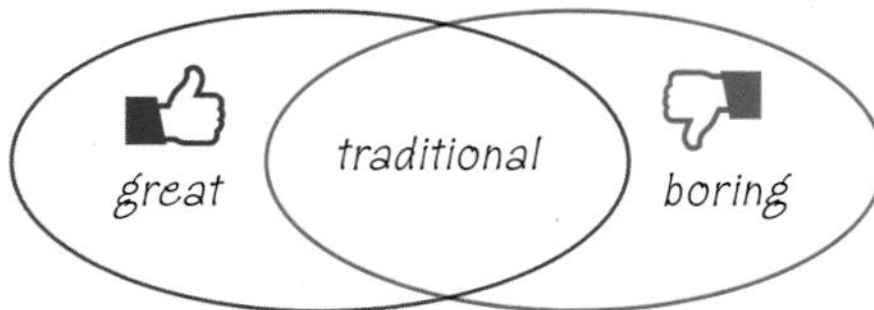

4 **Complete the sentences about songs you know. Use adjectives from exercise 1.**

1 I like … by … . It's … .
2 I don't like … . It's … .
3 … is number one at the moment in my country. In my opinion, it's … .

5 3.19 **Listen to a radio DJ talking about three new songs. Which one of the songs in exercise 2 does he mention?**

6 **Listen again. Which adjectives do you hear?**

original traditional emotional loud
lively unusual rubbish slow annoying

7 **Are the sentences true or false? Correct the false sentences.**

1 The first song has got vocals and a piano.
2 The DJ didn't like the first song.
3 The second song is by an American singer.
4 The DJ put the second song on his MP3 player.
5 The DJ bought the third song.

Exercise 7
1 True
2 False
3 False
The second song is by an Australian singer.
4 True
5 False
The DJ didn't buy the third song.

Fact box

Music and dance are very important in Scotland. Typical instruments include the fiddle, bagpipes, drums and harp.

Cultural awareness

Traditional music and dance

Exercise 1

1 c
2 b
3 a
4 d

1 3.20 **Listen to four traditional Scottish instruments. Match the music to the instruments in pictures a–d.**

a fiddle

b bagpipes

c drums

d harp

Exercise 2

bagpipes
drums

2 3.21 **Read and listen to the email. Which two traditional Scottish instruments did Lucy hear?**

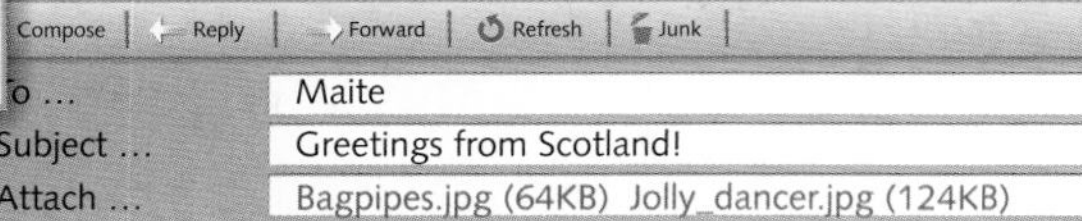

To ... Maite
Subject ... Greetings from Scotland!
Attach ... Bagpipes.jpg (64KB) Jolly_dancer.jpg (124KB)

Hi Maite,

Here are some photos from my summer holiday with my family in Scotland. I had a fantastic time!

First, we visited Edinburgh, which is a great city. We went to the Military Tattoo at Edinburgh Castle – it's an amazing show with traditional Scottish music. There were lots of pipers and drummers, all in traditional costume. My brother said the bagpipes were too loud and annoying, but I thought they were amazing! There were also some fantastic fireworks at the end of the show.

Then, we went to the Highland Games in Aberdeen. We saw some traditional Highland dancing, which was great fun. They wear kilts and tartan socks, and they dance with swords – it looks quite dangerous! We also went to Loch Ness, but we didn't see the monster!

What about you – did you have a good summer? Did you go to the beach?

Love to all the family.

Lucy

Word check

Exercise 3

1 a
2 a
3 b
4 b

3 **Read the email again and choose the correct answers.**

1 Where did they see the Military Tattoo?
a) In Edinburgh **b)** In Aberdeen
2 Did Lucy like the bagpipes?
a) Yes, she did. **b)** No, she didn't.
3 What did they do in Aberdeen?
a) They bought kilts and tartan socks.
b) They went to the Highland Games.
4 Did they see the Loch Ness monster?
a) Yes, they did. **b)** No, they didn't.

CULTURAL COMPARISON

4 **Copy and complete the sentences.**

In my country / region,

1 ... and ... are traditional types of music.
2 ... and ... are traditional instruments.
3 the traditional dances include ... and ... .
4 traditional dancers wear ... .
5 there is a traditional festival in ... .
6 the most popular type of music is ... .

Culture video: Music in the UK

Cultural awareness

Traditional music and dance

Lesson objectives

In this lesson students will:

- read an email about Scotland
- practise reading for gist and specific information
- talk about traditional types of music, instruments and dances

Warmer

Write *Scotland* on the board. Focus students on the Fact box. Then ask students to work in pairs and write down any other information they know about Scotland. Listen to their ideas as a class (eg *It's part of the UK, They speak English there, Edinburgh is the capital city*).

1 3.20

- Play the CD. Students listen and match the music to the instruments in pictures a–d.
- They compare answers in pairs.
- Check answers as a class.
- Point out that *fiddle* is another word for *violin*.

Culture note

Scotland is not the only country where bagpipes are a traditional musical instrument. Bagpipes can also be found in Ireland and have been played for centuries in many parts of Europe (including the north of Spain), Asia Minor and North Africa.

2 3.21

- Make sure students understand the task – to identify two instruments the writer heard.
- Play the CD. Students follow the email in their books. They write the answers.
- Check answers as a class.

Word check

Check students understand the words. A *piper* is someone who plays the *bagpipes*. Check understanding of *swords* by asking students to look at the picture of the dancer and translate the word into their language.

Culture note

Highland Games are held in various regions of Scotland. The main events are piping and drumming, dancing, and Scottish heavy athletics (eg tossing the caber – throwing a large tree trunk), but the games also include entertainment and exhibits related to other aspects of Scottish and Gaelic culture. The biggest Highland Games event in Scotland is held at Dunoon in August with 20,000 spectators and 3,500 competitors.

3

- Students read the questions and the alternative answers first.
- They read the email again and find the answers.
- They compare their answers in pairs or small groups.
- Check answers as a class.

CULTURAL  COMPARISON

4

- Students complete the sentences individually and write them into their notebooks.
- They compare their answers in pairs.
- Listen to their ideas as a class.

Language note

In exercise 4 students may not know the English word for some of the traditional local instruments they suggest. Unless the particular instrument is also used internationally, eg *castanets, tambourine*, there may not be a word in English for it and the local word is acceptable.

Culture video: Music in the UK

Grammar 

Past simple: questions and short answers

Lesson objectives

In this lesson students will:
- learn and use the past simple of regular verbs in questions
- ask and answer *wh-* questions

Warmer

Write these irregular past simple tense forms on the board: *began, wore, bought, gave, became, went, wrote, had*. Students work in pairs and write the negative form of each verb. The first pair to write all eight correct answers wins (*didn't begin, didn't wear, didn't buy, didn't give, didn't become, didn't go, didn't write, didn't have*).

1
- Students look at the tables and read the questions.
- They answer questions a–c.
- Check answers as a class.
- Highlight the fact that the main verb doesn't change at all. The past nature of the question is formed by the auxiliary verb *do* in the past simple.

2
- Read aloud the example question to the class.
- Students work individually and write the past simple questions.
- They compare answers in pairs.
- Check answers as a class.

3
- Students read Lucy's email on page 88 again.
- Nominate two students to read aloud the question and example short answer.
- Do the first answer with the whole class as an example. Elicit the question and short answer from the students and write them on the board (*Did Lucy's family visit Scotland? Yes, they did.*).
- Point out that we use the pronoun *they* when we talk about a family because it has several members.
- Students write the rest of the answers individually.
- They compare answers in pairs.
- Check answers as a class.

4
- Do the first example with the whole class as an example. Elicit the correct order from the class and write it on the board (*Where did you go on holiday?*).
- Students work individually and reorder the words to make questions.
- They compare answers in pairs.
- Check answers as a class.

EXPRESS YOURSELF

5
- Students write their own true answers to the questions in exercise 4.
- They work in pairs and ask and answer the questions.
- Listen to some pairs as a class.

CLIL Grammar in context: Music

6
- Ask students to read the whole text carefully first.
- Students work individually and complete the text with the past simple form of the verbs in brackets.
- They compare their answers in pairs.

7 3.22
- Play the CD. Students check their answers to exercise 6.
- Check students understand the verb *marry*.

CLIL task

Elicit the names of some well-known composers from the students' country and write them on the board. Students choose one of the composers to research. Encourage them to use the internet to find out about their composer's life and work. Ask them to write a short paragraph like the one about Beethoven.

Pronunciation lab: Diphthongs, page 125

Digital course: Interactive grammar table

Study guide: page 93

Exercise 1

a yes
b the infinitive without *to*
c no

Exercise 2

1 Did Lucy's family visit Scotland?
2 Did Lucy have a good holiday?
3 Did Lucy's brother like the bagpipes?
4 Did they watch the fireworks?
5 Did they dance with swords?

ercise 3

Yes, they did.
Yes, she did.
No, he didn't.
Yes, they did.
No, they didn't.

Grammar 

Past simple: questions and short answers

1 Study the tables. Then answer questions a–c.

questions		
Did	I / you / he / she / it / we / you / they	**have** a good summer?
		go to Scotland?

short answers		
Yes,	I / you / he / she / it / we / you / they	did.
No,		didn't.

a) Are past simple question forms the same for all subject pronouns?
b) What form is the verb after *did*?
c) Is it possible to translate *did* into your language?

2 Write past simple questions for 1–5.

Lucy / play the bagpipes?
Did Lucy play the bagpipes?

1 Lucy's family / visit Scotland?
2 Lucy / have a good holiday?
3 Lucy's brother / like the bagpipes?
4 they / watch the fireworks?
5 they / dance with swords?

3 Read Lucy's email on page 88 again and write true answers for the questions in exercise 2.

Did Lucy play the bagpipes? *No, she didn't.*

4 Order the words to make questions.

1 did / you / Where / go / on holiday ?
2 do / What / you / yesterday / did ?
3 listen / When / you / did / music / to ?
4 this / class / did / time / What / start ?
5 have / for / breakfast / What / you / did ?
6 did / travel / How / school / you / to ?

EXPRESS YOURSELF

5 Work in pairs. Ask and answer the questions in exercise 4.

Exercise 4

1 Where did you go on holiday?
2 What did you do yesterday?
3 When did you listen to music?
4 What time did this class start?
5 What did you have for breakfast?
6 How did you travel to school?

CLIL Grammar in context: Music

6 Complete the text with the past simple form of the verbs in brackets.

7  3.22 Listen and check your answers.

xercise 6

died
didn't have
did ... play
played
was
Did ... become
became
didn't stop
composed
wrote

Beethoven

Who was Beethoven?
Ludwig van Beethoven was a German composer and musician. He was born in Bonn in 1770 and he (1) ... (die) in 1827. He never married and he (2) ... (not have) any children.

Which instruments (3) ... he ... (play)?
Beethoven was a pianist. He also (4) ... (play) the organ and the violin. His first public performance (5) ... (be) when he was seven years old.

(6) ... Beethoven ... (become) deaf?
Yes, he did. He (7) ... (become) deaf when he was about 30, but he (8) ... (not stop) composing music. He (9) ... (compose) his famous Ninth Symphony when he was completely deaf.

What are his most famous works?
Beethoven's famous works include nine symphonies and sonatas for piano, cello and violin. He also (10) ... (write) an opera called *Fidelio*.

CLIL TASK
Go online. Find out about a famous composer from your country.
Write a paragraph about his / her life.

 3.23–3.24 Pronunciation lab: Diphthongs, page 125 

At a music festival

TEENFEST

ABOUT | NEWS | BUY TICKETS | BANDS | PHOTOS | FAQS | CONTACT US

TeenFest is Manchester's first music festival only for 13–17 year-olds*! For one day only, you can see loads of the UK's most popular bands in one place.

Date: Saturday 31st March
Place: Green Park, Manchester
Time: 11.00am–8.00pm
Price: £15.00

Artists: Billy Jean, Two Dimensions, Dan May, The Hipsters, Yo-Yo, The Kinetics and many more!

Food and drink available.

* Strictly no entry for under 13s or over 17s. Photo ID is obligatory.

Step 1: Read

1 Read the web page quickly. How old must you be to go to TeenFest?

2 Read the web page again and answer the questions.

1 When was the festival?
2 Where was it?
3 What time did it start?
4 What time did it finish?
5 How much were the tickets?

3 Do you think this festival sounds fun? Why (not)?

Exercise 1
between the ages of 13 and 17

Exercise 2
1 Saturday 31st March
2 Green Park, Manchester
3 11am
4 8pm
5 £15.00

Step 2: Listen

4 3.25 **Listen to three announcements. In what order do you hear them?**

a) Information about an African drumming class.
b) An announcement about the end of the festival.
c) Information about a Scottish pipe band.

5 **Listen again. Choose the correct answers.**

1 The pipe band starts at **5 o'clock** / **7.30**.
2 The drumming class is for **under 16s** / **adults**.
3 The festival closes in **ten** / **thirty** minutes.

Exercise 4
1 c
2 a
3 b

Exercise 5
1 five o'clock
2 under 16s
3 thirty

SKILLS BUILDER

Listening for specific information
When you listen, you don't need to understand every word. Before you listen, read the questions. Then listen for specific information.

Integrated skills

At a music festival

Lesson objectives

In this lesson students will:

- work on all four skills
- read a web page about a music festival
- listen to some announcements
- write a personalized dialogue
- act out their dialogue

Warmer

Write the word *music festival* on the board. Ask students if they know any famous music festivals around the world or in their country.

Step 1: Read

1
- Highlight James' speech bubble. Elicit answers to the question *What did you do last weekend?* from the class.
- Students read the web page and find out how old you must be to go to TeenFest.
- Check the answer as a class.

Culture note

The first Underage Festival for 13 to 17-year olds was held in Victoria Park in London in 2007. It was started by a young man called Sam Kilcoyne who had the idea after he was refused entry to a gig at the age of 14. The festival is held in August and many of the UK's most popular bands can be heard there. BBC Radio 1 broadcasts part of the festival live.

2
- Students read the questions carefully first.
- They look on the web page and find the answers.
- Check answers as a class.

3
- Elicit answers to the questions from the class.

Step 2: Listen

4 3.25
- Make sure the students understand the task.
- They copy the three announcements into their notebooks.
- Play the CD. Students put the announcements in the order in which they hear them.
- They compare answers in pairs.
- Check answers as a class.

5 3.25
- Students read the sentences and the alternative answers.
- Play the CD again. Students choose the correct answers.
- They compare their answers in pairs.
- Check answers as a class.

Skills builder

Listening for specific information

Encourage students to read all the questions carefully before listening. This will help them to identify the specific information they need. Explain that they do not necessarily need to understand every word when they listen.

3.25 Audioscript, exercises 4 and 5

1 Your attention please! The Scottish pipe band is starting soon on the Main Stage. That's the Scottish pipe band at five o'clock on the Main Stage.

2 Attention everyone! This is an announcement about classes and activities. The African drumming class is starting now at the activity tent. All children welcome – under 16s only please for this event!

3 Your attention please! Please make your way to the exits. The festival closes in 30 minutes. Please make your way to the exits now. Thank you.

Integrated skills - continued

Talking about past events

6 3.26

- Students read the words in the box.
- Play the CD. Students follow the dialogue in their books and write the correct answers in the gaps 1–5.
- They compare answers in pairs
- Check answers as a class.

Extra activity

Divide the class into two groups. One takes the part of Hazel and the other the part of James. Play the CD again. Each group reads their lines aloud in time with the recording. Swap roles and repeat the activity.

7
- Play the CD again, pausing after each speaker's part for students to repeat as a class.
- Note the stress on *amazing* and *fantastic*.
- Ask students to repeat the questions and responses several times both chorally and individually with the correct stress and intonation.
- Students practise the dialogue in pairs. Then swap roles and practise the dialogue again.

Step 3: Write

8
- Write the words *concert, football match, cinema* on the board.
- Students look at the tickets and choose one of the events.
- They invent answers to the two questions.

9
- Students work individually and write their dialogue, using the dialogue in the book as a model and the Communication kit: Talking about past events for key phrases.
- Monitor while they are writing and give help if necessary.

Step 4: Communicate

10
- Students practise their dialogues in pairs.
- For extra practice, they swap roles in both dialogues.

11
- Choose some pairs to act out their dialogue for the class.

Integrated skills: Workbook page 118

TALKING ABOUT PAST EVENTS

Hi! Did you have a good weekend?	Yes, I did. It was (1) ... !
What did you do?	I went to a music festival with my brother.
Really? How was it?	It was (2) ... ! I saw some (3) ... bands.
Wow! Cool.	Anyway, what about you? How was your weekend?
Oh, it was (4)	What did you do?
Nothing (5) ... . I went shopping.	Oh well. Next time you can come with us!

Exercise 6
1 amazing
2 fantastic
3 great
4 all right
5 special

6 3.26 **Listen and complete the dialogue with the words in the box.**

fantastic	all right	great	special	amazing

7 **Listen again and repeat. Practise your intonation.**

Step 3: Write

8 **Look at the tickets. Choose an event and imagine you went there last weekend. Invent answers to the questions.**

What did you do last weekend? *I went to ...*
How was it? *It was ...*

THE HIPPODROME
presents
THE HIPSTERS
£25 Doors open at 7.30

Arsenal vs Everton
Saturday 28 April
3.00pm Kick-off
The Emirates Stadium
NOT FOR RESALE NOT FOR RESALE NOT FOR RESALE NOT FO

Orion PICTURE HOUSE
ORION CINEMA PRESENTS
THE HOBBIT
ROW G
SEAT 16

9 **Write a dialogue about your weekend. Use your notes from exercise 8 and the dialogue in exercise 6 to help you.**

Step 4: Communicate

10 **Work in pairs. Take turns to practise your dialogues.**

Hi! Did you have a good weekend?
Yes, I did. It was ...

11 **Act your dialogue for the class.**

COMMUNICATION KIT

Talking about past events

Did you have a good weekend?
Yes, I did. It was great / amazing / fantastic!
No, not really. It was boring / terrible!
What did you do?
What about you?
I went to ... with ... .
Nothing special.

Writing

A personal profile

1  3.27 **Read and listen to the profile of Taylor Swift. Then answer the questions.**

1 Where is Taylor Swift from?
2 What does she do?
3 When was she born?
4 When did she become interested in music?
5 What prize did she win?
6 What is her fourth album called?

Exercise 1
1 the USA
2 She is a singer and musician.
3 1989
4 at the age of 12
5 the GRAMMY Award for album of the year
6 Red

TAYLOR SWIFT: SINGER AND MUSICIAN

Taylor Swift is a famous American singer and musician. She plays the guitar, piano and ukelele. Her favourite type of music is country. I think her songs are great – they're original and unusual.

Taylor was born in Pennsylvania in 1989. At the age of 12, she started to play the guitar. She wasn't happy at school and she began to write songs about her life. When she was 14, her family moved to Nashville – the home of country music.

In 2006, Taylor made her first album. Two years later, she made her second album, Fearless. Taylor won the GRAMMY Award for 'album of the year' when she was only 19 years old. Her third album, Speak Now, came out in 2010 and she made her fourth album, Red, two years later.

2 Study the Writing focus. How do you say the words in *italics* in your language?

WRITING FOCUS

Time expressions
At the age of 12, Taylor started to play the guitar.
When she was 14, her family moved to Nashville.
In 2006, Taylor made her first album.
Two years later, she made her second album.

Exercise 3
in 1989
when she was only 19 years old
in 2010

3 Read the profile again. Find three more examples of time expressions.

4 Match 1–4 with a–d to make sentences.

1 She began to write songs
2 Taylor was born
3 She won the GRAMMY Award
4 Taylor made her second album

a) in 1989.
b) in 2008.
c) at the age of 19.
d) when she was at school.

Exercise 4
1 d
2 a
3 c
4 b

Writing task

Write a personal profile of a famous singer or musician.

Plan Choose a famous singer or musician. Find out about his / her life. Make notes about the singer using the questions in exercise 1.

Write Write three paragraphs:
1 Introduction and your opinion
2 Information about his / her early life
3 Information about his / her work

Check Check your writing.

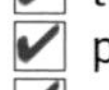

- ✔ time expressions
- ✔ past simple verbs
- ✔ vocabulary for instruments and adjectives of opinion

Build your confidence: Writing reference and practice. Workbook page 134

Writing

A personal profile

Lesson objectives

In this lesson students will:

- learn how to use time expressions in writing
- write a personal profile of a famous singer or musician

Warmer

Think of a singer that your students will know. They have to ask questions and guess the name of the singer. You can only answer using short answers with *Yes* or *No*, eg *Is he a man? No, she isn't. Is she Spanish? Yes, she is. Does she sing pop-rock songs?* Continue until the students have guessed who the singer is.

1 3.27

- Ask students to look at the picture. Ask if they know this singer.
- They read the questions.
- Play the CD. Students listen and follow the profile in their books. They write the answers to the questions.
- They compare answers in pairs.
- Check answers as a class.

Culture note

In addition to her musical career, Taylor Swift has appeared as an actress in the crime drama *CSI: Crime Scene Investigation* (2009), the romantic comedy *Valentine's Day* (2010), the animated film *The Lorax* (2012) and the TV series *New Girl* (2013).

2

- Students read the Writing focus.
- Elicit the translations for the time expressions in italics in their language.

Language note

These time expressions can be used either at the beginning or at the end of the sentence, eg *Taylor made her first album in 2006*. If they are used at the end of the sentence, there is no comma before the time expression.

3

- Students find three more time expressions in the profile.
- They copy them into their notebooks.
- Check answers as a class.

4

- Students match the parts of the sentences.
- They refer back to the profile to check their answers.
- Check answers as a class.

Writing task

The aim of this activity is for students to produce a piece of guided writing using time expressions, past simple verbs, vocabulary for instruments and adjectives of opinion appropriately. Ask the students to follow the stages in the Student's Book. Monitor while they are writing and give help with vocabulary if necessary. At the Check stage, ask them to swap notebooks and check each other's writing.

Writing reference and practice: Workbook page 134

Study guide

Grammar, Vocabulary and Speaking

Tell the students the Study guide is an important page which provides a useful reference for the main language of the unit: the grammar, the vocabulary and the functional language from the Integrated skills pages. Explain that they should refer to this page when studying for a test or exam.

Grammar

- Tell the students to look at the example sentences of the past simple and make sure they know how to form the tense correctly.
- Then tell students to look at the example sentences which contain past time expressions and ensure they understand the meaning. Get students to translate into their own language if necessary.
- Refer students to the Grammar reference on pages 98–99 of the Workbook for further revision.

Vocabulary

- Tell students to look at the list of vocabulary and check understanding.
- Refer students to the Wordlist on page 151 of the Workbook where they can look up any words they can't remember.

Speaking

- Check that students understand the phrases to use for talking about past events.
- Tell students to act out a conversation between two people talking about what they did last weekend.

Additional material

Workbook

- Progress check page 70
- Self evaluation page 71
- Grammar reference and practice page 98
- Vocabulary extension page 109
- Integrated skills page 118
- Writing reference and task page 134

Teacher's Resource File

- Pulse Basics worksheets pages47–52
- Vocabulary and grammar consolidation worksheets pages 31–34
- Translation and dictation worksheets pages 9, 19
- Evaluation rubrics pages 1–7
- Key competences worksheets pages 15–16
- Culture and CLIL worksheets pages 29–32
- Culture video worksheets pages 15–16
- Digital competence worksheets pages 15–16
- Macmillan Readers worksheets pages 5–6

Tests and Exams

- Unit 8 End-of-unit test: Basic, Standard and Extra
- CEFR Skills Exam Generator

Study guide

Grammar

Past simple: affirmative and negative

affirmative	
I / You / He / She / It / We / You / They	**watched** the band. **played** the guitar.
negative	
I / You / He / She / It / We / You / They	**didn't watch** the band. **didn't play** the guitar.

Past simple: questions and short answers

questions
Did I / you / he / she / it / we / you / they **go** to the concert ?
short answers
Yes, I / you / he / she / it / we / you / they **did**. **No,** I / you / he / she / it / we / you / they **didn't**.

LEARNING TO LEARN

Make sure you check if verbs are regular or irregular. Always look in the Irregular verb list on page 126 if you aren't sure. There aren't any rules for irregular verbs – you just have to learn them!

Past time expressions

last	night / weekend / month / year	
in	May / 2014	
two hours / days / months		**ago**

I played my guitar **last night**.
My friend went to a festival **in April**.
I went to a Maroon 5 concert **three months ago**.

Vocabulary

Instruments and musicians

bass — bass player
drums — drummer
guitar — guitarist
keyboards — keyboard player
piano — pianist
vocals — singer
choir
orchestra
conductor

Adjectives of opinion

amazing
annoying
boring
catchy
great
lively
loud
original
quiet
rubbish
surprising
terrible
traditional
unusual

Speaking

Talking about past events

Did you have a good weekend?
Yes, I did. It was great / amazing / fantastic!
No, not really. It was boring / terrible!
What did you do?
What about you?
I went to ... with ... .
Nothing special.

UNIT 9 SPECIAL DAYS

Unit objectives and key competences

In this unit the student will learn…

- understand, memorize and correctly use words related to celebrations **CLC CMST SCC**
- understand, memorize and correctly use a set of adverbs **CLC**
- understand and correctly use grammar structures related to the future and draw parallels to L1 **CLC L2L**
- about national days in the **UK CLC CMST CAE**
- about different ways to celebrate in the UK by watching a short video **CLC SCC CAE**

In this unit the student will learn how to ...

- identify specific information in a blog **CLC DC CAE**
- look for information about a coming-of-age ceremony **CLC DC CAE CIE**
- identify specific information in a news interview **CLC CMST CAE**
- speak about how people celebrate special days **CLC SCC**
- write an invitation **CLC SCC CAE**
- read a poster for a day trip, listen to a group of people talking about going on a day trip and
- make arrangements **CLC SCC**
- prepare to discuss a topic in a speaking exam **CLC L2L**

Linguistic contents

Main vocabulary

- Celebrations: *give presents, sing songs, send cards,* etc
- Adverbs: *quickly, hard, happily,* etc

Grammar

- *be going to*: affirmative, negative and question forms
- Present continuous for future plans

Functional language

- Expressions for making arrangements
- Phrases for interacting with your partner in a speaking exam

Pronunciation

- Rhythm and sentence stress

Skills

Reading

- Read a blog about special days
- Read a text about national days in the UK
- Read a leaflet about a festival

Writing

- Write a personalized dialogue
- Write an invitation in three steps: plan, write, check

Listening

- Listen to a news report extract about New Year resolutions
- Listen to people talking about day trips they are planning

Spoken interaction

- Exchange information about celebrating special days
- Ask and answer questions about future intentions

Spoken production

- Prepare and act out a dialogue about a planned day trip
- Prepare and discuss a topic in a speaking exam

Lifelong learning skills

Self-study and self-evaluation

- Study guide: Student's Book page 103
- Progress check and self-evaluation: Workbook pages 78–79
- Grammar reference and practice: Workbook pages 100–101
- Wordlist: Workbook pages 151–157

Learning strategies and thinking skills

- Identifying which tense is used for different purposes (making arrangements and intentions)

Cultural awareness

- Celebrations around the world
- National days in England, Ireland, Scotland and Wales
- National symbols in the UK
- Comparing local and national celebrations in the UK and Ireland with celebrations in students' own towns and countries

Cross-curricular contents

- ICT: searching the internet for information, making a glog
- Language and literature: Shakespeare, World Book Day, conventions for writing an invitation

Key competences

CLC	Competence in linguistic communication
CMST	Competence in mathematics, science and technology
DC	Digital competence
L2L	Learning to learn
SCC	Social and civic competences
SIE	Sense of initiative and entrepreneurship
CAE	Cultural awareness and expression

Evaluation

- Unit 9 End-of-unit test: Basic, Standard and Extra
- End-of-term test, Units 7–9: Basic, Standard and Extra
- CEFR Skills Exam Generator

External exam trainer

- Speaking: Discussing a topic

Digital material

Pulse Live! Digital Course including:

- Interactive grammar tables
- Audio visual speaking model: Making arrangements
- Audio visual cultural material: Ways to celebrate in the UK

Student's website

Digital competence

- Web quest: Project about coming-of-age ceremonies
- Digital competence worksheet: Comic creator tools

Reinforcement material

- Basics worksheets, Teacher's Resource File pages 53–58
- Vocabulary and Grammar: Consolidation worksheets, Teacher's Resource File pages 35–36

Extension material

- Fast-finisher activity: Student's Book page 95
- Extra activities: Teacher's Book page T94, T96
- Vocabulary and Grammar: Extension worksheets, Teacher's Resource File pages 37–38

Teacher's Resource File

- Translation and dictation worksheets pages 10, 20
- Evaluation rubrics pages 1–7
- Key competences worksheets pages 17–18
- Culture and CLIL worksheets pages 33–36
- Culture video worksheets pages 17–18
- Digital competence worksheets pages 17–18
- Macmillan Readers worksheets pages 5–6

SPECIAL DAYS

THINK ABOUT IT

Make a list of special days that people celebrate each month in your country.

January – New Year's Day

Exercise 2

The people are from the USA, the UK and Australia.

1 decorate
2 sing
3 watch
4 watch
5 wear
6 have
7 send
8 give
9 go
10 visit

Vocabulary and Speaking

Celebrations

1 3.28 **Listen and repeat the words in the box. Which things do you do for someone's birthday?**

eat special food   visit relatives   watch street parades   send cards
give presents   have a party   go to church   decorate the house
sing songs   watch fireworks   wear a costume   have fun

2 **Read the article. Where are these people from? Complete the text with verbs from exercise 1.**

Special days around the world

4th July – Independence Day

On Independence Day, we often (1) ... the house in the colours red, white and blue and we have a party at home. We (2) ... special songs, (3) ... street parades and (4) ... fireworks in the evening.

31st October – Halloween

At Halloween I always (5) ... a costume – this year I'm a witch. My friends and I go to a party at the youth club – we always (6) ... fun!

25th December – Christmas

Here, Christmas is in the summer holidays – it's often 30°C! We usually (7) ... cards and (8) ... presents and we eat special food. Some people (9) ... to church, but in my family, we usually (10) ... relatives and have a picnic on the beach!

3 **Read the Look! box. Then write the dates of the special days from Think about it.**

New Year's Day is on 1st January.

LOOK!

Ordinal numbers

We use ordinal numbers for dates.

1st = first	12th = twelfth
3rd = third	23rd = twenty-third

EXPRESS YOURSELF

4 **Choose three celebrations. Write them on a piece of paper and give them to your partner.**

18th March: my birthday

5 **Work in pairs. Ask and answer questions about your celebrations from exercise 4.**

How do you usually celebrate your birthday?

I usually have a party and ...

Vocabulary extension: Workbook page 110

Vocabulary and Speaking

Celebrations

Lesson objectives

In this lesson students will:

- learn vocabulary for activities on special days
- revise ordinal numbers for dates
- talk about celebrations

Warmer

Write four or five months of the year on the board with the letters in the wrong order, eg *s u g t a u* (*August*), *o e r b c t o* (*October*). Students work in pairs and write the correct spellings.

Think about it

Elicit the months of the year in the correct order and write them on the board. Students work in pairs and make a list of special days that people celebrate for each month in their country.

1 

- Students read the words in the word pool.
- Play the CD. Students listen to the words and repeat them.
- Ask which of these things they usually do for someone's birthday.

2

- Students read the article and look at the pictures. Elicit where the people are from (the USA, the UK, Australia).
- Students work individually and fill the gaps in the text by using words from the word pool from exercise 1.
- They compare their answers in pairs.
- Check answers as a class.

Culture note

American independence from the UK was declared on 4th July 1776. The first President of the United States was George Washington, who took office in 1789. Today Independence Day is a federal holiday celebrated across the whole of the USA. It is usually called Fourth of July and it is also the American National Day.

3

- Students read the information about ordinal numbers and dates in the Look! box.
- Revise the ordinal numbers from *first* to *tenth*, paying particular attention to the irregular ordinal numbers.
- Students write the dates next to the special days they listed in the Think about it activity earlier in the lesson.
- Check answers as a class.

Language note

Remind students that we can say dates in two ways. You can say *the third of August* or *August the third*. You can write dates in three ways: *3rd August*, *August 3rd* or *3 August*. You don't need to write *the* or *of* when you write dates but you must use them when you say dates.

4

- Students choose three celebrations (eg *their birthday, Christmas, New Year's Eve*).
- They write the three dates and events on a piece of paper.
- Put students into pairs.
- They give their paper to their partner.

5

- Nominate two students to read aloud the model question and the beginning of the model answer to the class.
- Pairs ask and answer their questions about their celebrations.
- Listen to some pairs as a class.

Extra activity

Students work in pairs and play a guessing game. They think of the best birthday or Christmas present they ever received. They have to guess what their partner's present is by asking questions. Their partner can only answer using short answers with *Yes* or *No*, eg *Was it a bicycle? No, it wasn't. Was it connected with sport? Yes, it was.*

Vocabulary extension: Workbook page 110

Reading

Text type: A blog

Lesson objectives

In this lesson students will:

- read a blog
- talk about birthday celebrations

Warmer

All the students come to the front of the class and stand in a line side by side with their backs to the classroom wall. They rearrange the line from 1st January on the left to 31st December on the right, according to their birthday. They have to ask the question *When's your birthday?* and give the date in English, eg *the tenth of January*. Check that the order is correct by getting each student to say their birthday.

1 3.29

- Students read the question.
- Play the CD. Students follow the blog in their books and find the answer to the question.
- Check the answer as a class.

Word check

Check students understand all the new words.

Culture note

In many countries 13 is a special age as it is when children become teenagers and 18 is also a special age as it is when young people officially become adults. In England, 21 is a special birthday too as until 1970 it was the age when young people became adults.

2

- Write on the board *I watched a film on TV last night. It was really good*.
- Ask what the word *It* refers to (*the film*).
- Students look at the words in green in the blog and the example.
- They write down what the words in green refer to.
- Check answers as a class.

3

- Students read the questions carefully first. Make sure they understand them.
- They read the blog again and find the answers.
- They compare their answers in pairs.
- Check answers as a class.

EXPRESS YOURSELF

4

- Students work individually and answer the questions.
- They compare their answers in pairs.
- Check answers as a class.

Finished?

Ask fast finishers to make a list of 13 things they would like to do this year. They can refer back to James' list of 13 new adventures for ideas.

Web quest

Students do a class project about coming-of-age ceremonies. Highlight the Web quest tip.

1
- Students work in groups of girls and boys and find out about their coming-of-age ceremony.
- Ask students to open an internet web browser such as Internet Explorer. Students open a search engine (eg Google) and type in the name of their ceremony.

2
- They find as much information as they can about their ceremony by answering the *wh-* questions (*Where? What? Why? When? Who?*) and share their information with the group.

3
- Groups of girls and groups of boys work together and share their research.
- Students report back to the class.

Reading
A blog

Exercise 1
Because it's his 13th year.

1 3.29 **Read and listen to the blog. Why has James chosen to have 13 adventures during the next year?**

13 adventures for my 13th year …

▶ June (2)
▼ July (1)
About me
View my profile
Photo album

My 13 adventures
1 Visit London
2 Go to Wembley
3 Try 13 new sports
4 Go camping
5 Join a band
6 Run a 5 k race
7 Learn Spanish
8 Read 13 books
9 Learn to juggle
10 Learn to cook
11 Travel by plane
12 Do voluntary work
13 Get a dog!

25th June Next Saturday I'm going to be 13 …
… and I'm having a big party! After that, it's going to be a special year. I'm going to have 13 new adventures (click on the links to see more about **them**). Enjoy my blog and please send **me** your comments!

Posted by Hazel at 20:32
Great idea, James – I love your list of adventures! Your blog looks great and I'm looking forward to reading **it**. Are you going to put more photos in the album?

29th June Tomorrow's the big day!
My brother's decorating the house – he's going to fill **it** with balloons! And my sister's making an enormous chocolate cake. ☺

Posted by Aunt Anne at 17:12
Happy birthday, James! Have a great day. Sorry I can't come to your party. ☹

1st July It's official: I'm a teenager!
The party was fantastic! Thanks to all my friends and relatives for the amazing presents. Now my year of adventure begins … with a trip to London!
My aunt lives there and I'm going to visit **her**. She's going to take me to watch Manchester United play at Wembley!

Posted by John at 10:52
Congratulations on becoming a teenager! Have fun in London. What are you going to do for your next adventure?

Word check
look forward to (+ *-ing*) balloon trip teenager Congratulations!

Exercise 2
me – James
it – James' blog
it – the house
her – James' aunt

2 Look at the green words in the blog. What or who do they refer to?
them = James' new adventures

Exercise 3
1 He's going to have 13 (new) adventures.
2 His brother's decorating the house by filling it with balloons and his sister's making an enormous chocolate cake.
3 James' Aunt Anne.
4 In London.
5 They're going to watch Manchester United play at Wembley.

3 Read the blog again and answer the questions.
1 What is James going to do to celebrate being 13?
2 What are James' brother and sister doing on 29th June?
3 Who can't come to James' birthday party?
4 Where does James' aunt live?
5 What are James and his aunt going to do?

4 Answer the questions.
1 How did you celebrate your last birthday?
2 How are you going to celebrate your next birthday?
3 Which birthdays are most important in your country?

FINISHED?
Write a list of 13 things you would like to do this year.

WEB QUEST
Make a class project about coming-of-age ceremonies.
1 **Girls:** Find out about the Apache sunrise dance.
Boys: Find out about the Satere-Mawe tribe's bullet ant gloves.
2 Answer these questions: Where? What? Why? When? Who?
3 Work together in your group and share your research. Then tell the rest of the class.

Web Quest tip!
A librarian can help you find information in books and on the internet. Ask for help!

Grammar

be going to

Exercise 1
1 're going to
2 isn't
3 Are
We use *be going to* for the future.

Exercise 2
1 I'm going to sing songs. I'm not going to sing songs.
2 My friend's going to go to church. My friend isn't going to go to church.
3 We're going to decorate the house. We aren't going to decorate the house.
4 My mum's going to make a cake. My mum isn't going to make a cake.
5 They're going to have a party. They aren't going to have a party.

Exercise 3
2 Are you going to have
3 'm going to have
4 are you going to cook
5 'm not going to cook
6 're going to have
7 's going to pay
8 aren't going to tell
9 Are you going to invite

1 Read the table. Then copy and complete 1–3. Do we use *be going to* for the past, present or future?

affirmative	
I'm going to have a party.	
You're going to have fun.	
He / She / **It's going to** make a cake.	
We / You / They (1) ... **going to** send cards.	
negative	
I'm not going to visit relatives.	
You're not going to eat special food.	
He / She / It (2) ... **going to** sing songs.	
We / You / They **aren't going to** celebrate.	
questions and short answers	
(3) ... you **going to** watch fireworks?	Yes, I **am**. / No, I**'m not**.
Is he / she / it **going to** celebrate?	Yes, he / she / it **is**. No, he / she / it **isn't**.
Are we / you / they **going to** have fun?	Yes, we / you / they **are**. No, we / you / they **aren't**.

2 Order the words to make affirmative sentences. Then make them negative.

watch / to / parades / We / the / are / going .
+ *We are going to watch the parades.*
– *We aren't going to watch the parades.*

1 sing / I'm / going / songs / to .
2 go / is / My / friend / going / to / church / to .
3 going / We're / decorate / to / house / the .
4 cake / make / mum's / My / to / going / a .
5 party / a / They're / going / have / to .

3 Complete the dialogue with the affirmative, negative or question forms of *be going to*.

Ben: How (1) *are you going to celebrate* (you / celebrate) your birthday? (2) ... (you / have) a party?
Ann: No, I (3) ... (have) dinner with friends.
Ben: Really? What (4) ... (you / cook)?
Ann: I (5) ... (not cook)! We (6) ... (have) dinner in a restaurant. My grandad (7) ... (pay)!
Ben: Wow! Which restaurant?
Ann: I don't know – it's a surprise. They (8) ... (not tell) me until my birthday.
Ben: Cool. (9) ... (you / invite) me?!

EXPRESS YOURSELF

4 Write questions about your intentions.

Where / live / when you're older?
Where are you going to live when you're older?

1 How / you / celebrate / your next birthday?
2 What presents / you / ask for?
3 you / travel / this summer?
4 What / you / do / during the holidays?
5 you / study English / at university?

5 Work in pairs. Ask and answer your questions from exercise 4.

Where are you going to live when you're older?
I'm going to live in Paris!

Exercise 4
1 How are you going to celebrate your next birthday?
2 What presents are you going to ask for?
3 Are you going to travel this summer?
4 What are you going to do during the holidays?
5 Are you going to study English at university?

Object pronouns

6 Look at the table. How do you say the blue words in your language?

subject pronouns							
I	you	he	she	it	we	you	they
object pronouns							
me	**you**	**him**	**her**	**it**	**us**	**you**	**them**
We use object pronouns to replace nouns that are the object of a sentence. *My aunt lives in London. I'm going to visit her.*							

7 Copy and complete the sentences with your own ideas and an object pronoun.

My aunt lives in London. I sometimes visit *her*.

1 In my country, we often eat ... at Christmas. I love ... !
2 In my town, there are fireworks on ... . I sometimes / never watch ... .
3 Our English teacher's name is ... . He / She doesn't usually give ... homework in the holidays.
4 My best friend often goes to the ... . I sometimes go with ... .

Exercise 7
1 students' own answers; it / them
2 students' own answers; them
3 students' own answers; us
4 students' own answers; her

Is the word order for *be going to* sentences similar or different in your language?

Pronunciation lab: Rhythm and sentence stress, page 125

Grammar 

be going to

Lesson objectives

In this lesson students will:

- learn and use the *be going to* form of the future in the affirmative, negative and in questions and short answers
- revise subject and object pronouns

Warmer

Write *a card, a present, the house, fun, a party, special food, a cake* on the board. Students work in pairs and write verbs that can go with these nouns to make expressions we use for celebrations like birthdays. Elicit examples from the class and write the verbs on the board, eg *send, give, decorate, have, have, eat, make*.

1
- Tell students that we use the verb *be* in the present simple tense in the *be going to* form.
- Students copy the tables and complete 1–4.
- Check answers as a class.
- Elicit that we use *be going to* for the future.

Language note

Short answers to questions with *be going to* are the same as short answers with the present continuous, eg *Is she making a cake? Yes, she is. Is she going to come to the party? Yes, she is*. We don't use *going to* in the short answers.

2
- Students read the example sentences.
- Students write affirmative sentences by reordering the words.
- They write negative forms of the sentences.
- Check answers as a class.

3
- Students read the dialogue carefully first.
- They fill the gaps with the affirmative, negative or question forms of *be going to* using the verbs in brackets.
- They compare their answers in pairs.
- Check answers as a class.

EXPRESS YOURSELF

4
- Read the example question aloud to the class.
- Students use the prompts to write more questions using *be going to*.
- They compare answers in pairs.
- Check answers as a class.

5
- Nominate two students to read the example question and answer aloud to the class.
- Students write their own answers to the questions in exercise 4.
- They work in pairs and ask and answer the questions.
- Listen to some pairs as a class.

Extra activity

Students work in pairs and write two or three further questions using *going to* to add to those in exercise 4, eg *What are you going to do next weekend?* They work with another pair and ask and answer their questions.

Object pronouns

6
- Students look at the table.
- They translate the blue words into their language.
- Highlight that we use object pronouns to replace nouns that are the object of a sentence.
- Write the example sentences on the board.
- Elicit that *I* is the subject of the second sentence.
- Highlight that we use object pronouns to replace nouns or noun phrases that are the object of the sentence.

7
- Focus students on the example and make sure they understand the task.
- Students complete the first sentences in each pair with their own ideas and the second sentences with the correct object pronouns.
- Check answers as a class.

Analyse

Ask students to translate *I am going to* into their language. Ask if the word order is the same or different.

Pronunciation lab: Rhythm and sentence stress, page 125

Digital course: Interactive grammar table

Study guide: page 103

Vocabulary and Listening

Adverbs

Lesson objectives

In this lesson students will:
- learn some adverbs
- listen for specific information

Warmer

Write these adjectives on the board: *quiet, difficult, safe, unhappy, good, fast*. Students work in pairs and write the opposites. The first pair to write all six correctly wins (*loud, easy, dangerous, happy, bad, slow*).

1 3.32
- Check students understand *intention* and *resolution.*
- Students read the quiz.
- Play the CD. Students listen and repeat the adverbs in blue.
- Highlight the pronunciation and stress of *regularly* /ˈregjələlɪ/.

2
- Students read the quiz again and choose an answer a or b to each question.
- They calculate their total score.
- They read the comment that corresponds to their score.
- Students compare their total scores in pairs.
- Find out which students are going to do very well this year.

Look!

Check students understand the concept of an adverb – a word that shows how we do something.

3
- Students read the adverb spelling rules on page 103.
- They copy the table into their notebooks and add the adverbs from the quiz to the correct column.
- They write the adjectives for these adverbs in the adjective column.
- They compare answers in pairs.
- Check answers as a class. Highlight the irregular adverbs – *hard* and *well*.

4
- Students copy the adjectives into the adjective column in the table.
- They write the equivalent adverbs in the adverb column.
- They compare answers in pairs.
- Check answers as a class. Highlight the irregular adverbs *far* and *fast*, the spelling change from *-y* to *-i* in *noisily*, the disappearing *-e* in adverbs whose adjective ends in *-le*, eg *terribly*, and the double *l* in *wonderfully*.

5
- Students read the resolutions and identify the adverbs.
- Check answers as a class.

6 3.33
- Students copy the resolutions from exercise 5 into their notebooks.
- Play the CD. Students put the resolutions in the order they hear them.
- Check answers as a class.

7
- Students read the questions carefully first.
- Play the CD again. Students write the answers.
- Students compare answers in pairs.
- Check answers as a class.

3.33 Audioscript, exercises 6 and 7

Newsreader Now it's over to Rob Porter live in London.
Rob Thanks, Sophie! I'm here next to the River Thames, waiting for the fireworks! There are thousands of people here to celebrate the New Year. While we wait for the fireworks, I'm going to ask a few people if they've made any resolutions. Hello! What are your resolutions for the new year?
Person 1 I'm going to learn a new language – I want to learn Spanish!
Rob Spanish? Great! And what about you?
Person 2 I'm going to exercise more regularly.
Rob Great idea! How about you?
Person 3 I'm going to eat well and be more healthy!
Rob So many good intentions!
Person 4 Yeah – I'm going to study hard and pass all my exams this year!
Rob And how about you?
Person 5 Me? I'm going to be happy and have more fun!
Rob And that starts now, right? It's nearly midnight. Here's Big Ben ... Happy New Year everyone!!

Vocabulary and Listening

Adverbs

1 3.32 **Read the quiz. Listen and repeat the adverbs in blue.**

2 Do the quiz. What's your score?

LOOK!

We use adverbs to describe how we do things.
*I'm **happy**. I'm going to live **happily**!*

3 Read the spelling rules on page 103. Then copy and complete the table with the adverbs from the quiz.

Adverb	Adjective
quickly	*quick*
hard	*hard*

4 Add the adjectives in the box and their adverb form to the table in exercise 3.

noisy	quiet	brave	safe
fast	terrible	wonderful	

5 Read the resolutions. How many adverbs can you find?

a) I'm going to study hard and pass all my exams this year.
b) I'm going to exercise more regularly.
c) I'm going to learn a new language.
d) I'm going to be happy and have more fun!
e) I'm going to eat well and be more healthy.

6 3.33 **Listen to an extract from the news. In what order do you hear the resolutions in exercise 5?**

7 Listen again and answer the questions.

1 What day is it?
2 Where is the reporter?
3 What are the people waiting for?
4 Which language does the woman want to learn?
5 What time is it at the end of the report?
6 What do you hear at the end of the report?

Exercise 3

adverbs
oudly, nicely, healthily, regularly, well, easily, dangerously, happily, badly

adjectives
oud, nice, healthy, regular, good, easy, dangerous, happy, bad

Exercise 4

adverbs
noisily, quietly, bravely, safely, fast, terribly, wonderfully

Exercise 5

a hard
b regularly
e well

Exercise 6

1 c
2 b
3 e
4 a
5 d

Exercise 7

1 New Year's Eve
2 in London next to the River Thames
3 the fireworks
4 Spanish
5 It's nearly midnight.
6 Big Ben (striking midnight) and the fireworks

Today is a good day to reconsider your resolutions for the year!

1 School

What's your attitude to school this year?

a) Maximum results with minimum effort. I'm going to do my homework as **quickly** as possible so I can go out with my friends!
b) I'm going to work **hard** and practise my English every day!

2 Home and family

Are you an angel or a little devil at home? Choose your resolution:

a) My room is my space … I'm going to play my music as **loudly** as I want!
b) I promise to tidy my room and speak **nicely** to my brother or sister.

3 Health and fitness

Are you planning to be healthier this year?

a) No way! My health regime starts next year …
b) Yes – I'm going to eat **healthily**, relax more and do sport **regularly**.

4 Friends

Are you a good friend?

a) Who needs real friends? I've got hundreds on Facebook!
b) Friends are precious! I'm going to treat my old friends **well** and make new friends more **easily**.

5 The year ahead

What's your motto for the year ahead?

a) Live **dangerously** – you're only young once!
b) Live **happily** – that's the most important thing!

Points: a = 2 b = 3

Your score:

10–12 What a disaster! Do you really want to behave so **badly** this year?

13–15 Great! You've got so many good intentions. You're going to do very well this year!

Cultural awareness

National days

Exercise 1
a St Patrick's Day
b St Andrew's Day
c St David's Day

1 Look at pictures a–c. Which special days do they show?

2 3.34 Read and listen to the text. Find these words.

1 The adjectives for Ireland, Scotland, Wales and England.
2 The name of a religion.
3 The name of a flower.

Exercise 2
1 Irish, Scottish, Welsh, English
2 Christianity
3 daffodil

Fact box

Ireland
St Patrick's Day
17th March

Wales
St David's Day
1st March

Scotland
St Andrew's Day
30th November

England
St George's Day
23rd April

Let's celebrate our special days!

It's St Patrick's Day and everybody is wearing green clothes and painting their faces! This afternoon we're watching the street parades in the city centre. Did you know that the Irish patron saint was actually born in Wales? He travelled far from home and brought Christianity to Ireland in the 5th century.

Here in Scotland, St Andrew's Day is a national holiday and most people celebrate it. This evening my friends and I are going to a ceilidh – a big party with traditional music and dancing. Guess what? Saint Andrew wasn't Scottish! He was from Israel and he became one of Christ's 12 apostles.

It's St David's Day and many Welsh people wear a daffodil, the national flower of Wales, and traditional clothes. Our patron saint was a Welsh monk. He was born in the 6th century, and legend says that he worked very hard and lived happily to the age of 100!

England's patron saint is Saint George. In the legend, he killed a dragon and rescued a princess. St George's Day isn't a national holiday in England, but there are folk festivals and celebrations in some English towns and villages.

a

b

c

Word check
patron saint century apostle monk legend

Exercise 3
1 They wear green clothes, paint their faces and watch or take part in street parades.
2 He was one of Christ's 12 apostles.
3 A daffodil and traditional clothes.
4 In the 6th century.
5 He killed a dragon and rescued a princess.

3 Read the text again and answer the questions.

1 How do people celebrate St Patrick's Day?
2 Who was Saint Andrew?
3 What do people wear on St David's Day?
4 When was Saint David born?
5 In the legend, what did Saint George do?

CULTURAL COMPARISON

4 Answer the questions.

1 Has your town or village got a patron saint?
2 How do people celebrate your town or village's special day?
3 Is there a national day in your region / country?

Culture video: Ways to celebrate in the UK

Cultural awareness

National days

Lesson objectives

In this lesson students will:

- read about national days in the four countries of the UK
- practise reading for specific information
- talk about their special days and national days

Recommended web links

www.projectbritain.com

Warmer

Books closed. Write *the UK* on the board and elicit what it stands for (*the United Kingdom*). Ask students to tell you the names of the four countries that make up the UK (*England, Scotland, Wales, Northern Ireland*). Ask students to spell each country's name and write it on the board.

1
- Focus students on the Fact box and point out the names and dates of the four countries' national days.
- Students match pictures a–c with three of the national days in the Fact box.
- They compare answers in pairs.
- Check answers as a class.

Word check

Check students understand the new words. Check the word *century* by asking what century we are in now – the 21st century. Ask them to translate the words into their language.

Culture note

The daffodil is only one of the national symbols of Wales. The others are the *leek*, a long green and white vegetable that is similar to an onion, and the *red dragon*, which also appears on the Welsh flag.

2  3.34
- Check students understand the task.
- Play the CD. Students follow the text in their books and find the words.
- They write the answers.
- Check answers as a class.

3
- Students read the questions first.
- They read the text again and find the answers.
- They compare their answers in pairs or small groups.
- Check answers as a class.

CULTURAL COMPARISON

4
- Students answer the questions individually.
- They compare their answers in pairs.
- Listen to their ideas as a class.

Culture video: Ways to celebrate in the UK

Grammar 

Present continuous for future plans

Lesson objectives

In this lesson students will:

- learn and use the present continuous for future plans
- read a short text about Shakespeare

Warmer

Write on the board two or three sentences in the present continuous tense with the words in the wrong order, eg *the at I reading book a moment am* (*I am reading a book at the moment*); *sister now doing homework her is my* (*My sister is doing her homework now*). Students work in pairs and write the sentences in the correct order. Check answers as a class. This will help to prepare students for the next activity.

1
- Students read sentences a–d.
- They look at the information in the table and decide which two sentences refer to the future.
- Check answers as a class.
- Highlight the fact that the present continuous can refer to the present and the future. We usually know which time the present continuous refers to because of the adverbials of time that are used with it (eg *at the moment* = present time; *this weekend* = future time).

2
- Do the first question with the whole class as an example. Elicit the question from the students and write it on the board (*Where are you going on holiday this year?*).
- Students work individually and complete the rest of the dialogue.
- They compare answers in pairs.
- Check answers as a class.

EXPRESS YOURSELF

3
- Do the first question with the whole class as an example. Elicit the question from the class and write it on the board.
- Students work individually and write the remaining questions.
- They compare answers in pairs.
- Check answers as a class.

4
- Students write their own true answers to the questions in exercise 3.
- Focus students on the example dialogue.
- They work in pairs and ask and answer the questions.
- Listen to some pairs as a class.

 Grammar in context: History

5
- This activity practises the present continuous for future plans and object pronouns.
- Ask students to read the text carefully first.
- Do the first example with the whole class to demonstrate the activity (the answer is *'m going*).
- Students work individually and choose the correct word or words from the three possibilities.
- They compare their answers in pairs.

6 3.35
- Play the CD. Students check their answers to exercise 5.
- Check students understand *school trip* (a special excursion with your class to a place of interest).

Culture note

Stratford-upon-Avon is a small, historic market town with a population of around 25,000. It is situated about 35 km south-east of Birmingham and 160 km north-west of London. Stratford is extremely popular with tourists. It is estimated that more than five and a half million visitors come to Stratford each year.

CLIL task

Students research World Book Day. Encourage them to use the internet to find out about World Book Day in their country. Ask them to report back to the class at the start of the next lesson.

Digital course: Interactive grammar table

Study guide: page 103

Grammar 

Present continuous for future plans

Exercise 1
c and d

1 Read the table. Then choose two sentences from a–d which refer to the future.

a) What are you doing at the moment?
b) I'm studying English grammar.
c) What are you doing this weekend?
d) I'm playing football on Sunday morning.

present continuous for future plans
We use the present continuous to talk about specific plans with a fixed date or time in the near future. This afternoon I'**m watching** the parades. This weekend we'**re visiting** our cousins.

Exercise 2
1 are you going
2 're going
3 Are you flying
4 's driving
5 'm not going
6 'm working

2 Complete the dialogue with the correct form of the present continuous.

Kay: Where (1) ... (you / go) on holiday this year, Dan?
Dan: We (2) ... (go) to Spain – to the Costa del Sol.
Kay: Wow! That sounds great. (3) ... (you / fly) to Málaga?
Dan: No – my dad (4) ... (drive) there. It takes about three days.
Kay: Really? Well, have fun! I (5) ... (not go) on holiday this summer. I (6) ... (work) at the café for five weeks.
Dan: Oh dear. I'll send you a postcard from the beach!

EXPRESS YOURSELF

Exercise 3
1 Where are you going this evening?
2 What are you doing tomorrow morning?
3 What are you doing on Sunday afternoon?
4 Where are you going in the summer holidays?
5 Are you doing anything special next week?

3 Write questions for 1–5. Use the present continuous for future plans.

1 Where / you / go / this evening?
2 What / you / do / tomorrow morning?
3 What / you / do / on Sunday afternoon?
4 Where / you / go / in the summer holidays?
5 you / do / anything / special / next week?

4 Work in pairs. Ask and answer your questions from exercise 3.

What are you doing this evening?
I'm watching a DVD. What are you doing?

CLIL Grammar in context: History

5 Read the text and choose the correct answers.

6 3.35 **Listen and check.**

Exercise 5
1 'm going
2 are we going to
3 're visiting
4 is
5 us
6 her
7 easy
8 're going
9 it
10 good

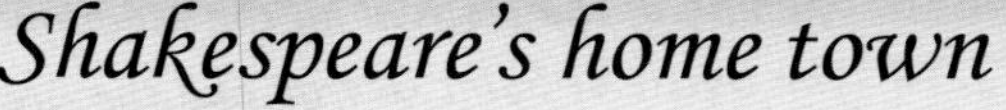

Shakespeare's home town

Tomorrow I (1) **'m going / go / went** on a school trip to Stratford-upon-Avon – the town where Shakespeare lived. What (2) **are we going to / we are going to / do we** do there? In the morning, we (3) **visit / 're visiting / visited** Shakespeare's house. Our history teacher (4) **am / is / are** going to be our guide. Our English teacher is coming with (5) **we / us / them** too. We're studying *Hamlet* with (6) **she / her / it** at the moment. It isn't (7) **easy / easily / hardly**!

In the afternoon, we (8) **'re going / go / went** to the Swan Theatre to see *Romeo and Juliet*. That's my favourite Shakespeare play – we studied (9) **it / him / them** last year. It's going to be a (10) **badly / good / well** day!

CLIL TASK

World Book Day is celebrated on 23rd April because Miguel de Cervantes and Shakespeare both died on 23rd April 1616.

Go online. Find out about World Book Day in your country.

Going on a day trip

Next Saturday I'm going on a day trip to Nottingham – there's a festival for Saint George's Day. Do you ever go on day trips?

Saint George's Day Festival in Nottingham

Saturday 10.30–4.30

10.30 Opening of the festival by the Mayor of Nottingham
11.30 'The Battle of Saint George and the Dragon' at Nottingham Castle
12.30 Morris dancers in the Market Square
1.30 Archery and jousting at Nottingham Castle
2.30 Brass band in the Market Square
3.30 Scout parade through the city

FUN FOR ALL THE FAMILY!

There is also a Medieval market all day in the Market Square.
All events are FREE!

Exercise 1
jousting
the battle of Saint George and the dragon

Exercise 2
1 the Mayor of Nottingham
2 12.30
3 at Nottingham Castle
4 in the Market Square
5 4.30
6 There's going to be a Scout parade through the city.

Step 1: Read

1 Look at the poster. Which of the activities in the box can you see in the pictures?

Morris dancing · brass band · jousting · archery · Scout parade · Medieval market · The battle of Saint George and the dragon

2 Read the information in the poster and answer the questions.

1 Who is opening the festival?
2 What time are the Morris dancers starting?
3 Where are they going to do the archery and jousting?
4 Where is the brass band going to play?
5 What time does the festival finish?
6 What is happening at 3.30?

Step 2: Listen

3 3.36 Listen to four teenagers talking about going on a trip. Which four trips do they talk about?

a) A school trip to an exhibition in London.
b) A day trip to Windsor Castle.
c) A trip to visit relatives in Manchester.
d) A Scout trip to the mountains in Wales.
e) A day trip to the beach at Blackpool.
f) A day trip to an amusement park.

4 Listen again and choose the correct answers.

1 Ann is going to visit the **Science Museum** / **National Art Gallery**.
2 Ben is going to stay with his **cousins** / **grandparents**.
3 Charlotte is going to stay at a **youth hostel** / **campsite**.
4 David is going to travel by **car** / **bus**.

Exercise 3
a A school trip to an exhibition in London.
c A trip to visit relatives in Manchester.
d A Scout trip to the mountains in Wales.
f A day trip to an amusement park.

Exercise 4
1 Science Museum
2 grandparents
3 campsite
4 car

Integrated skills

Going on a day trip

Lesson objectives

In this lesson students will:

- work on all four skills
- read a poster about a festival
- listen to people talking about going on a trip
- write a personalized dialogue
- act out their dialogue

Warmer

Elicit the names of the four countries of the UK from the students and write them on the board (*England, Scotland, Wales, Northern Ireland*). Then ask them to tell you the names of the patron saints of each country. Elicit the names (*George, Andrew, David, Patrick*) and write them next to the countries.

Step 1: Read

1
- Highlight Hazel's speech bubble. Elicit answers to the question *Do you ever go on day trips?* from the class.
- Students look at the poster and read the list of activities. Point out that in *jousting*, people fight with long, sharp sticks while riding horses.
- They look at the pictures and say which activities they can see.
- Check answers as a class. Point out that *archery* is an Olympic sport.

2
- Students read the questions carefully first.
- They look at the information and find the answers.
- Check answers as a class. Make sure students understand the word *mayor*, the official head of a town or city.

Culture note

Historical events like archery and jousting are popular in Nottingham because of the city's long association with the legend of Robin Hood, an outlaw who robbed the rich to give to the poor. Robin Hood was a skilled archer and lived in Sherwood Forest, just to the north of the city of Nottingham.

Step 2: Listen

3  3.36
- Make sure the students understand the task.
- They read the descriptions of the six trips carefully.
- Play the CD. Students identify the four trips they hear in the recording.
- They compare answers in pairs.
- Check answers as a class.

4
- Students read the sentences and the alternative answers.
- Play the CD again. Students choose the correct answers.
- They compare their answers in pairs.
- Check answers as a class.

3.36 Audioscript, exercises 3 and 4

1 Ann Next Wednesday I'm going on a school trip to the Science Museum in London. We're going to see an exhibition about space and the universe and all that ...

2 Ben Next weekend I'm going on a trip to Manchester to visit my relatives. We're all going to stay at my grandparents' house and we're going to celebrate my grandma's 60th birthday with all the family.

3 Charlotte I'm going on a Scout trip to Wales. We're going to stay on a campsite right in the mountains – it's going to be amazing! We're going to climb the highest mountain in Wales. I'm so excited!

4 David On Saturday I'm going on a day trip with my best friend Peter and his parents. They're going to drive to a fantastic amusement park called Alton Towers. I'm going to go on the biggest rollercoaster! It's going to be fun!

Integrated skills - continued

Making arrangements

5 3.37

- Play the CD. Students follow the dialogue in their books and choose the correct answers.
- They compare answers in pairs.
- Check answers as a class.

6
- Play the CD again, pausing after each speaker's part for students to repeat as a class.
- Note the main stress on the *wh-* questions: *What are you up to? Who else is going?*
- Ask students to repeat the questions and responses several times both chorally and individually with the correct stress and intonation.
- Students practise the dialogue in pairs. Then swap roles and practise the dialogue again.

Step 3: Write

7
- Students choose a place to go on a trip.
- They write answers to the four questions individually.

8
- Students work individually and write their dialogue, using the dialogue in the book as a model and the Communication kit: Making arrangements for key phrases.
- Monitor while they are writing and give help if necessary.

Skills builder

Talking about arrangements and intentions
Remind students that we use the present continuous for arrangements and *be going to* + verb for intentions.

Step 4: Communicate

9
- Students practise their dialogues in pairs.
- For extra practice, they swap roles in both dialogues.

10
- Choose some pairs to act out their dialogue for the class.

Integrated skills: Workbook page 119

Hi there. What are you up to?	Oh, nothing special. I'm just (1) **going to class / going to the library**.
Listen, are you free on (2) **Saturday / Sunday**?	Yes, I think so. Why?
I'm going to a Saint George's Day festival in Nottingham. Do you want to come?	That sounds fun. Who else is going?
My brother and my (3) **friend / cousin** Harry.	Great! What time are you going?
We're leaving at (4) **10 o'clock / half past ten.**	OK. Shall I come round to your house?
Yes, great. See you soon.	See you (5) **tomorrow / on Saturday**!

Exercise 5
1 going to class
2 Saturday
3 cousin
4 10 o'clock
5 on Saturday

5 3.37 **Listen to the dialogue and choose the correct answers.**

6 **Listen again and repeat. Practise your intonation.**

Step 3: Write

7 **Imagine you are going on a day trip. Answer the questions in your notebook.**

1 Where are you going?
2 When are you going?
3 Who else is going?
4 What time are you leaving?

8 **Prepare a new dialogue about your day trip. Write both parts. Use your notes from exercise 7 and the dialogue in exercise 5 to help you.**

Hi there. What are you up to?
Oh, nothing special. I'm ...

SKILLS BUILDER

Talking about arrangements and intentions

Remember to use the present continuous for arrangements and *be going to* for intentions.

*We**'re going** to the beach on Saturday.*
*I**'m going to swim** in the sea.*

Step 4: Communicate

9 **Work in pairs. Take turns to practise your dialogues.**

Hi there. What are you up to?
Oh, nothing special. I'm ...

10 **Act your dialogue for the class.**

COMMUNICATION KIT

Making arrangements

Are you free on ... ?
Yes, I think so. / No, I'm not – sorry!
I'm going to ... . Do you want to come?
That sounds fun. / Sorry, I can't.
Who else is going?
What time are you going?

Hello all,

It's Independence Day on 4th July and we're having a party – we hope you can come!

The party is at our house in Washington on Saturday. It starts at 5 o'clock in the afternoon. Dad's going to do a barbecue (he can cook really well!). After that, we're going to watch the fireworks. The weather should be good. It's always warm and sunny in July!

All my cousins from Florida are coming too. It's going to be a lot of fun! Let me know if you can come. And don't forget to wear red, white and blue!

See you soon!

Brad

PS We're decorating the garden in the morning – do you want to come and help?

Writing

An invitation

Exercise 1

1 at Brad's house
2 Saturday 4th July
3 5 o'clock
4 barbecue
5 watch the fireworks

1 3.38 **Read and listen to Brad's invitation. Copy and complete the notes about Brad's party.**

Brad's Independence Day party
1) Where? ...
2) When? ...
3) What time? ...
4) Food ...
5) Activity ...

2 Look at the Writing focus and translate the examples. Do you always use a preposition in your language?

WRITING FOCUS

Prepositions of time and place

in	towns, cities and states months / seasons parts of the day	*in Washington* *in July / in the summer* *in the afternoon*
on	days dates	*on Saturday* *on 4th July*
at	places times	*at our house* *at 5 o'clock*

3 Complete the sentences with *in*, *on* or *at*.

1 It's my birthday ... 3rd March.
2 We're having dinner ... eight o'clock.
3 My relatives are coming ... the morning.
4 What are you doing ... Friday?
5 He's on holiday ... Paris.
6 We're going to have a party ... the youth club.

Exercise 3

1 on
2 at
3 in
4 on
5 in
6 at

Writing task

Imagine it's your birthday next week. Write an invitation to your friends.

Plan Decide when and where you're going to have a party. Make notes like the ones in exercise 1.

Write Write your invitation. Use your notes and the invitation to help you.

Check Check your writing.

- ✔ *in, on, at*
- ✔ correct forms of *be going to* or present continuous for future plans
- ✔ vocabulary for celebrations

Build your confidence: Writing reference and practice. Workbook page 136

Writing

An invitation

Lesson objectives

In this lesson students will:

- learn how to use prepositions of time and place in writing
- write an invitation

Warmer

Ask students to imagine they can invite a famous person to their birthday party. Students work in pairs and discuss who they are going to invite and why. Listen to their ideas as a class.

1 3.38

- Students read the notes about Brad's party and copy them into their notebooks.
- Play the CD. Students listen and follow Brad's email in their books. They complete the notes.
- They compare answers in pairs.
- Check answers as a class. Check students understand *barbecue*.

2

- Students look at the Writing focus.
- They translate the example phrases.
- Ask students if they always use a preposition of time and place in the example phrases in their language.

Language note

We use *at* with buildings, especially public buildings, eg *at the station, at the library, at the airport*. We also use *in* with years (*in 2010, in 2014*).

3

- Students find one more preposition in the email.
- Check the answer as a class.

4

- Students complete the sentences using *in, on* or *at*.
- They refer back to the list in exercise 2 to check their answers.
- Check answers as a class.

Writing task

The aim of this activity is for students to produce a piece of guided writing using prepositions of time and place, *be going to* + verb for intentions and the present continuous for future plans appropriately. It also gives them practice in using vocabulary for celebrations. Ask the students to follow the stages in the Student's Book. Monitor while they are writing and give help with vocabulary if necessary. At the Check stage, ask them to swap notebooks and check each other's writing.

Writing reference and practice: Workbook page 136

Study guide

Grammar, Vocabulary and Speaking

Tell the students the Study guide is an important page which provides a useful reference for the main language of the unit: the grammar, the vocabulary and the functional language from the Integrated skills pages. Explain that they should refer to this page when studying for a test or exam.

Grammar

- Tell the students to look at the example sentences of *be going to* and make sure they know how to form the verb correctly.
- Then tell students to look at the example sentences of object pronouns and ensure they understand the meaning. Get students to translate into their own language if necessary.
- Tell students to look at the example sentences of the present continuous for future plans and ensure they know how to form the tense correctly. Get students to translate into their own language if necessary.
- Refer students to the Grammar reference on pages 100–101 of the Workbook for further revision.

Vocabulary

- Tell students to look at the list of vocabulary and check understanding.
- Refer students to the Wordlist on page 151 of the Workbook where they can look up any words they can't remember.

Speaking

- Check that students understand the phrases to use for making arrangements.
- Tell students to act out a conversation between two friends making plans for next weekend.

Additional material

Workbook

- Progress check page 78
- Self evaluation page 79
- Grammar reference and practice page 100
- Vocabulary extension page 110
- Integrated skills page 119
- Writing reference and task page 136

Teacher's Resource File

- Pulse Basics worksheets pages 53–58
- Vocabulary and grammar consolidation worksheets pages 35–38
- Translation and dictation worksheets pages 10, 20
- Evaluation rubrics pages 1–7
- Key competences worksheets pages 17–18
- Culture and CLIL worksheets pages 33–36
- Culture video worksheets pages 17–18
- Digital competence worksheets pages 17–18
- Macmillan Readers worksheets pages 5–6

Tests and Exams

- Unit 9 End-of-unit test: Basic, Standard and Extra
- CEFR Skills Exam Generator
- End-of-term test: Basic, Standard and Extra

Study guide

Grammar

be going to

affirmative
I'm **going to** visit London.
He / She / It's **going to** buy a ticket.
We / You / They're **going to** watch football.
negative
I'm **not going to** visit Nottingham.
He / She /It **isn't going to** buy two tickets.
We / You / They **aren't going to** watch cricket.

questions and short answers	
Am I **going to** visit London?	Yes, I **am**. No, I'**m not**.
Is he / she / it **going to** go camping?	Yes, he / she / it **is**. No, he / she / it **isn't**.
Are we / you / they **going to** watch football?	Yes, we / you / they **are**. No, we / you / they **aren't**.

Object pronouns

subject pronouns							
I	you	he	she	it	we	you	they
object pronouns							
me	you	him	her	it	us	you	them

We use object pronouns to replace nouns that are the object of a sentence.
My aunt lives in London. I'm going to visit her.

Present continuous for future plans

present continuous for future plans
This afternoon I'**m watching** a film.
This evening we'**re playing** football.

Speaking

Making arrangements

Are you free on ... ?
Yes, I think so. / No, I'm not – sorry!
I'm going to .... Do you want to come?
That sounds fun. / Sorry, I can't.
Who else is going?
What time are you going?

Vocabulary

Celebrations

decorate the house
eat special food
give presents
go to church
have a party
have fun
send cards
sing songs
visit relatives
watch fireworks
watch street parades
wear a costume

Adverbs

badly
dangerously
easily
happily
hard
healthily
loudly
nicely
quickly
regularly
well

Adverb spelling rules

- For most adverbs add *-ly* to the adjective
  bad → badly
- For adjectives that end in *-e*, omit the *-e* and add *-ly*
  terrible → terribly
- For adjectives that end in *-y*, omit the *-y* and add *-ily*
  healthy → healthily
  easy → easily
- Some adverbs are irregular. They don't follow any rules!
  good → well fast → fast

LEARNING TO LEARN

Don't confuse *well* and *good*.
You speak English well (adverb).
You are good at English (adjective).

Progress check: Workbook page 78
Grammar reference: Workbook page 100

COLLABORATIVE PROJECT 

Step 1: Think — Step 2: Listen and plan — Step 3: Create — Step 4: Evaluate

Making a presentation

TASK

Work in pairs to prepare a presentation about a singer or a group.

DIGITAL LITERACY

When you make a presentation, remember to:

- have an overview, introduction and conclusion.
- organize the information into slides.
- carefully edit the material and make it look attractive – use photos, headings, different fonts and colours.

Step 1: Think

1 Look at the slides from the presentation. Find an example of:

1 a video clip
2 the overview of the presentation
3 headings
4 photos
5 facts about the group
6 the cover of a CD

All about Little Mix

Overview

6 cover of a CD

1) Introduction
2) Who are Little Mix?
3) How they became famous
4) More about the members
5) About their music
6) A song
7) Conclusion

2 the overview of the presentation

3 a heading

Who are Little Mix?

1 a video clip

- Little Mix are a British girl band.
- There are four girls in the band: Perrie Edwards, Jesy Nelson, Leigh-Anne Pinnock and Jade Thirlwall. They all sing.
- Little Mix are very popular in the UK.

How they became famous

4 a photo

- Little Mix started in 2011. They formed on a talent show called *The X Factor*. Everyone thought they were fantastic, and they won. They were the first group ever to win the show!
- After the show, Little Mix got a record deal. Then they released their first single in December 2011. Their first album came out in November 2012.

5 Facts about the group

Collaborative project 3

Making a presentation

Lesson objectives

In this lesson students will:
- create a presentation about a singer or pop group
- identify features of a presentation
- listen to a group planning a presentation
- read and complete dialogue extracts

Warmer

Write the word *music* on the board. Elicit some words related to the topic, eg *singer, guitar, band,* etc. In teams, students brainstorm and write down as many words related to the topic as they can. The team with the most words writes them on the board. Other teams then add any other words they have on their lists. Check spelling and pronunciation and practise the words as necessary.

TASK

Read the task with the class and check students understand. NOTE: If students do not have access to computers, they can do a short oral presentation about a singer or group instead. If they have any pictures they can stick them on the board. If there is time, they could play a song or song extract on a CD player.

Step 1: Think

1
- Discuss digital presentations with the class. Have they seen any? Have they ever made one? What things can you include?
- Read the list of items students have to identify and help with any vocabulary. Point out that *a heading* is a page title and *a slide* is a single page from a presentation.
- Ask students to read the slides and find an example of each item.
- Check answers as a class.
- Read the Digital literacy box with the class and check students understand.

Step 2: Listen and plan

2 3.39
- Ask students to read the questions carefully.
- Play the CD. Students listen and answer the questions.
- Check answers as a class.

3
- Read the Useful language box with the class and help with any vocabulary.
- Students read the conversation extracts and complete them in pairs.
- Play the CD again. Students listen and check their answers.
- Check answers with the class. Students practise the extracts in groups.

4
- Explain to the class that they are going to plan a presentation in pairs.
- Ask students to read the list of things they need to do to plan their presentations.
- Students work in pairs and plan their presentations. Ask one or two pairs to report back to the class to explain their plans.

Step 3: Create

5
- Read the steps with the class to give students a clear idea of what they have to do.
- Monitor while they are writing and give help where necessary.

Share information

Students share their information in their pairs. They discuss their work and how to improve it. They check for errors.

Create the presentation

Each pair creates their presentation. Encourage them to be creative and to try to make the presentation as attractive as possible. Remind them to use a variety of colours and styles. Students practise giving their parts of the presentation to their partner. Alternatively, they can record themselves and then listen and correct any problems.

Show and tell

Each pair gives their presentation. Allow time for the other students to ask questions and comment on the presentation. If you like, the class can vote for their favourite presentation.

Step 4: Evaluate

6
- Look at the evaluation grids with the class.
- Read through the different options and help with any vocabulary as necessary.
- Students complete their self-evaluation. Give help if necessary.

Extra activity

Give out empty wordsearch grids. Individually or in pairs, students write 5–10 words related to music in their grid. Then they complete the wordsearch with other random letters. Students or pairs swap their wordseach grids. Then they find and circle the music-related words.

3.39 Audioscript, exercises 2 and 3

Mario OK, so let's practise the introduction and conclusion. You start the introduction…
Ana Hello, everyone. Today we're doing a presentation about a British pop group called Little Mix. We chose this group because we think it's interesting that some pop groups start from talent shows.
David As you can see on this overview slide, in the presentation, first we're going to tell you about the group, then we're going to explain how they became famous.
Laura After that, we're going to tell you something about their music and finally, you can listen to one of their best songs. So, to begin, who are Little Mix?
…
Mario In conclusion, we think Little Mix are a good example of British pop music. We hope you enjoyed the presentation and that you learned a bit about Little Mix.
Ana Has anyone got any questions?

Step 2: Listen and plan

2 3.39 **Listen to Mario, Ana, Silvia and David discussing their presentation and answer the questions.**

1 In what order do they do these things in the introduction?
a) say what the presentation is about
b) explain the overview page
c) say why they chose the group

2 In what order do they do these things in the conclusion?
a) say they hope people enjoyed the presentation
b) ask if there are any questions
c) give an opinion about the group

Exercise 2
1 c, a, b
2 c, a, b

3 Complete the conversation extracts with the words in the box. Listen again and check your answers.

chose example today first think finally see hope explain questions

Introduction

Mario: OK, so let's practice the introduction and conclusion. You start the introduction.
Ana: Hello everyone. (1) ... we're doing a presentation about a British pop group called Little Mix. We (2) ... this group because we think it's interesting that some pop groups start from talent shows.
David: As you can (3) ... on the overview slide in the presentation, (4) ... we're going to tell you about the group, then we're going to (5) ... how they became famous.
Silvia: After that, we're going to tell you about their music and (6) ... you can listen to one of their best songs. So, to begin, who are Little Mix? ...

Conclusion

Mario: In conclusion, we (7) ... Little Mix are a good (8) ... of British pop music. We (9) ... you enjoyed the presentation, and that you learned a bit about Little Mix.
Ana: Has anyone got any (10) ... ?

Exercise 3
1 Today
2 chose
3 see
4 first
5 explain
6 finally
7 think
8 example
9 hope
10 questions

4 Work in groups. Plan your presentation. Use the Useful language box to help you.

- Choose a person or group to write about.
- Decide what information to include.
- Decide how to share the work. Make sure everyone contributes.
- Decide when to meet again to share your information.

Step 3: Create

5 Follow the steps to create your presentation.

Share information
Read or listen to each other's work. Discuss your work. Check these things:

- Is it in your own words?
- Have you got all the information you need?
- Have you got photos, video clips, etc?
- Is the grammar and vocabulary correct?
- Is the spelling and punctuation correct?

Create the presentation
Create the presentation using an appropriate tool. Make sure all the information is complete and in the correct place. Add your photos and video clips. Then, check the grammar, vocabulary, spelling and punctuation again. Practise giving the presentation.

Show and tell
Give your presentation to the class.

Step 4: Evaluate

6 Now ask your teacher for the group and individual assessment grids. Then complete the grids.

USEFUL LANGUAGE
For the introduction
Today, we're doing a presentation about … .
We chose this group because … .
First, we're going to tell you about ... .
Then we're going to explain how ... .
After that, we're going to tell you about … .
For the conclusion
In conclusion, we think … .
We hope you enjoyed the presentation.
Has anyone got any questions?

External exam trainer

Your exam preparation

1 Read questions 1–5 in the Model exam. Translate the questions into your language.

2 3.40 Read and listen to the Model exam. Does Miguel give any one-word answers?

Exercise 2
No, he doesn't.

EXAM TIP: Give full answers

Don't give one-word answers! Try to give as much information as possible.

Where do you live? Coslada. ✗
I live in Coslada. It's near Madrid. ✓

About the exam

Giving personal information
The examiner asks you questions about yourself, your family, your school or your interests. This tests your ability to understand and answer questions.

3 3.41 Match 1–6 with a–f. Then listen, check and repeat.

1 first name
2 surname
3 birthday
4 address
5 email address
6 phone number

a) 628 134 759
b) the 18th of January
c) M-I-G-U-E-L
d) 23, Calle Betis
e) G-O-M-E-Z
f) mgomez@mail.com

Exercise 3
1 c
2 e
3 b
4 d
5 f
6 a

EXAM TIP: The alphabet and numbers

You often need to spell your name or give your telephone number or email address. Practise the English alphabet and numbers!

MODEL EXAM

1 What's your name?
My name's Miguel.
2 Can you spell that, please?
Yes, of course. It's M-I-G-U-E-L.
3 How old are you?
I'm twelve years old.
4 Where do you live?
I live in Coslada. It's near Madrid.
5 Have you got any brothers and sisters?
Yes, I have. I've got two sisters.

UNIT 1

Your exam preparation

Lesson objectives

In this lesson students will:
- practise giving full answers
- practise using the alphabet and numbers

Target exams

This section will prepare your students for the following external exams:
- KET speaking part 1
- EOI A2

1
- Students look at the Model exam.
- They read questions 1–5 and translate them into their language.
- Check answers as a class.

2 3.40
- Play the CD.
- Students read and listen to the Model exam.
- Highlight the fact that none of the answers are one-word answers.

Exam tip

Point out that it is important for students not to simply give one-word answers as this can sound rude or abrupt in English, eg *Where do you come from? Spain*. Encourage them to give more information, eg *Where do you come from? I come from Oviedo. It's in the north of Spain*. Ask them to read the Exam tip and highlight the extra information in the ticked sentences.

3 3.41
- Explain the task. Students match 1–6 with the answers a–f.
- They work individually to complete the task.
- They compare answers in pairs.
- Play the CD. Students listen, check their answers and repeat.
- Make sure students pronounce the numbers and letters correctly. In the email address, point out that @ is *at* and .com is *dot com*.

Exam tip

Point out that it is important for students to be able to say letters, numbers and email addresses correctly.

Extra activity

For extra practice, dictate a fictional address, telephone number and email address to the class. Then ask students to read them back to you, spelling the address and pronouncing the numbers correctly. Then put students into pairs and ask them to dictate their telephone number and email address to their partner.

3.41 Audioscript, exercise 3

Examiner Can you spell your first name?
Miguel Yes, it's M-I-G-U-E-L.
Examiner And can you spell your surname, please?
Miguel Yes, it's G-O-M-E-Z.
Examiner When's your birthday?
Miguel It's on the 18th of January.
Examiner What's your address?
Miguel It's 23, Calle Betis.
Examiner What's your email address?
Miguel It's mgomez@mail.com.
Examiner And what's your phone number?
Miguel It's 628 134 759.

Your exam practice

4
- Explain the task. Students match the answer beginnings a–f with the questions in Your exam.
- They work individually to complete the task.
- They then copy and complete the answer beginnings with true information.
- Check answers as a class.

5
- Students copy and complete the table with their personal details. Ask students to look at the Useful vocabulary box if necessary.
- Ask individual students to spell names and addresses and to say their phone numbers, email addresses and birthdays.
- Make sure they pronounce the letters and numbers correctly.

6
- Go through the Useful expressions box.
- Students look again at the questions in Your exam.
- They work in pairs and ask and answer the questions, using the information from the table in exercise 5.

Speaking: Giving personal information

Your exam practice

Exercise 4
1 b
2 d
3 a
4 f
5 e
6 c
students' own answers

4 **Match answers a–f with questions 1–6 in Your exam. Then copy and complete the answers with information that is true for you.**

a) I'm from … .
b) My surname is … .
c) Yes, I have. It's … .
d) Yes, of course. It's … .
e) My phone number is … .
f) My birthday is on … .

5 **Copy and complete your personal information. Practise spelling the names and saying the numbers and dates.**

My personal information	
First name:	
Surname:	
Address:	
Phone number:	
Email address:	
Birthday:	

6 **Work in pairs. Ask and answer the questions in Your exam.**

Exam kit: Useful vocabulary

Personal information

(first) name — surname
address — phone number
at = @ — email address

Months of the year

January February March April May June July August September October November December

Countries and nationalities

Spain – Spanish — China – Chinese
Morocco – Moroccan — Mexico – Mexican

Exam kit: Useful expressions

My name / surname is … .
I'm from … .
I live in … .
My address is … .
I've got … brothers / sisters.
My email address is … .
I'm … years old.
My birthday is on … .
My phone number is … .

1 Giving personal information
2 True or False activity
3 Pairwork activity
4 Gap-fill activity
5 Describing a photo
6 Multiple-choice pictures
7 Role-play activity
8 Multiple-choice answers
9 Discussing a topic

UNIT 2

External exam trainer

Your exam preparation

Exercise 1
Sally and Paul

About the exam

True or False activity
You listen to a conversation. You decide if five sentences are true or false. This tests your ability to understand people talking about their experiences and opinions.

1 **Read the instructions and the example. Who are you going to hear?**

Example
Listen to a conversation between Sally and Paul. Decide if each sentence is true or false.

Sally's favourite subject is PE. TRUE / FALSE

2 **Read the example sentence in exercise 1 again. Is it about Paul or Sally? Translate the key words into your language.**

Exercise 2
Sally

Sally's favourite subject is PE. TRUE / FALSE

We are interested in **Sally's** favourite subject – not Paul's.	We are interested in Sally's **favourite** subject – not the subjects that she doesn't like.	Is Sally's favourite class PE? Or does she prefer a different subject?

EXAM TIP: Key words
When you read the questions, underline the names and the important words (key words). This helps you know what to listen for.

MODEL EXAM

Exercise 3
False

3 3.42 **Read and listen to Sally and Paul's conversation. Is the example sentence in exercise 1 true or false?**

UNIT 2

Your exam preparation

Lesson objective

In this lesson students will:
- practise listening for key words

Target exams

This section will prepare your students for the following external exams:
- PET listening part 4
- EOI A2

1
- Ask students to read the instructions and the example sentence carefully.
- Ask who they are going to hear.
- Check the answer as a class.

Exam tip

Point out that with listening exercises it is very important for students to read the questions carefully before they begin the task. Highlight the importance of underlining key words as this will help students to know what information to listen for.

2
- Ask students to read the example sentence in exercise 1 again.
- Ask if the sentence refers to Paul or Sally and check the answer (*Sally*).
- Students translate the underlined key words into their language.
- Check students' translations of key words as a class.
- Go through the notes on each underlined word as a class.

3 3.42
- Explain the task. Students read and listen to the conversation and say if the example sentence in exercise 1 is true or false.
- Play the CD. Students follow the conversation in their books.
- Check the answer as a class.

Your exam practice

UNIT 2

Step 1:

4
- Students read the instructions for Your exam.
- They answer the question.
- Check the answer as a class.

Step 2:

5
- Students read the five sentences in Your exam.
- They copy them into their notebooks.
- They underline the names and the key words, eg *Laura usually goes skiing in the winter holidays*.
- Listen to students' suggestions for key words as a class.

Steps 3 and 4:

6 
- Check students understand the task – they should decide if each sentence is true or false.
- Play the CD.
- Give students time to choose the correct answer.
- Play the CD again.
- Students compare answers in pairs.
- Check answers as a class.

Exam tip

Point out that with listening tests like this, the recording is always played twice so students should not panic if they do not understand the recording the first time.

3.43 Audioscript, exercise 6

Simon Do you usually go away during the winter holidays, Laura?
Laura Yes, I do. I usually go skiing!
Simon Wow! Really? You're lucky!
Laura Yeah – my aunt and uncle live in Scotland, near a ski station! We usually stay with them during the holidays. What about you? Do you usually go on holiday?
Simon No, we usually stay at home during the winter holidays. We always go away in the summer, though.
Laura Yeah? So what do you usually do in the winter holidays, when you stay at home?
Simon Well, it often snows in my town too, so I can play in the snow with my friends. We don't go skiing, but we go sledging! I love the snow.
Laura Yes, me too. I love skiing. I get up early in the holidays and go skiing all day!
Simon Hmm – well, I don't like getting up early during the holidays. When I'm not at school, I usually get up late. Sometimes I don't get up until midday!
Laura Well, enjoy the holidays, Simon.
Simon Yes – you too. Have a great time skiing!

Your exam practice

Exercise 4
Laura and Simon

Step 1: Read the instructions.

4 Read the instructions for Your exam. Who are you going to hear?

Step 2: Read all the sentences.

5 Copy sentences 1–5 from Your exam into your notebook. Then <u>underline</u> the names and the key words.

Exercise 5

1. Laura usually goes skiing in the winter holidays.
2. Laura's aunt and uncle live in Austria.
3. Simon stays at home in the winter holidays.
4. Simon and Laura both like the snow.
5. Laura gets up late during the holidays.

Step 3: Listen to exercise 6 and choose the correct answers.

Step 4: Listen again and check your answers.

EXAM TIP: Listen twice

Don't panic if you don't understand the first time. You always hear the conversation twice.

YOUR EXAM

6 3.43 Listen to a conversation between Laura and Simon. You will hear the conversation twice. Decide if each sentence is true or false.

1. Laura usually goes skiing in the winter holidays. TRUE / FALSE
2. Laura's aunt and uncle live in Austria. TRUE / FALSE
3. Simon stays at home in the winter holidays. TRUE / FALSE
4. Simon and Laura both like the snow. TRUE / FALSE
5. Laura gets up late during the holidays. TRUE / FALSE

Exercise 6

1. True
2. False
3. True
4. True
5. False

External exam trainer

Your exam preparation

Exercise 1
a is 1
b What 4
c How 5
d do 3
e much 2

Exercise 2
a It's on Friday the eighth of December.
b We leave at quarter to nine in the morning.
c You can ask the PE teacher – Mrs White – if you've got any questions.
d We go by bus.
e They cost £7.50.

About the exam

Pairwork activity
Students work in pairs of A and B. Student B has a card with information on it. Student A has a card with ideas for questions about the information. This tests your ability to ask and understand questions, and to interpret information.

1 Choose the correct words in questions a–e. Then match them with 1–5 in the Model exam.

a) When **is** / **are** the trip?
b) **What** / **When time do we leave?**
c) **How** / **Who** can I get more information?
d) How **does** / **do** we travel there?
e) How **much** / **many** do the tickets cost?

2 Carlos and Rafa are doing the Model exam. Read the information and their conversation. Then answer the questions from exercise 1.

3  3.44 Read Carlos and Rafa's conversation again. Then listen and check. Who asks their partner to repeat the question?

Exercise 3
Rafa

Exam tip: Repetition
If you don't hear or understand your partner's questions, it's OK to ask them to repeat.

Sorry, can you repeat that, please?

MODEL EXAM

Student A: your questions

School trip to Activity Centre

1 when / trip?
2 tickets / £?
3 how / travel?
4 we / leave?
5 how / information?

Student B: your information

School trip to Activity Centre

Friday 8th December
Bus leaves school at 8.45 and returns at 4.30
Tickets cost £7.50
Any questions?
Ask Mrs White (PE teacher).

Carlos: Hi, Rafa. I'd like to ask you some questions about the school trip. First, when is the trip?

Rafa: It's on Friday the 8th of December.

Carlos: OK, thanks. How much do the tickets cost?

Rafa: Let's see. They cost £7.50.

Carlos: Great! And how do we travel to the Activity Centre?

Rafa: Sorry, can you repeat that, please?

Carlos: Yes – how do we travel to the Activity Centre? Do we go by train?

Rafa: Ah, no. We go by bus.

Carlos: I see. What time do we leave?

Rafa: We leave at quarter to nine in the morning.

Carlos: Oh, that's early! Thanks for your help.

Rafa: That's OK.

UNIT 3

Your exam preparation

Lesson objectives

In this lesson students will:

- practise asking and answering questions
- practise interpreting information

Target exam

This section will prepare your students for the following external exams

- KET speaking part 2

1
- Students read the questions.
- They work individually and choose the correct words.
- They match the questions with prompts 1–5 in the Model exam.
- Check answers as a class.

2
- Students read the information and the conversation between Carlos and Rafa.
- They work individually and answer the questions from exercise 1.
- They compare answers in pairs.
- Check answers as a class.

3 3.44
- Make sure students understand the task – they need to find who asks for repetition.
- Play the CD.
- Students listen to the conversation and read it again. They answer the question.
- Check the answer as a class.

Exam tip

Point out that it is a good idea to ask for repetition if you cannot hear or you do not understand your partner's questions. Focus students on the Useful expressions: Asking for repetition on page 111. Point out that two ways to ask for repetition are *Sorry, can you repeat that, please?* or *Could you say that again, please?* Ask students to repeat the questions chorally and individually and encourage them to use them.

Your exam practice

4
- Students look at the poster in Your exam.
- They work individually and write the words in 1–4 in the correct order to make questions. Ask students to look at the Useful grammar box if necessary.
- They compare answers in pairs.
- Check answers as a class.

Exam tip

Encourage students not to use *er* or *um* if possible. Ask students to look at the Useful expressions box: Giving yourself time to think. Point out that we can use these expressions when we need time to think.

5
- Students look at the information in Your exam.
- They use the information to prepare answers to the questions in exercise 4 by completing sentences 1–4.
- They compare answers in pairs.
- Check answers as a class.

6
- Ask students to close their books or cover exercises 4 and 5.
- Put them into pairs.
- They practise Your exam and take it in turns to be Student A and Student B.
- Choose some pairs to do the activity again for the class.

Your exam practice

xercise 4
1 Where are the karate classes?
2 How often are the classes?
3 What time do they start?
4 How much do the classes cost?

4 Look at Your exam. Then order the words in 1–4 to make questions.

1 classes? / karate / Where / the / are
2 often / How / classes? / are / the
3 start? / time / they / do / What
4 much / classes / do / cost? / How / the

EXAM TIP: Give yourself time to think

Try not to say *er* or *um* too often! Learn the Useful expressions to give yourself time to think.

5 Look at the information in Your exam. Then prepare answers to the questions in exercise 4 by completing sentences 1–4.

1 They're at ... .
2 They're every ... .
3 They start ... .
4 The classes cost ... .

6 Now cover exercises 4 and 5. In pairs, practise Your exam. Take turns to be Student A and Student B.

Exercise 5
1 They're at Belview Sports Centre.
2 They're every Monday evening.
3 They start at 5.15.
4 The classes cost £5.

Student A: your questions

Karate classes

1 where?
2 how often?
3 time / start?
4 cost?

Student B: your information

EXAM KIT: Useful grammar

***be* questions**

question word	*be*	subject	other words
	Is	the trip	on Wednesday?
When	is	the trip?	

***Do* / *Does* questions**

question word	*do* / *does*	subject	verb	other words
	Do	we	travel	by bus?
What time	does	the bus	leave?	

EXAM KIT: Useful expressions

Asking for repetition
Sorry, can you repeat that, please?
Could you say that again, please?

Giving yourself time to think
Let's see.
Well, ...
OK, ...

4 Gap-fill activity
5 Describing a photo
6 Multiple-choice pictures
7 Role-play activity
8 Multiple-choice answers
9 Discussing a topic

External exam trainer

Your exam preparation

About the exam

Gap-fill activity
You listen to a conversation or a monologue. You have to complete five gaps with a number, time, date or word. This tests your ability to listen for specific information.

Exercise 1
Bath

1 Read the information. In which city is the Fashion Museum?

FASHION Museum
visitor information

Location: (1) ... Street, Bath

Ticket prices: Adults: £7.50

Children: (2) ... Family ticket: (3) ...

Opening times:

1 April – 31 October: 10.00 until (4) ...

1 November – (5) ... : 10.30 until 4.30

2 Study gaps 1–5 in exercise 1. What type of information is in each gap?

1 = a name

a time a name a price a date

Exercise 2
2 a price
3 a price
4 a time
5 a date

EXAM TIP: Analyse the gaps
Study the missing information carefully. What kind of word or number do you need? Is it a name, a date, a price or a time?

3 3.45 Read and listen to the Model exam. Can you complete all five gaps in exercise 1?

Exercise 3
1 Bennett
2 £5.50
3 £21
4 5.00
5 31st March

Lucy: So where is the Fashion Museum, exactly?

Rick: It's on Bennett Street.

Lucy: How do you spell that?

Rick: It's B-E-N-N-E-T-T. Bennett Street.

Lucy: OK, thanks! And how much does it cost?

Rick: Well, it's £7.50 for adults and £5.50 for children. Or you can get a family ticket for £21.

Lucy: What are the opening times?

Rick: From the 1st of April until the 31st of October, it's open from 10 in the morning until 5. Then from the 1st of November until the 31st of March, it's open from 10.30 in the morning until 4.30 in the afternoon.

Lucy: Great, thanks!

UNIT 4

Your exam preparation

Lesson objective

In this lesson students will:

- practise listening for specific information

Target exams

This section will prepare your students for the following external exams:

- KET listening part 4 / 5
- PET listening part 3
- EOI A2

1
- Ask students to read the question carefully.
- They look in the visitor information and find the answer.
- Check the answer as a class.

2
- Ask students to look again at the visitor information.
- They work in pairs and decide if the words in gaps 1–5 are a time, a name, a price or a date.
- Check answers as a class.

Exam tip

Point out that with listening exercises like this it is very important for students to know the kind of word or number they are listening for. If they know in advance that it is a name, a date, a price or a time, this will make the listening task easier.

3 3.45
- Play the CD.
- Students read and listen to the Model exam.
- They complete the five exercise 1.
- Check answers as a class.

Your exam practice

UNIT 4

Step 1:

4
- Students read the instructions in Your exam carefully.
- They answer the questions.
- Check answers as a class.

Step 2:

5
- Ask students to read the information in Your exam.
- Make sure they understand that their task is to find which of these things is not mentioned in the information about Madame Tussauds.
- They read the information and find the answer.
- Check the answer as a class.

Step 3:

6
- Students look at gaps 1–5 in Your exam.
- They choose one of the two options for each gap.
- Check answers as a class.

Steps 4 and 5:

7 3.46
- Play the CD.
- Students write the correct words in the gaps.
- Play the CD again.
- Students compare answers in pairs.
- Check answers as a class.

3.46 Audioscript, exercise 7

Maria Oh, hello. I'm thinking about visiting Madame Tussauds – can you give me some information, please?
Man Yes, of course.
Maria What are the opening times?
Man Let's see … well, from Monday to Friday it's open from half past nine in the morning, until half past five. Then at the weekend it's open from nine until six.
Maria OK. And how much are the tickets?
Man Er – the prices are from £22.50 for adults and £19 for children. Or you can get a family ticket for £81.
Maria Oh, OK. It's quite expensive! Er, and where is it, exactly?
Man Madame Tussauds is on Marylebone Road.
Maria How do you spell that?
Man It's M-A-R-Y-L-E-B-O-N-E. Marylebone Road.
Maria Thanks. What's the best way to get there?
Man Well, it's only a short walk from Baker Street underground station.
Maria Ah, OK! And how much time do you need to see everything, do you think?
Man Oh, I think you need about two hours. There are more than 300 wax figures to see!

Your exam practice

Step 1: Read the instructions carefully.

4 Read the instructions in Your exam and answer the questions.

1 Where is Emily?
2 What is she asking about?

Step 2: Read all the information.

5 Read the information in Your exam. Which one of these things is not mentioned?

opening times	ticket prices	location	food and drink	transport

Step 3: Analyse the gaps.

6 Look at gaps 1–5 in Your exam. What kind of answer do you need? Choose a) or b).

1 **a)** a price **b)** a time
2 **a)** a name **b)** a price
3 **a)** a number **b)** a name
4 **a)** a date **b)** a number
5 **a)** a number **b)** a price

Step 4: Listen carefully and write the answers.

Step 5: Listen again and check your answers.

7 3.46 **Emily is at the Tourist Information Office. She's asking for information about visiting Madame Tussauds. Listen to the conversation and complete the information. You will hear the information twice.**

Madame Tussauds: Visitor information

Opening times:

Monday–Friday from 9.30 until **(1)** ...
Weekends from 9.00 until 6.00

Location:

(3) ... Road, London

Transport:

a short walk from Baker Street underground station

Notes:

You need about **(4)** ... hours to visit Madame Tussauds – there are more than **(5)** ... wax figures!

Ticket prices:

Adults from £22.50
Children from **(2)** ...
Family ticket £81

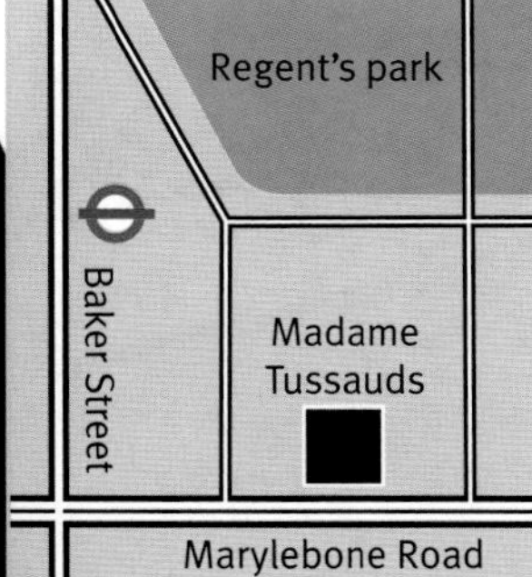

External exam trainer

Your exam preparation

About the exam

Describing a photo
The examiner shows you a photo, and asks you to describe it. This tests your vocabulary of different topics, and your ability to organize language clearly.

Exercise 1
beach
guitar
surfboard
umbrella
sand
sky
smile
take a photo
relax
chat

1 **Look at photo A in the Model exam. Which words from the Useful vocabulary box on page 115 can you use to describe it?**

EXAM TIP: Say where things are in a photo

For this type of exam, you need to learn to describe the position of things in a photo. Study the phrases in the Exam kit.

2 **Look at photo A again. Match 1–4 with a–d to make sentences.**

1 In the middle of the photo
2 On the right
3 At the top of the photo
4 In the background

a) I can see the blue sky.
b) there are five friends at the beach.
c) there's a house and some trees.
d) I can see a guitar and an umbrella.

Exercise 2
1 b
2 d
3 a
4 c

3 3.47 **Read and listen to Pablo's description of photo A. How many of the Useful expressions on page 115 does he use?**

Exercise 3
four –
In the middle of the photo …
On the right …
In the background …
At the top …

In this photo, I can see five teenagers at the beach. There are two boys and three girls. One boy is taking a photo, and the others are smiling. I think it's the weekend, and they are relaxing. In the middle of the photo, there's a blue and white surfboard. Perhaps they're going surfing. On the right I can see a guitar and an umbrella. In the background there's a house and some trees. I can see the sea, and there are some big rocks too. At the top of the photo I can see the blue sky.

UNIT 5

Your exam preparation

Lessson objectives

In this lesson students will:
- practise describing a photo
- organise their thoughts

Target exams

This section will prepare your students for the following external exams:
- PET speaking part 3

1
- Students look at photo A in the Model exam and the words in the Useful vocabulary box on page 115.
- Check that they understand all the words. If necessary, ask them to translate the words into their language.
- They look at the photo and say which words from the Useful vocabulary box they can use to describe the picture.
- Check answers as a class.

Exam tip

Point out that to describe a photo, you need to use phrases that describe the position of objects. Ask students to look at the expressions in the Useful expressions box on page 115. Check they understand them. If necessary, ask them to translate the expressions into their language.

2
- Students look at photo A and match 1–4 with a–d.
- They compare answers in pairs.
- Check answers as a class.

3 3.47
- Play the CD.
- Students read and listen to the description of the picture.
- They underline the expressions from the Useful expressions box used in the description.
- They compare answers in pairs.
- Check answers as a class.

Your exam practice

4
- Ask students to look at photo B in Your exam.
- They read questions 1–3 referring to the people and questions 4–6 referring to the place carefully.
- Students work individually and write answers to the questions.

Exam tip

Point out that when describing a photo, it is important to organize ideas clearly. Tell students that in a photo with people and a place, it is a good idea to describe the main 'character(s)' and what they are doing first, and then to say what you can see in the background.

5
- Students write a description of photo B.
- Encourage them to use their answers from exercise 4, the Useful vocabulary and Useful expressions boxes, and The Model exam to help them.
- Monitor while they are writing and give help if necessary.

6
- Students cover their description from exercise 5.
- They practise describing photo B.
- Choose some students to describe photo B for the class.

Your exam practice

4 **Look at photo B in Your exam. Write answers to these questions.**

The people

1 Who can you see in the photo?
2 What are they doing?
3 Describe the people.

The place

4 Where are they?
5 What can you see on the table?
6 What can you see in the background?

Exam Tip: Organize your thoughts

Before you start speaking, it's a good idea to organize your ideas clearly. Describe the main character(s) first and then what you can see in the background.

5 **Write a description of photo B. Use these things to help you:**

- Your answers from exercise 4.
- The Exam kit.
- The Model exam on page 114.

6 **Cover your writing from exercise 5 and practise describing the photo.**

B

Exam kit: Useful vocabulary

beach burger fast food guitar
surfboard umbrella sand sky
pins bowling alley smile take a photo
relax chat laugh

Exam kit: Useful expressions

Describing where things are in a photo

In the middle of the photo ...
On the left / right ...
In the background ...
At the top / bottom ...

External exam trainer

Your exam preparation

About the exam

Multiple-choice pictures
You listen to five short conversations. You select one picture to answer each question. This tests your ability to listen for important information in conversations.

Exercise 1
c

1 Read the example question. What is it about?

a) Sam's home now.
b) Sam's house when he was young.
c) Sam's ideal home.

Example question
Which of these is Sam's perfect home?

A

B

C

Exercise 2
A villa
B farm
C apartment

2 Look at pictures A–C. Which three places can you see?

farm villa castle apartment caravan

Exam tip: Predict vocabulary
When you look at the pictures, think about all the vocabulary you might hear.

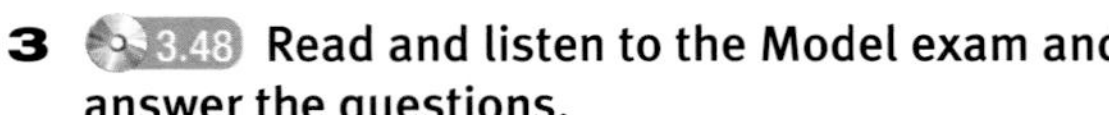

3 3.48 **Read and listen to the Model exam and answer the questions.**

1 Which three places do Elena and Sam mention?
2 Which of the pictures is Sam's perfect home? Why?

Exercise 3
1 farm apartment villa
2 C The picture shows a luxury apartment in the city.

Exam tip: Be careful!
The listening probably mentions all of the illustrated options, but only one is the correct answer.

MODEL EXAM

UNIT 6 Your exam preparation

Lesson objective

In this lesson students will:

- practise listening for important information in conversations

Target exams

This section will prepare your students for the following external exams:

- KET listening part 1
- PET listening part 1

1
- Ask students to read the example question and the three possible answers to what the example question is about.
- They choose the correct answer.
- Check the answer as a class.

2
- Students look at pictures A–C and say which three places they can see, choosing from the five words in the box.
- Check answers as a class.

Exam tip

Prediction is a very important skill when listening. If students know the topic, it is a good idea to think about what words might be used in the conversation as this will make listening comprehension easier when they hear the conversation.

3 3.48
- Play the CD.
- Ask students to read the two questions carefully first. The second question refers to the question in exercise 1.
- They read and listen to the Model exam and answer the questions.
- They compare answers in pairs.
- Check answers as a class.

Exam tip

Tell students to be careful. Although the conversations probably mention all the options shown in the pictures, only one is the correct answer.

Your exam practice

Step 1:

4
- Students read the five questions in Your exam carefully.
- They underline the key words.
- They compare answers in pairs.
- Check answers as a class.

Step 2:

5
- Students look at the pictures in Your exam and decide which options in each list are not possible answers to questions 1–5.
- They compare answers in pairs.
- Check answers as a class.

Steps 3 and 4:

6 

- Play the CD.
- Students listen to the conversations and choose the correct pictures.
- Play the CD again.
- Students compare answers in pairs.
- Check answers as a class.

3.49 Audioscript, exercise 6

1 Where does Sally usually do her homework?
Fred Where do you usually do your homework, Sally?
Sally Oh, usually on the big table in the dining room – it's quieter there than in the living room when everybody is watching TV!
Fred Haven't you got a desk in your bedroom?
Sally Well, yes – but I can't concentrate there, because I share a room with my sister.

2 What time does John usually get up?
Anna Do you get up early on school days, John?
John Hmm … quite early. But later than my mum! She gets up at quarter to seven, to take the dog for a walk.
Anna So what time do you get up then?
John At seven o'clock, then I have breakfast at about half past seven.

3 Which of these is David's new house?
Jane How's your new house, David?
David Oh, it's great, thanks! So much better than my old flat!
Jane Is it bigger?
David Yes, it's much bigger and it's got a garden! I didn't have a garden before.

4 Where is Liz's notebook?
Liz Mum, where's my notebook? I can't find it anywhere!
Mum Isn't it on the kitchen table?
Liz No, I can't see it.
Mum What about on the bookshelf?
Liz Hmm …
Mum Oh – here it is, look! On the floor under the chair!

5 When is the party at David's new house?
David Hey, Sally. I'm having a party next Saturday at my new house. Do you want to come?
Sally That sounds great. This Saturday?
David No, next Saturday – the fifteenth of April.
Sally Oh, I'm sorry – I can't. It's my mum's birthday on the fifteenth of April and we're going out for dinner.

Listening: Multiple-choice pictures

Your exam practice

Exercise 4

<u>Where</u> does <u>Sally usually</u> do her <u>homework</u>?
<u>What time</u> does <u>John</u> usually <u>get up</u>?
<u>Which</u> of these is <u>David's new house</u>?
<u>Where</u> is <u>Liz's notebook</u>?
<u>When</u> is the <u>party</u> at <u>David's new house</u>?

Step 1: Read all the questions.

4 Read questions 1–5 in Your exam. What are the key words?

Step 2: Look at all the pictures.

5 Look at the pictures in Your exam. Which options are not possible answers to questions 1–5?

1 living room / bedroom / bathroom / dining room
2 quarter to seven / seven o'clock / quarter past seven / half past seven
3 farm / house / log cabin / flat
4 shelf / table / chair / wardrobe
5 the fifth / the sixth / the twelfth / the fifteenth

Step 3: Listen and choose the correct answers.

Step 4: Listen again and check your answers.

Exercise 5

1 bathroom
2 quarter past seven
3 farm
4 wardrobe
5 the twelfth

6 3.49 Listen to the conversations and choose the correct pictures. You will hear each conversation twice.

Exercise 6

C
B
A
C
C

1 Where does Sally usually do her homework?

A

B

C

2 What time does John usually get up?

A

B

C

3 Which of these is David's new house?

A

B

C

4 Where is Liz's notebook?

A

B

C

5 When is the party at David's new house?

A

SATURDAY 6th APRIL

B

SATURDAY 15th APRIL

C

6 Multiple-choice pictures
7 Role-play activity
8 Multiple-choice answers
9 Discussing a topic

External exam trainer

Your exam preparation

About the exam

Role-play activity
The examiner describes a situation to you and your partner. He / She gives you a card with some pictures to help you. This tests your ability to interact in an everyday situation.

Exercise 1
1 b
2 b

1 3.50 **Listen to the examiner describing the Model exam. Choose the correct answers.**

1 It's … birthday next week.
a) your
b) your friend's

2 You and your partner must …
a) say which things you want
b) decide which present to buy

EXAM TIP: Listen carefully to the instructions

It is very important to listen carefully to the instructions and understand what you have to do. The examiner usually reads the situation twice.

2 **Read suggestions 1–3. Which picture A–C in the Model exam does each suggestion refer to?**

1 Let's give him a computer game!
2 How about giving him cinema tickets?
3 Why don't we give him a gift voucher?

Exercise 2
1 A
2 C
3 B

3 3.51 **Rosa and Pedro are discussing the Model exam. Read and listen to their dialogue. Which present do they decide to buy?**

Exercise 3
a gift voucher

MODEL EXAM

Your exam preparation

Lesson objectives

In this lesson students will:
- practise listening carefully to instructions for a role-play
- interact with a partner in a role-play

Target exams

This section will prepare your students for the following external exams:
- PET speaking part 2
- EOI A2

1 3.50
- Students read the sentences and the different possible answers to fill the gaps.
- Play the CD.
- They listen to the examiner describing the Model exam.
- They choose the correct answers.
- Check answers as a class.

Exam tip

Emphasise that it is very important to understand the instructions so that you know exactly what you have to do. Point out that the examiner usually reads the situation twice.

2
- Students read the three suggestions.
- They match them to the pictures in the Model exam.
- Check answers as a class.

3 3.51
- Make sure students understand the task.
- Play the CD.
- Check the answer as a class.

3.50 Audioscript, exercise 1

I am going to describe a situation to you. It's your friend Daniel's birthday next week and you want to buy him a present. Talk together about what you should give him. Here are some pictures to help you decide. I'll say that again.
I am going to describe a situation to you. It's a friend's birthday next week and you want to buy him a present. Talk together about what you should give him.
All right? Now, talk together.

Your exam practice

4
- Students read the instructions for Your exam carefully.
- They translate them into their language.
- Make sure the translation is correct.

5
- Ask students to look at the expressions in the Useful expressions box. Highlight the fact that we use these expressions to make suggestions and to respond to suggestions.
- Students then look at the pictures in Your exam and the example suggestions for the restaurant.
- Students work individually and write the suggestions for the two other places in the pictures (A the cinema, C a concert) using the vocabulary in the Useful vocabulary box where necessary.

Exam tip

Remind students always to respond when someone makes a suggestion. Ask students to look again at the typical responses to suggestions in the Useful expressions box.

6
- Ask students to look at Your exam.
- They work in pairs and make suggestions for the pictures in Your exam and respond to the suggestions.
- Encourage them to use their ideas from exercise 5 and the exam kit boxes and the Model exam to help them.
- Listen to some pairs as a class.

Your exam practice

4 **Read the examiner's instructions for Your exam. Translate the instructions into your language.**

> I am going to describe a situation to you. An English student is coming to your school for a week. Talk together about the places you can take her. Decide which is the best place. Here are some pictures to help you decide.

5 **Look at pictures A–C in Your exam. Complete suggestions 1 and 2. Give a reason for each suggestion.**

Let's take her to a traditional restaurant. She can try some typical food!

1 How about ...
2 Why don't we ...

6 **Work in pairs. Discuss Your exam. Use these things to help you:**

- your ideas from exercise 5.
- the model exam on page 118.
- the Exam kit.

EXAM TIP: Respond to suggestions

When someone makes a suggestion, you should always respond!

A

B

C

EXAM KIT: Useful expressions

Making suggestions
Let's ...
How about ... ?
Why don't we ... ?

Responding to suggestions
Good idea!
I'm not sure about that.
No, I don't think so.

EXAM KIT: Useful vocabulary

computer game cinema tickets gift voucher
go to the cinema / watch a film
go to a restaurant / have dinner
go to a concert / listen to music
He likes ... / She doesn't like ... /
We don't know what she likes.
He can choose ...
It's (too) expensive.

External exam trainer

Your exam preparation

Exercise 1
Lisa's weekend

1 **Read the example question. What is it about?**

Example question
What did Lisa do at the weekend?
a) She stayed at home.
b) She went to a concert.
c) She went to London.

Exercise 2
All the answers are possible.

2 **Read answers a–c in exercise 1. Translate them into your language. Are they all possible?**

About the exam

Multiple-choice answers
You listen to a conversation and choose the correct answer for five questions. There are three options for each question. This tests your ability to understand a conversation and select the important information.

3 3.52 **Read and listen to part of the conversation in the Model exam. Is the correct answer to the question in exercise 1 a), b) or c)? Why?**

Exercise 3
c
She saw lots of famous places in London, like Big Ben and Buckingham Palace.

Exam Tip: Order of questions
The questions are always in the same order as the information in the recording.

MODEL EXAM

Ben: Hi Lisa! Did you have a good weekend with your cousins?

Lisa: Yeah, thanks – it was great! We had an amazing time.

Ben: What did you do?

Lisa: We saw lots of famous places in London, like Big Ben and Buckingham Palace!

UNIT 8

Your exam preparation

Lesson objective

In this lesson students will:
- practise understanding a conversation and selecting important information

Target exams

This section will prepare your students for the following external exams:
- KET listening part 3
- PET listening part 2
- EOI A2

1
- Ask students to read the example question.
- They decide what the question is about.
- Check the answer as a class.

2
- Ask students to read the possible answers to the question in exercise 1.
- They translate the answers into their language.
- Check that they have translated the answers correctly.
- Ask students if all the answers are possible (they are).

3 3.52
- Play the CD.
- Students read and listen and choose the correct answer.
- They compare answers in pairs.
- Check the answer as a class and elicit why it is correct.

Exam tip

Point out to students that it sometimes happens that they do not know the answer. In this situation the best solution is to guess. They have a one in three chance of being right and do not lose marks for the wrong answer.

Your exam practice

Step 1:

4 • Students read the instructions for Your exam.
- They answer the three questions.
- Check answers as a class.
- Make sure they understand the situation.

Step 2:

5 • Point out that students do not need to know the answer to one of the six questions in exercise 5.
- They read the questions in Your exam.
- They decide which five questions they need to answer.
- Check answers as a class.

Step 3:

6 • Give students time to read all the answer options before you play the recording.
- Make sure they understand all the vocabulary in the answers.

Exam tip

Highlight that the questions are always in the same order as the information in the recording.

Steps 4 and 5:

7 3.53
- Play the CD.
- Students choose the correct answers.
- Play the CD again.
- Students compare answers in pairs.
- Check answers as a class.

Exam tip

Point out that sometimes the words in the answers can be different from the words in the recording. For example, *great* is similar to *fantastic*.

3.53 Audioscript, exercise 7

Ben Hi Lisa! Did you have a good weekend with your cousins?
Lisa Yeah, thanks – it was great! We had an amazing time.
Ben What did you do?
Lisa We saw lots of famous places in London, like Big Ben and Buckingham Palace! Oh, and we went to a great exhibition about the history of pop music!
Ben Yeah? Where was that?
Lisa At the British Music Experience. It was fantastic!
Ben What was it like?
Lisa Well, it was really interactive. You could listen to all kinds of music and watch music videos … you could even play different instruments!
Ben Sounds cool! So did you learn a lot?
Lisa Yeah, I learnt about all the different music styles in Britain … from The Beatles in the 1960s … to punk in the 1970s … and Britpop in the 1990s.
Ben So what was your favourite part of the museum?
Lisa My favourite part? Oh, they had this cool room where you could dance – you could dance all the different styles, like disco and heavy metal!
Ben Wow! It sounds fun. Glad you had a good time!
Lisa Yeah. How about you? Did you have a good weekend?

Your exam practice

ercise 4
wo
3en and
.isa
.isa's
isit to
ne British
Music
Experience
Museum
luring
er trip to
.ondon.

Step 1: Understand the situation.

4 Read the instructions for Your exam and answer the questions.

1 How many people are talking?
2 Who are they?
3 What are they talking about?

Step 2: Read all the questions.

5 Now read all the questions in Your exam. Which five things do you need to know?

a) Who was Lisa with last weekend?
b) Did she like the British Music Experience?
c) What could you do at the museum?
d) When did people listen to the Beatles?
e) What did Lisa enjoy most?

Step 3: Read all the answers.

6 Read all the answer options (a, b and c). Think about the meaning of the words.

Exam Tip: Use synonyms

Remember that the words in the answers and in the recording could be different. For example, *great* is similar to *fantastic* or *very interesting*.

Step 4: Listen and choose the correct answers.

Step 5: Listen again and check your answers.

Exercise 5

a Who was Lisa with last weekend?
b Did she like the British Music Experience?
c What could you do at the museum?
d When did people listen to The Beatles?
e What did Lisa enjoy most?
f Students do not need to know the answer to question c 'When was punk music popular?'.

Exercise 7

1 b
2 a
3 c
4 a
5 c

7 3.53 **Listen to Ben and Lisa's conversation about Lisa's trip to London. For each question choose the correct answer (a, b or c). You will hear the conversation twice.**

1 Who did Lisa spend the weekend with?
a) her sister
b) her cousins
c) Ben

2 What was Lisa's opinion of the British Music Experience?
a) it was great
b) it was boring
c) it wasn't very interactive

3 Which activity could you do at the museum?
a) try on different clothes
b) meet famous singers
c) play different instruments

4 When were the Beatles popular?
a) in the 1960s
b) in the 1970s
c) in the 1990s

5 What was Lisa's favourite part of the museum?
a) the café
b) the shop
c) the dance room

External exam trainer

Your exam preparation

Exercise 1
c

1 **Study the examiner's instructions in the Model exam. What must you do?**

a) Describe two pictures
b) Discuss how children usually celebrate their birthday
c) Talk about how we celebrated our birthdays when we were younger

Exercise 2
past

2  **Read and listen to the Model exam. Which tense do David and Elena use: past, present or future?**

Exam Tip: Use the correct tense

When you're discussing a topic, remember to use the correct tense to talk about the present, past or future.

About the exam

Discussing a topic
The examiner shows you and your partner two pictures and asks you to discuss a particular aspect of the topic. This tests your ability to have a more complex conversation and talk about your own experiences.

3 **Check the meaning of the words in the Useful vocabulary box on page 123. Which ones can you find in the Model exam?**

Exercise 3
birthday cake
party
celebrate

Exam Tip: Discuss, don't describe!

In this type of exam, you mustn't *describe* the pictures. You must *discuss* what the examiner tells you.

In the first picture I can see some children at a party. ✗
When I was younger, I usually had a party with all my friends. ✓

Examiner's instructions

These pictures show young children celebrating their birthdays.

Now, talk together about how you celebrated your birthday when you were young.

David: So, how did you celebrate your birthday when you were young?

Elena: I usually had a party with all my friends.

David: And did you have a birthday cake?

Elena: Yes, my mum always made a chocolate cake! What about you? What did you do for your birthday when you were younger?

David: I didn't have a party at home. I usually did an activity with my friends.

Elena: Really? What kind of activities did you do?

David: Oh, we went to the swimming pool or to an activity centre. It was fun!

UNIT 9

Your exam preparation

Lesson objective

In this lesson students will:
- practise describing their own experiences

Target exam

This section will prepare your students for the following external exam:
- PET speaking part 4

1
- Students look at the examiner's instructions in the Model exam.
- They decide which of the three options best describes what they have to do.
- Check the answer as a class.

2 3.54
- Students read and listen to the Model exam.
- They decide which tense the speakers use in the dialogue.
- They compare their answer in pairs.
- Check the answer as a class.

Exam tip

The time reference of this topic is in the past so students need to use the past tense to talk about it. Remind students that it is very important to know the time reference of the topic so that they can choose the correct tense.

3
- Ask students to look at the words in the Useful vocabulary box on page 123.
- Make sure they understand all the words. If necessary, ask them to translate the words into their language.
- They find and underline any of the words from the box that are in the Model exam.
- They compare answers in pairs.
- Check answers as a class.

Exam tip

Remember that in this type of exam, the task is not to describe the pictures. The examiner will use the pictures to introduce the topic students have to discuss.

Your exam practice

4
- Students look at Your exam.
- They read the three options and decide which tense they must use for Your exam.
- Check the answer as a class.

Exam tip

Refer students to the questions and response in the Useful expressions box. Point out that when we have a discussion, we do not just listen in silence to our partner but we respond with interest to what they say to keep the discussion going.

5
- Students work individually and prepare their discussion for Your exam.
- They answer questions 1–6 in exercise 6.
- Encourage them to use their answer from exercise 4, the Useful vocabulary and Useful expressions boxes, and the Model exam to help them.

6
- Students work in pairs and do Your exam.
- When they have finished, listen to some pairs as a class.

Your exam practice

4 **Look at the instructions and questions in Your exam. Which tense must you use?**

- use the past simple to talk about past experiences
- use the present simple to say what we usually do
- use *going to* to discuss our future plans

EXAM TIP: Interact with your partner

When you're having a discussion, you must interact with your partner. Don't forget to ask questions and respond to what your partner says!

5 **Prepare your discussion for Your exam. Use these things to help you:**

- Your answer from exercise 4.
- The Model exam.
- The Exam kit.

6 **In pairs, do Your exam. Follow the examiner's instructions. Answer questions 1–6.**

Examiner's instructions

These pictures show different ways that young people celebrate their birthdays. Now, talk together about how you're going to celebrate your next birthday.

On your next birthday, ...

1 how old are you going to be?
2 are you going to celebrate with family or friends?
3 are you going to have a party?
4 who are you going to invite?
5 are you going to eat any special food?
6 what presents are you hoping to get?

EXAM KIT: Useful vocabulary

birthday cake   candles   balloons   party
presents   cards   invite   celebrate

EXAM KIT: Useful expressions

Interacting with your partner

Really?
What about you?
Tell me about ...

PRONUNCIATION LAB

UNIT 1

» /h/

1 1.11 **Listen and repeat the words.**

has hasn't have haven't hair

Exercise 2
1 b
2 a
3 a
4 b

2 1.12 **Listen and choose the correct answer.**

1 a) is b) his
2 a) and b) hand
3 a) ear b) hear
4 a) air b) hair

» Rhythm and intonation

1 1.19 **Listen and repeat. Pay attention to the intonation.**

1 Are you English? ⟶
2 Yes, I am. ⟶
3 What's your favourite film? ⟶
4 I like adventure films. ⟶

Exercise 2
b *yes / no* questions

2 Look at the sentences in exercise 1 again. Complete the rule with the correct answer.

Rule: Intonation goes up ⟶ in ...
a) affirmative and negative sentences
b) yes / no questions
c) other questions
d) short answers

UNIT 2

» Syllables and word stress

Exercise 2
French
Eng lish
Wednes day
time ta ble
e du ca tion

1 1.26 **Listen and repeat the words. Pay attention to the stress of the syllables.**

French English Wednesday timetable education

Exercise 2
1 syllable
art
maths
2 syllables
subject
Spanish
3 syllables
physical
afternoon
4 syllables
technology
activities

2 1.27 **Copy and complete the table with the words in the box. Then listen and check.**

~~art~~ subject technology Spanish activities physical maths afternoon

1 syllable	2 syllables	3 syllables	4 syllables
art			

» Third person verb endings

1 1.33 **Listen and repeat the verbs. Can you hear the difference?**

/s/ or /z/		/ɪz/
goes	lives	misses
costs	loves	practises

2 1.34 **Listen and repeat the words. Which two have the /ɪz/ sound?**

1 teaches
2 starts
3 likes
4 performs
5 watches
6 gets

Exercise 2
1 teaches
5 watches

UNIT 3

» *can*

Exercise 1
a /kən/
b /kæn/
c /kən/
d /kæn/

1 1.43 **Listen and repeat.**

a) Can you ski?
b) Yes, I can.
c) What team sports can you play?
d) I can play football and volleyball.

2 Listen again. Which two use the weak form /kən/ and which two use the strong form /kæn/?

a) yes / no questions
b) other questions
c) short answers
d) affirmative sentences

Exercise 2
c Short answers
d affirmative sentences

UNIT 4

» *-ing* endings

1 2.04 **Listen and repeat the words.**

wear – wearing
go – going
carry – carrying
do – doing

2 2.05 **Listen and repeat the sentences.**

1 What are you wearing?
2 I'm wearing blue jeans.
3 She isn't going to a party.
4 Is she going to school?

Pronunciation lab

UNIT 1

»/h/

1 1.11 Play the CD, pausing after each word. Students repeat the words chorally.
- Play the CD again. Students repeat the words chorally and then individually. If students have problems producing the /h/ sound in English, ask them to whisper the words. Then ask them to gradually increase the volume.

2 1.12 Ask students to read the pairs of words aloud.
- Play the CD. Students choose the correct answer. Check answers as a class.

»Rhythm and intonation

1 1.19 Play the CD. Students listen and repeat the questions and answers.
- Make sure students copy the rhythm and intonation correctly.

2
- Students look at the questions and answers in exercise 1 and complete the rule. Check the answers as a class. Point out that in short answers the stressed word is always the last word, eg *Yes, it is, No, she isn't,* etc.

UNIT 2

»Syllables and word stress

1 1.26 Write the word *English* on the board. Ask how many syllables it has got. Elicit that it has two syllables: *Eng – lish*.
- Ask students which syllable is stressed. Elicit that *English* is stressed on the first syllable.
- Play the CD. Students listen and repeat chorally and individually. Point out that *Wednesday* /ˈwenzdeɪ/ only has two syllables and that the first syllable is stressed.

2 1.27 Students work individually and write the words in the correct column in the table.
- They underline the stressed syllable in each word.
- Play the CD so they can check their answers. Highlight in compound nouns formed by putting two nouns together, the first syllable is normally stressed, eg *timetable*.

1 »Third person verb endings

1.33 Play the CD. Students listen and repeat the verbs.

2
- Highlight the verbs ending in /ɪz/.
- Play the CD again for students to hear the difference.

1.34 Play the CD. Students listen and repeat chorally and individually.
- Students identify the two verbs ending in /ɪz/.
- Check answers as a class. Point out that verbs ending in the sounds /s/, /z/, /tʃ/, /dʒ/, /ʃ/ and (the very rare ending) /ʒ/ have the /ɪz/ sound for third person verb endings.

UNIT 3

»*can*

1 1.43 Students read the four sentences.
- Play the CD. Students listen and repeat chorally and individually.

2 1.43 Ask students to read the question carefully.
- Play the CD again.
- Students listen and decide which two use the weak form /kən/ and which two use the strong form /kæn/.
- Check answers as a class. Make sure the students do not stress *can* in *yes* / *no* questions and other questions. Unstressed *can* is always pronounced /kən/.

UNIT 4

»*-ing* endings

1 2.04 Write *sleep* on the board followed by three dashes to indicate three missing letters: *sleep* _ _ _ . Mime sleeping and elicit the missing letters (*ing*) from the class.
- Ask students how *sleeping* is pronounced.
- Play the CD. Students listen and repeat chorally and individually. To help students pronounce /ŋ/ correctly have them say /n/ and then /g/ aloud chorally. Ask them to repeat the sounds several times one after the other. Then ask them to speed up so that they blend into one. This will be very close to /ŋ/.

2 2.05 Play the CD. Students listen and repeat the sentences chorally and individually.
- Make sure they pronounce /ŋ/ correctly.

UNIT 5

»Difficult sounds: /ɪ/ and /i:/

1 2.18 Students copy the table into their notebooks.

- Play the CD. Students listen and repeat the words chorally and individually.
- Point out that the vowel sound in the first column is short and the one in the second column is longer. For the longer /i:/ sound the lips are more spread, almost in a smile. For the shorter /ɪ/ sound, the lips are much less spread.

2 2.19 Play the CD. Students listen and repeat the words chorally and individually.

- Play the CD again. They write the words in the correct column in the table in exercise 1.
- Check answers as a class. Point out that the *ea* spelling is often pronounced /i:/.

UNIT 6

»/ə/

1 2.27 Ask students to notice the unstressed schwa /ə/ sound in the second (final) syllable.

- Play the CD. Students listen and hear the /ə/sound. The *-er* endings in comparative adjectives and in other words ending in *-er* and *-or* (eg *teacher, doctor,* etc) are always pronounced /ə/.

2 2.28 Students copy the words into their notebooks.

- Play the CD. Students underline the unstressed /ə/ sound in each word.
- Check answers as a class.

»Contractions: *can't* and *mustn't*

1 2.33 Students read the four sentences.

- Play the CD. Students listen and choose the correct answers.
- Check answers as a class.

2 2.34 Play the CD. Students listen and repeat the senteces chorally and individually.

- Make sure they pronounce *can*, *can't*, *must* and *mustn't* correctly.

UNIT 7

»*was* and *were*

1 3.04 Play the CD. Students listen and repeat the sentences chorally and individually.

2 3.04 Ask students to read the question carefully.

- Play the CD again. Students listen and decide which two are weak forms.
- Check answers as a class. Point out that *was* is usually pronounced /wəz/ and *were* as /wə/. However in short answers and affirmative sentences, both *was* and *were* are stressed, so they are pronounced in their strong forms /wɒz/ and /wɜ:/.

»Past simple endings

1 3.09 Students copy the table into their notebooks.

- Play the CD. Students listen and repeat the verbs chorally and individually.
- Point out that *asked* and *played* only have one syllable.

2 3.10 Students read all the verbs in the box.

- Play the CD. Students listen and repeat the verbs chorally and individually.
- Students write the verbs in the correct column in exercise 1. Check answers as a class. The *-ed* ending is pronounced in three ways. Highlight the Look! box and point out that in verbs that end in *t* or *d*, it is pronounced /ɪd/, eg *wanted* /wɒntɪd/. In verbs ending in a voiceless consonant sound /t/, eg *helped* /helpt/. In verbs ending in a voiced consonant or a vowel or diphthong sound, it is pronounced /d/, eg *arrived* /ə'raɪvd/, *played* /pleɪd/.

UNIT 5

» Difficult sounds: /ɪ/ and /iː/

1 2.18 **Copy the table into your notebook. Then listen and repeat the words.**

/ɪ/	/iː/
it gym crisps	eat he cheese

2 2.19 **Listen and repeat. Add the words to the correct column in the table in exercise 1.**

meat chicken fish peas beans milk

Exercise 2
/ɪ/
chicken, fish, milk
/iː/
meat, peas, beans

UNIT 6

» /ə/

1 2.27 **Listen to the words. Can you hear the /ə/ sound?**

better cooker faster
tidier cheaper sofa

2 2.28 **Copy the words into your notebook. Then listen and underline the /ə/ sound.**

1 bigger
2 mirror
3 older
4 richer
5 easier
6 dinner

Exercise 2
1 bigger
2 mirror
3 older
4 richer
5 easier
6 dinner

» Contractions: *can't* and *mustn't*

1 2.33 **Listen and choose the correct answers.**

a) You **must** / **mustn't** wait here.
b) You **must** / **mustn't** run.
c) I **can** / **can't** ride a bike.
d) I **can** / **can't** ride a horse.

Exercise 1
a must
b mustn't
c can
d can't

2 2.34 **Listen and repeat the sentences.**

1 I can speak English.
2 I can't speak Japanese.
3 You must listen in class.
4 You mustn't be noisy.

UNIT 7

» *was* and *were*

1 3.04 **Listen and repeat.**

1 **Were** you happy?
2 Yes, I **was**.
3 Where **were** you born?
4 I **was** born in London.

Exercise 1
/wə/
/wɒz/
/wə/
/wɒz/

2 **Listen again. Which two are weak forms?**

a) yes / no questions
b) short answers
c) other questions
d) affirmative sentences

Exercise 2

» Past simple endings

1 3.09 **Copy the table into your notebook. Then listen and repeat the past simple verbs.**

/t/	/d/	/ɪd/
asked	played	invented

Look!
We use the /ɪd/ sound after 't' and 'd'.

2 3.10 **Listen and repeat the verbs. Then write them in the correct column.**

wanted watched arrived
studied helped started liked

Exercise 2
/t/
watched
helped
liked
/d/
arrived
/ɪd/
wanted
studied
started

UNIT 8

» Diphthongs

1 3.23 **Copy the table into your notebook. Then listen and repeat the words.**

/eɪ/	/aɪ/	/əʊ/	/aʊ/
play	sign	grow	now
bass	die	ago	our

2 3.24 **Add the words in the box to the table in exercise 1. Then listen and check.**

great sound like hate go
nice loud slow

Exercise 2
/eɪ/
great
hate
/aɪ/
like
nice
/əʊ/
go
slow
/aʊ/
sound
loud

UNIT 9

» Rhythm and sentence stress

1 3.30 **Copy the sentences into your notebook. Then listen and repeat. Pay attention to the stressed words.**

1 What are you going to do?
2 I'm going to make a cake.
3 We aren't going to buy a present.

2 3.31 **Listen and repeat the sentences. Which words are stressed?**

1 Are you going to visit your relatives?
2 She's going to have a party.
3 They aren't going to watch the fireworks.

Exercise 2
a Are you going to visit your relatives?
b She's going to have a party.
c They aren't going to watch the fireworks.

UNIT 8

»Diphthong:

1 3.23 Students copy the table into their notebooks.

- Play the CD. Students listen and repeat chorally and individually.

2 3.24 Students work individually and write the words in the box in the correct column in the table in exercise 1.

- Play the CD. Students check their answers. Draw students' attention to common patterns in the relationship between sounds and spelling, eg the combination *ou* is often pronounced /aʊ/; *i* followed by a consonant and then *e* is often pronounced /aɪ/.

UNIT 9

»Rhythm and sentence stress

1 3.30 Students copy the sentences with the underlined stressed words into their notebooks.

- Play the CD. Students listen and repeat the sentences chorally and individually.
- Point out that we do not stress words like *to* and *a*.

2 3.31 Play the CD. Students listen and repeat the sentences chorally and individually.

- Play the CD again. Students write the sentences and underline the stressed words.
- They compare their answers in pairs.
- Check answers as a class. The last stressed word in each of these sentences carries the main stress (it is stressed more strongly than the others).

WORKBOOK ANSWER KEY

STARTER UNIT

Vocabulary

1
1 grandma
2 dad
3 mum
4 uncle
5 aunt
6 sister
7 brother
8 cousins

Grammar

2
1 Those
2 This
3 That
4 That
5 These, those

3
1 He
2 He
3 It
4 I
5 you

4
1 Our
2 Their
3 Its
4 her
5 my, His

5
1 My name is … . I am … years old.
2 These are my parents. Their names are … and … .
3 This is my … (eg grandad / grandma / aunt / uncle / cousin). My mum is … (eg his / her daughter / sister / aunt).
4 This my cousin. He / She is … years old.

Vocabulary

1
1 Sunday
2 Monday
3 Tuesday
4 Wednesday
5 Thursday
6 Friday
7 Saturday

2
1 February
2 March
3 April
4 May
5 June
6 July
7 August
8 September
9 October
10 November
11 December

Grammar

3
1 rabbit's
2 Jandro's
3 Jada's
4 friends'

4
1 Today's date is …
2 My birthday is …
3 My mum's birthday is …

Vocabulary

5
1 Poland
2 Japanese
3 Chinese
4 Australia, (New) Zealand
5 Portuguese, Brazilian, Portuguese
6 American, Argentinian, Spanish
7 France, Moroccan, French

Grammar

1
1 You're
2 He's
3 We're
4 They're
5 I'm not
6 You aren't
7 She isn't
8 We aren't
9 They aren't

2
1 's
2 aren't
3 's
4 'm not
5 're
6 aren't

3
1 Her name isn't Sophie.
2 We're English.
3 I'm not from London.
4 This isn't my brother.
5 It is Monday.
6 They aren't 13 years old.
7 You aren't American.

4
1 Are your friends from Liverpool?
Yes, they are.
2 Are they English?
No, they aren't.
3 Is he from South Africa?
Yes, he is.
4 Is this cat your pet?
No, it isn't.
5 Are we in your class?
Yes, you are. Yes, we are.

5
1 Is your mum from the UK?
2 What are your parents' names?
3 When is your birthday?

Integrated skills

1
1 pen
2 pencil
3 pencil case
4 pencil sharpener
5 rubber
6 ruler
7 schoolbag

2
1 say
2 repeat
3 mean
4 page

3
1 Can you repeat that, please?
2 What page are we on?
3 How do you say *estuche* in English?
4 How do you spell that?

4
1 Where are you from?
2 Welcome to the class!
3 Hello. What's your name?
4 My name's Belén.
5 I'm from Badajoz.
6 Nice to meet you too!

5
1 name's …
2 to meet you
3 Nice to meet you too
4 Where are you from
6 Welcome
7 Thanks / Thank you

UNIT 1

Vocabulary 1

1

M	O	A	V	E	R	A	G	E
L	O	N	G	R	W	A	V	Y
U	T	U	K	G	R	E	Y	E
L	I	P	S	O	L	C	D	B
S	H	O	R	T	T	I	A	R
L	I	F	W	F	A	I	R	O
I	S	P	R	U	L	C	K	W
M	T	C	U	R	L	Y	H	S
B	E	A	R	D	C	E	R	E

2
2 dark
3 long
4 lips
5 average
6 fair
7 curly
8 slim
9 tall
10 slim
11 eyebrows
12 hair
13 beard

3
2 long
3 dark
4 tall
5 beard
6 grey
7 slim
8 fair
9 curly

Grammar 1

1
1 hasn't
2 've
3 've
4 haven't
5 have

2
2 e
3 a
4 c
5 d

3
1 They haven't got black hair.
2 I've got a dictionary.
3 My aunt hasn't got a big house.
4 We've got a ruler.
5 My grandad hasn't got grey hair.

4
1 Have you got a brother?
2 Has she got brown eyes?
3 Has he got dark hair?
4 Have you got a dog?
5 Have they got a new teacher?

5
1 Have you got a pet?
2 Has your dad got a beard?
3 Have your grandparents got grey hair?
4 Have you got curly hair?

Vocabulary 2

1 toes, feet, legs, hands, neck, head

2
1 tooth
2 horn
3 wing
4 finger
5 arm
6 tail

3
1 neck
2 fingers
3 legs
4 hands
5 tooth

4
1 head
2 horns
3 wings
4 toes
5 tail

5
1 I have got long / short legs.
2 My pet has got a long / short tail.
3 My dad has got big / small hands.
4 My hair is long / short.
5 My fingers are long/short.
6 I have got big / small feet.

Grammar 2

1
2 c
3 f
4 b
5 a
6 d

2
1 What
2 Where
3 When
4 How
5 How

3
2 Where
3 How old
4 When
5 What
6 How many

4
1 What is your school's name?
2 Who is your best friend?
3 How old are you?
4 How many DVDs have you got?
5 When is your friend's birthday?
6 Where are your parents from?
7 What is your favourite film?
8 What are your favourite colours?

Reading

1 b

2 Students' own answers

3
1 Almería
2 tourists
3 has
4 *Die Another Day*
5 Kazakhstan

4
1 The town in the Western is in Almería.
2 The tours are in the summer.
3 A famous actor in Westerns is Clint Eastwood.
4 The small town has got one cinema (with two screens).
5 Cádiz is a 'Cuban' port in the Bond film.

Listening

03 Audioscript, exercises 1 and 2

Welcome to Cambridge Cinema. In Screen 1 today we have got the new adventure film, *Wings of a Bird*, about a father's search for his children. This film starts at 2.30. For children, the new cartoon *Snake Eyes* is on in Screen 2 at three o'clock. It's in 3D and it's a very funny film! At four o'clock we have got *Sister Mystery* in Screen 3. Buy your tickets and 3D glasses at the reception desk. Ladies and gentlemen, we've got a missing child at the reception desk. Her name's Ruby. She's seven years old. She's got long, fair hair and blue eyes. She says she's with her mum today. If you are her mother, please come to reception. *Snake Eyes* is on now. Please go to Screen 2. And thank you: Ruby is with her mother now. Are you hungry or thirsty? When you've got your tickets, go to the café. It's on floor 2 and it's open now. It's got lots of drinks and snacks. The doors are now openfor *Wings of a Bird*. Please go to Screen 1. And enjoy the film!

1 screen, film, children, cartoon, 3D, tickets, blue eyes, mother

2
1 b
2 b
3 c
4a
5b

3
1 *Snake Eyes* starts at three o'clock.
2 *Wings of a Bird* is about a father's search for his children.
3 The cinema has got three screens.
4 Ruby is seven years old.
5 Ruby's mother is at the cinema with Ruby.
6 The café is on floor 2.

Speaking

4
2 What
3 How
4 much
5 glasses
6 Here
7 change

Writing

5
1 is
2 has
3 is
4 is
5 has
6 P

Progress check

1
1 short
2 grey
3 tall
4 fair
5 moustache
6 beard
7 average
8 dark
9 long
10 wavy

2
1 neck
2 hands
3 toes
4 wings
5 legs
6 horn

3
1 Andy has got a beard.
2 They haven't got a pet.
3 Have you got a brother?
4 I haven't got two pens.
5 Have we got an English lesson?

4
1 How many sisters have you got?
2 Where is he from?
3 Who is your English teacher?
4 When is the football match?
5 What is your favourite film?

5
1 Who
2 Where
3 How
4 What
5 've
6 Have
7 got
8 've
9 haven't
10 What

Extension

1
1 My
2 How
3 Where
4 sisters'
5 're
6 brother's
7 He's
8 have you
9 'm
10 What's
11 His
12 What's
13 haven't got
14 have
15 Who

UNIT 2

Vocabulary 1

1

C	H	M	E	N	G	L	I	S	H	P
A	I	C	T	S	H	T	B	C	I	N
M	A	T	H	S	U	M	P	Y	S	I
O	S	C	I	E	N	C	E	P	T	M
N	P	E	K	Z	G	D	L	Y	O	S
Z	A	I	F	A	E	A	R	C	R	H
R	N	W	R	X	R	N	A	A	Y	P
G	I	J	E	U	M	C	S	C	M	R
A	S	U	N	L	A	E	A	H	C	A
R	H	L	C	M	N	M	U	S	I	C
T	E	C	H	N	O	L	O	G	Y	P

2
1 history
2 maths
3 PE
4 drama
5 dance

3
1 French
2 citizenship
3 Art
4 science
5 music

4
1 On Wednesday morning I have got maths and science.
2 The extra activity at lunchtime is art club.
3 The first lesson after lunch is history.
4 I have got PE at 2.30 in the afternoon.
5 I go to drama club after school.

Grammar 1

1
2 plays
3 teaches
4 studies
5 misses

2
1 teaches
2 study
3 have
4 goes
5 finish

3
1 They don't like Mondays.
2 He has got a bike.
3 We don't go shopping at the weekend.
4 She tries to work hard.
5 The film doesn't finish at eight o'clock.

4
1 goes
2 don't like
3 study
4 doesn't think
5 don't play

5
1 go
2 starts
3 finishes
4 plays
5 sing
6 have
7 don't go
8 don't see
9 travel
10 watch

Vocabulary 2

1
1 have a shower
2 have lunch
3 do sport
4 meet friends
5 go to bed

2
2 a
3 g
4 f
5 b
6 c
7 e

3
1 my homework
2 have
3 my room
4 up
5 do

4
1 get up
2 have breakfast
3 get dressed
4 go to school
5 have lunch
6 watch TV
7 go to bed

Grammar 2

1
1 Does
2 Do
3 Does
4 Do

2
2 e
3 b
4 a
5 f
6 d

3
1 Do … think
2 Does … start
3 Do … get
4 Does … listen
5 Do … wear
6 Does … teach

4
1 No, I / we don't.
2 Yes, it does.
3 Yes, I / we do.
4 No, she doesn't.
5 No, I / we don't.
6 Yes, he does.

5
1 Do you like
2 I do.
3 Do you listen
4 I do
5 Do you have
6 I don't
7 Does Kelly write
8 she does
9 Does she come
10 she doesn't

6
1 Do you go to a large secondary school?
2 Do you live in a city?
3 Do you and your friends do sport?

Reading

1 c

2
2 a
3 g
4 c
5 d
6 e
7 b

3
1 **F** The boys are from Liverpool or nearby.
2 **T**

3 **F** He does his homework at the Academy, but he goes to school because the boys who study at the Academy are over 15.
4 **T**
5 **T**

4
1 Harry is 14 years old.
2 No, he doesn't.
3 Harry has football training after school.
4 They come from Liverpool or nearby.
5 They train for an hour every day.
6 They play in the youth league.
7 Yes, they do.
8 No, they aren't.

Listening

05 Audioscript, exercises 1 and 2

Max Hi Sophie! Have you got your new timetable?
Sophie Yes, but I don't like it. I've got science all morning on Mondays and on Fridays.
Max I've got science on Monday and Friday mornings too, with Mr Martin. Are you in Mr Martin's group?
Sophie No, I'm not. I've got Miss Benson.
Max Who is your maths teacher?
Sophie Mrs Potter. I've got her for maths on … Wednesday afternoons.
Max Me too! Great! We can sit together. What about English? I've got English on Thursday mornings.
Sophie Er, let's see … No, I've got English on Tuesday mornings and Friday afternoons with Mr Davies.
Max Oh, I've got Spanish in the morning on Tuesdays, and French on Friday afternoons.
Sophie Wow! French and Spanish! You're good at languages, aren't' you?
Max Well, I really like them.
Sophie I'm not very good at languages. I prefer English.
Max English is a language!
Sophie I know! I mean foreign languages. I like English because I like reading. I like drama too.
Max There's a drama club after school.
Sophie Really? What day is it on?
Max Look, here's a list of all the after-school clubs. The drama club is on Wednesdays.
Sophie Great! Do you want to do drama with me?
Max No, not really. I'm too shy.

1 science, maths, English, Spanish, French, drama

2
1 science
2 Spanish
3 maths
4 English
5 French

3
1 isn't
2 different
3 Mrs Potter
4 likes
5 Wednesdays

4
1 Mrs Potter
2 maths
3 English
4 French and Spanish
5 no

Speaking

5
1 up
2 on
3 What
4 Where

6
1 I'd like to sign up for
2 What day is it on
3 Where is it
4 What time does it finish

Writing

7
2 .
3 ?
4 ,
5 ?
6 !
7 ?
8 ,

Progress check

1
1 PE
2 English
3 ICT
4 art
5 maths

3
1 wears
2 have
3 live
4 don't study
5 play
6 doesn't start

4
1 Do you go to bed early at weekends? Yes, I do. / No, I don't.
2 Does your best friend do sport? Yes, he / she does. / No, he / she doesn't.
3 Do you play the piano? Yes, I do. / No, I don't.
4 Do you meet friends at the cinema? Yes, I do. / No, I don't.

5
1 've got
2 are
3 gets up
4 tidies
5 Do you like
6 No, we don't
7 studies
8 Do you speak
9 Yes, I do
10 speak
11 do
12 Yes, we do
13 meet

Extension

1
1 Are
2 have
3 Have you got
4 What
5 don't
6 your
7 meet
8 Do
9 've got
10 Do
11 wants
12 do
13 Are you good
14 haven't got
15 watch

UNIT 3

Vocabulary 1

1
1 horse-riding
2 yoga
3 mountain-biking
4 cycling
5 athletics
6 surfing
7 swimming

2
1 play
2 goes
3 do
4 do
5 plays

3
1 athletics
2 swimming
3 cycling
4 surfing

4
2 go mountain-biking
3 do judo
4 go skateboarding
5 do aerobics
6 do yoga

Grammar 1

1
1 never does
2 rarely watches
3 are sometimes
4 often play
5 usually go
6 are always

2 1 We often play football in the winter.
2 Sara sometimes goes to yoga classes.
3 Swimming is rarely dangerous.
4 I am usually happy.
5 Dad never goes roller-skating.
6 We do aerobics twice a week.

3 1 How often does your grandad play tennis?
2 How often do you do judo?
3 How often do your friends go skateboarding?
4 How often do you do gymnastics?

4 1 doing 3 wearing
2 watching 4 going

5 1 Do you like doing yoga?
2 I don't mind going swimming.
3 Does he love playing tennis?
4 They don't like doing sport.
5 I hate tidying my room.

Vocabulary 2

1 run, ride, jump, throw, catch, hit, score, kick, lift, ski, dive, skate

2 1 catch 4 jumps
2 throw 5 rides
3 score 6 hit

3 1 ride 4 skate
2 lift 5 ski
3 kick

4 1 lifts 5 catches
2 jumps 6 ski
3 dives 7 rides
4 score 8 throws

Grammar 2

1 1 Where 4 Have
2 Am 5 When
3 Do

2 2 a 5 c
3 d 6 b
4 e

3 1 Do you do a lot of sport?
2 ✓
3 When has he got PE today?
4 ✓
5 When do you do exercise / When do you exercise?

4 1 Where are the tennis balls?
2 Are the players excited?
3 When have we got training?
4 Where do they go surfing?

5 1 When are the Olympic Games?
2 Where do you do judo?
3 Do you like cycling?
4 What is your favourite sport?
5 When do you go skateboarding?

Reading

1 team sports

2 1 d 4 a
2 f 5 c
3 e 6 b

3 1 **T**
2 **F** She has got some friends, but they don't choose her for their teams.
3 **T**
4 **F** She has got a bike and she cycles to school.
5 **F** She says she loves dancing in her bedroom.
6 **F** She says aerobics is fun.

4 1 She wants to be healthy.
2 No, she isn't.
3 No, she doesn't.
4 She cycles to school every day in Week 3.
5 Daisy also wants to try running.

Listening

Audioscript, exercises 1 and 2

Hello and welcome to the programme. Today on Sports Scene we've got a feature on an American speed skater. His name is Apolo Ohno, and he's an Olympic® champion. He's got eight Olympic medals and two of them are gold medals.

How does Apolo stay at the top of his sport? He trains hard – he never stops! He's got an incredible training programme. He often trains all day. Apolo usually starts his training session with some jumping. He jumps up 25 stairs, then runs back down, and then jumps up each step again. He does this for an amazing 45 minutes! Then, to rest his legs, he runs 1.5 km.
After jumping and running, Apolo skates … and he skates fast. He skates at 60 km per hour. He goes around the track again and again. About three times a week Apolo lifts weights to build his strength.
With so much training, has Apolo got time to relax? Well, yes, he has. Apolo thinks it's important to relax. He loves his home city of Seattle, and he especially loves being in the beautiful parks there. The parks are good places for him to go cycling.
In the USA, Apolo is famous for speed skating and for something else too. Millions of Americans know him as a dancer. He's one of the champions on the TV show *Dancing with the Stars*. Where does he dance? … That's right – on the ice!

1 2 Olympic medals
3 training programme
4 jumping
5 runs
6 lifts weights
7 relax
8 parks
9 cycling
10 dancing

2 1 two 4 1.5 km
2 starts 5 60 km
3 45 6 lifts weights

3 1 Apolo is from the USA.
2 He runs 1.5 km.
3 He lives in Seattle.
4 He cycles in the parks.
5 Because they are beautiful and they are good places for him to go cycling.
6 The other activity he is famous for is dancing on ice.

Speaking

4
2 Sure. Go ahead.
3 The questions are for a survey about the park.
4 Oh, OK.
5 How often do you go to the park?
6 I usually go about three times a week.
7 What do you do in the park?
8 I go skateboarding. I love it!
9 That's all. Thanks for your time.
10 No problem. Bye!

Writing

5
1 My class has got 25 students.
2 We all go swimming once a week in the summer.
3 Two students are never happy doing exercise.
4 Most of the students play football twice a week in the winter.
5 Some of the students go cycling after school.

Progress check

1
1 athletics
2 mountain-biking
3 aerobics
4 yoga
5 horse-riding
6 judo
7 surfing

2
1 ride
2 jump
3 throw
4 score
5 hit
6 ski
7 run

3
1 I rarely do gymnastics.
2 We usually watch football on Saturdays.
3 He's always happy in the snow.
4 I often go cycling early.
5 He never goes horse-riding.

4
1 Jade loves reading.
2 She doesn't mind going swimming.
3 She doesn't like playing tennis.
4 She likes doing sport.
5 She hates watching football.

5
1 What is your favourite sport?
2 Are you tired after PE?
3 Has he got a ticket?
4 When have you got basketball training?
5 Do you do judo?

6
1 What's
2 often
3 Once
4 usually do
5 doing judo
6 Do you
7 often go
8 don't

Extension

1
1 What
2 Is
3 Where
4 finishes
5 usually
6 doing
7 doesn't
8 Does
9 loves
10 always

UNIT 4

Vocabulary 1

Across

1
1 trainers
3 shirt
4 boots
6 jacket
7 socks
10 cap
12 trousers
13 jeans

Down

1 T-shirt
2 shorts
5 skirt
6 jumper
8 coat
9 shoes
11 dress
12 tie

3
1 The man is wearing trousers, a shirt and a tie.
2 The boy is wearing jeans, trainers, a T-shirt and a jacket.
3 The girl is wearing a skirt, boots and a jumper.

Grammar 1

1
1 riding
2 having
3 winning
4 reading

2
1 is talking
2 isn't wearing
3 isn't helping
4 is buying
5 is looking

3
1 We're driving to school.
2 I'm looking at some pictures.
3 You aren't tidying your bedroom.
4 He's writing an email.

4
2 Am, b
3 Are, a
4 Are, c

5
1 Is Ben talking to Sophie? No, he isn't.
2 Is Sophie choosing a dress? No, she isn't.
3 Is Sophie carrying a bag? No, she isn't.
4 Is Ben standing next to the table? Yes, he is.

6
1 Are … calling
2 Yes, I am
3 'm sitting
4 isn't sharing
5 are cleaning
6 's working
7 Are … doing
8 No, you aren't
9 'm talking

Vocabulary 2

1

2
1 proud
2 jealous
3 funny
4 lazy
5 clever

3
1 friendly
2 selfish
3 confident
4 unfriendly
5 shy
6 adventurous

Grammar 2

1
1 're wearing
2 travel
3 Do you watch
4 are they going
5 designs

2
1 is buying
2 Do you meet
3 'm not going
4 wear
5 aren't listening

3
1 Freya doesn't wear jeans every day.
2 I'm buying some clothes at the moment.
3 My mum isn't using the computer now.
4 ✓
5 We do sport every Saturday.

4
1 I work in a large fashion store.
I'm not working at the moment.
2 I'm buying a coat now.
Do you buy clothes every week?
3 My sister is making a skirt today.
She often makes her clothes.
4 They rarely go shopping.
Are they going shopping now?

Reading

1

2	d	4	e
3	a	5	c

2

1	d	4	a
2	c	5	b
3	f	6	e

3
1 teenagers
2 Some
3 entertainment
5 teaches

4
1 The course lasts for two weeks.
2 The students study for six hours a day.
3 After classes there are discos, film nights, talent shows and quizzes.
4 Students can go swimming or play tennis in their free time.
5 Students learn drawing and designing, T-shirt printing, using a sewing machine and decorating garments.

Listening

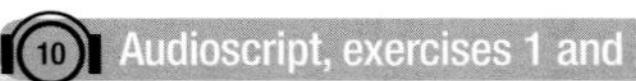

Presenter Hello! Well, it's London Fashion Week. We're backstage at one of the shows. Let's meet one of the designers here at the show. I've got Paul Brady here with me. Paul, how are you feeling about your show today? Are you feeling confident?

Paul Yes and no … I'm feeling nervous, too. Everyone is looking at my designs today.

Presenter What's your collection like?

Paul I create classic designs. I don't use lots of colour. I prefer a lot of black and white.

Presenter Wow! These dresses are great! You're very clever.

Paul Thank you. I'm very proud of the clothes.

Presenter OK, thank you, Paul. With me here backstage I've also got Jade Edwards, one of the stylists at the show. Now, Jade, can you describe your job for the listeners?

Jade Yes, of course. The stylists look at the clothes and decide which clothes look good together. So, for example, this shirt looks nice with those grey trousers, but it looks really great with these pink trousers!

Presenter Yes, I see … it's like you're getting dressed for a big party.

Jade Yes, something like that! Then I make decisions about the show itself. A good fashion show needs a theme, a sort of story, to make it really exciting.

Presenter What do you mean by a theme?

Jade Well, we've got the clothes, but we also need to think about all the make-up and the hairstyles, and the music – that's important, too. All these things are connected by the theme.

Presenter Hmm, yes, I see. So, what's the theme for Paul's show?

Jade Black and white Hollywood films! When I look at Paul's black and white collection, I think of those amazing old films.

Presenter So the models look like Hollywood film stars, is that right?

Jade Yes, exactly! Oh, look … let's watch them rehearse …

1 confident, dresses, clever, proud, shirt, nice, trousers, great

2
1 **F** Paul isn't very confident about the fashion show.
2 **F** Paul's clothes are classic designs.
3 **T**
4 **T**
5 **F** The models are made up to look like film stars.
6 **T**

3
1 Paul is feeling nervous.
2 No, it isn't.
3 Jade is a stylist.
4 Jade decides the theme for the show.
5 The theme for Paul's show is black and white Hollywood films.

Speaking

4
1 I'm looking for a shirt.
2 Can I try it on?
3 You can pay over there.
4 What size are you?
5 It's too big.
6 It looks great!

Writing

5
1 She's carrying a beautiful bag.
2 They look amazing.
3 He's a funny actor.
4 His shorts are black.
5 Madonna is very famous.

Progress check

1

1	dress	5	trousers
2	tie	6	cap
3	trainers	7	shorts
4	socks	8	T-shirt

2

1	f	5	g
2	d	6	e
3	h	7	a
4	b	8	c

3
1 are playing
2 is wearing
3 aren't going
4 aren't having
5 're smiling

4
1 Is Anna buying some shoes? Yes, she is.
2 Is Jake wearing a hat? No, he isn't.
3 Are they cycling in the park? No, they aren't.
4 Are the boys doing their homework? Yes, they are.
5 Are you tidying your room? No, I'm not/we aren't.

5
1 'm reading
2 like
3 don't know
4 's got
5 designs
6 comes
7 has got
8 talks

Extension

1
1 are you
2 'm doing
3 What
4 We're
5 looking
6 've
7 's wearing
8 raining
9 your
10 sitting
11 She's wearing
12 Do
13 I do
14 Have you got

UNIT 5

Vocabulary 1

1
1 café
2 swimming pool
3 gym
4 shopping centre
5 park
6 bowling alley
7 library
8 football stadium
9 cinema
10 restaurant
11 skate park

2
1 football stadium
2 restaurant
3 shopping centre
4 library
5 bowling alley
6 skate park

3
1 swimming pool
2 café
3 gym
4 shopping centre
5 park

4
1 skate park
2 shopping centre
3 gym
4 swimming pool
5 football stadium
6 cinema
7 café

Grammar 1

1
1 some
2 isn't
3 a
4 an
5 any
6 any
7 an

2
1 C
2 P
3 C
4 C
5 P
6 U
7 U
8 U
9 C
10 C

3
1 There is a
2 There aren't any
3 There is a
4 There aren't any

4
1 are
2 a
3 an
4 are
5 a
6 some
7 some
8 a
9 isn't
10 a
11 isn't
12 any

Vocabulary 2

1

P	O	T	A	T	O	E	S	E	S
E	R	F	I	S	H	C	A	K	E
A	I	U	B	S	J	H	A	M	O
S	C	H	I	C	K	E	N	H	R
S	E	C	S	J	M	I	L	K	A
A	N	E	C	R	I	S	P	S	N
L	U	J	U	I	C	E	O	N	G
A	T	O	I	H	E	T	Y	A	E
D	S	N	T	C	H	E	E	S	E
Y	O	G	H	U	R	T	P	O	A

2
1 Chicken
2 cheese
3 Oranges
4 cakes
5 Nuts

3
1 Rice
2 fish
3 salad
4 milk
5 peas
6 ham

Grammar 2

1
1 Are
2 Is
3 Is
4 Are
5 Is

2
1 Are there any sandwiches in your bag?
2 Is there a bowling alley near your school?
3 Is there some juice in the school cafeteria?
4 Is there a sports centre in your town?

3
1 Are there any cafés in Sanford? Yes, there are.
2 Is there a cinema? No, there isn't.
3 Is there a library? Yes, there is.
4 Is there a park? Yes, there is.
5 Are there any gyms? Yes, there are.
6 Is there a shopping centre? No, there isn't.

4
1 many
2 much
3 many
4 much

5
1 How many calories are there in this yoghurt?
2 How much juice is there in the bottle?
3 How many gyms are there in the sports centre?
4 How many people are there in the café?

6
1 How much water do you drink every day?
2 How many vegetables do you eat for lunch?
3 How much fish do you eat every week?
4 How many bags of crisps do you eat at weekends?

Reading

1 c

2
1 c
2 e
3 b
4 f
5 a
6 d

3
1 **T**
2 **F** She often has a baked potato, bread or brown rice with fish, meat or other proteins like pulses.
3 **T**
4 **F** She thinks it is OK if you have a small amount of it.
5 **F** She drinks coffee, water and special energy products on competition days.
6 **T**

4 1 Chrissie has two meals in the morning.
2 She eats a baked potato, bread or brown rice at lunchtime.
3 She eats vegetables twice a day.
4 When she has a race she has rice cereal and coffee for breakfast.
5 After a competition she eats high-energy, high-fat food like chips, pizza and burgers.

Listening

12 Audioscript, exercises 1 and 2

Oliver Are you enjoying your visit to the UK?
Grace Yes, I am. It's very different from the USA. But it's fun.
Oliver Who are you staying with?
Grace My aunt and cousins.
Oliver Let's sit here.
Grace OK. Wow, this is a great park.
Oliver Yes, it is. I usually come here every weekend and go skateboarding.
Grace Oh, is there a skate park here then?
Oliver Yes, it's over there. Do you like skateboarding?
Grace No, I'm not very good at it. I like other sports though, like swimming and tennis. Is there a sports centre in the town?
Oliver Yes, there is. It's very good. It's got a swimming pool and a gym. There's even a bowling alley there. Would you like to go bowling one day?
Grace Yes, that sounds good. Are there any cinemas here?
Oliver Yes, there's a cinema in the shopping centre.
Grace Do you want to see a film this Saturday?
Oliver Yeah, sure. There's a nice café next to the cinema. Let's go there first and have something to eat.
Grace OK. What time?
Oliver Six o'clock? The films usually start at seven.
Grace Great. Come on. Let's walk in the park a bit …

1 c

2 1 the USA
2 park
3 skate park
4 sports centre
5 swimming pool
6 gym
7 bowling alley
8 cinemas
9 shopping centre
10 café

3 1 **T**
2 **T**
3 **F** She doesn't like skateboarding and she isn't very good at it.
4 **F** She does want to go bowling.
5 **T**

4 1 Grace is from the USA.
2 She is staying with her aunt and cousins.
3 Oliver goes skateboarding every weekend.
4 Yes, there is.
5 The café is next to the cinema.
6 They are meeting at six o'clock on Saturday.

Speaking

5 1 Can I help you?
2 Yes, I'd like some pasta, please.
3 OK, some pasta. Would you like anything to drink?
4 Have you got any apple juice?
5 Yes, here you are. Is that everything?
6 Yes. How much is it?
7 That's £5.55, please.
8 Here you are.
9 Thanks. Enjoy your meal!

Writing

6 1 First 3 Next / Then
2 Then / Next 4 Finally

Progress check

1 1 park
2 skate park
3 sports centre
4 swimming pool
5 library
6 cinema
7 shopping centre

2 1 nuts 4 cake
2 rice 5 cheese
3 crisps 6 juice

3 1 is a 4 are some
2 aren't any 5 isn't any
3 isn't a

4 1 Is there an apple in the bowl?
2 Is there any rice in the cupboard?
3 Is there a swimming pool here?
4 Are there any children in the cinema?

5 1 How many calories are there in pizza?
2 How much rice do you want?
3 ✓
4 How many people go to your school?
5 How many potatoes are there?
6 How much sugar is there in the dessert?

6 1 much 6 many
2 some 7 a
3 some 8 Are
4 any 9 any
5 is 10 some

Extension

1 1 What do you have
2 How often do you eat
3 Are there any
4 Is there anything
5 Are you
6 How many days
7 How much fruit
8 Have you got
9 There are some
10 There aren't many
11 There isn't
12 are sometimes

UNIT 6

Vocabulary 1

1 desk, chair, cupboard, shelf, lamp, mirror

2
1 sofa
2 armchair
3 wardrobe
4 bed
5 fridge
6 cooker
7 table
8 bath
9 sink
10 toilet

3
1 chair
2 wardrobe
3 shelves
4 sofa
5 sink
6 table

4
1 mirror
2 lamp
3 cooker
4 armchair

Grammar 1

1
1 bigger
2 cheaper
3 more difficult
4 shorter
5 more expensive
6 better
7 worse

2
1 easier
2 smaller
3 more comfortable
4 more popular
5 longer

3
1 more expensive than the mirror
2 cheaper than the armchair
3 older than the table

4
1 My dad is / isn't taller than me.
2 My bedroom is / isn't smaller than our living room.
3 My phone is / isn't newer than my dad's phone.
4 I'm / I'm not quieter than my friend.

5
1 is under
2 are in
3 is on
4 is between
5 is in front of
6 is opposite
7 is next to
8 behind

Vocabulary 2

1 **Across**
2 castle
4 (+ 5 down) youth
7 log cabin
11 apartment
12 hotel

Down
1 mobile home
2 caravan
3 lighthouse
5 (+ 4 across) hostel
6 farm
8 villa
9 tent
10 barge

2
1 tent
2 log cabin
3 caravan
4 villa
5 apartment

3
1 hotel
2 lighthouse
3 youth hostel
4 barge
5 castle

Grammar 2

1
1 can't
2 must
3 mustn't
4 Can
5 can't

2
2 can't
3 can
4 can
5 must
6 mustn't

3
1 can't phone
2 must show
3 can't be
4 mustn't use
5 can do

4
1 d You can rent this villa between May and October.
2 c You can't go shopping here on Sundays.
3 a You mustn't listen to music at school.
4 b You can make a fire next to your tent.

Reading

1 b

2
2 g
3 a
4 b
5 h
6 c
7 e
8 f

3
1 six
2 part of the year
3 visit
4 some
5 Sand Island

4
1 The duties of a volunteer keeper are to show tourists the lighthouses and help them set up camp on the islands' campsites.
2 Michigan Island is especially quiet.
3 People on Michigan Island use a pump to get water from Lake Superior.
4 Sand Island is good for sociable people to work on.

Listening

14 Audioscript, exercises 1 and 2

Callum Mum! Where's my school bag?
Mum I don't know, Callum. Why?
Callum I want to call Tom, but I can't find my phone. It's usually in my school bag.
Mum Where do you usually put your bag?
Callum Under my desk in my bedroom.
Mum And it's not there now?
Callum No.
Mum Try the kitchen. Is your bag there?
Callum Oh yes, here it is, opposite the door ... Oh, but my phone isn't in it.
Mum Well, look on the table. You sometimes leave your phone there.
Lisa Hi, Mum.
Mum Oh, hello Lisa. Do you know where your brother's phone is? Callum can't find it.
Lisa No, er, sorry – no idea. Is it in the bathroom?
Mum Don't be silly, Lisa. It can't be in the bathroom. He's not looking there. Oh, I know … Callum, why don't you look next to the computer in the dining room?
Callum OK.
Callum No, it's not in the dining room.
Mum Callum, I can hear your phone ringing here in the living room!
Callum Ah, there it is! It's on this shelf, between the books. How strange! Why is it there …? Ooh, Lisa!
Callum Lisa! Come back here!

1 He wants to find his phone.

2
1 his bedroom
2 the kitchen
3 the bathroom
4 the dining room
5 the living room
He doesn't look in the bathroom.

3
1 under, desk
2 opposite, door
3 on, table
4 in, dining room
5 between, books

4
1 Callum needs his phone because he wants to call Tom.
2 He usually puts his bag under his desk in his bedroom.
3 Lisa is Callum's sister.
4 No, she isn't.
5 I think the phone is on the shelf in the living room because Lisa put it there.

Speaking

5
2 tell
3 get
4 straight
5 turn
6 cross
7 past
8 right
9 far
10 minute

Progress check

1
1 bed
2 desk
3 lamp
4 wardrobe
5 mirror
6 sofa
7 shelf
8 cupboards

2
1 castle
2 tent
3 lighthouse
4 log cabin
5 farm
6 youth hostel
7 apartment
8 villa

3
1 You're not faster than me.
2 Millie is older than Alex.
3 My book is better than your book.
4 Your room is tidier than my room.
5 Her bag is not heavier than his bag.

4
1 in
2 next to
3 under
4 opposite

5
1 You can come to my house.
2 Gemma must finish her homework.
3 We mustn't use mobile phones at school.
4 I can't do PE today, I forgot my kit.
5 You must wear a uniform at school.

6
1 better
2 bigger
3 more comfortable
4 in
5 under
6 opposite
7 can
8 must

Extension

1
2 are
3 many
4 sharing
5 Our
6 next
7 smaller
8 opposite
9 isn't
10 can
11 twice
12 better
13 rides
14 every
15 much
16 must

UNIT 7

Vocabulary 1

1

S	T	R	A	T	E	G	Y	I	D	R
A	I	S	O	Q	T	N	P	V	A	E
D	A	M	F	L	U	Q	U	A	N	F
V	G	A	U	I	E	I	Z	U	C	E
E	D	C	O	L	T	P	Z	S	I	R
N	C	T	G	T	A	N	L	Z	N	E
T	R	I	V	I	A	T	E	A	G	N
U	R	O	D	N	T	R	I	S	Y	C
R	A	N	C	Z	Z	T	N	O	S	E
E	N	N	I	D	R	A	C	I	N	G

2
1 dancing
2 trivia
3 racing
4 role-play

3
1 fitness
2 quizzes
3 action
4 strategy
5 simulation

Grammar 1

1
1 were
2 was
3 weren't
4 wasn't
5 wasn't

2
1 That quiz wasn't interesting.
2 I was good at chess.
3 Those computer games weren't fun.
4 Were you pleased with them?
5 She wasn't happy at school.
6 The people in my game were funny.

3
1 Was your English lesson easy yesterday? Yes, it was. / No, it wasn't.
2 Were you busy last weekend? Yes, I was. / No, I wasn't.
3 Was your holiday fun last summer? Yes, it was. / No, it wasn't.
4 Were you and your family at home yesterday evening? Yes, we were. / No, we weren't.

4
2 There wasn't
3 There were
4 there were
5 there was
6 There weren't

5
1 Were there mobile phones? No, there weren't.
2 Was there a games console? No, there wasn't.
3 Was there a TV? Yes, there was.

Vocabulary 2

1
1 chat show
2 weather forecast
3 game show
4 the news
5 sports programme
6 advert
7 music programme

2
1 soap opera
2 comedy
3 documentary
4 film
5 drama

3
1 music programme
2 documentary
3 sports programme
4 chat show
5 soap opera
6 drama
7 the news

Grammar 2

1
2 watched
3 studied
4 played
5 finished
6 liked
7 pushed
8 started

2
1 We all tidied the house at the weekend.
2 They started school at eight o'clock this morning.
3 ✓

4 He watched TV last night.
5 ✓

3
1 lived
2 listened
3 stayed
4 cooked
5 looked

4
1 discovered
2 used
3 phoned
4 asked
5 agreed
6 worked
7 helped
8 finished

Reading

1
1 The beginnings
2 Worldwide success
3 Positive judges
4 Listening not looking
5 Working together

2
2 f
3 a
4 g
5 e
6 b
7 d

3
1 **T**
2 **T**
3 **F** The judges usually give very positive comments to the contestants.
4 **F** The judges aren't interested in what the singers look like.
5 **T**

4
1 The first name of *The Voice* was *The Voice of Holland*.
2 *The Voice* is a reality TV show.
3 The judges usually give very positive comments to the contestants.
4 At first, the judges only judge the singers on how they sound, not on how they look.
5 *The Voice* is more about collaboration, but other reality shows are more about competition.

Listening

16 Audioscript, exercises 1 and 2

Presenter This morning I'm in a shopping centre and I'm finding out about toys and games. What's popular now and what was popular in the past? … Excuse me, sir. Can I ask you some questions?
Man Of course!
Presenter Thanks. What did you play with when you were a child? What sort of toys and games?
Man Ah, that was a long time ago – I'm 64! Well, my favourite game was probably playing football in the street with my friends.
Presenter Was that a bit dangerous?
Man Not really. There weren't many cars, so it was quite safe then.
Presenter What about toys? What did you have?
Man Oh, I had a fantastic train set.
Presenter Thank you … Now, moving over here … Hello. Here's a mother with her teenage son. Can I ask you both about your favourite toys and games?
Mum and Sam OK.
Presenter Great. OK, Mum first!
Mum When I was very little I played with my dolls a lot.
Presenter And what about when you were a teenager? Did you have any computer games then?
Mum Yes, I did. My brother and I had a computer with a very simple game. It wasn't like the computer games today. It was a type of tennis. I loved it, although it was very simple compared with the ones you can play today.
Presenter Did you play chess?
Mum Oh yes! I loved playing chess. It was hard, though, and my brother was very good at it!
Presenter And, what about you? What's your name?
Sam Sam.
Presenter So, Sam, what did you play with when you were younger?
Sam I don't remember!
Mum What about plastic building bricks? You really loved building things when you were little.
Sam Oh yeah! I played with bricks a lot. I built tall towers and castles. And I had lots of toy cars. I loved racing them, too.
Presenter Did you play computer games?
Sam Well, I had a hand-held games console and I played action games, stuff like that.
Presenter And what about now?
Sam I've got a laptop computer now. I quite like strategy games, but I don't play computer games very often, actually. I prefer meeting my friends.
Mum Um, Sam … that's not exactly true. You play computer games all the time!
Sam Hmm, maybe … But I play them with my friends!

2 football, train set, dolls, tennis, chess, building bricks, toy cars, games console

3
1 b
2 a
3 b
4 a
5 c
6 b

4
1 The man played football in the street.
2 She played computer games and chess.
3 She played chess with her brother.
4 He made tall towers and castles with the bricks.
5 They play computer / strategy games together.

Speaking

5
1 ready
2 minute
3 explain
4 first
5 must
6 How
7 win
8 Good

Writing

6
1 I also enjoy going to the cinema.
2 There were also a lot of children at the park.
3 There was also some food at the party.
4 He also listens to music programmes.

Progress check

1
1 action / adventure
2 adventure / action
3 racing
4 fitness
5 dancing
6 puzzle
7 quiz
8 role-play

2
1 chat show
2 Soap operas
3 Adverts
4 documentary
5 Cartoons
6 weather forecast
7 game show

3
1 Computer games weren't very good in 1985.
2 Were soap operas popular in 1960?
3 The weather forecast was terrible last night.
4 Was your brother tired after school?
5 They were happy this morning.

4
1 There was
2 Were there
3 There were
4 There weren't
5 Was there

5
1 there were
2 worked
3 cooked
4 tidied
5 cleaned
6 listened
7 There were
8 were
9 called
10 used

Extension

1
1 older
2 Some
3 can't
4 discovered
5 was
6 played
7 created
8 Inside
9 are
10 many
11 play
12 is
13 are

UNIT 8

Vocabulary 1

1 **Across**
1 conductor
5 choir
8 pianist
9 (+ 6 down) key
10 drummer

Down
2 orchestra
3 guitar
4 bass player
6 (+ 9 across) boards
7 singer

2

	drums	piano	guitar	singer	conductor
classical	✓	✓	✓	✓	✓
country	✓	✓	✓	✓	
heavy rock	✓		✓	✓	
jazz	✓	✓	✓	✓	✓
Latin	✓	✓	✓	✓	
opera	✓	✓		✓	✓
pop	✓	✓	✓	✓	
rap	✓			✓	

3
1 piano
2 drummer
3 bass guitar
4 choir
5 orchestra

Grammar 1

1
1 went
2 became
3 have
4 wore

2
1 bought
2 went
3 performed
4 had
5 listened

3
1 I didn't study music last term.
2 Mum didn't go to work a week ago.
3 We didn't buy the DVD last weekend.
4 I didn't wear a uniform when I was younger.

4
2 d
3 a
4 f
5 c
6 b

He joined an R&B group called NuBeginnings in 1987 and competed in a TV talent competition in 1991. He became famous in 1997 with the album *My Way*. He recorded '*OMG*' with will.i.am for the *Raymond v. Raymond* album and sold more than 300,000 copies of *Raymond v. Raymond* in one week. He travelled around the world in 2010–2011 on the *OMG* tour.

5
1 I had … for lunch yesterday.
2 I went to … last weekend.
3 I bought … last month.

Vocabulary 2

1

S	B	A	M	L	I	V	E	L	Y
L	U	N	U	S	U	A	L	G	C
T	E	R	R	I	B	L	E	R	A
L	T	E	P	I	Q	U	I	E	T
O	Q	B	O	R	I	N	G	A	H
U	A	M	A	Z	I	N	G	T	C
D	R	Q	N	G	A	S	T	E	Y
G	A	N	R	U	B	B	I	S	H
O	R	I	G	I	N	A	L	N	Z
S	B	A	N	N	O	Y	I	N	G

2
1 amazing
2 Rubbish
3 Unusual
4 Lively / loud, quiet
1 lively

3
2 annoying
3 boring
4 surprising
5 catchy
6 unusual
1 original

4
2 loud
3 quiet
4 rubbish
5 lively
6 fantastic

Grammar 2

1
1 listen
2 know
3 have
4 buy
5 give

2
1 ✓
2 Did you want to talk to me?
3 No, he didn't.
4 ✓
5 Did she watch a film last night?

3
1 What did you play?
2 Where did you go?
3 Where did you live?
4 When did you buy it?

4
1 Did you see Becky?
2 What did they see?
3 Did MP3 players exist?
4 Where did your family live?

5
1 Did you listen
2 Did you see
3 did you buy
4 Did she like
5 Did she have

Reading

1 c

2
1 d
2 a
3 e
4 f
5 c
6 b

3
1 **F** They used drums hundreds of years ago.
2 **T**
3 **F** DJs played funk and soul records at parties in the Bronx.
4 **F** The Sugarhill Gang released the first rap single.
5 **T**

4
1 Poets and storytellers used drums when they told stories in West Africa.
2 Rap music developed in the 1970s in the Bronx in New York.

3 People met in houses and in the streets to have parties.
4 They listened to funk and soul music at these parties.
5 The people at the parties sang about their lives.

Listening

18 Audioscript, exercises 1 and 2

Presenter Hello and welcome to Classic Radio, the programme that's all about music. And today in the studio I'm talking to three young musicians from the New City Youth Orchestra. OK, first, can you tell me who you are and what you play?
Tom Hi, I'm Tom and I play the piano.
Sarah Hello. I play the violin. Oh, and, um, my name is Sarah.
Presenter Hi Tom, hi Sarah. And so you must be Fiona. You play the guitar, don't you?
Fiona That's right. I'm not usually part of the orchestra, but a year ago they asked me to tour with them because they wanted a guitarist. One of the pieces they played was Rodrigo's *Concierto de Aranjuez*. I played the solo part on a traditional Spanish guitar.
Presenter It was an important tour, wasn't it? I believe you travelled to five different countries. Er, Tom, is that right?
Tom Yes, that's right. We started in the UK, then we performed in Paris and Madrid.
Presenter What was it like to perform the *Concierto* in Spain?
Fiona Oh, it was absolutely amazing!
Presenter What other countries did you go to? Sarah …?
Sarah We went to Germany and then we flew to the USA for a concert in New York. It was great. It's a really lively city.
Presenter And how did you travel with all your instruments?
Fiona Well, in Europe we had a tour bus with a trailer. It carried all the instruments.
Tom Except my piano! I played a different one in every city.
Fiona When we flew to New York, I bought a ticket for my guitar. It's very expensive, you see. I wanted it next to me all the time!
Presenter Good idea. So, Fiona, why are you back with the orchestra again at the moment?
Fiona We're making a CD. The orchestra invited me back to play the Concierto with them at the recording studio.
Presenter Great! Well, thank you, all of you. And good luck with the CD. Let's hear a bit of the *Concierto* now …

1
1 c
2 a
3 b

2
1 c
2 b
3 a
4 c
5 b

3
1 They wanted a guitarist.
2 A traditional Spanish guitar.
3 The UK, France, Spain, Germany and the USA.
4 They are making a CD.

Speaking

4
1 have
2 really
3 terrible
4 did
5 about
6 How
7 Nothing
8 went

Writing

5
1 in
2 At
3 When
4 later
5 In
6 at
7 In

Progress check

1
1 singer
2 guitarist
3 guitar
4 bass player
5 orchestra
6 pianist
7 conductor

2
1 boring
2 rubbish
3 lively
4 annoying
5 catchy
6 surprising

3
1 I enjoyed the festival.
2 Lisa didn't buy Kanye West's first album.
3 Tim sold his MP3 player.
4 We went to school yesterday.

4
1 Where did you buy your coat?
2 Did he go to Edinburgh last year?
3 When did you see the film?
4 Who did you see at the music festival?
5 Why did she stop learning the piano?

5
1 Did you like
2 I did
3 loved
4 bought
5 did you start
6 saw
7 grew
8 wanted
9 Did you look
10 I didn't
11 didn't look

Extension

1
1 Did you go
2 Do you remember
3 saw
4 was
5 gave
6 didn't come
7 don't know
8 bought
9 tried
10 weren't
11 don't live
11 not doing

UNIT 9

Vocabulary 1

1
2 d
3 g
4 b
5 k
6 h
7 a
8 e
9 l
10 c/f
11 f/c
12 j

2
1 send cards
2 go to church
3 decorate the house
4 watch fireworks
5 go to / have a party
6 eat special food
7 sing songs
8 give presents
9 visit relatives
10 wear a costume
11 watch street parades

3
1 went
2 has
3 watched
4 watching
5 wore

4
1 decorate the house
2 send cards
3 give presents
4 eat special food
5 sing songs

Grammar 1

1
1 'm not
2 's
3 Are
4 're
5 not going to

2
1 Elliot is going to sell the tickets.
2 I'm going to phone the DJ.
3 Mr Clark isn't going to buy the fireworks.
4 Mr Clark and Miss Martin aren't going to go shopping on Saturday.
5 We're going to decorate the school hall on Friday.

3
1 Is Tom going to phone the DJ? No, he isn't. I'm going to phone the DJ.
2 Are Tom and Holly going to choose some music with me? Yes, they are.
3 Am I going to buy the fireworks? No, I'm not. Mrs Knight is going to buy the fireworks.
4 Are we going to tidy the hall on Saturday? No, we aren't. We're going to tidy the hall on Sunday.

4
1 her
2 me
3 it
4 you
5 us

5
2 them
3 him
4 us
5 me

Vocabulary 2

1
1 carefully
2 dangerously
3 easily
4 happily
5 hard
6 healthily
7 loudly
8 nicely
9 quickly
10 regularly
11 well

2
1 healthily
2 easily
3 badly
4 well
5 quickly
6 happily
7 carefully
8 regularly
9 nicely
10 dangerously
11 hard

3
1 regularly
2 badly
3 well
4 proudly
5 carefully

Grammar 2

1
2 d
3 e
4 b
5 a

2
1 is wearing
2 're playing
3 aren't travelling
4 Are you decorating
5 isn't giving

3
1 ✓
2 Ethan is having a party at his house on Saturday night.
3 Are we leaving the theatre at ten?
4 The train is arriving at 9.40pm.
5 ✓
6 I'm not watching the fireworks tonight because I don't like loud noises.

4
1 're practising
2 are you doing
3 helping
4 'm revising
5 are buying

Reading

1 b

2
2 g
3 a
4 e
5 h
6 f
7 d
8 c

3
1 **F** It is about King James the First of England and Scotland.
2 **T**
3 **F** The king's guards discovered Guy Fawkes in the House of Lords.
4 **T**
5 **T**
6 **F** Lots of bands are going to play all evening.

4
1 They were going to start a fire / make an explosion under the Parliament building.
2 5th November.
3 People light huge bonfires and watch fireworks. Many people make large models of Guy Fawkes.
4 People in Lewes can watch street parades and fireworks.

Listening

20 Audioscript, exercises 1 and 2

I'm Nisha and I live in Birmingham in the UK. We celebrate the Hindu festival of Diwali every year in the autumn. It's the start of our new year and it makes us think of new beginnings. We're getting ready for this year's festival at the moment. Today we're cleaning the house well. It's something the family do together. We make the house clean because we want the goddess Lakshmi to come into our homes. We believe she brings us good luck and wealth, or money.
Another important part of Diwali is buying new clothes. I'm going to choose some new clothes with my mum tomorrow.
On Thursday our family is going to make lots of sweets and special food. We give these sweets as presents to our family and friends. We also send special Diwali cards. I'm going to write my cards this evening.
Perhaps my favourite part of Diwali is when we decorate the house. We're going to decorate our house on Friday. We're going to put lots of little lamps and lights all around it. It always looks very beautiful. We put the lights in our homes to guide Lakshmi. She doesn't come if the house is dark.
At the weekend we're visiting my grandparents and then some more of our relatives are coming to visit us. Our cousins are arriving on Saturday afternoon. We are going to eat special food together. In the evening, we're going to watch fireworks. My dad and my uncles are going to do a fireworks display in our garden. The lights and the fireworks are the things which make Diwali so special for me.

1 new year, give presents, send cards, lights, visit relatives, eat special food, watch fireworks

2
1 Clean
2 write
3 Buy
4 Make
5 Decorate
6 Watch

3 1 Diwali is in the autumn.
2 People clean the house before Diwali because they want the goddess Lakshmi to come into their homes.
3 They believe Lakshmi gives them good luck and wealth, or money.
4 They decorate the house with little lamps and lights.
5 They are going to eat special food together and watch fireworks.

Speaking

4 2 I'm not – sorry!
3 Are you free in the evening?
4 Who else is going?
5 See you on Saturday.

Writing

5 1 in 5 in
2 on 6 at
3 at 7 in
4 at 8 at

Progress check

1 1 go 5 fun
2 cards 6 watched
3 going to / having 7 give
4 wears 8 special food

2 1 healthily 3 regularly
2 quickly 4 well

3 1 You aren't going to like the film.
2 Jo's going to travel to the USA next summer.
3 Are they going to visit regularly next year?
4 I'm going to learn German next year.
5 Are you going to go to Adam's party?

4 1 him 4 it
2 us 5 you
3 them

5 1 is leaving
2 're finishing
3 Are … meeting
4 'm not watching
5 are playing

6 1 Have you got
2 visiting
3 are
4 going
5 aren't arriving
6 Are you going
7 visit
8 'm going
9 You're
10 You're going to have
11 'm staying

Extension

1 've 8 'm dancing
2 practising 9 in front of
3 are 10 was
4 started 11 watched
5 was 12 older
6 than 13 can
7 have 14 me

GRAMMAR EXERCISES

STARTER UNIT

1 1 That 4 This
2 This 5 That
3 Those

2 1 their 4 her
2 It 5 His
3 They

3 1 Jim's eyes are very green.
2 My grandparents' house is in Scotland.
3 My sister's boyfriend is very nice.
4 All the teachers' cars are very old.
5 Your cousins' names are unusual.
6 Her best friend's name is Jane.

4 1 'm 4 are
2 are 5 's
3 is

5 1 I'm not from France
2 My friends aren't Moroccan.
3 My dad isn't in New Zealand.
4 You and your cousins aren't 11 years old.
5 She isn't English.

6 1 Is your house in Bilbao? No, it's not.
2 Are your best friends in your class? Yes, they are.
3 Are your parents Colombian? No, they aren't.
4 Is his teacher German? Yes, he is.
5 Are you and your cousins 13 years old? No, we're not.
6 Is her mum a doctor? Yes, she is.

UNIT 1

1 1 've got 4 've got
2 have got 5 've got
3 's got 6 have got

2 1 They've got three dogs.
2 I've got English homework.
3 We've got a favourite film.
4 She's got green eyes.
5 It's got four legs.

3 1 hasn't got 4 haven't got
2 hasn't got 5 haven't got
3 haven't got 6 hasn't got

4 1 We have got 3D glasses.
2 Gollum hasn't got much hair.
3 Has she got a favourite teacher?
4 My dad hasn't got a beard.
5 They haven't got tickets for the film.

5 1 Has your friend Mike got a pet? Yes, he has.
2 Have you got a favourite actor? Yes, I have.
3 Has she got green eyes? No, she hasn't.
4 Have they got beautiful voices? No, they haven't.
5 Has it got a long neck? Yes, it has.
6 Have dragons got two wings? Yes, they have.

6 2 f 5 g
3 e 6 b
4 a 7 d

7 1 What's your dad's name?
2 Where is she from?
3 How many houses have they got?
4 When is the film festival?
5 How old is your grandad?

UNIT 2

1 1 hates 4 say
2 live 5 like
3 wears 6 go

2 1 watches 5 sleeps
2 studies 6 does
3 has 7 finishes
4 goes

3 1 sleeps
2 doesn't watch
3 finishes 4 does
5 goes 6 have
7 don't study

4 1 I don't go to ballet school.
2 My friend doesn't sing very well.
3 Julie doesn't go to bed very late.
4 My sister doesn't meet her friends on Sundays.
5 We don't do a lot sof sport at my school.
6 They don't wear a school uniform.
7 He doesn't study performing arts.

5 1 Do you like ICT and history?
2 Do you start school at 6am?
3 Does your grandma use a computer?
4 Do your parents play cricket?
5 Do your friends do their homework every day?
6 Does Richard live near you?
7 Does your brother play the guitar?

6 1 Yes, she does.
2 No, they don't.
3 Yes, she does.
4 No, I don't.
5 No, they don't.
6 Yes, I do.
7 Yes, he does.

UNIT 3

1 1 I always watch the Olympics on TV.
2 He never wins a race.
3 The Winter Olympics are usually in February.
4 We often go to a football match.
5 She sometimes does exercise before school.
6 I rarely lose a game.

2 1 Jane often goes to the gym.
2 Paul never plays tennis at the weekend.
3 I usually do my homework after school.
4 My dad always watches Manchester United matches on TV.
5 We sometimes go skiing in winter.

3 1 How often does he play in the school team?
2 Does she sometimes win a match?
3 Do they usually do winter sports?
4 Do you always skate on ice?
5 How often does your brother lift weights?

4 1 We love playing football in the rain.
2 They hate going to the gym.
3 My father doesn't mind training every day.
4 I don't like watching sport on TV.
5 My friend likes skateboarding in the park.

5 1 How many medals has she got?
2 Do they go surfing in the holidays?
3 Where do your family go horse-riding?
4 Does your sister like running?
5 How many people play in a football team?

6 1 does she live
2 she got a pet/any pets
3 does she run
4 she like her sport
5 does she like doing in her free time

UNIT 4

1 1 're 4 's
2 'm 5 're
3 're

2 1 is / are winning 3 're wearing
2 are listening 4 're going
5 's carrying

3 1 I'm not celebrating my birthday.
2 They aren't playing basketball.
3 My dad isn't feeling energetic!
4 We aren't dancing at the prom.
5 You aren't studying.
6 Anne and Rob aren't making new clothes.

4 1 riding 5 lying
2 swimming 6 sleeping
3 visiting 7 dancing
4 carrying

5 1 Are they walking to school? No, they aren't.
2 Is your friend going home? No, he / she isn't.
3 Are you studying English? Yes, I am.
4 Are we celebrating her birthday? No, we aren't.
5 Are Carol and Matt competing in the TV show? Yes, they are.
6 Am I playing basketball? Yes, you are.
7 Is Gerry riding a horse? No, he isn't.
8 Are you listening to music? Yes, I am.

6 1 're wearing 2 does 3 isn't smiling 4 don't study 5 's learning 6 'm not playing 7 buy 8 see

UNIT 5

1 1 There are 2 There is 3 There are 4 There are 5 There is 6 There is

2 1 There aren't 2 There isn't 3 There isn't 4 There aren't 5 There isn't 6 There aren't

3
1 Is there a café next to the swimming pool?
2 How many calories are there in a chocolate cake?
3 Is there a drinks machine here?
4 How much milk is there in the fridge?
5 Are there any strawberries for dessert?
6 Is there some fruit on the table?

4 1 any 2 some 3 an 4 an 5 any 6 a 7 any

5

countable	uncountable
friend	fruit
group	meat
library	money
orange	rice
potato	spinach
school	water
people	pasta

6 1 friends 2 meat 3 money 4 apples 5 people 6 eggs

UNIT 6

1
1 stronger
2 more intelligent
3 worse
4 later
5 wider
6 redder / more red
7 tidier
8 more comfortable
9 more popular

2
1 more modern
2 better
3 tidier
4 more comfortable
5 more expensive

3
1 Chinese is more difficult than English.
2 Everest is higher than Annapurna.
3 Vegetables are healthier than hamburgers.
4 A hotel is more expensive than camping.
5 A barge is slower than a car.

4 1 in 2 on 3 in front of 4 between 5 opposite

5
1 He can't stay out late.
2 Can you be noisy in class?
3 We can't have a party in the street.
4 She can have pets.
5 Can we go to the concert this Saturday?
6 We can watch TV before dinner.
7 You can't use your mobile phone in class.

6 1 mustn't 2 must 3 mustn't 4 must 5 must 6 must

UNIT 7

1 1 was 2 were 3 were 4 was 5 was 6 were

2
1 We weren't at the sports club. We were at the museum.
2 My friends weren't in the garden. They were in my house.
3 My dad wasn't in Bilbao. He was in Cádiz.
4 They weren't opposite the shopping centre. They were next to it.
5 Tim wasn't at school. He was at my party.

3
1 Were your parents at the football match? Yes, they were.
2 Was Dave in the library at 11am? No, he wasn't.
3 Were we in our English class at 10pm? No, we weren't.
4 Was Paula in Seville two days ago? Yes, she was.
5 Were they at the party last weekend? No, they weren't.
6 Were you and your brother in London last month? Yes we were.
7 Was the film good last night? No, it wasn't.

4 1 was 2 were 3 was 4 were 5 was

5 1 Was, wasn't 2 Were, were 3 Was, was 4 Was, was 5 Were, weren't

6 1 arrived 2 loved 3 played 4 talked 5 listened 6 watched

7 1 studied 2 lived 3 planned 4 stopped 5 tried 6 permitted 7 started

UNIT 8

1 1 had 2 gave 3 made 4 knew 5 met 6 left 7 took

2 1 became 2 began 3 went 4 wore 5 saw

3
1 He didn't play the drums when he was younger.
2 We didn't watch a great programme last night.
3 The festival didn't start at 10pm.
4 Adele didn't write the lyrics for that song in 2012.
5 Her hit song didn't sell one million copies.

4 1 How did they go to the concert?
2 Why did Caroline like that song?
3 Where did she learn to sing?
4 What time did you leave school?
5 Did she go to the festival?

5 1 Did Lucy see a concert? No, she didn't.
2 Did Lucy stay in Edinburgh? Yes, she did.
3 Did Rick go to Manchester? Yes, he did.
4 Did Rick play in a band? No, he didn't.
5 Did Jim and Alison play in an orchestra? Yes, they did.

6 1 Last night he studied until 11pm.
2 Yesterday, we met our friends at the cinema.
3 She didn't buy any concert tickets.
4 He didn't compose that opera.
5 Did she have a good time?
6 Where did they go last holiday?

UNIT 9

1 1 are going to 4 is going to
2 is going to 5 is going to
3 am going to

2 1 We are going to give our teacher a present.
2 The festival is going to be fantastic.
3 She is going to sing in a new band next month.
4 I am going to do more sport next year.
5 My parents are going to travel to Thailand next summer.

3 1 They aren't going to watch a film. They're going to do their homework.
2 Pete isn't going to sing at the party. He's going to sing in church.
3 We aren't going to send a card. We're going to buy a present.
4 Sue isn't going to come for dinner. She's going to go to the cinema.
5 You aren't going to study French. You're going to study English.

4 1 Is your sister going to eat pasta for dinner? No, she isn't.
2 Are your classmates going to watch a film? No, they aren't.
3 Is your brother going to celebrate his birthday? No, he isn't.
4 Are we going to travel by car? Yes, we are.
5 Are you going to invite me to the party? Yes, I am.
6 Am I going to meet them at the airport? No, I'm not.

5 1 it 4 them
2 us 5 us
3 them

6 1 I'm going to visit my grandparents this evening.
2 He's going to do an exam tomorrow.
3 My cousin is going to fly to Germany next weekend.
4 We're going to watch TV tonight.
5 We're going to meet them at the restaurant tomorrow.

VOCABULARY EXTENSION

UNIT 1

2 a knight f king
b dragon g queen
c wizard h princess
d spell i hero
e witch j villain

3 1 d 4 a
2 f 5 c
3 b 6 e

4 1 wizard 5 king
2 spells 6 princess
3 hero 7 witch
4 heroine 8 dragon

UNIT 2

2 1 get a good mark
2 revise
3 underline
4 test
5 listen
6 cheat

3 1 revise 5 underline
2 test 6 check
3 make notes 7 cheat
4 learn

UNIT 3

1 1 goggles 8 swimming cap
2 bat 9 boxing gloves
3 net 10 helmet
4 racket 11 nose clip
5 ball 12 headband
6 flippers
7 knee-pads

2

tennis	net racket headband ball
skateboarding	helmet skateboard knee-pads
swimming	flippers nose clip goggles swimming cap

3 1 bat, b
2 goggles, c
3 nose clip, c
4 rackets, a
5 net, b
6 headbands, a
7 gloves, b
8 cap, c

UNIT 4

2 a belt
b necklace
c hat
d handbag
e sunglasses
f backpack
g bracelet

3 1 gloves
2 handbag
3 sunglasses
4 earrings
5 watch
6 belt

4 1 scarf
2 cap
3 sunglasses
4 backpack
5 necklace
6 watch / bracelet
7 bracelet / watch
8 earrings
9 rings

UNIT 5

2 1 do exercise / get fit
2 drink water
3 eat fruit and vegetables
4 sleep for eight hours
5 avoid fast foods
6 go to the gym

3 1 eat a balanced diet
2 sleep
3 do exercise
4 avoid fast food
5 lose weight
6 drink water

4 2 drink water
3 eat a balanced diet
4 Avoid fast foods
5 put on weight
6 fit
7 exercise
8 gym
9 sleep

UNIT 6

2 b windows
c roof
d ceiling
e door
f chimney
g garden
h garage
i floor
j fireplace
k balcony
l stairs

3 1 wall
2 stairs
3 door
4 chimney
5 windows
6 garage

4 2 fireplace
3 garage
4 garden
5 ceiling
6 balcony

UNIT 7

1 1 webcam
2 console
3 speakers
4 racing wheel
5 microphone
6 headset
7 charger
8 keyboard
9 joystick
10 remote control
11 screen
12 memory card

2 1 microphone
2 joystick
3 screen
4 consoles

3 1 headset
2 speakers
3 racing wheel
4 webcam
5 screen
6 keyboard
7 charger
8 memory card

UNIT 8

1 1 recorder
2 trumpet
3 cymbol
4 flute
5 harp
6 tuba
7 clarinet
8 castanets
9 xylophone
10 double bass
11 trombone
12 violin

2

strings	violin harp
brass	trumpet tuba trombone
woodwind	clarinet recorder flute
percussion	cymbal xylophone castanets

3 3 trumpet
4 trombone
5 flute
6 cymbal
7 violin

UNIT 9

2 1 Harvest Festival
2 Valentine's Day
3 Bonfire Night
4 Chinese New Year
5 Thanksgiving
6 bar mitzvah

3 2 Chinese New Year
3 Thanksgiving
4 bar mitzvah
5 wedding
6 wedding anniversary

INTEGRATED SKILLS

UNIT 1

1 1 yes
2 yes
3 one
4 Lady Gaga
5 Taylor Swift

30 Audioscript, exercises 1 and 2

Ticket seller Next please.
Joe Hello. Have you got tickets for the Coldplay concert?
Ticket seller Yes, of course, which date?
Joe Umm, what are the dates?
Ticket seller The 13th and 14th of November.
Joe Oh, OK, the 13th please.
Ticket seller How many people?
Joe Two adults please, I want to surprise my friend, Anna.
Ticket seller OK, I've got two seats in Row A, near the stage.
Joe That's great! How much is it?

Ticket seller It's £120.
Joe Oh, that's expensive. How much are the other seats?
Ticket seller I've got two seats in Row T for £60.
Joe Right, two seats in Row T please. Here you go.
Ticket seller Thanks, here's your change.
Joe Thanks. One last question. What time does the concert start?
Ticket seller It starts at 9pm and finishes around 11pm. Have fun!

2 1 13 3 £120
2 friend 4 Row T

3 2 Have you got tickets
3 Which date
4 How many
5 two
6 How much are the
7 £25 each
8 Here you are
9 here's your
10 What time

UNIT 2

1 1 F 3 T
2 T 4 F

32 Audioscript, exercises 1 and 2

Danny Hello Leila. Do you want to join a club?
Leila Yes, I want to join the dance club. I love dancing.
Danny Well, I don't, I love football.
Leila Oh, come on Danny, dancing's great fun. Why don't you try it?
Danny Well, OK. What day is it on?
Leila It's on Mondays.
Danny What time does it start?
Leila It starts at 5pm.
Danny And what time does it finish?
Leila I think it finishes about 6.30pm.
Danny So, where do they meet?
Leila In the gym.
Danny Oh, where's the gym?
Leila It's next to the dining hall.
Danny OK. I think I'd like to sign up.
Leila OK, see you there!

2

name of club	dance club
day	Monday
start time	5pm
finish time	6.30pm
place	gym

3 1 Can I help you?
2 What day is it on?
3 What time does it start?
4 What time does it finish?
5 Where is it?

UNIT 3

1 1 No, she doesn't. She goes less than once a week.
2 Once a month.
3 online
4 headbands and rackets
5 tennis

34 Audioscript, exercises 1 and 2

Sam Excuse me, can I ask you a few questions?
Jane Sure. Go ahead!
Sam Thanks! It's for a survey about the Sports Centre.
Jane Oh, OK.
Sam Do you play any sports at the sports centre?
Jane Yes, I do. I play tennis a lot and I also go swimming with my friends on Fridays.
Sam How often do you come to the sports centre?
Jane Very often, about three times a week.
Sam And how often do you visit the sports centre café?
Jane I rarely visit the café, it's expensive!
Sam What other sports do you do?
Jane I love judo so I sometimes go to judo classes.
Sam OK, great. That's all. Thanks for your time!
Jane No problem. Bye!

2 1 tennis 4 expensive
2 three 5 judo
3 rarely

3 2 It's for a survey
3 How often do you
4 once a week
5 never watch
6 usually watch
7 Thanks for your time!

UNIT 4

1 1 The clothes sale is in the afternoon.
2 The sale is at Colston School.
3 You can buy clothes for everybody: for men, women, babies, children and teenagers.
4 You can buy shoes at the clothes sale.
5 The sale is on Saturday 18th February.

36 Audioscript, exercises 1 and 2

Jane Hi Sonia, what are you looking at?
Sonia I'm looking at a poster for a clothes sale at the community centre. It looks great.
Jane When is it?
Sonia It's on every day this week after school.
Jane What are the opening times?
Sonia It starts at half past three after school and finishes at 6 o'clock and on Friday it finishes at 8 o'clock.
Jane Are there any student discounts?
Sonia No, there aren't. The clothes are really cheap though – look £5 for a T-shirt.
Jane That's great! Are you going?
Sonia Yes, I am.
Jane See you there!

2 1 every day 4 8pm
2 3.30pm 5 aren't any
3 6pm

3 1 orange 3 big
2 medium 4 £5

UNIT 5

1 1 The Blues Café
2 Mario's Pizza Parlour
3 The Blues Café
4 Mario's Pizza Parlour

Audioscript, exercises 1 and 2

Elsa This is great – I love pizza, but I don't eat it very often.
James I come here every Saturday with my friends after the football match.
Elsa Really? So what's good here? Remember I'm a vegetarian so I don't eat meat …
James They make a delicious tomato, mushroom, onion and apple pizza with four different types of cheese. It's called Mario's Special.
Elsa That sounds great! Let's order!
Assistant Hi, can I help you?
James Yes – a Mario's Special for my friend, please. And I'd like a carbonara pizza, please.
Elsa Carbonara pizza? What's that?
James It's got mushrooms, bacon, cream, onions and lots of cheese.
Assistant OK. Would you like anything to drink?
James Yes, a bottle of water for me …
Elsa And a cola for me, please.
Assistant Thank you. Enjoy your meal.
Elsa & James Thanks!

2
1 friends
2 apple
3 Mario's Special
4 bacon
5 a cola

3
2 I'd like a
3 chicken
4 Would you like
5 apple
6 Is that everything
7 How much
8 Enjoy your meal

UNIT 6

1
1 going by car
2 Benson Road
3 two minutes
4 miles

Audioscript, exercises 1 and 2

Kate So, what's the address of the museum?
Mark 32 Old Bridge Road.
Kate Which way is it?
Mark I don't know.
Kate Where's the map?
Mark I haven't got it. I left it in the hotel.
Kate Right. Let's ask someone. Excuse me, can you tell us how to get to the Museum of Modern Art, please?
Man The Museum of Modern Art? Let me think. Ah, yes. I know where it is. Go straight on, then turn left, no sorry, turn right. Then cross the road and go past the sports centre. The museum is on the right.
Kate OK. Is it far?
Man Yes, it's a 15 minute walk.
Kate Thank you.
Man No problem.
Mark That's easy! Straight on, then turn left, cross the roundabout …
Kate No! You turn right! And you cross the road! Mark!

2
1 The map is in the hotel.
2 They are looking for the Museum of Modern Art.
3 The museum is near the sports centre.
4 They must walk for about 15 minutes.

3
2 way
3 library
4 right
5 far
6 5

UNIT 7

1
1 Sudoku is a numbers logic game.
2 You can only use each number once in Sudoku.
3 You use numbers 1–9.
4 To win, you must complete the puzzle with the correct missing numbers.

Audioscript, exercises 1 and 2

Tom What are you playing?
Emily Dream Town – it's brilliant!
Tom Oh, I don't know that game, what's it about?
Emily Well, it's a new game and you can create your own town! Do you want to play?
Tom Yes, it sounds fun. How do you play?
Emily Well, first you have to work very hard to buy your first house. Then you can start building your dream town.
Tom OK … then what?
Emily Then, you must decide where to put your new cinema, your school and your restaurants. It's all about strategy!
Tom I see. And how do you win?
Emily Oh, that's easy. You just continue building your dream town so it becomes a big city! Are you ready to play?
Tom No – wait a minute! Yes, I'm ready now.
Emily Good luck!
Tom Thanks!

2
1 doesn't know
2 house
3 restaurants
4 strategy
5 city

3
2 first you must
3 Then what
4 how do you win
5 To win,
6 don't forget

UNIT 8

1
1 Russia.
2 £50 per adult and £10 per child with family discounts available.
3 Yes, they were.
4 No, there was free camping.

Audioscript, exercises 1 and 2

Paula Hi! Did you have a good weekend?
Mark No, not really. It was boring!
Paula What did you do?
Mark Oh, nothing special. I painted my sister's bedroom.
Paula Oh well.
Mark Anyway, what about you? How was your weekend?
Paula Oh, it was amazing!
Mark What did you do?
Paula I went to a dance festival with all my family.
Mark Really? How was it?
Paula It was fantastic! We saw some great performances. There were dance groups from all over the world… India, Turkey, America… They were brilliant!
Mark Wow! That sounds like fun.
Paula Oh well. Next month there's a music festival in the same place. You can come with us then!
Mark OK. Thanks!

2 1 bedroom
2 amazing
3 family
4 dance
5 music

3 2 What did you do
3 How was it
4 It was fantastic
5 what about you
6 Where did you go

UNIT 9

1 1 F
2 F
3 F
4 T
5 T

46 Audioscript, exercises 1 and 2

Kristen Hi there Robert. What are you up to?
Robert Oh, nothing special. I'm watching TV.
Kristen Listen, are you free on the 4th of July?
Robert Yes, I think so? Why?
Kristen Well, it's Independence Day and there's going to be a big celebration in the park. Do you want to come?
Robert That sounds fun. What kind of celebration is it?
Kristen There's going to be a parade and fireworks, and then traditional American food!
Robert Great, I love hamburgers and hot dogs! Who else is going?
Kristen All my American friends and family!
Robert Great! What time does it start?
Kristen It starts at 9 o'clock, so we're leaving at 8.30.
Robert OK. Shall I come to your house about 8.15?
Kristen Yes, great. See you then.
Robert Yes, see you then!

2 1 Kristen has plans for 4th July.
2 The celebration is going to be at the park.
3 They're going to eat traditional American food.
4 Kristen's American family will be at the celebration.
5 Robert is going to go to Kristen's house at 8.15pm.

3 2 are you free
3 Yes, I think so
4 Do you want to come
5 else is going
6 What time are you going

WRITING REFERENCE

UNIT 1

1

	Wolverine	Storm
build	strong	strong
height	short	tall
hair	brown	white
special powers	animal senses	can fly and control the weather

2 1 has
2 has
3 possession
4 is

3 1 's got
2 's
3 's
4 's
5 's got
6 '

Step 1

2 Physical description: hair, eyes, build
3 Other characteristics
4 Special powers / abilities
5 Films and actors

UNIT 2

1 1 9am
2 She plays tennis and football.
3 She goes to the park and the shopping centre.
4 On Sundays.
5 She has chicken, salad and potatoes.
6 10.30pm
7 Sunday

2 1 What time does your class start?
2 Saturday is my favourite day!
3 For lunch I eat a sandwich (my favourite is chicken), a salad and a banana.
4 My favourite subjects are English, history and PE.
5 After lunch, I do my homework.

3 1 What time do you get up on Sundays?
2 After lunch we do our homework.
3 My favourite subjects are French, technology and citizenship.
4 I get up at 7.30am. My sister gets up late, at 12 o'clock!
5 Do you go to drama classes? Yes, I do.

UNIT 3

1 1 3
2 Yes, the football team.
3 12
4 basketball, football, snowboarding and skiing
5 15
6 football teams and ice skating clubs

2 1 Do
2 Where
3 How often
4 Are
5 What

3 1 We usually go snowboarding at the weekend.
2 They are sometimes tired after playing football.
3 I rarely go swimming in the winter.
4 She is always first in the sports competition.
5 My brother never plays basketball on Fridays.

Step 1

2 Think of vocabulary you need for the topic, eg summer sports.
3 Plan ideas for your survey.
4 Make a list of question words.
5 Write your questions.

UNIT 4

1

1	3	**4**	3
2	1	**5**	2
3	2	**6**	1

2
1. He's my favourite footballer!
2. He's wearing a red football shirt.
3. His clothes are casual.
4. He looks serious
5. He's playing football.
6. He's wearing a grey and white jumper.

3
1. loves
2. is wearing
3. casual trousers
4. looks confident and friendly
5. blue jeans
6. are competing

UNIT 5

1
1. eggs, mushrooms, tomatoes and baked beans
2. sausages and bacon
3. baked beans
4. orange juice

2
1. First, cut the bread.
2. Then, add some butter and mayonnaise / mayonnaise and butter.
3. Next, add some chicken and a tomato.
4. Then, put some cheese on top.
5. Finally, enjoy your sandwich.

3

1	First	**4**	Then
2	Then	**5**	Finally
3	Next		

UNIT 6

1

1	F	**4**	F
2	F	**5**	T
3	F		

2
1. I like rock climbing because it's exciting.
2. I travel by plane because it's faster than by car.
3. They love the sea because they can swim very far!
4. My cousin lives in a caravan because he likes to travel.
5. We stay in hotels because they're more comfortable than going camping.

3
1. In my opinion
2. because you can
3. because it's more comfortable
4. dancing in the disco
5. because they aren´t
6. are more boring than

UNIT 7

1
1. A teen drama programme.
2. 9pm
3. Because there was a lot of drama.
4. No, it was great last night.
5. *Beverly Hills, 90210*.

2
1. We watched a film and we also read a book.
2. The show was funny and there were also some great jokes.
3. My friends sang a song and I also danced.
4. The singer was terrible and the guitarist was also bad.
5. The characters were interesting and they were also funny.
6. They studied all morning and they also did an exam.

3

1	watched	**5**	also danced
2	was	**6**	was
3	it was also	**7**	also watched
4	was also		

UNIT 8

1
1. singer and dancer, Colombia
2. when she was eight
3. in Columbia in 1977
4. when she was 24
5. in 2007
6. 28 years old

2
1. Three years later they moved house.
2. When he was 18 he went to university.
3. At the age of 23 she recorded her first album.
4. In 2012 they went to Ireland.
5. When they were young they played in a band.

3
1. The singer Ed Sheeran was born in 1991.
2. He started writing songs when he was at school.
3. Ed recorded his first album at the age of 14.
4. He moved to London in 2008 and started to play concerts.
5. Three years later, he released his first single.
6. In 2012, he won a BRIT award.

UNIT 9

1
1. Midsummer's Eve
2. It's the longest day in the summer.
3. At Kevin's house.
4. They're going to have a barbecue, light a bonfire and watch fireworks.
5. All Kevin's friends from school.
6. They're decorating the house.

2

1	on	**5**	are
2	are	**6**	come
3	at	**7**	in
4	at	**8**	Write

3
1. The fireworks display is in the evening.
2. In London, there is a big carnival every year.
3. The barbecue is going to be at my house.
4. My birthday is on 19 May.
5. It is usually very cold in the winter.

EXTERNAL EXAM TRAINER

EXAM 1

1 You have to match the sign to the correct meaning.

2 **a** 4 **c** 1
b 3 **d** 2

3 **a** 1 **c** 3
b 4 **d** 2

5 **1** b
2 a
3 c
There are five notices.

6 **1** d

7 **2** c **5** a
3 e
4 b

EXAM 2

1 The word *toast*.

2 You can eliminate options b and c in question 1 and options a and c in question 2.

3 **1** a **2** b

4 **1** b **3** c
2 b **4** b

EXAM 3

1 d

2 Students' own answers

4 **1** adjective
2 verb
3 personal pronoun
4 possessive adjective
5 verb
6 verb

5 **1** well
2 hope
3 you
4 My
5 think
6 See

EXAM 4

1 They are about Sara Baras.

2 **1** a (true) **2** b (false)

3 **1** b (false) **3** a (true)
2 a (true) **4** a (true)

4 **1** b (false) **3** a (true)
2 b (false) **4** b (false)

EXAM 5

1 Before: small house, garden, cycled to school
Now: apartment, big city, balcony, building, travel to school by bus

2 **1** b
2 c
3 a

4 **1** Yes, he does.
2 Yes, it is.
3 Yes, he does.
4 No, he answers everything.

6 Students' own answers

7 Students' own answers